THE GOD
WHO IS
TRIUNE

Revisioning the Christian Doctrine of God

Allan Coppedge

IVP Academic

An imprint of InterVarsity Press
Downers Grove, Illinois

InterVarsity Press
P.O. Box 1400, Downers Grove, IL 60515-1426
World Wide Web: www.ivpress.com
E-mail: email@ivpress.com

InterVarsity Press® is the book-publishing division of InterVarsity Christian Fellowship/USA®, a student movement active on campus at hundreds of universities, colleges and schools of nursing in the United States of America, and a member movement of the International Fellowship of Evangelical Students. For information about local and regional activities, write Public Relations Dept., InterVarsity Christian Fellowship/USA, 6400 Schroeder Rd., P.O. Box 7895, Madison, WI 53707-7895, or visit the IVCF website at <www.intervarsity.org>.

The Scripture quotations quoted herein are from the Revised Standard Version of the Bible, *copyright 1946, 1952, 1971 by the Division of Christian Education of the National Council of the Churches of Christ in the U.S.A. Used by permission. All rights reserved.*

Design: Cindy Kiple
Images: Art Resource/Réunion des Musées nationaux

ISBN 978-0-8308-2596-7

Printed in the United States of America ∞

Library of Congress Cataloging-in-Publication Data

Coppedge, Allan.
    The God who is Triune: resolving the Christian doctrine of God/
    Allan Coppedge.
        p. cm.
    ISBN 978-0-8308-2596-7 (pbk.: alk. paper)
    1. Trinity. I. Title.
    BT111.3.C67 2007
    231'.044—dc22

                                                                2007021570

P 21 20 19 18 17 16 15 14 13 12 11 10 9 8 7 6 5 4 3 2 1

Y 25 24 23 22 21 20 19 18 17 16 15 14 13 12 11 10 09 08 07

To my daughter Christiane Ann Albertson, with deep appreciation for the privilege of working together as father and daughter on the Trinity and the family language that comes from a heavenly father and gives direction to all Christian theology. It has been a rich blessing as an intergenerational family team to have Cricket's love, encouragement and critical assistance in crafting the theology of this book. No father could be more proud than I am of her ability to think, shape ideas and articulate truth in writing while applying the theology of a holy loving triune God in her personal life, in her family and in her ministry to others. In gratitude for being her father and for all she has done to make this work possible, I dedicate it to her with the love of a father's heart.

CONTENTS

PREFACE

Behind every book is a personal story. That is certainly true of this book. While much academic writing treats ideas in the abstract, a biblical precedent exists for addressing truth in relationship to personal experience. In Scripture, truth is never encountered in the abstract but in the concrete. The Bible does not just present ideas, it pictures people experiencing truth in their own lives.

In our age very few people would pretend that their thinking is not shaped by their own experiences. This book is the result of some major influences on my life, and in turn it has had a profound effect on my walk with God. As we understand truth and appropriate it, we become different persons. If Jesus' pattern is to be ours, then this is the way it ought to be.

This book begins with Jesus, moves to an understanding of the Trinity and then develops the implications of a triune beginning point for understanding how God works in the world. Jesus' relationship with God as his Father is the key piece of biblical data that structures all theology. For a time I thought God borrowed the concept of fatherhood from our world. Now I am convinced that the reverse is true. Human fathers are an analogue of who God is within his own triune being—Father, Son and Spirit. Fatherhood is a universal experience in our world, and it becomes one of the great object lessons God uses to describe who he is and how he works. My appreciation of this role of God, both within himself and in relationship to us, has been influenced by Scripture and my own personal experience.

A significant portion of this book was written in a cottage at a camp-meeting location that I have attended all my life and that has had a profound impact on my intellectual and spiritual development. My paternal grandparents started coming to this camp almost a hundred years ago. Later, they brought my father and his brothers and sisters. I am part of a third generation who have come every summer for spiritual retreat and family time. Grandmother, aunts, uncles and cousins—all delightfully enjoying each other as well as hearing from God. My wife Beth's paternal grandfather found Christ at the same camp, and when he later brought his son—Beth's father—he too came to faith in the Lord Jesus. So Beth and I, and now our children and grandchildren, have been marked profoundly by the theology and spiritual life that has blossomed in this atmosphere.

This camp meeting has for many years called people to intimacy with God, and its preaching has been theologically connected to Jesus, who brings us to the holy Father, and is wrapped in the dynamic work of the Holy Spirit. The Father, Son and Spirit, who give themselves in unconditional love, have set the tone for the transforming experiences of grace that we and other generations of our family have experienced.

I experienced my first intellectual awakening to God's grace at this camp. Many of the preachers were college and seminary faculty, a number of whom preached from their Greek New Testaments. The bookstore provided the first serious Christian literature that I encountered. It was delightful to have head *and* heart encouraged to reflect the life of God as made known in Jesus Christ. When my grandparents, laity from Atlanta, first came to this place, they undoubtedly had no idea that one day a grandson would write on the nature and character of God because of their choices. But in the economy of God, parents have the privilege of setting some things in motion that have implications far beyond their wildest imagination.

At this camp I first began to hear about the experience of the new birth, about loving God with all my heart and about growing in maturity from a babe to a child, to a young man and on to a father in the faith. And our heavenly Father's character was modeled in this family context. The profound experience of fatherhood is intricately intertwined in my own life with my understanding of the role of a triune God who is Father, Son and Spirit. A positive experience of God as Father, wrapped in a solid family context and reinforced by the experience of being a father myself has deepened my appreciation of how profoundly certain ideas and concepts shape lives, family, the church and the world. This enormously powerful experience of knowing God moves beyond natural families. It creates a spiritual family very similar to that modeled by Jesus' relationship to his disciples.

The Lord providentially brought together one such spiritual family several years ago. As several of us gathered in a retreat setting, we asked the Spirit to guide our thinking about how we might more fully contribute to what he was doing. He impressed on us the need for some fresh theological work. After much prayer, thinking and sharing together, we conceived of a theological project that would begin with Jesus, move to a triune understanding of God and then address the main themes of Christian theology. The senior member of this group was my father-in-law, Dennis Kinlaw. Two of us, John Oswalt and myself, had been his students. Almost all of the others had been students of the three of us or students of our students. Not only were we related by academic connections, but after leaving our educational institutions, the entire group has stayed in touch while serving in local churches and other ministry projects. So our lives in this close spiritual family have been intertwined for quite a few years.

Out of our deep theological and spiritual confidence in each other, we conceived the idea of writing a systematic theology. Accordingly, we assigned responsibilities within the group for the different segments of Christian theology. The members then committed to meet together twice a year to review the work that each had done. My first assignment, of which this book is the result, was on the doctrine of God. I am deeply indebted to this group for the hours of corrections, suggestions and personal conversations about the content of this volume. I am responsible for the end result, but the book as a whole is as much a product of a close-knit theological community as any I have ever known. Working together through these materials, paragraph by paragraph, page by page, over several years has certainly marked my life and thinking, and it has put me further in debt to each member of this fellowship.*

The group includes Harold Burgess, professor of Christian education, Asbury Theological Seminary; Mary Fisher, former associate professor of biblical theology, Asbury Theological Seminary; Paul Blair, president, Francis Asbury Society; Paul Vincent, professor of English, Asbury College; Bill Ury, professor of theology, Wesley Biblical Seminary; Gareth Cockerill, professor of New Testament, Wesley Biblical Seminary; Steve Blakemore, associate professor of philosophy and pastoral theology, Wesley Biblical Seminary; Ron Smith, president, Wesley Biblical Seminary; Tom McCall, assistant professor of theology, Trinity Evangelical Divinity School; Chris Bounds, professor of theology, Indiana Wesleyan University; and my daughter, Cricket Albertson,

---

*This fellowship has affected not only my thinking but my writing style, in that I speak relationally for this group and not on my own. Consequently, I will normally use the pronoun *we* rather than *I*.

research assistant for the Francis Asbury Society.

Two laypeople who have given us the impetus for this project complement this academic family. They are Burt Luce and his father, Joe. With his father's encouragement, Burt first called the group together and began to challenge us to dream about what we might do to help raise up godly leadership in the church. These laymen have continued to meet with the group, encourage us and make it possible for us to do the theological work that underlies the vital spiritual experience of knowing and loving God with all our hearts.

A word of special thanks goes to Juanita Ostroske, Michael Paulson and my niece Anna Key for their assistance in the details of typing, correcting and proofing this manuscript. I am also indebted to the Barnabas Foundation's board of directors for its encouragement and assistance in helping make possible a theological articulation of the basis for making disciples of Jesus. Further, I am grateful to Asbury Theological Seminary for a sabbatical to work on this project and for the privilege of teaching students from this theological perspective.

Finally, I would like to express my deep appreciation to my wife, Beth, for her support in the long process of writing this book. In addition to her personal encouragement, she has created a platform for many of the ideas to first be articulated around her kitchen table. It was here, at meal times with her father, Cricket and other members of my family (my son Billy, my nephew Laurence and others), that we discussed the ideas we were seeing in Scripture. The fruit of those multiple conversations not only have had an effect on my personal life, teaching, discipleship groups and this book, but also on Beth's ministry through the Titus Women's Bible Study, of which she is the principal teacher and retreat speaker. So God has a variety of venues for using his ideas, and beginning with family he seems to regularly find ways to multiply them in the lives of others.

Thinking correctly about God has enormous personal and ministry implications for me *and* my family, both natural and spiritual. This is God's way! Good theology produces fruit. Accordingly, it is my hope that this volume assists others in the same way. If God the Father and the Son are working in this world, as I believe they are, then may God the Spirit quicken our minds and assist us in drawing out the implications in order that we may get God's best individually, in our families, in the church and in the world.

Indian Springs, Georgia

INTRODUCTION

It is time to return to Jesus as the center of the Christian faith! The fact that he *is* the center should be obvious to all those who are in the Christian tradition, but in the church many things keep pushing him into secondary places and sometimes to the margin. This has not always been the case. Biblically he stands at the center of God's revelation. All that God reveals through the history of Israel finds its culmination in the person of Jesus. His story is found in the Gospels, and the meaning and significance of his life, death and resurrection are elaborated and worked out more fully in Acts and the Epistles. Finally, his return to gather together his church closes Scripture in the book of Revelation. The centrality of Christ has been a recurring focus throughout history. This is particularly true of the early church—during its first four centuries the dominant theological question was, Who is Jesus?

Grappling with the question of Jesus' identity and his relationship to the Father and the Spirit forced the church to work out the doctrine of the Trinity. Jesus compels us to reconceptualize the nature of God, which has widespread implications for every believer. Jesus is the center—biblically, historically, theologically and personally—of the Christian faith.

As the early followers of Jesus came to understand his divine nature, they had to do so in the context of Jewish monotheism. How can the one God have a Son who also shares the divine nature? How does the Holy Spirit fit into this picture? As the early church studied the Scriptures in order to understand the relationships of the Father, Son and Spirit within the framework of Old Testament monotheism, they carefully established the doctrine of the Trinity.

The centrality of Jesus meant a theological shift for Christians from the strict monotheism of the Old Testament to a trinitarian monotheism for the church. This entailed a rethinking of how God works, how he has made persons, how sin affects persons and how the full Trinity was involved in Christ's atoning work. Trinitarian thought is carried out in salvation, the Christian life, the sanctifying and maturing work of the Spirit in believers, and in our understanding of the church and God's final purposes for his created order. In other words, a triune understanding of God has shaped all of Christian theology by setting a different context for the major theological themes introduced in Scripture.

Thus those who have faith in Jesus Christ have a relationship with the triune God that affects all of Christian life and experience. They are no longer just disciples of Jesus but also disciples of the Father and the Holy Spirit (Mt 28:19). Properly understood, this view of God also affects the collective body of believers who know God in the saving work of Christ through the sanctifying work of the Spirit. Within a trinitarian context the people of God corporately live out their worship in service and outreach to each other and to the world.

Reframing our theology by starting with Jesus and the triune nature of God will help us understand more fully who God is and how he works in creation. This will set the stage for a clearer conception of the work of all three persons of the Trinity. Approaching the Christian faith through Jesus and the triune God not only relates to biblical, historical, theological, personal and corporate dimensions of the faith, it is also tied to three contemporary movements in theology.

The first is the revived interest in trinitarian studies. This fresh interest was begun by Karl Barth in the early part of the twentieth century and reinforced by Karl Rahner in mid-century. But by the end of the century a significant number of persons from a wide variety of theological traditions had made fresh explorations of the doctrine of the Trinity and its implications for the rest of Christian theology.[1]

This focus on the Trinity inevitably led to revisiting the fourth century, the

---

[1]For contemporary discussions regarding the Trinity see T. F. Torrance, *The Christian Doctrine of God* (Edinburgh: T & T Clark, 1996); and *The Trinitarian Faith* (Edinburgh: T & T Clark, 1995); Colin Gunton, *The Promise of Trinitarian Theology* (Edinburgh: T & T Clark, 1991); and *The One, the Three, and the Many* (Cambridge: Cambridge University Press, 1993); Walter Kasper, *The God of Jesus Christ*, trans. Matthew J. O'Connell (New York: Crossroad, 1999; W. J. Hill, *The Three-Personed God* (Washington, D.C.: Catholic University of America Press, 1982); C. Schwöbel and Colin Gunton, eds., *Persons, Divine and Human* (Edinburgh: T & T Clark, 1992); John D. Zizioulas, *Being as Communion* (Crestwood, N.Y.: St. Vladimir's Seminary Press, 1997; R. J. Feenstra and Cornelius Plan-

standard formulation of the doctrine in the Nicene Creed and the writings of the leaders of the early church as they worked to express trinitarian beliefs. The Scriptures were the church fathers' starting point and foundation for shaping the Christian doctrine of the Trinity. Following Barth's and Rahner's lead, recent studies have renewed theological interest in the threeness of the Trinity rather than the oneness of God.

Today, significant theological work is being done across denominational lines, a reality that is possible because every major Christian church has a commitment to trinitarian faith. Its potential fruitfulness for ecumenical dialogue is significant because the focus is not on ecclesiology, as has been the case for so many years, but rather on theology. For generations theological questions have been shunned in ecumenical dialogue because they seemed too divisive. Thus the focus has been on organizational and structural issues. With a return to trinitarian thinking as a part of the classical theology of the church, a new approach may be unfolding.[2]

This fresh outburst of trinitarian studies has opened the door for a new appreciation of God. While all of the implications of this reexamination of the Trinity have not yet been fully explored, a number of them have significant value for other theological discussions.[3] The purpose in writing this book is to join this rising interest in trinitarian studies. It is my conviction that beginning with the Trinity reorients our working conception of God and our understanding of how he accomplishes his work in creation, re-

---

tinga Jr., *Trinity, Incarnation, and Atonement* (Notre Dame: University of Notre Dame Press, 1989); C. Schwöbel, *Trinitarian Theology Today* (Edinburgh: T & T Clark, 1965); T. A. Smail, *The Forgotten Father* (Eugene, Ore.: Wipf and Stock, 2001); Jürgen Moltmann, *Trinity and the Kingdom of God* (San Francisco: HarperSanFrancisco, 1991; Minneapolis: Fortress, 1993); A. F. Kimmel, *Speaking the Christian God* (Grand Rapids: Eerdmans, 1992); James R. White, *The Forgotten Trinity* (Minneapolis: Bethany House, 1998); Karl Rahner, *The Trinity* (New York: Crossroad, 1997); C. M. LaCugna, *God For Us: The Trinity and Christian Life* (San Francisco: HarperSanFrancisco, 1991); Robert W. Jenson, *Systematic Theology*, vol. 1, *The Triune God* (New York: Oxford University Press, 1997); Wolfhart Pannenberg, *Systematic Theology*, vol. 1 (Grand Rapids: Eerdmans, 1991); David Coffey, *Deus Trinitas: The Doctrine of the Triune God* (New York: Oxford University Press, 1999); Boris Bobrinskoy, *The Mystery of the Trinity: Trinitarian Experience and Vision in the Biblical and Patristic Tradition* (Crestwood, N.Y.: St. Vladimir's Seminary Press, 1999).

[2]See T. F. Torrance, *Theology in Reconciliation* (Grand Rapids: Eerdmans, 1975), pp. 15-81, 215-66; *The Incarnation: Ecumenical Studies in the Nicene-Constantinopolitan Creed* (Edinburgh: Handsel Press, 1985); *Theological Dialogue Between Orthodox and Reformed Churches* (Edinburgh: Scottish Academic Press, 1985), pp. 79-156; *Trinitarian Perspectives: Toward Doctrinal Agreement* (Edinburgh: T & T Clark, 1994), pp. 77-102.

[3]For a review of a portion of this revived interest in the Trinity, see Stanley, J. Grenz, *Rediscovering the Triune God: The Trinity in Contemporary Theology* (Minneapolis: Fortress, 2004).

demption and providence. Ultimately, it reshapes all the themes of Christian theology.

A second relevant theological issue is the current debate between classical and open theism. Open theism is an attempt to articulate a position between classical theism and process theology.[4] This position is defined by its reaction to the traditional view of God articulated throughout the history of Western Christianity by Augustine, Thomas Aquinas and John Calvin. Classical theism begins with the role of God as sovereign King and emphasizes the oneness of his triune being.[5]

Openness theologians believe that the classical view of God overemphasizes God's transcendence to the detriment of his immanence. Their hope is to redress the balance between transcendence and immanence without overemphasizing immanence.[6] From the open theist's perspective classical theism has made God remote and unresponsive to people and their needs, deemphasizing his relational character and failing to give enough attention to his love and interaction with persons. The open theists are particularly concerned that the classical position does not provide enough room for human freedom and makes God static and distant. Further, they contend that God's impassability is not an appropriate way to describe the God of Scripture, who identifies with the suffering and pain of his people.

In reaction to the classical theist position, the open theists propose a view of God that makes him more relational and capable of interacting with persons. It accentuates his love rather than his sovereignty and power, and emphasizes human free will as opposed to God's arbitrary choices for human beings. In turn, the open theists limit God's omniscience, so the concept of God's foreknowledge is confined to what he knows about the past and the present. This means God has to take significant "risks" and remain "open" to an uncertain future. Open theists maintain that this perspective allows God to more adequately identify with the

---

[4]Clark Pinnock, *The Openness of God* (Downers Grove: InterVarsity Press, 1994). In the words of Pinnock, one of its most articulate advocates, "Let us seek a way to revise classical theism in a dynamic direction without falling into Process Theology" (p. 107).

[5]Richard Rice, *On the Openness of God* (Downers Grove: InterVarsity Press, 1994), pp. 10-11; Pinnock, *Openness of God*, pp. 103-4. Contemporary and widely used examples of classical theism in the study of the doctrine of God include John Feinberg, *No One Like Him* (Wheaton, Ill.: Crossway, 2001); and John Frame, *The Doctrine of God: The Theology of Lordship* (Phillipsburg, N.J.: P & R, 2002).

[6]Pinnock, *Openness of God*, pp. 105-7, 111-13.

suffering and turmoil of the world.

The chief contributors to trinitarian studies and openness theology come from different orientations within the church. The revived interest in trinitarian studies comes from a broadly based orthodox commitment to the Christian faith. It runs across denominational lines but centers on those who have a conservative bent in their theology, generally falling under the rubric of a "generous orthodoxy." On the other hand, the debate between classical and open theism has been primarily within the evangelical community of the church. Some from both positions are also in the trinitarian debate.

Does a deeper and fuller understanding of the doctrine of the Trinity assist us in sorting through the debate between the open and classical theists? I believe so. Trinitarian theism carries significant implications for this debate and has the potential to resolve many of the concerns of Classical and Open theism. Part of this stems from the fact that both sides of the debate are trinitarian in their presuppositions. The question is whether taking more seriously a trinitarian *starting point* would address some of their major issues concerning the nature and work of God. I hope that this fresh approach to trinitarian theism will contribute significantly to this interaction.[7]

A third contemporary theological issue relates to the exploration of Jesus and the doctrine of the Trinity. There is a rising interest in reconnecting biblical studies with Christian theology. This includes connecting Old Testament and New Testament studies, and connecting both with systematic theology. Francis Watson has correctly identified major splits in academic circles between Old Testament scholars and New Testament scholars, and both of these from Christian theologians. Appropriately, he is calling for reunification a of these three disciplines, which are currently operating as separate entities,[8] and he is being joined by others who also

---

[7]The proposal of a trinitarian theism as a mediating position between classical and open theism is not to suggest that either of these other positions is not basically trinitarian. Nevertheless, the trinitarianism of the classical position, influenced by Augustine, Aquinas and Calvin, is not a controlling paradigm for the rest of their theology. On the other side, open theism's early presentation (Pinnock, *The Openness of God*) says little about the Trinity and far more about God's love and his relationality. Pinnock's later work (*Most Moved Mover* [Grand Rapids: Baker Academic, 2001]) redresses the balance somewhat by suggesting that the Trinity is essential to the open theism model (p. 84). In this presentation, the Trinity seems to get a bit more accent, but not nearly as much as God's personal nature and love as the center of who God is. Trinitarian theism proposes a much firmer base from which to address some of the concerns of open theism and a more articulate way to maintain the relational God within a more traditional and orthodox position of the faith.

[8]Francis Watson, *Text and Truth* (Grand Rapids: Eerdmans, 1997), pp. 1-9.

see creative ways to unite the three.[9] Many believe that for Christian theology to be credible, it must first demonstrate its scriptural foundation.
Theology does not begin with philosophy, tradition or experience, but
with revelation. But how does this revelation from the Old Testament lead
to the New Testament, and how do both flow into Christian theology?

One of the values of trinitarian studies is that it gives us the opportunity
to see the interconnectedness between the Old Testament, the New Testament and Christian theology that was so much a part of early Christianity. In the first centuries of the church, there were no Old or New Testament scholars as we know them today. There were elders, pastors and
bishops who knew both Testaments intimately and saw them wrapped together in the wholeness of Christian theology. The same authors who were
writing theological treatises to defend the faith, address heretics and pro-
mote the truth in the church were those who were writing commentaries
on the Old and New Testaments. They saw no disjunction in the wholeness of revelation because they viewed the Old Testament as culminating
in the New. They understood the New Testament as the fulfillment of
God's plans, purposes and revelation in the Old, and therefore as incom-
prehensible without the Old Testament background. But they knew that
after there had been a diachronic unveiling of God's truth, there needed to
be a holistic account of all the themes of Scripture for preaching, teaching
and appropriation by individuals and the church. In other words, to apply
biblical truth, theology needed to see both the unity and coherence of the
data revealed in both Testaments.

The contemporary movement toward unity, sometimes described under the
rubric of theological hermeneutics, is a welcome addition to the divisiveness
of academic disciplines that have separated the Old Testament from the New,
and biblical studies from Christian theology.[10] The blend of biblical, historical
and theological readings of Scripture allows the whole of biblical truth to have

---

[9]Joel B. Green and Max Turner, *Between the Horizons: Spanning New Testament Studies and Systematic
Theology* (Grand Rapids: Eerdmans, 2000); Christopher R. Seitz, *Word Without End* (Grand Rapids:
Eerdmans, 1998); G. O'Collins and D. Kendall, *The Bible for Theology: Ten Principles for the Theolog-
ical Use of Scripture* (New York: Paulist Press, 1997); Trevor A. Hart, *Faith Thinking: The Dynamics of
Christian Theology* (Downers Grove: InterVarsity Press, 1995); Charles J. Scalise, *From Scripture to
Theology: A Canonical Journey into Hermeneutics* (Downers Grove: InterVarsity Press, 1996); and N. T.
Wright, *The New Testament and the People of God* (Minneapolis: Fortress Press, 1992), pp. 121-44.
[10]For a valuable contribution to this enterprise see, Kevin J. Vanhoozer, ed., *Dictionary for Theological
Interpretation of the Bible* (Grand Rapids: Baker, 2005).

its full weight in the lives of individuals, the church and the world.[11] This is particularly true when the whole is wrapped in a full understanding of God as the triune One who relates to others as Father, Son and Holy Spirit. This holistic approach to revelation will inform our approach to the doctrine of the Trinity. Accordingly, we will address the biblical understanding of the Trinity, explore its historical development to illuminate its theological components, and along the way try to work out the practical implications of this for all Christians.

In addition to the three contemporary theological concerns, we would like to provide an intellectual foundation for Christians in their personal walk with the Lord, in their desire to contribute to the church of Jesus Christ and in their longing to be used by God to influence their cultures. Relating personally to Jesus and through him to the triune God is foundational for everyone who desires to be a disciple of Jesus, and so these theological underpinnings are incredibly significant for all those who are involved in church leadership—pastors and laypeople alike—and the missionary enterprise.

Most theology in the West has followed the pattern of Aquinas by discussing the existence and the attributes of God before the Trinity. I reverse this method. We first address the doctrine of the Trinity and then let this trinitarian perspective affect the definition and explication of the attributes, roles and work of God, particularly in creation and providence.

Chapters one and two lay out the biblical foundations with two suggestions about organizing the data. First, we should not limit our study to the passages of Scripture that refer to all three persons of the Trinity. Rather, starting with the early church's handling of biblical materials, we will study any passage that relates two persons of the Trinity together. Further, in discussing the passages that include all three persons, it is not necessary that they all be in the same verse or with a triune formula or triadic structure. Within the same thought

---

[11]For more on the approaches to theological hermeneutics of Scripture, see Richard E. Burnett, *Karl Barth's Theological Exegesis: The Hermeneutical Principles of the Römerbrief Period* (Grand Rapids: Eerdmans, 2004); Ellen F. Davis and Richard B. Hayes, eds., *The Art of Reading Scripture* (Grand Rapids: Eerdmans, 2003); Steven E. Fowl, ed., *Theological Interpretation of Scripture: Classic and Contemporary Readings* (London: Blackwell, 1997); L. Gregory Jones and James J. Buckley, eds., *Theology and Scriptural Imagination* (Oxford: Blackwell, 1998); Jens Zimmermann, *Recovering Theological Hermeneutics: An Incarnational-Trinitarian Theory of Interpretation* (Grand Rapids: Baker Academic, 2004); John David Dawson, *Christian Figural Reading and the Fashioning of Identity* (Cambridge: Cambridge University Press, 2002); and Telford Work, *Living and Active: Scripture in the Economy of Salvation* (Grand Rapids: Eerdmans, 2002).

context, a biblical author may casually refer to the different members of the Trinity, and we will study how this contributes to trinitarian data.

The second contribution under biblical foundations is the observation that most of the New Testament books begin and end with references to two or three persons of the Trinity. If we take the literary *inclusio* seriously, this means that the view of God included in these materials brackets the books of the New Testament. This argument is significant in making the case that there is a triune overview of God that dominates all the New Testament material.

The third chapter begins with a discussion of the divinity of Christ and the Spirit. It addresses how the church dealt with the heresies of adoptionism, modalism and Arianism. Then we look at the church's constructive response, beginning with its development of theology and creeds as some of the conceptual tools its leaders used to handle the biblical material. The contributions of key theological church leaders are identified. The chapter closes with a discussion of two historical approaches to the Trinity: (1) the East, beginning with the focus on the three divine persons and the diversity within the triune God, and (2) the West, focusing on the unity and the oneness of God. The implications of each are briefly discussed.

Chapters four and five begin with an outline of key historical terms. This is followed by a review of the two different approaches to discussing the doctrine of the Trinity. The Trinity may be approached in terms of God's relationships to the created order (chap. 4) or it may be approached in terms of the interrelationships between the three members of the Godhead (chap. 5). In discussing God's relationship to creation (traditionally referred to as the economic Trinity), special attention is given to the differences between the three persons, followed by a discussion of their unity in relationship to God's plan for the created order. In describing God's interrelationships (this is usually referred to as the ontological Trinity), the distinction of persons is followed by the discussion of their equality, oneness and unity. Chapter five closes with a discussion of the mystery of the Trinity.

Chapters six, seven and eight take a different approach to the attributes of God. By addressing the attributes after the doctrine of the Trinity, the significance of the attributes is changed. The concepts of God's holiness and love are extracted from their usual niche within the moral character of God and described in terms of God's essential being (chap. 6). Then a major move is made to reorder the attributes of God from the traditional classification (absolute, relative, personal and moral). The new trinitarian approach places the personal attributes first. Then the moral attributes are discussed (chap. 7). In the light of these two, the relative and absolute attributes are introduced (chap. 8). By making the personal and moral characteristics primary, the role of the relative and absolute attributes is modified. In particular, omnipotence, omniscience (foreknowledge), infinity and immutability are reframed. The other significant element in these chapters is an expansion of the personal attributes of God. This prepares the way for a greater discussion of personhood in anthropology.

Chapter nine discusses the roles of God in terms of how the Trinity relates to the cosmos. The primary roles introduced are those of Creator, King, Personal Revealer, Priest, Judge, Father, Redeemer and Shepherd, with particular emphasis on God as Father and Personal Revealer. The triune context shows how the Father, Son and Spirit are described as working in each of the eight roles.

Chapters ten and eleven explore the relationship between the triune God and the world he created. We begin by discussing worldviews, particularly the questions of naturalism and supranaturalism. This is followed by an analysis of the triune Creator's personal and moral attributes in relation to creation. Chapter eleven closes with a natural versus supranatural approach to the nature of God in relationship to creation and how this affects other doctrines in the Christian faith.

The doctrine of providence is the topic of chapters twelve and thirteen. The three traditional components of providence—preservation, concurrence and government—introduce the discussion (chap. 12). Jesus, the key to understanding the Trinity, is also the key to comprehending God's providence. This entails seeing God through Jesus' eyes. Thus God is viewed as our Father rather than as sovereign King. The Father's direction of the world, allowing freedom and encouraging growth and maturity, sets the stage for a different approach to the doctrine of providence.

A discussion of persons and freedom prepares the way for exploring foreknowledge, freedom and providence (chap. 13). This chapter explores living within triune providence and its practical and pastoral implications, and concludes with a review of how trinitarian theism addresses issues raised by classical, open and process theism.

Having introduced the chapters to this Christian triune theology, we need to say a word about the twofold nature and purpose of theology. People need truth in order to deal with reality. We cannot deal with the reality of who God is and how we relate to him if we do not know the truth, which is found in Christian theology. But making truth known is only the first step. The second is applying the truth. This begins with a receptivity to what God is saying, which then leads to faith. After faith come other proper responses such as obedience, love, thanksgiving and confronting sin. In other words, application is the second stage of Christian theology. Truth must not only be understood, it must be appropriated. God does not teach us just so we can think more clearly about who he is, but so that our hearts and lives might respond accordingly. This means all theology is designed to come in two stages: First, an intellectual understanding of the truth; second, the application of that truth to personal lives and to the church.

On occasion individuals and sometimes the church believe that when the first task is completed, that is, there is a right understanding of the truth, then the work of theology is done. But theology is not an end in itself; it is God's means of transforming individuals, the church and the world. If it is not applied, it has not served God's purpose in the world.

Of course the reverse is also true. We cannot have application without the truth. There are some who would like to skip the tough work of thinking through the implications of God's revelation. God's design is that head should go with heart and mind should be coupled with will to yield appropriate responses to God.

This twofold nature of theology—truth plus application—is particularly accented in Scripture. Jesus is our model: truth is wrapped up in his personhood. So truth is never abstract but always personal. This means that as we learn the truth about the triune nature of God and how he relates to the world, we must apply it appropriately to our lives. Accordingly, the challenge is not only to understand what is being said but to continually ask how it may be put into practice. Receptivity is the first stage, faith in the One being revealed is the next, and then other appropriate responses follow. A work of Christian theology that is read but not appropriated might as well have been left unread. So your challenge is not only for a receptive, evaluative reading, but to respond to the truth as the Spirit is ready to apply it in your life.

1

THE NEW TESTAMENT
FOUNDATIONS FOR THE TRINITY

The theological focus of the Christian faith—the triune God who has made himself known in Jesus Christ—sets the tone for this book. Christians believe that the monotheism of the Old Testament does not make God a strictly unitary being as in Judaism and Islam. Rather, Old Testament monotheism is a monotheism of the triune God, who reveals himself more fully in the New Testament as Father, Son and Holy Spirit. The best way to describe this view of God is "triune theism," which begins with the one God of Jewish theism but accents his triune nature. Jesus is our way into this expanded understanding of God.

The historic Christian church ties our understanding of who God is to the person of Jesus. The church bases its belief in Scriptures such as the first chapter of the Gospel of John, which says, "In the beginning was the Word, and the Word was with God, and the Word was God," and that Word became flesh and dwelled among us so we might behold Jesus as "the only Son from the Father." Therefore, although "no one has ever seen God; the only Son, who is in the bosom of the Father, he has made him known" (Jn 1:1, 14, 18). Jesus' own statement to Thomas is illustrative of this general principle, "He who has seen me has seen the Father" (Jn 14:9). If Jesus is our way of knowing God, then he becomes our key to organizing the New Testament material about the nature and personhood of God.

I. ORGANIZING THE BIBLICAL DATA
Jesus Christ is the center of all of the Gospel stories, the heart of the preaching in Acts as well as the primary focus of the Epistles and the book of Revelation. Who is Jesus? This is a central question addressed by all of the New Testament.

Context: "Hear, O Israel: The Lord Our God Is One Lord"

The monotheistic faith of ancient Israel is the background for understanding who Jesus is. In distinction from the polytheistic faith of the peoples around them, Israel had come to believe in only one God (Deut 6:4). Yet the Gospels open with references to Jesus as the Son of God in a unique way (Mt 1:18, 20; 2:15; Lk 1:35; Jn 1:14-18). How can Yahweh, who is the only God, have a son, especially if the implication is that the son in some way shares the divinity of God? How can a monotheistic God be plural?

Accounts of Jesus' birth and baptism, which appear in all four Gospels, as well as John's prologue, introduce Jesus and alert readers that Jesus is not just a man but in fact has a unique relationship with God. A divine dimension to the nature of Jesus is implied.

Hints of this plurality of divinity are apparent in the Old Testament. One hint is the promise of a new covenant, which includes the coming of a messiah with the Spirit of God, along with reference to the personal presence of God coming in a new way among his people (Ezek 37). Thus the Old Testament and the early chapters of the Gospels set the biblical stage for passages about the Trinity in the New Testament.[1]

A New Way of Thinking

The coming of Jesus at the incarnation, coupled with the work of the Spirit at Pentecost, made it possible for the apostles to lead the New Testament church into an triune understanding of God. This new conceptualization of God underlay their whole way of thinking. Sometimes this is consciously expressed and at other times unconsciously presupposed.[2]

This trinitarian view of God appears when the writers of the New Testament connect Jesus with the Father.[3] For example, all but three New Testament epistles begin by referring to God as Father and to his relationship to Jesus. Of the three that initially do not refer to God as Father, two do so later in their first chapter (James and 2 Peter). Only 3 John does not refer to God

---

[1] For an expanded treatment of the Old Testament preparation for a trinitarian understanding of God, see chap. 2.

[2] For a theological evaluation of the biblical materials beginning with Jesus and leading to the triune God, see T. F. Torrance, *The Christian Doctrine of God* (Edinburgh: T & T Clark, 1996), pp. 32-72.

[3] Wolfhart Pannenberg insists that the basis of the doctrine of the Trinity must be understood in terms of the relationship between Jesus and the Father (*Systematic Theology*, 3 vols., trans. Geoffrey W. Bromiley [Grand Rapids: Eerdmans, 1991-97], 1:304, 308).

as Father.[4] So the norm for every apostolic epistle is that we now understand God as Father and Jesus as his Son.

The Problem with the Trinitarian Data

A common approach to presenting the biblical data on the Trinity is to examine the New Testament passages that closely relate all three persons of the Trinity. Trinitarian formulas include Matthew 28:19-20 (the Great Commission), 2 Corinthians 13:14 (the blessing of the triune God) and Revelation 1:4-6 (God and the future). Triadic forms of Scripture that include all three members are Ephesians 4:4-6 (the Trinity and the church), 1 Corinthians 12:3-6 (the Trinity and spiritual gifts) and 1 Peter 1:2 (the Trinity and salvation). Finally, there are cases where all three divine persons are mentioned in close proximity without following a trinitarian formula or triadic form. Sometimes these passages are minimized because their structure is not explicit. Nevertheless, all three persons are mentioned in this way by every New Testament book except James, 2 John and 3 John.

Unfortunately such an approach is entirely inadequate. This method of presenting a biblical foundation for the Trinity may suggest that the concept is confined to a few passages of Scripture, which therefore can be quickly dispensed with as of only passing interest to the church. The quantity of material mentioned above raises serious questions about this approach.

This approach to the trinitarian data carries with it several other problems. The first is that the literary structure (and a very restricted literary structure at that) controls the discussion. Only passages that refer to all three persons are included. When this strict formula is followed, the more generalized references to the three persons of the Trinity within a passage are not extensively used.

The second and more significant problem is that the theology behind the passages is not appropriately considered. The theology of how the Father, Son and Spirit are related to one another within the literary structure is not fully explored. If the New Testament and the early church's way of handling the data serve as our model, then using the trinitarian formula and triadic form is far too limited.

---

[4]Even 3 John uses family language like "brethren," borrowed from the concept of God as Father.

Fresh Approaches to Trinitarian Data

In order to adequately handle the significant data of the New Testament on the trinitarian nature of God, three proposals are in order. First, we must broaden our understanding of the literary structure to include the theology of the persons of the Trinity in the selection of data. Second, we will consider the literary structure of whole New Testament books in the light of trinitarian references. Third, Jesus' challenge to his disciples in the Great Commission will serve as a lens for organizing other trinitarian passages that refer to all three persons of the Trinity. In combination these three guidelines will allow us to use literary structure to understand the meaning and theology of the passages.

II. BROADEN THE LITERARY STRUCTURE

Following the New Testament and early church, we need to do justice to all of the scriptural material, so *four* kinds of passages will be examined. These include those passages that include (1) Jesus and the Father, (2) Jesus and the Spirit, (3) the Father and the Spirit, and (4) all three persons.[5] This approach considerably strengthens the biblical basis for our discussion. But it also gives us a more realistic appraisal of the data the New Testament church's understanding of the nature of God.

Of course, the relationship of Jesus to the Father is crucial to the discussion of the Trinity. Who this Jesus is and how he is related to God is a central issue of gospel proclamation. These questions forced the early church to formulate the doctrine of the Trinity in the fourth century. If Jesus is divine, then the whole understanding of a monotheistic God must be transformed. But we must also consider the relationships of the other two persons of the Trinity. This means we must discover how Jesus and the Father each relate to the Spirit.

Jesus and the Father

The passages that identify the relationship of Jesus to his Father in the

---

[5]For alternative ways of organizing the biblical materials, see Wayne Grudem, *Systematic Theology* (Grand Rapids: Zondervan, 1994), pp. 231-48; and Thomas Oden, *The Living God* (San Francisco: Harper & Row, 1987), pp. 194-208.

Gospels may be grouped under six headings.[6] First comes the introduction to Jesus in Matthew 1—2. The Father-Son connection begins with the fulfillment of the messianic prophecy: "Behold, a virgin shall conceive and bear a son, and his name shall be called Emmanuel (which means, God with us)" (Mt 1:23; see Is 7:14). This identification of Jesus as Emmanuel, "God with us," introduces not only Matthew's Gospel but the whole New Testament.

This connection of Jesus to God is complemented by the introduction of family language to describe Jesus' relationship to God. This language is used when Joseph is led to bring Jesus back from Egypt, which fulfills an Old Testament prophecy: "This was to fulfill what the Lord had spoken by the prophet, 'Out of Egypt I have called my Son' " (Mt 2:15; see Hos 11:1). To the Jews whom Matthew was addressing his Gospel, this passage would bring to mind God being Father to Israel. The first reference to God dealing with Israel as his son comes when God is about to deliver the Hebrews from Egypt (Ex 4:22). This role of God as Father is now alluded to in the opening paragraphs in the New Testament. This is particularly significant in the light of the rest of the New Testament, which views Jesus as the representative of Israel as son to God.

Second, Jesus' often refers to Yahweh—the God of Israel—as "my Father." "Not everyone who says to me, 'Lord, Lord,' shall enter the kingdom of heaven, but he who does the will of my Father who is in heaven" (Mt 7:21; see also Mt 10:32-33; 12:50; 18:10, 20:23; 25:34; 26:29, 39, 42). Very early, then, Jesus' role as Messiah is being modified by the dominant use of family language in which he refers to God's rule as "my Father's kingdom" (Mt 26:29). The intimacy of the connection between Son and Father is accented in a special way in the garden of Gethsemane when Jesus refers to his Father as "Abba" (Mk 14:36).

When Jesus speaks of God as Father, he is implying that he is divine, an implication that is not lost on those around him. Once, when Jesus said, "My Father is working still, and I am working," those around him attempted to take his life because he "called God his Father, making himself equal with God" (Jn 5:17-18).

Jesus' relationship to God is also described in terms being God's Son. This

---

[6]For the theological implications of these passages, see Ralph Del Colle, "The Triune God," in *The Cambridge Companion to Christian Doctrine*, ed. Colin Gunton (Cambridge: Cambridge University Press, 1997), pp. 123-25.

is the other side of the coin that depicts God as Jesus' Father.[7] In the Gospel of John, Jesus is first called the Son of God by Nathaniel (Jn 1:49), and in the Synoptic Gospels even the demonic world acknowledge Jesus' unique relationship to the Father as Son (Mt 8:29). When Jesus walks on the water and stills the storm, his disciples' respond in worship and acknowledge, "Truly you are the Son of God" (Mt 14:33). In response to Jesus' question about his own identity, Peter identifies him as the Messiah, "the Son of the living God" (Mt 16:16).[8] The connection between Jesus as the Son of God and as the promised Messiah is made throughout the New Testament (Mt 26:63; Jn 11:27; 20:31). In addition to the disciples, others identified Jesus as the Son of God (Mt 27:40, 54), and Jesus himself claims, "I am the Son of God" (Mt 27:43; Jn 10:36; 11:4).[9]

Jesus' relationship to the Father also comes through the way the Son reveals the Father. The key passage in the Synoptics, which heavily influenced the early church fathers, is Matthew 11:25-27. Here Jesus says the Father keeps certain things hidden from those who are wise in earthly ways but reveals them to "babes" who are open to God's revelation. "All things have been delivered to me by my Father; and no one knows the Son except the Father, and no one knows the Father except the Son and anyone to whom the Son chooses to reveal him" (Mt 11:27). Note the intimate connection between Father and Son; the Son knows the Father as no one else knows him, making it possible for the Son to reveal him to others.

---

[7]On whether Father-Son language is time bound, see Pannenberg, *Systematic Theology,* 1:262-65.

[8]N. T. Wright discusses the three possible meanings of the "Son of God" in the first century. The first, a description of the Messiah as son of God, might not necessarily carry divine overtones. The second occurred in the pagan world where the Roman emperor was described as son of god. Finally, because of the implications of the resurrection of Jesus, the title "Son of God" does carry divine overtones. Wright concludes that because of the resurrection the use of this title is a divine indicator, which is symbolized in particular by Thomas's confession in John 20:28. In light of this discussion it is possible that some of the references to Son of God in the Gospels may not initially have been understood as carrying reference to Jesus' divine nature. Others seem more convincing, such as the passage mentioned above in John 5:17-18. However, what is clear is that by the time that the Gospels were written, the early church had concluded that the Jesus' and others' use of "Son of God" did carry implications of divine nature, even if that meaning was veiled for its initial hearers. It was not intended to be veiled for those who read the Gospel stories in light of the total revelation of the New Testament. See N. T. Wright, *The Resurrection of the Son of God* (Minneapolis: Fortress Press, 2003), pp. 673, 723-36.

[9]For the centrality of the role of the Son in the understanding of the New Testament data on the Trinity, see Emil Brunner, *The Christian Doctrine of God,* Dogmatics, 3 vols., trans. Olive Wyon (London: Lutterworth, 1949), 1:209-14.

John makes it clear that Jesus, the Word, gives us a picture of what God the Father is really like: "The Word became flesh and dwelt among us, full of grace and truth; we beheld his glory, the glory as the only Son from the Father" (Jn 1:14). It is the role of the Son to make the Father known: "No one has ever seen God; the only Son, who is in the bosom of the Father, he has made him known" (Jn 1:18). Jesus makes the case that he is the only one who has seen God and has come from God (Jn 6:40, 47; 8:18-19, 38; 10:15; 13:3). On his last night with the disciples Jesus declares to Thomas that to know Jesus is also to know the Father (Jn 14:7). This is followed by his declaration to Philip, "He who has seen me has seen the Father" (Jn 14:9).

The close relationship of the Father and the Son is depicted in Jesus doing what the Father does. In chapter nine this will be explored in more detail in our discussion of how both the Son and the Spirit fulfill the same roles as God the Father. But Jesus declares, "My Father is working still, and I am working" (Jn 5:17). This work, he claims, includes the divine prerogatives of giving life and exercising judgment (Jn 5:19-29). That Jesus brings life from the Father is a consistent theme throughout the Gospel of John (e.g., Jn 6:27, 32-35, 40; 20:31).

The intimate relationship between Jesus and the Father comes into perspective when toward the end of his time with disciples, Jesus says, "That you may know and understand that the Father is in me and I am in the Father" (Jn 10:38; see also 14:10-11; 17:21). Jesus also says, "I and the Father are one" (Jn 10:30). His hearers understand the implication and accuse him of blasphemy, "because you being a man, make yourself God" (Jn 10:33; cf. 10:36, 38; 17:11, 21-22).

Finally, against the backdrop of Yahweh's declaration "I AM WHO I AM" (Ex 3:14), Jesus' "I am" sayings seal his identification with the Father. When Jesus declares, "Before Abraham was, I am," the Jewish leaders attempt to stone him for blasphemy. They clearly understand he is identifying himself with Yahweh of the Old Testament (Jn 8:58-59).

In light of what he has seen and heard, the writer of the Fourth Gospel begins by identifying Jesus with God before the creation of the world: "In the beginning was the Word, and the Word was with God, and the Word was God" (Jn 1:1). This identification of Jesus with God the Father is so strong that the New Testament repeatedly affirms it (e.g., Phil 2:5-11; Col 1:15-20; Heb 1:1-8; 2 Pet 1:16-17; 1 Jn 1:2-3; 2:22-24). This is nowhere clearer than when Paul affirms the oneness of God to the Corinthians: "There is no God but one" (1 Cor 8:4). But he goes on, "Yet for us there is one God, the Father, from whom are all things and for whom we exist, and one Lord, Jesus Christ, through whom are all things and through whom we exist" (1 Cor 8:6). Paul identifies one God, but then in the same breath he identifies the Father with the one Lord Jesus Christ. And both are identified as divine Creator. Clearly for Paul this monotheistic God includes both Father and Son.[10]

Jesus' relationship with the Father is the focal point of the church's fourth-century debate with the Arians over the divine nature of Jesus. While many of these passages do not discuss all three members of the Trinity, the relationship of Jesus to the Father is central in the development of trinitarian thinking in the early church.[11] The conclusion demanded by these materials is that, along with the Father, Jesus is divine.

Jesus and the Spirit

There are also six kinds of passages that address the relationship between Jesus and the Spirit. First we will look at the incarnation. Jesus is conceived by the Holy Spirit (Mt 1:18, 20; Lk 1:35). Matthew and Luke use this miracle to indicate that the story of Jesus begins with a divine-human interaction. This virgin birth reveals two significant facts: Jesus' human nature (he was born of a woman), and Jesus' divine nature (he was conceived by the Holy Spirit).

Jesus' divine nature is confirmed by the angel's statement to Mary that Jesus will "be called holy" (Lk 1:35). Luke also adds that the Father's essential name/nature is also holy (Lk 1:49). The Lukan birth narrative demonstrates that Jesus shares in the essential nature of a holy God and that Jesus' holiness is shared with both the Father and the Spirit.

Second, just as the birth narratives clarify the close relationship between Jesus and the Spirit in the incarnation, Jesus' baptism does the same with his ministry. As Jesus is being introduced as the Son by the Father (Mt 3:17; Lk 3:22), the Spirit visually descends as a dove, symbolizing the anointing and guiding work of God the Spirit in the life of Jesus. And John the Baptist bears

---

[10]For the discussion of the role of God as Father in relationship to Jesus, see Arthur Wainwright, *The Trinity in the New Testament* (London: SPCK, 1962), pp. 44-50.

[11]For discussion of how the New Testament focus on God as Father leads to the significance of the role of God as Father for Christian theology, see Walter Kasper, *The God of Jesus Christ,* trans. Matthew J. O'Connell (New York: Crossroad, 1999), pp. 50-51.

witness that the one on whom he saw the Spirit descend as a dove will baptize others with the Spirit (Jn 1:32-33; cf. Mt 3:11; Mk 1:8; Lk 3:16).

Third, the life and ministry of Jesus also connect with the Spirit. After Jesus' desert experience of resisting temptation in the Spirit (Lk 4:1-14), he begins his teaching in Nazareth with the explanation, "The Spirit of the Lord is upon me, because he has anointed me to preach good news to . . ." (Lk 4:18; see Is 61:1-2). There is quite a list of things that the Spirit is anointing him to do in ministry. Luke makes the case very early that the ministry of Jesus is being done under the full control of God through his Spirit, and since this is expressed so strongly in the introduction to the Gospel, it does not need repeating throughout the rest of the story.

Fourth, Jesus specifically teaches about the Spirit. While rejoicing in the Holy Spirit, Jesus explains his relationship with the Father (Lk 10:21-24). Jesus teaches that one comes into a relationship with the Spirit by asking the Father for the Holy Spirit (Lk 11:13).[12] Jesus also explains that he casts out demons by the Spirit of God (Mt 12:28; Lk 11:20), and he warns that blasphemy against the Spirit will not be forgiven (Mt 12:22-37; Mk 3:28-30). Further, Jesus alerts the disciples that the Spirit will speak through them when they are called on to bear witness in unexpected situations (Lk 12:11-12), and this is related to the Spirit's work of revelation. This is why, from Jesus' perspective, the Spirit clearly carries a role in the inspiration of Scripture (Mt 22:43). Jesus also views the Spirit as the agent of the new birth (Jn 3:3-8) and looks forward to the time when the Spirit will flow out of the hearts of believers after his own glorification (Jn 7:37-39).

Fifth, Jesus and the Spirit are closely connected in his final farewell to his disciples. Here he both explains the fuller work of the Spirit and promises to send the Spirit. Part of the promise is that the Spirit will be another Counselor like Jesus (Jn 14:16). The Spirit will replace the physical presence of Jesus in their lives. These passages do not exclusively tie Jesus to the Spirit, because they also relate the Father to this work (Jn 14:16-17, 26; 15:26; 16:7-15). However, it is clear that one of the Spirit's chief tasks in relationship to the disciples is to teach them and bring to remembrance Jesus' own words (Jn 14:26; 16:13-14).

Finally, Jesus is connected with the Spirit in sending forth the disciples. As

---

[12]Note the context: Lk 10:21—11:13.

he sends them out to do the work he was sent to do, he breathes on them, symbolizing the breath or Spirit of God. Then he says, "Receive the Holy Spirit" (Jn 20:21-23).

Among these references we should note that two of them bracket the Gospel story: the role of the Spirit in the incarnation (Mt 1:18, 20) and Jesus' sending forth disciples in the same way that the Father sent him (Jn 20:21-22). This same close connection between Jesus and the Spirit continues throughout the New Testament. Paul strengthens this connection by identifying the Holy Spirit as "the Spirit of the Lord" (2 Cor 3:17-18; see also Acts 2:33; 10:38; Rom 8:2; 9:1; Gal 3:14; 5:5-6, 22-24; Eph 1:13-14; 3:5-6; 1 Pet 1:11). These passages from the Gospels, Acts and Epistles guided the early church leaders as they tried to see the coherence of the biblical data related to all three members of the Trinity. They could not divorce the divinity of the Father from the Spirit, and when Jesus and the Spirit are so closely identified with each other, the divinity of both is reinforced.

The Spirit and the Father

The Gospels not only speak of Jesus' relationship to the Father and the Spirit, but also point to the special relationship between the Spirit and the Father. While this relationship does not receive the same attention as the others already mentioned, it is an important part of the data that relate all three members of the Trinity to one another.

When Jesus teaches the disciples how to pray, he explains that the Father longs to send his Spirit to those who ask him: "If you then, who are evil, know how to give good gifts to your children, how much more will your Father who is in heaven give the Holy Spirit to those who ask him" (Lk 11:13). And when disciples are called to bear witness to their faith, Jesus says that it will not be they who speak but "the Spirit of your Father speaking through you" (Mt 10:20). "The Spirit of your Father" means the two persons are closely identified. This of course parallels the significant Old Testament data that identifies this Spirit with the Spirit of Yahweh.

Jesus statement that "God is spirit" (Jn 4:24) may have a double meaning. It certainly refers to the fact that God is a spiritual being, but it may also be implying that God is the Spirit; that is, God has a Spirit. If Jesus' statement includes the second meaning, it is a strong affirmation of the shared divine nature between the Father and the Spirit.

The Father sent the Spirit in answer to Jesus' prayer (Jn 14:16), and in sending forth his disciples Jesus identifies the "promise of the Father" (Lk 24:48-49) with the baptism of the Holy Spirit (Acts 1:4-5). This is surely related to the promise of the Father under the old covenant that connects the coming role of the Spirit under the new covenant (Is 59:21; Ezek 11:19; 36:26-27; 37:14).

This connection between the Spirit and the Father is made not only in the Gospels but also in the rest of the New Testament. Paul identifies the work of God with the Spirit: "God's love has been poured out into our hearts through the Holy Spirit which he has given us" (Rom 5:5). He reiterates the point by describing the Spirit of God as the one who reveals the thoughts of God (1 Cor 2:10-14). Just as the spirit of a person knows and reveals the thoughts of that person, so the Spirit of God knows and reveals his thoughts to us. And Paul reinforces this with the identification of God's temple with God's indwelling Spirit: "Do you not know that you are God's temple and that God's Spirit dwells in you?" (1 Cor 3:16; cf. 1 Cor 6:19). Other New Testament passages reinforce this strong connection between the Father and the Spirit (Rom 8:27; 15:13; 1 Cor 2:4-5; 14:2; 2 Cor 5:5; Eph 6:17; 1 Thess 4:8; 2 Pet 1:21). The close identification between Father and Spirit is part of the data the early church used in establishing the full trinitarian understanding of the nature of God.[13]

Implications

The Trinity—all three divine persons—are intimately involved in the Gospels' narratives of Jesus' life. Sometimes all three are grouped together, but often only two of them are described in their relationship to each other. There are four kinds of trinitarian passages: those that discuss (1) Jesus' relationship to the Father, (2) Jesus' relationship to the Spirit, (3) the Spirit's relationship to the Father, and (4) the relationship of all three. The interweaving of these four kinds of trinitarian passages and their implications stand behind the development of the doctrine of the Trinity in the early church.

After the Spirit comes at Pentecost, the relationships between Father, Son and Spirit receive additional emphasis throughout the rest of the New Testa-

---

[13]For a discussion of the biblical materials indicating the unique personhood of the Spirit see Wainwright, *Trinity in the New Testament*, pp. 200-204.

ment. The apostles gain significant insight about who God is from their time with Jesus, but their comprehension increases after Pentecost as the Spirit directed their thinking. When Jesus asserts that the Spirit will guide them into all truth, surely he intends this to include the truth about the triune nature of God (Jn 14:26; 16:13). In their interpretation of both the life of Jesus and the nature of God, the New Testament authors have a much fuller understanding about the divine nature of each of the three members. This oneness of the three divine persons is seen in the common way the apostles describe the names, attributes, works, roles and worship of all three members. The four kinds of trinitarian passages may be summed up in four statements:

> The Father is God.
> Jesus is God.
> The Spirit is God.
> God is one.[14]

III. THE TRINITARIAN STRUCTURE OF THE NEW TESTAMENT BOOKS

The first proposal for managing the New Testament materials related to broadening the structure to include references to any two persons of the Trinity. The second proposal has to do with the trinitarian structure of many New Testament books.

Here the key for discerning how trinitarian thinking influences the whole New Testament is to observe how many trinitarian references bracket individual books. Several begin and end with references to all three persons of the Trinity. This includes Matthew (1:20-23; 28:19), Luke (1:35; 24:49), John (1:32-34; 20:21-22); Acts (1:3-5, 7-8; 28:23, 25), Romans (1:1-4; 15:30), 2 Corinthians (1:21-22; 13:14), 1 Thessalonians (1:3-5; 5:18-19) and Revelation (1:4-6; 22:17-18). This approach does not demand that trinitarian references only appear in the opening and closing verses of a book but that they come within the introductory and concluding passages of the argument of the book. So in the Gospel of John, for example, there is a prologue before all three persons are mentioned and an appendix after the three are related in a resurrection appearance.

The data get even stronger if passages that relate to two members of the Trinity are included. Several books either begin (or end) with reference to all

---

[14]Oden, *Living God*, pp. 194ff.

three persons, then either end (or begin) with references of two members of the Trinity, including Mark (1:10-11; 16:19 [longer ending]), 1 Corinthians (2:1-4; 15:57), 1 Peter (1:2; 5:10) and Jude (1; 20-21). Other books have references to two members of the Trinity that also bracket the entire book. These include Galatians (1:3; 6:7-8, 16-17), Ephesians (1:3; 6:23), Philippians (1:2; 4:19-20), Colossians (1:2; 4:12), 2 Thessalonians (1:2; 3:5), 1 Timothy (1:2; 6:14-15), 2 Timothy (1:2; 4:1), Titus (1:4; 3:4-6), Hebrews (1:1-2; 13:20), 1 John (1:3; 5:20), and 2 John (3; 9). Three other books open with a reference to two persons of the Trinity: Philemon (1:3), James (1:1) and 2 Peter (1:2). Only 3 John has a reference to God without any specific reference to the Father, the Son or the Spirit.

These passages are particularly significant if we treat introductions and conclusions as more than formalities. If in fact they are introducing theological elements that set the context for understanding the content between the opening and closing of a book, then the trinitarian references are setting the stage for understanding all of the material in the book in light of the persons of the Godhead. In other words the reader is alerted to the fact that what is being said is profoundly influenced by a new way of understanding God.

The literary structure strengthens this conviction. The principle used here is *inclusio*, and material included between the brackets of the trinitarian references must be interpreted as influenced by the enclosing ideas. Matthew is an excellent illustration (Mt 1:20-23; 28:19), and it is no accident that this book comes first in the New Testament, thereby setting the stage for the view of God that is going to be unpacked in the rest of the New Testament.

A second literary tool also assists us, that is, the law of generalization and particularization. These statements about the Trinity (either two- or three-person references) provide a general statement about the Godhead, allowing the readers to expect particulars (further details or explanations) following or preceding the generalization. This approach greatly increases the theological significance of the material thus included and demonstrates how pervasive implicit trinitarianism was for the New Testament church. John and Romans are illustrations of how this understanding of generalization-particularization works.[15]

---

[15]For discussion of the literary laws of structure see Robert A. Traina, *Methodical Bible Study* (New York: Ganis & Harris, 1952), pp. 49-59.

In sum, if introductions and conclusions help set the stage theologically for books in the New Testament, then the trinitarian framework for New Testament thinking is extensive. Further, if we do not demand that Scripture refers to all three persons to make it a trinitarian passage, then the data is impressive indeed. This indicates that, without explicitly spelling it out, the early church viewed the three persons as divine, sharing the nature of the Godhead. This underlying presupposition governed their proclamation of the gospel and their own spiritual lives. They worshiped the triune God.

IV. TRIUNE LIFE REVEALED IN THE MAKING OF DISCIPLES

In the light of the foregoing observations regarding trinitarian data, there is a third proposal for the organization of trinitarian passages in the New Testament that speak of all three persons. The purpose is to try to get a better feel for how significantly these passages affected the theology of the New Testament church and the way the church approached all relationships with God.[16] Here, the key is not the literary form (i.e., trinitarian formula or triadic form) but in the theology behind Jesus' central command to make disciples.[17] The challenge of Jesus (Mt 28:19-20) is particularly significant in the light of what he wants his disciples to do with their lives. After investing three years in them, Jesus now wants them similarly to assist others in developing their relationship with God. The theology behind this climactic command of Jesus becomes our third major way of organizing the triune data in Scripture.[18]

Making Disciples of the Triune God

In the last of the resurrection appearances mentioned by Matthew, Jesus meets his disciples and reminds them of the authority he has from the Father, and then he charges them, "Go, therefore, and make disciples of all nations, bap-

---

[16]Robert Jenson asserts that behind the passages that have a threefold reference to the triune God there is a full trinitarian logic at work. This means that even when a triune formula or triadic form are not used, the logic of talking about God in relationship to Father, Son and Spirit compels the authors to mention how all three persons are included. Jenson formulates the rule of this trinitarian logic: "When the specific relation to God is opened by the Gospel as thematic, God the Father and Christ and the Spirit all demand dramatically coordinating mentions" (*Systematic Theology*, 2 vols. [New York: Oxford University Press, 1997-2001], 1:92).

[17]For an alternative method of organizing the biblical materials, see T. F. Torrance's use of 2 Cor 13:14 in *The Christian Doctrine of God*, pp. 50-67.

[18]For a more traditional listing of major passages used in the early church with reference to all three persons of the Trinity see Oden's list of twelve *locus classicus* texts in his *Living God*, pp. 202-8.

tizing them in the name of the Father, the Son, and the Holy Spirit, teaching them to observe all that I have commanded you; and lo, I am with you always, to the close of the age" (Mt 28:19-20). Jesus is giving them a life assignment. It is a reasonable supposition that whatever he wants them to give the rest of their lives to is of primary importance. If the challenge contains an underlying principle that applies to all future disciples, as well as to the Twelve, then it makes it all the more urgent that we pay careful attention to his direction for their lives.

The focus of Jesus' exhortation is to *make disciples*. There is only one main verb in the passage (i.e., "make disciples") and three participles that are secondary and subsidiary dimensions of that process ("going," "baptizing," "teaching"). Clearly Jesus wants his disciples to go and make other disciples. They will do for others the same kind of things that Jesus has been doing for them. So this commandment is about how people relate to Jesus and what their lives will look like as a result of this relationship.[19]

The standard way of using this passage in relation to trinitarian thinking is to highlight the clause "baptizing them in the name of the Father, the Son and the Holy Spirit." Frequently, this is described as a "baptismal formula."[20] Unfortunately, this approach obscures the fact that this reference is a part of something much bigger than baptism. The problem is exacerbated when the subject being symbolized by baptism (i.e., a new relationship with the triune God) is replaced with the symbol (baptism). So for many, baptism becomes the focus instead of a relationship with the triune God.

The problem gets worse when baptism is only associated with public worship. Then the focus centers on a sacrament and becomes limited to a worship context instead of connecting it with Jesus' larger purpose of shaping the whole lives of future disciples.

A much more adequate understanding of the role of baptism is to see it as the initial part of making disciples of Jesus. Those who want to be disciples of Jesus must understand that he connects them with both the Father and the Spirit as well as himself. Thus their commitment to Jesus involves a commitment to all three persons of the triune God. The key ingredient is not so much the formality of a sacrament but the establishment of a relationship with God.

---

[19]Robert E. Coleman, *The Master Plan of Evangelism* (Old Tappan, N.J.: Fleming Revell, 1973), pp. 108-9.

[20]Oden, *Living God*, p. 202; Edmund J. Fortman, *The Triune God* (Grand Rapids: Baker, 1972), p. 15.

The process of beginning to relate to the triune God has three components: (1) proclamation of the gospel, (2) response of faith and (3) public declaration by baptism (cf. Acts 2:14-41).

The key to making disciples is introducing them into a relationship with the three-personed God. Baptism serves as a symbol that an initial relationship has been established. This relationship, like all person-to-person relationships, must be developed, which leads us to the second half of the Great Commission: "teaching them to observe all that I have commanded you" (Mt 28:20). This means that the newly formed relationship with the triune God must be developed in the same way that Jesus developed his relationships with his disciples.[21] This takes time and involves teaching, life transference, knowledge of the purposes of God, and continual growth by faith. Disciples are not made at baptism. Jesus took three years to develop his relationships with the Twelve. At the end of his time on earth with them, they knew the Father, and through the Father and the Son they would come to know the Holy Spirit. Further, these relationships are ongoing, even when Jesus is no longer physically present. This is what he discusses on his last evening with them (Jn 14—16).[22]

So the Great Commission is not primarily about the formal act of baptizing. Neither should it merely be used when the church discusses its responsibilities in evangelism and missions. Instead, it is a description of the way people learn to relate to God. It begins with an understanding of who God is (triune) and then wraps our relationship with him within becoming disciples of Jesus. From this point on, therefore, being a disciple of Jesus means being a disciple of the triune God. This begins with a public witness (baptism) and continues with ongoing teaching about knowing and following God. Thus referring to Matthew 20:18-20 as "a baptismal formula" alone does not do justice to Jesus' intention.

What Disciples Should Know

Jesus took three years to educate his disciples about himself, the Father and

---

[21]For more on the Great Commission as the center of the new Jesus movement in both outreach and training, see Allan Coppedge, *Biblical Principles of Discipleship* (Grand Rapids: Zondervan, 1986), pp. 114-18.

[22]Cf. Pannenberg's conviction that Matthew 28:19 is not primarily about baptism but about catechizing. In the development of the church's teaching, the trinitarian nature of God was to be central (Pannenberg, *Systematic Theology*, 1:268).

the Spirit. Thus his disciples had a trinitarian structure to follow when they
were instructed to make other disciples, baptize them and then teach them
further. To understand what Jesus wants new disciples to know, we will look
at the New Testament passages that refer to all three persons of the Trinity.
This should indicate how these teachings shape the thinking of new disciples.

As Jesus finishes his own time with the Twelve, he entrusts them to the
Spirit, who will guide them into all the truth they need to know (Jn 16:13).
This certainly includes what they need to know about the triune God, and
how that knowledge affects all of God's purposes for their lives. The trinitarian
passages may be grouped as follows:

- Jesus' model for disciples: Life with the Father and the Spirit
- Becoming a disciple of the triune God
- Living as a disciple of the triune God
- The disciples' relationship to disciples: The Trinity and the church
- Disciples serving a triune God: The church in the world

Jesus' teaching so reoriented the apostles' understanding of God that an implicit trinitarianism undergirds the way they understand God and how they relate to him. Their transformed vision of God is so deep that when they discuss
an important issue, they seem to walk around it, relating it first to one member
of the Trinity, then another and finally the third. This apparently casual approach to the Trinity may in fact represent a deep-seated, if implicit, conviction
that the subject under discussion can be approached from the perspective of the
Father, the Son or the Spirit. This reveals that the mindset of the writers of the
New Testament is much more deeply trinitarian than if they had repeatedly
used an explicit trinitarian formula. The pervasive trinitarian conviction of the
New Testament did not escape the attention of the teachers of the early church
as it began to formulate the doctrine of the Trinity. Let's look at how each of
the five groups of trinitarian passages guide Jesus' disciples.

Jesus' model for disciples: Life with the Father and the Spirit. Up to the giving of the Great Commission, the disciples received from Jesus information
about the nature of God, a fact that is crucial to understanding their personal
relationships with Jesus, and through him the Father and the Spirit. They
were responsible for knowing at least seven key events in the life of Jesus that
are wrapped in trinitarian language. Whether or not the disciples were present
for all of these events, Jesus made sure that they were aware of them. Through

these occasions, the disciples clearly understood that Jesus revealed the triune nature of God.

1. Matthew and Luke make it clear that all three persons of the Trinity are involved in the coming of the Messiah to fulfill God's purposes in history through Israel. Yahweh of the Old Testament has promised a new covenant ushered in by the Messiah, and through the birth announcements the Gospels reveal that Jesus is the fulfillment of this plan. In Matthew, God sends an angel to let Joseph know that the conception of Jesus is through the Holy Spirit and that he will be called Emmanuel, which means "God with us" (Mt 1:20-23). In Luke the angel declares that God's presence—all three persons of the Trinity—will be with Mary: "The Holy Spirit will come upon you, and the power of the most high will overshadow you; therefore the child to be born will be called holy, the Son of God" (Lk 1:35). The birth stories of Jesus have tremendous theological significance because they present the divine nature of God in relation to the conception of Jesus by the Holy Spirit, and the human nature of Jesus in terms of his being born of a human mother. So in his role as the God-man Jesus models what the disciples ought to be like as human beings. But before that can happen, he models what God is like, and the trinitarian context in which he is introduced sets the stage for what he is going to make known.

2. At the inauguration of his public ministry—connected with his baptism—the Spirit and the Father witness to who Jesus is: "He saw the Spirit of God descending like a dove, and alighting on him; and lo, a voice from heaven, saying, 'This is my beloved Son, with whom I am well pleased'" (Mt 3:16-17; Mk 1:9-11; Lk 3:21-22; Jn 1:32-34). The significance of this event for understanding the life and ministry of Jesus is enhanced by the fact that it is recorded by all four Evangelists. Closely connected to this event, John the Baptist reports that through Jesus' baptism God alerted him that Jesus is the Son of God and will baptize others with the Holy Spirit (Mt 3:11; Mk 1:8; Lk 3:16; Jn 1:33-34).

3. After Jesus' baptism he is led by the Spirit into the wilderness to be tempted by the devil. The temptations begin with the question of whether he is the Son of God (Lk 4:1-3). The story illustrates how Jesus trusts the Father, walks in obedience and is faithful to God's way of working. These references to faith, obedience and faithfulness are bracketed with references to

the work of the Spirit, which tells us that Jesus is committed to the will of God as God enables him to do the work through his Spirit (Lk 4:1-14).

4. The temptation story closes with the statement that Jesus returns in "the power of the Spirit" and begins his ministry of teaching, preaching, healing and making disciples (Lk 4:14—5:11). Here Jesus goes into the synagogue in Nazareth and reads the passage from Isaiah 61: "The Spirit of the Lord is upon me" (Lk 4:18). The Spirit of Yahweh is upon him for a variety of ministries, and this passage sets the stage for all the subsequent activities that will be described in the Gospel story. It is a declaration that Jesus intends to serve his Father through life in the Spirit.

5. The week following Peter's confession of Jesus as the Messiah, "the Son of the living God" (Mt 16:16), Jesus is transfigured before three of the disciples. Here the Father reaffirms Peter's witness, saying, "This is my beloved Son with whom I am well pleased; listen to him" (Mt 17:5). The voice is parallel to the voice of the Father at the baptism, and it is possible that the cloud that overshadowed the mountain may be a symbolic representation of the Holy Spirit. (The presence of God is represented by a cloud at times in the Old Testament [Ex 19]). But since there is no explicit connection made between the cloud and the Spirit in this passage, the possibility must remain tentative. Nevertheless, the transfiguration is an explicit event in the life of Jesus where his Father witnesses to him as his Son.

6. While in the Gospels the work of Jesus in his death is primarily connected to his role as the Son of the Father (Mt 26:63-64; 27:40, 43, 54; Mk 14:36, 61-62; Lk 23:34, 46; Jn 19:7), after Pentecost the disciples understand this to be the work of the all three persons of the Trinity. So Peter, on the day of Pentecost, describes how Jesus was delivered up according to God's plan, was raised from the dead, and sent the Spirit: "This Jesus God raised up, and we are all witnesses. Being therefore exalted the right hand of God, and having received from the Father the promise of the Holy Spirit, he has poured out this which you see and hear" (Acts 2:23-24, 32-33). Paul says the same when he talks about Jesus as "designated Son of God in power according to the Spirit of holiness by his resurrection from the dead, Jesus Christ our Lord" (Rom 1:4). The resurrection is definitely understood as a trinitarian event.

7. On Jesus' final day with his disciples, he explains their future relationship

with the Father and himself, telling them of the coming of the Spirit: "I will pray the Father, and he will give you another Counselor, that will be with you for ever, even the Spirit of truth" (Jn 14:16-17). The whole evening's discussion (Jn 14—16) is about the coming of the Spirit and how this will affect the disciples' future relationship with both Jesus and the Father. Jesus reiterates this point right before his ascension when he instructs them to wait for the promise of the Father and identifies it with John's promise that Jesus will baptize them with the Holy Spirit (Acts 1:4-5). The fulfillment all takes place on the day of Pentecost (Acts 2:33).

These seven events in the life of Jesus give the disciples some understanding of the nature of the God. Following Jesus has connected them with the triune God at major events throughout his life and ministry. This knowledge of God's nature begins to supply them with the intellectual content for understanding what it is like to be a disciple of the Father and of the Son and of the Holy Spirit.

Becoming a disciple of the triune God. The disciples first needed to know and share with others the nature of the God whom Jesus made known to them. Next they needed to share what it is like to be a disciple of Jesus and therefore of the triune God. A number of trinitarian passages flesh out the relational dimension of the disciples' connection to the trinitarian God. The place to begin is in knowing how to become a disciple.

1. Hebrews makes it clear that all three persons of the Trinity are involved in the atoning work that stands behind our salvation: "How much more shall the blood of Christ, who through the eternal Spirit offered himself without blemish to God, purify your conscience from dead works to serve the living God" (Heb 9:14; cf. Heb 10:12-18). The same triune basis of the atonement is alluded to in a later warning:

   How much worse punishment do you think will be deserved by the man who has spurned the Son of God, and defamed the blood of the covenant by which he was sanctified, and outraged the Spirit of grace? For we know him who said, 'Vengeance is mine, I will repay.' And again, 'the Lord will judge his people.' It is a fearful thing to fall in the hands of the living God. (Heb 10:29-31)

2. As soon as the disciples have experienced the coming of the Holy Spirit on Pentecost, Peter, speaking for the group, begins to fulfill the Great Commission by making other disciples. He invites people to come into a rela-

tionship with this triune God and be baptized: "Repent and be baptized every one of you in the name of Jesus Christ for the forgiveness of your sins; and you shall receive the gift of the Holy Spirit. For the promise is to you and to your children and to all that are far off, everyone whom the Lord our God calls to him" (Acts 2:38-39).

3. This initial relationship with God is often referred to as the work of God in salvation and is consistently described in trinitarian categories. Peter identifies it in one of the clearest trinitarian passages on the purposes of God, the atonement of Jesus and sanctification by the Spirit: "Chosen and destined by God the Father and sprinkled by the Spirit for obedience to Jesus Christ and for sprinkling with his blood" (1 Pet 1:2). Paul describes salvation by grace through faith in Jesus when he says, "for through him we both have access in one Spirit to the Father" (Eph 2:18). Paul likens this salvation to the inhabitation of the triune God in believers who are a holy temple: "In whom the whole structure is joined together and grows into a holy temple in the Lord; in whom you also are built into it for a dwelling place of God in the Spirit" (Eph 2:21-22). Paul also talks about the death of Jesus as that which stands behind God's love, which is poured out in our hearts through the Holy Spirit (Rom 5:5-6). Elsewhere he identifies the Spirit as both the Spirit of God (the Father) and the Spirit of Christ, so there is a triune work that provides the life of God to those who are his children (Rom 8:9, 11).

4. Paul bears witness to this saving work of God in trinitarian terms: "You were washed, you were sanctified, you were justified in the name of the Lord Jesus Christ and in the Spirit of our God" (1 Cor 6:11). Even more explicitly Hebrews says all three persons have born witness to the great salvation God has provided: "It was declared at first by the Lord, and it was attested to us by those who heard him, while God also bore witness by signs and wonders and various miracles and by gifts of the Holy Spirit distributed according to his own will" (Heb 2:3-4).

5. Four different times in the New Testament the question of assurance of salvation is described in trinitarian categories. Two of these deal with receiving the Spirit of sonship. The most well known is Paul's declaration:

> All who are led by the Spirit of God are sons of God. For you did not receive the spirit of slavery to fall back into fear, but you have received the spirit of

sonship. When we cry, "Abba! Father!" it is the Spirit himself bearing witness with our spirit that we are children of God, and if children, then heirs, heirs of God and fellow heirs with Christ. (Rom 8:14-17; see also Gal 3:3-6; 4:6)

The other two references discuss the way the Father and the Son give the Spirit as a guarantee of our salvation: "It is God who establishes us with you in Christ, and has commissioned us; he has put his seal upon us and given us his Spirit in our hearts as a guarantee" (2 Cor 1:21-22; see also 2 Cor 5:5-6).

Living as a disciple of the triune God. Not only is it important to know how to *become* a disciple, it is also vital that we learn how to *live* as a disciple. This particularly relates to the second half of the Great Commission; Jesus wants those who have made an initial commitment, expressed through baptism in the triune name, to be taught all the things that he communicated to the Twelve. A number of triune passages are related to various components of a life of discipleship.

1. Twice the New Testament specifically deals with the role of the Trinity and prayer in the life of a disciple. The first instance is the request by Paul: "I appeal to you, brethren, by our Lord Jesus Christ and by the love of the Spirit, to strive together with me in your prayers to God on my behalf" (Rom 15:30). In the second instance, Paul is aware that a disciple needs supernatural assistance, often in knowing how to pray, so he speaks about the Spirit interceding for us according to the will of God and Jesus praying for us at the right hand of God (Rom 8:26-27, 34).

2. In the life of a disciple who has a growing relationship with the triune God, Paul says that all three persons are involved in making spiritual things known, such as the gifts bestowed by God:

> Now we have received not the spirit of the world, but the Spirit which is from God, that we might understand the gifts bestowed on us by God. And we impart this in words not taught by human wisdom but taught by the Spirit, interpreting spiritual truths to those who possess the Spirit. . . . "For who has known the mind of the Lord so as to instruct him?" But we have the mind of Christ. (1 Cor 2:12-13, 16)

Developing the mind of Christ means thinking as the triune God thinks, especially about spiritual blessings, such as the gifts of the Spirit.

3. On Jesus' last night with his disciples he begins his teaching by talking about how they will continue to relate to all three members of the Trinity

(Jn 14). Then he expresses how they will abide in him so that he can work through them to bear fruit (Jn 15:1-11). There is a trinitarian context set for learning to abide in Jesus, who himself abides in the Father. John gives us even more explicit explanation: "By this we know that we abide in him and he in us, because he has given us of his own Spirit. And we have seen and testified that the Father has sent his Son as the Savior of the world. Whoever confesses that Jesus is the Son of God, God abides in him, and he in God" (1 Jn 4:13-15).

4. Even though John describes the Spirit witnessing to us regarding our abiding relationship with the Father and the Son, he is aware that the enemy is at work, and so there are false spirits abroad. To help disciples develop discernment about which spirit is from God and which is not, he gives them this trinitarian test: "By this you know the Spirit of God: every spirit which confesses that Jesus Christ has come in the flesh is of God, and every spirit which does not confess Jesus is not of God. This is the spirit of antichrist" (1 Jn 4:2-3).

5. Positively, growing as a disciple also means building oneself up in faith. This is where the trinitarian challenge of Jude is so pertinent: "But you, beloved, build yourselves up on your most holy faith; pray in the Holy Spirit; keep yourselves in the love of God; wait for the mercy of our Lord Jesus Christ until eternal life" (Jude 20-21).

6. After Paul explains to the Ephesians the trinitarian nature of the salvation God has made available to them (Eph 2:18, 21-22), he prays that they would come into a deeper experience with God. He summarizes his prayer with the hope that they "may be filled with all the fullness of God" (Eph 3:19). This fullness has a triune focus; Paul includes the Father, the Spirit and Christ in his prayer for God to work in their lives (Eph 3:14-19). The trinitarian nature of this experience is emphasized again later when he challenges the Ephesians to attain "to the measure of the stature of the fullness of Christ" (Eph 4:13) and to "be filled with the Spirit" so that they can be "always and for everything giving thanks in the name of our Lord Jesus Christ to God the Father" (Eph 5:18, 20). Thus, the experience of the fullness of the Spirit, like that the apostles experienced at Pentecost (Acts 2:4), is actually the fullness of the triune God. To experience the fullness of one person of the Trinity is to experience the fullness of all three.

7. The book of Revelation reminds us that God, who has made himself known
   in the person of Jesus, is in charge not only of the present but also of the future. So John introduces his revelation with a triune vision of God:

> Grace to you and peace from him who is and who was and who is to come,
> and from the seven spirits [an apocalyptic reference to the Holy Spirit] who
> are before his throne, and from Jesus Christ the faithful witness, the first-
> born of the dead, and the ruler of kings on earth. To him who loves us and
> has freed us from our sins by his blood and made us a kingdom, priests to his
> God and Father, to him be glory and dominion for ever and ever. (Rev 1:4-6)

This triadic introduction to God is reinforced when John tells us that it is the
threefold God who has given him the revelation. He relates that he was "on
the island called Patmos on account of the word of God and the testimony of
Jesus. I was in the Spirit on the Lord's day, and I heard behind me a loud voice
like a trumpet saying, 'Write what you see in the book and send it to the seven
churches'" (Rev 1:9-11).

The trinitarian cast that follows is emphasized in the messages to the seven
churches. Each message comes from Jesus and closes with a reference to the
Spirit. "He who has an ear, let him hear what the Spirit says to the churches"
(Rev 2:7, 11, 17, 28; 3:6, 13, 22). Five of the seven letters carry references to
all three members of the Trinity, and the last of them closes with the invitation
of Jesus to a relationship with himself, an invitation that also includes the Father and the Spirit:

> Behold, I stand at the door and knock; if anyone hears my voice and opens the
> door, I will come into him and eat with him, and he with me. He who conquers,
> I will grant him to sit with me on my throne, as I myself conquered and sat down
> with my Father on his throne. He who has an ear, let him hear what the Spirit
> says to the churches. (Rev 3:19-22)

A disciple needs to know that the triune God is providentially in charge of the
future.

A disciple's relationship to disciples: The Trinity and the church. Disciples of
the triune God not only must learn to relate to him, but they also have a special
relationship with each other. This is the foundation of the church. Made in
the triune God's own image, they must learn to relate to one another, person-
to-person, in reflection of the God whom they serve. So discipleship naturally
leads to discussion of the church of the triune God.

1. When Jesus commands his own disciples to go and make other disciples (Mt 28:19-20), we must remember that the Twelve themselves reflect something of the nature of the triune God. This is seen in the way Jesus went about making the Twelve into disciples. Therefore, Jesus' command is plural in form; it is given to a group in whom Jesus has invested his life for three years. Being a disciple means participating collectively with other like-minded believers who follow after the triune God. Jesus does not make disciples one at a time but in a group where there is the essential ingredient of relatedness and therefore fellowship with a few other persons.[23] Together they cultivate a deep relationship with Jesus. Being a disciple is not a solitary experience.

   For Jesus' disciples to reflect the triune nature of a relational God, they have to be in close relationship with other persons. This principle is foundational for understanding the church of the New Testament. The triune nature of God is personal, and Jesus reflects that personhood in his own being. So Jesus' method is rooted in the social nature of human personhood, which is a mirror of divine personhood. Jesus is modeling for the Twelve what it means to be a true disciple, that is, close relationships with a few others that reflect the shared life and experience in relationship to him.

2. After Paul has explained to the disciples the trinitarian nature of their salvation (Eph 2:18, 21, 22) and prayed that each of them might be filled with all the fullness of the triune God (Eph 3:14-19), he challenges them to "lead a life worthy of the calling to which you have been called" (Eph 4:1). The first dimension of this life is how they relate to one another in the church. Paul begins his discussion of the church with the reference to "one Spirit," "one Lord," and "one God and Father of us all" (Eph 4:4-6). The Trinity functions for Paul as the model for how the church should work in both its unity and diversity. So Paul challenges them to "maintain the unity of the Spirit," which parallels the unity of the triune God (Eph 4:3-5). Then he discusses diversity within the church in terms of Christ's gifts to his church (Eph 4:7-14). The gifts help us function within the same body, similarly to the way the different members of the Trinity interact within the triune God.

---

[23]This certainly does not mean that Jesus did not have personal time with them as individuals.

3. The role of spiritual gifts receives even more explicit attention in 1 Corinthians 12. Here Paul begins with the declaration that no one professes their allegiance to Jesus except through trinitarian empowerment: "Therefore I want you to understand that no one speaking by the Spirit of God ever says 'Jesus be cursed!' and no one can say 'Jesus is Lord' except by the Holy Spirit" (1 Cor 12:3). Thus begins a discussion of the varieties of gifts that are clearly tied to the threefold nature of God. "Now there are varieties of gifts, but the same Spirit; and there are varieties of service, but the same Lord; and there are varieties of working, but it is the same God who inspires them all in every one" (1 Cor 12:4-6). Though the church usually describes spiritual gifts as "gifts of the Spirit," Paul is careful to set them within a trinitarian framework so that the work of the Spirit is not separated from the work of the Father or the Son. The gifts are always used under the direction of the triune God who gives them.

4. At the conclusion of one the epistles, where Paul gives instruction to the church and individuals and describes the way he is working in ministry, he closes with a trinitarian blessing: "The grace of the Lord Jesus Christ and the love of God and the fellowship of the Holy Spirit be with you all" (2 Cor 13:14). This is frequently referred to as a trinitarian "doxology" because it is used as such in church worship. While this certainly is appropriate, Paul actually summarizes the *means* that the triune God has made available to disciples to accomplish the things he is exhorting them to do.

Paul is saying that three significant means for getting God's best are *grace*, *love* and *fellowship*. These three terms are woven throughout 2 Corinthians and characterize the inner life of the triune God. So while in this final blessing Paul connects each of the means with one member of the Trinity, in reality all three persons share each of these in their interpenetrating relationship. The triune God makes these things available to enable us to follow after him and reflect his likeness, and to enjoy them as a part of reflecting his image. So while Paul's statement comes as a benediction and may be used as a doxology, the heart of this blessing is really a statement about the inner life of the triune God, which is made available to us that we might reflect God's likeness in our own lives of grace, love and fellowship. Paul's benediction serves as a summary of several other places where Paul makes reference to the work of the Trinity (2 Cor 1:21-22; 3:3-6; 3:17—4:1; 4:5-6).

Disciples serving a triune God: The church in the world.

1. Jesus begins his own ministry of service to believers and nonbelievers alike within a trinitarian perspective. He begins "in the power of the Spirit" and attributes this to the fulfillment of God's promise when he quotes the prophet, "the Spirit of the Lord is upon me, because he has anointed me to preach good news" (Lk 4:14, 18).

   Not surprisingly, out of this trinitarian sending forth of Jesus, he in turn does the same with his own disciples. John describes this at the close of his Gospel. Jesus announces, "As the Father has sent me, even so I send you," and then he breathes on the disciples with the exhortation, "Receive the Holy Spirit" (Jn 20:21-22). Without the fullness of the Holy Spirit, the disciples are no more ready to do the work of God than Jesus was. This is reinforced when Jesus indicates that they are being sent to do the same things that the Father sent him to do. This must include the public ministry of Jesus in preaching, teaching, healing, confronting evil and personally encountering individuals. But it also includes discipleship ministry with a small group, much like Jesus did with the Twelve. Clearly, this is a trinitarian enterprise.

2. Ministry that includes the whole work of the triune God is passed on to future generations of disciples. Paul writes that the kingdom of God entails "righteousness and peace and joy in the Holy Spirit." Serving Christ in this way is pleasing to God and even humans approve of it (Rom 14:17-18). Paul connects this with his own ministry, describing what a privilege it is "to be a minister of Christ Jesus to the Gentiles in the priestly service of the gospel of God, so that the offering of the Gentiles may be acceptable, sanctified by the Holy Spirit" (Rom 15:16). He sees his work as trinitarian ministry.

3. The trinitarian nature of ministry, both to God and with him to others, is twice mentioned by Paul in describing his work among the Corinthians. He says to them, "You are a letter from Christ delivered by us, written not with ink but with the Spirit of the living God, not on tablets of stone but on tablets of human hearts" (2 Cor 3:3). And Paul's confidence in ministry is based on the Trinity:

Such is the confidence that we have through Christ toward God. Not that we are competent of ourselves to claim anything as coming from us; our competence is from God, who has made us competent us to be ministers of a new covenant, not in a written code but in the Spirit; for the written code kills but the Spirit gives life. (2 Cor 3:4-6)

An analysis of the trinitarian passages. If this analysis of trinitarian passages in the New Testament is correct, what we have is a trinitarian context both for being and making disciples of Jesus. The data scattered throughout the New Testament indicate what the disciples should know about God, revealing a trinitarian foundation at every stage. This material accentuates the nature of the God with whom disciples identify at their baptism. It focuses on what it means to be a disciple of Jesus and the steps a disciple must take to grow in relating to the triune God. It shows the trinitarian nature of the church and how disciples relate to each other. The New Testament indicates that disciples serve God, the church and the world out of a trinitarian enablement.

The following is an outline of all the New Testament trinitarian passages,[24] seen from the perspective of making disciples of a triune God:

1. Jesus' Model for Disciples: Life with the Father and the Spirit
   A. Birth of Jesus (Mt 1:20-23; Lk 1:35)
   B. Baptism of Jesus (Mt. 3:16-17; Mk 1:9-11; Lk 3:21-22; Jn 1:32-34)
   C. Temptation of Jesus (Mt 4:1-3; Lk 4:1-14)
   D. Jesus Begins Public Ministry (Lk 4:14—5:11)
   E. Transfiguration of Jesus (Mt 17:5)
   F. Death and Resurrection of Jesus (Acts 2:23-24, 32-33; Rom 1:4)
   G. Jesus and the Father Promise the Spirit (Jn 14:16-17; Acts 1:4-5)

2. Becoming a Disciple of the Triune God
   A. Triune Atonement (Heb 9:14; 10:29-31)
   B. Invitation to Know the Triune God (Acts 2:38-39)
   C. Trinitarian Salvation (Rom 5:5-6; 8:9, 11; Eph 2:18, 21-22; 1 Pet 1:2)
   D. Trinitarian Witness of Salvation (1 Cor 6:11; Heb 2:3-4)
   E. Trinitarian Assurance of Salvation (Rom 8:14-17; Gal 3:3-6; 4:6)

---

[24]For alternative organization of the passages in threefold form see Wainwright, *Trinity in the New Testament*, pp. 237-47.

3. Living as a Disciple of the Triune God
   A. Praying with Triune Intercession (Rom 15:30; Rom 8:26-27)
   B. A Triune Understanding of Spiritual Things (1 Cor 2:12-13, 16)
   C. Abiding in the Triune God (1 Jn 3:23-24; 4:13-15)
   D. Trinitarian Test of the Spirits (1 Jn 4:2-3)
   E. Triune Building up of Faith (Jude 20-21)
   F. Disciples and Fullness of the Triune God (Eph 3:14-19; 5:18, 20)

4. A Disciple's Relation to Disciples: The Trinity and the Church
   A. Making Disciples with Disciples (Mt 28:19-20)
   B. The Trinity and the Church of Disciples (Eph 4:3-5)
   C. The Trinity and Spiritual Gifts of Disciples (1 Cor 12:3-6)
   D. Triune Doxology as a Means of a Ministry of Discipleship (2 Cor 13:14)
   E. The Future in Trinitarian Hands (Rev 1:4-6; 9-11)

5. Disciples Serving a Triune God
   A. Sending Forth Disciples (Jn 20:21-22)
   B. Trinitarian Ministry (Rom 14:17-18; 15:16)
   C. Fruit and Confidence of Trinitarian Ministry (2 Cor 3:3-6)

The significant number of passages that refer to three members of the Trinity also provide added weight to the conviction that there was a trinitarian mindset among the writers of the New Testament and in the early church. They were not constrained to use a triune formula or triadic structure to describe the relationship of the three persons. When talking about components of the Christian life, the authors sometimes describe it in terms of the Son, sometimes the Father and sometimes the Spirit. They mix the order without any self-consciousness. There is no evidence that they saw contradiction in this approach, but rather that they thoroughly understood God in this triune way. Thus it was appropriate sometimes to describe God's working from the perspective of the Father, sometimes from that of the Son, and sometimes from that of the Spirit.

The widespread explicit and implicit reference to the Trinity and how this God undergirds what it means to be a disciple clearly indicates the critical importance of the trinitarian perspective to the early church. It guided the way they thought about themselves in relationship to God, to each other, to the church and to the world. No wonder the church did not settle until it was able to formulate more explicitly the widespread understanding of the nature of this triune God in the New Testament.[25]

---

[25]J. N. D. Kelly describes it this way: "If the trinitarian creeds are rare, the trinitarian pattern which was to dominate all later creeds was already part and parcel of the Christian tradition of doctrine" (*Early Christian Creeds* [New York: D. McKay, 1960], p. 23; see also his *Early Christian Doctrines* [London: Adam & Charles Black, 1965], pp. 88-90).

2

THE BIBLICAL FRAME
FOR THE TRINITY

Jesus' disciples' understanding of the nature of God was transformed by the incarnation and Pentecost. While the Twelve started out seeing themselves as disciples of Jesus, it soon became clear that through him they were committed to the triune God, and this understanding permeates the New Testament. A large part of their new understanding came from the Old Testament, which had prepared the way for Jesus and hinted at the plurality in God. They saw who God is and what he is doing more fully after Jesus and the Spirit had come.

I. THE OLD TESTAMENT

Before we begin to review the Old Testament preparation for understanding God in a triune sense, a word is in order about the relationship between the Old Testament and the New Testament.

The Relationship Between Old and New Testaments

The New Testament writers, taking their cue from Jesus' attitude toward the Old Testament, stood in the tradition of what God had been doing through the life of Israel. They saw the life of Jesus and the work of the Spirit as a continuation and fulfillment of God's plans and purposes recorded in the Old Testament. So the most clear ideological preparation for understanding what God is doing in the New Testament comes from the Old.

While it is obvious that the Old Testament prepared the way for the New Testament, we need to explore the effect the further revelation of the New Testament has on our understanding of the Old. Do Christians read the Old

Testament any differently than Jews? For the early church the answer was yes. Christians have more information about how God works, so they could see more clearly how he was preparing for Christ in the Old Testament.

This illustrates the fact that we read our Bibles in two different ways. One is with the "order of knowing," that is, how God unfolds his revelation in a progressive way through time and history. Each successive generation receives additional revelation that builds on what God has said before. So in most biblical studies that use a historical-grammatical approach to Scripture, the first question is, what did the people who first heard this truth understand God to be saying in light of their historical situation, which included previous revelation? In other words, every part of the unfolding of Scripture builds on what has been given before but is read primarily in terms of the context of its immediate hearers.

This is a good place to begin, but not a satisfactory place to stop. We need to include all of God's revelation. By the end of the New Testament, God's people have a much better idea of the way God's plans and purposes unfold and a much clearer perspective on everything he revealed. We do the same in reading literature. Every book has a beginning, a middle and an end. Until we see the relationship of all the parts, we do not fully understand the whole picture.[1] When we have the whole perspective, our view of the book—and particularly the author's message—is more complete. The same principle applies to the Bible.

Once we have the whole perspective, we shift from the order of knowing to what may be called the "order of being." The order of being is holistic; it is God's overarching truth derived from all Scriptures. We have the responsibility to put the parts together into a whole. Once the whole is seen, each part takes on a fuller significance. When God's revelation is complete, truth transcends the historical situations of the individual parts.

Nowhere is this twofold reading of Scripture more obvious than with the doctrine of the Trinity. In light of the fuller revelation of God about himself (incarnation and Pentecost), we discover a threefold character to Yahweh in the Old Testament. The monotheism of God's revelation to Israel is now understood more fully; God is not the unitary being that Judaism (or Islam) worships. Rather, there is a plurality in God, which is now much more evident in

---

[1]Cf. Mortimer Adler, *How to Read a Book* (New York: Simon and Schuster, 1967).

light of the New Testament. For example, even though we do not have a full picture of the triune God creating the universe in the Old Testament, by the end of the New Testament we see that all three persons were involved in the act of creation. Christians now know that the Creator God is the triune God! If this was not crystal clear in the order of knowing, it becomes evident when we put the pieces together in the order of being. The God who created the universe is the triune God. All three persons of the Trinity were involved.

We can no longer read the Old Testament solely in terms of the order of knowing. This historical unfolding of God's revelation is valuable, but it must be coupled with the completed picture. This is why Christians do not read their Bibles in the same way that Jews do. Accordingly, the church has always spoken of the revelation of God to Israel as the Old Testament, not just the Hebrew Bible or Torah. The Old Testament is a preparation for the New, and now that the New Testament has come, the Old Testament not only has been superseded in some ways, it has been expanded into a larger revelation of God. This means as Christians now read the Old Testament, the fuller light of revelation expands and enriches their understanding of what God has been saying, sometimes in veiled ways, under the old covenant.

This shift from the order of knowing to the order of being was not lost on the early church. They were so excited to see Scripture as a whole that sometimes they read back into the Old Testament more things than were justified. Because of some of the early Christians' allegorical interpretations, contemporary scholars tend to shy away from their exegesis. The early church sometimes overstated its case in seeing the Trinity or other "Christian truth" in places in the Old Testament where it does not appear.

This means that our task is slightly more complicated. We need to be sure we understand the text as it was given to its original hearers. So the order of knowing is very important. Careful attention needs to be given to historical-grammatical exegesis of each text. But if we are going to be faithful to the holistic theological task (i.e., the order of being), then we must read all Scripture in light of the total revelation. Therefore we read the Old Testament to see if there are things God says, particularly about himself as a triune God, that become more explicit in the New Testament.

Two examples from the New Testament will help us understand this interpretive task. The first comes in Paul's description of Moses putting a veil over his face so that the Israelites would not have to encounter directly the splendor of God that was shining on his face. Paul uses this event to suggest that the Hebrews of his own day could not comprehend the Scripture because of the "veil" over their hard hearts (i.e., their unreceptivity to additional revelation in Christ). That veil is only removed when a person turns to the Christ, which brings intellectual and spiritual freedom. Paul ties this clearer understanding of what God is doing to both the work of the Spirit and to the work of the Lord (2 Cor 3:12-18). If we are to begin with Paul's analogy regarding the veil, we can understand better how trinitarian thought is veiled within the monotheism of ancient Israel. During a time of rampant polytheism, God went to great lengths to indicate that there is only one God. So it is not surprising that hints of this one God's threefold nature were not obvious to the Jews. But reading backward in light of New Testament revelation, we can see some indicators that the God of the Old Testament is not a unitary being.

The second New Testament example that may assist us with this interpretive task is Paul's concept of mystery. Paul speaks of "the mystery of Christ, which was not made known to the sons of men in other generations as it has now been revealed to his holy apostles and prophets by the Spirit; that is, how the Gentiles are fellow heirs, members of the same body, and partakers of the promise in Christ Jesus through the gospel" (Eph 3:4-6). The mystery is that God's saving grace includes Gentiles. As Paul makes explicit in other places, God had certainly spoken about this to Israel (e.g., Rom 15:8-12), but this revelation had not been well received or clearly understood. But now God has made it crystal clear that the inclusion of the Gentiles is a part of his plan, so what was hidden—a mystery—in the past has now been made known. Here the order of being (God's inclusion of the Gentiles) takes precedence over the order of knowing (where the hints at God's purposes have not been fully understood or received). But Paul's perspective is that this was part of what God was saying all along, and certainly a part of what he intended to do.

The parallel with the Trinity is obvious. There were some things that God was saying about the plurality of his own being that were vaguely or not at all understood under the old covenant. But in light of the incarnation and Pentecost, God's revelation is much more explicit, so now we read what he said earlier in a fuller light. Just as we now can pick out more clearly the passages in the Old Testament that reveal God's concern for the whole world, not just Israel, and see this was a part of his covenant promise all the way back to Abraham (see Gen 12:3), so by parallel we are able to look back on God's revelation and see places where he indicated something of the plurality of his nature as one God.

The Promises of a New Covenant Prepare the Way for Triune Theism

How did New Testament believers understand Jesus? They were rooted in God's revelation to Israel through the Old Testament, which finds its focus in God's covenantal relationship with his people. This covenant told Israel about the one God who is holy, who has created the universe and who desires to rule over them. It also told Israel that they, like God, were to be holy, and gave them the standard for holy living. But as Israel tried to live with God, they found it impossible to fulfill the covenant demands for holiness in their own strength. So a time came time when they cried out for some means to deal with their own stubbornness and inability to keep God's precepts.

God then promised the new covenant by which he would make it possible for them to be holy and to fulfill his plans and purposes for their lives. The means of realizing the new covenant relate to God himself and have three key characteristics: (1) the promise of the Messiah, (2) the Messiah will come with the Spirit of God and (3) God himself will dwell with his people. We will look at each of these.

The new covenant related to the coming Messiah. The promise of the new covenant is closely connected to God's sending of the Messiah. As Isaiah puts it, "There shall come forth a shoot from the stump of Jesse, and a branch shall grow out from his roots. And the Spirit of the LORD shall rest upon him" (Is 11:1-2). This is a regular theme of Isaiah (Is 32:1; 42:1; 61:1-4).

The same concept is reiterated in Ezekiel's discussion of the new covenant (Ezek 36—37; 39). In the midst of God's promise to work among his people in a new way, he declares:

> My servant David shall be king over them; and they shall all have one shepherd. They shall follow my ordinances and be careful to observe my statutes. They shall dwell in the land where your fathers dwelt; . . . and David my servant shall be their prince for ever. I will make a covenant of peace with them; it shall be an everlasting covenant with them. (Ezek 37:24-26)

Whether the coming Messiah is described as servant, king, shepherd, prince or branch, it is clear the Old Testament prophets saw an intimate connection between his coming and the promised new covenant.

The new covenant will be inaugurated by the Spirit. Many of the same Old

Testament passages that describe the coming of the Messiah also indicate that the Spirit will be a part of the Messiah's work (cf. Is 11:1-2). In the same context in which Ezekiel describes the coming of the Messiah, God promises, "I will put my Spirit within you, and you shall live" (Ezek 37:14; cf. Ezek 39:25-29).

The New Testament certainly sees Jesus' life as the fulfillment of the promised Messiah, who is closely connected with the Spirit of God. It begins with the announcement to Joseph about the birth of Jesus, indicating that he will be conceived by the Holy Spirit and will be called Emmanuel (Mt 1:18, 20). This is a clear reference to Isaiah's prophecy about the coming Spirit-anointed Messiah (Is 9:1-7; 11:2-3).

John the Baptist prepares the way for the coming of Jesus as the expected Messiah by promising that Jesus will baptize them with the Spirit (Mt 3:11; Mk 1:8; Lk 3:16; Jn 1:33; Acts 11:16). The early church understood this within the context of the promise in Joel 2 that God's Spirit would be made available to all his people, which Peter quoted on the day of Pentecost (Acts 2:17-21, 38-39; see Joel 2:28-29).

At the baptism of Jesus, the Father witnesses to his Son and the Spirit falls upon Jesus in a visible way (Mt 3:16; Mk 1:10; Lk 3:22; 4:1; Jn 1:32), fulfilling God's promise of a Messiah (Is 11:2-3; 42:1-4). Jesus' baptism is closely related to his ministry as the servant of God, anointed by God in fulfillment of the promises that the Spirit would rest on the servant of God. For example, "Behold my servant, whom I uphold, my chosen, in whom my soul delights; I put my Spirit upon him, and he will bring forth justice to the nations" (Is 42:1). Matthew 12:17-21 cites this passage as being fulfilled in Jesus. Luke makes the same connection: "The Spirit of the Lord God is upon me, because the Lord has anointed me to preach good news to the poor. He has sent me to proclaim release to the captives and recovering of sight to the blind, and set at liberty those who are oppressed, to proclaim the acceptable year of the Lord" (Lk 4:17-21; see Is 61:1-2).

Jesus is also deliberately called with the Holy One of God (Mk 1:24; Lk 4:34). The weaving of these three together—the Messiah, the Spirit and the Holy One—is done right after the baptism of Jesus, when the Spirit comes upon him and then Jesus begins his ministry. These events are related to Isaiah 11—12, which connect the Messiah with the Spirit of God and identify him as the Holy One of Israel (Is 11:2-3; 12:6).

The kingly Messiah, the Spirit and the Holy One of Israel are intimately related to the new covenant in Isaiah 30—32 as well as Isaiah 61:1-3, which comes in the larger context of consistent identification of God as the Holy One of Israel (Is 60:9, 14). The witness of the Old Testament is that the Messiah is to reflect the character of a holy God, and the Holy Spirit coming upon Jesus is seen by the New Testament writers as part of the manifestation of the holiness of God in the Messiah.

The new covenant related to the coming of God to dwell among his people. The Old Testament also depicts God coming to dwell with his people. Thus, though God promises his Spirit and his Messiah in Ezekiel 37, he also says, "My dwelling place shall be with them; and I will be their God, and they shall be my people" (Ezek 37:27). While this is not developed in any detail in the Old Testament, it is treated more fully in the New Testament. From the perspective of the order of being, the promised new covenant obviously relates to three divine persons.

The language describing the coming of God. So the promised new covenant focuses on the coming of the Spirit-filled Messiah who is closely tied to the immediate presence of God. The Old Testament clearly identifies the Messiah as a kingly figure. First-century Christians therefore understood Jesus' significance in royal terms. King David is the prototype of the promised Messiah, who is anointed by God to rule.

Jesus is identified in a kingly role even from the time of his conception (Lk 1:32-33) and birth (Mt 2:2). But the picture of the Messiah as a purely political figure is significantly modified by the use of the family language in the Old Testament. Until the time of David, the references to God as Father in the history of Israel had been in reference to his role as Father of the nation (e.g., Ex 4:22-23). With the establishment of the monarchy, however, God becomes the Father of the king in a special way. So David cries unto God, "Thou art my Father, my God" (Ps 89:26; cf. 2 Sam 7:14). This means that while King David represented God's sovereign rule over his people, he also modeled what it is like to understand God as a Father. Now God is not only the Father of the nation but of an individual.

Jesus brings to the fore this second dimension of messiahship. While Jesus gets the attention of first-century Judaism through his identification as the Messiah, he adds to the kingly role of Messiah the concept of sonship. Royal language very early is laden with family language, and Jesus ultimately transforms the first by the second. Thus the emphasis on God as King is radically transformed by God as Father. The former gets people's attention for Jesus, but the latter is part of Jesus' larger purpose in unfolding the full nature of who God is and how we relate to him. In a sense Jesus is both like and unlike the expectations of Second Temple Judaism. Like David, the prototype of the Messiah, he comes to reign, but he reigns as God's Son.

David also has a special relationship with the Spirit of Yahweh. As with other leaders, the Spirit of God comes upon him at the time of his inauguration so that he can function fully under God's direction. The earthly king is to be aligned with the heavenly King through the anointing of the Spirit of Yahweh (1 Sam 16:13). Surely, this is a factor behind the multiple places where the promise of the coming Messiah connects his work with the Spirit of Yahweh. Jesus' coming is seen by the Gospel writers as the fulfillment of the promised Messiah, who is anointed with the Spirit (Lk 4:18 = Is 61:1-2; Mt 12:18-21 = Is 42:1-4). In addition, the Messiah is explicitly identified by the Father as his Son (Mt 3:16-17; Mk 1:10-11; Lk 3:22; Jn 1:32-34). Jesus therefore met first-century messianic expectations in the sense that he came to rule, but sonship is also added to the equation. His sonship ultimately carries with it an element of divinity that is beyond anything envisioned by the Old Testament messianic prototype.

We now turn our attention to other specific ways the plural nature of the triune God is suggested in Old Testament monotheistic faith.

Plurality Within Unity

The writers of the Old Testament battled to maintain Israel's monotheistic faith. One weapon in this intellectual and spiritual warfare was the Hebrews' reiteration of the Shema: "Hear, O Israel: The LORD our God is one LORD" (Deut 6:4). To counter the polytheistic world of the ancient Near East, God emphatically declared his oneness to and through Israel. There is only one Creator, and people need to look to him alone for direction. This monotheism was the most significant intellectual revolution to this point in human history. While all other peoples struggled to balance one god against other gods, Israel looked to the one God who created the world. Everything is found in and explained by this one God.

Nonetheless, there is a richness in the manifestation of this one God. He is not a deistic God who creates the world and then leaves it on its own. The Old

Testament deftly balances God's transcendence (Creator, King, Judge, Redeemer) and immanence (Revealer, Teacher, Prophet, Friend, Priest, Physician, Father, Shepherd, Bridegroom).[2] The tension between God's transcendence and immanence is valuable, and the various figures used to describe God help keep them in balance.[3]

In Scripture, God relates to people in a variety of ways, and several of these include intimations of plurality within the Godhead.[4] Usually these are connected with the immanence of God, that is, when he comes into his world and makes himself known. We will look at several places where these roles suggest a plurality within monotheism.

God as Father. The earliest references to God as a Father are indirect, and they speak of him as one who has children. Thus God instructs Moses, "You shall say to Pharaoh, 'Thus says the LORD, Israel is my first-born son, and I say to you, "let My son go that he may serve me"; if you refuse to let him go, behold I will slay your first-born son'" (Ex 4:22-23). God is also likened to a father who corrects his son: "As a man disciplines his son, the LORD your God disciplines you" (Deut 8:5). The people who are "holy to the LORD your God" are described as "the sons of the LORD your God" (Deut 14:2, 1). Elsewhere in the Old Testament the people of God are described as his children. Isaiah quotes the Lord as saying:

> Sons have I reared and brought up,
> but they have rebelled against me. . . .
> They have forsaken the LORD,
> they have despised the Holy One of Israel,
> they are utterly estranged. (Is 1:2, 4)

The first explicit reference to God as Father comes in the Song of Moses. Moses sets out to "proclaim the name of the LORD," and the Lord reminds him at the close of the song that the Lord's name is holy (Deut 32:3, 51). Moses declares this God to be

---

[2]The transcendence of God refers to his separateness from creation. He stands outside the created universe of space and time as a supranatural being. But in his immanence he enters the universe in order to share life and relationships with human persons.

[3]More detail on the trinitarian function of these roles comes in chap. 9.

[4]For a fresh, contemporary assessment of the possibility of plurality within monotheism see Richard Bauckham, *God Crucified: Monotheism and Christology in the New Testament* (Grand Rapids: Eerdmans, 1998). Bauckham states, "The second Temple Jewish understanding of the divine uniqueness . . . does not make distinctions within the divine identity inconceivable" (p. 13).

> A God of faithfulness and without iniquity,
> just and right is he.
> They have dealt corruptly with him,
> they are no longer his children.

To these foolish and senseless people he asks:

> Is he not your father who created you,
> who made you and established you?" (Deut 32:4-6)

He reminds Israel that they are the heritage of the Lord (Deut 32:8, 9), and he rebukes them for forgetting "the God who gave you birth." "His sons and his daughters" provoke the Lord to hide his face from them "for they are a perverse generation, children in whom there is no faithfulness" (Deut 32:18-20).

This picture of a holy Father is expressed again by the psalmist: "Father of the fatherless and protector of widows / is God in his holy habitation" (Ps 68:5). Again, the Holy One of Israel says of David:

> He shall cry to me, "Thou art my Father,
> my God, and the rock of my salvation."
> And I will make him the first-born,
> the highest of the kings of the earth. (Ps 89:26-27)

While blessing God's holy name, David exclaims, "As a father pities his children, / so the LORD pities those who fear him" (Ps 103:13).

The prophets also speak of God as a loving Father. Isaiah recounts God's love to sons who deal falsely with him. In the same passage that describes God as having a Holy Spirit, Isaiah records the cry of God's people:

> For thou art our Father,
> though Abraham does not know us
> and Israel does not acknowledge us;
> thou, O LORD, art our Father. (Is 63:16)

Isaiah also likens God's role as Father to that of a potter:

> Yet, O LORD, thou art our father;
> we are the clay, and thou art our potter;
> we are all the work of thy hand. (Is 64:8)

Jeremiah describes God's evaluation of Judah:

> I thought
> how I would set you among my sons,

and give you a pleasant land,
a heritage most beauteous of all nations.
And I thought you would call me, My Father,
and would not turn from following me. . . .
Return, O faithless sons,
and I will heal your faithlessness. (Jer 3:19, 22)

But while Israel was faithless in responding properly to God as Father, he continues to fulfill this role in the restoration of his people.

With weeping they shall come,
and with consolations I will lead them back; . . .
for I am a father to Israel,
and Ephraim is my first-born. (Jer 31:9; cf. 20, 22)

This familial figure of speech is not only picked up in the prophets but also in the wisdom literature. In Proverbs we read, "For the LORD reproves him whom he loves, / as a father the son in whom he delights" (Prov 3:12).

Our survey of the figure of God as Father in the Old Testament indicates that there are a number of direct references to God as Father. Many of these refer to his role as the Father of Israel (Deut 32:6, 18; 1 Chron 29:10; Is 63:16; 64:8; Jer 3:14, 19; 31:9; Mal 1:6; 2:10). But it is also evident that God may be understood as the Father of certain individuals within the nation of Israel (2 Sam 7:14; Ps 68:5; 89:26-27; 103:1,13). In particular, the king is referred to explicitly as God's son, representing the nation as a whole, but so are other individuals within the nation who must directly relate to God (2 Sam 7:14; Ps 89:26-27).

The indirect references to God as Father come with allusions to his "sons" or "children." Israel is his "first-born son" (Ex 4:22; Jer 31:9). Clearly Israel, both as a people and as individuals, is sometimes understood as having a family relationship with God.[5]

This use of *Father, son* and *children* seems to be the basis for personal relationships. This will become far clearer when the Son of God appears in the New Testament in the person of Jesus, giving a much fuller picture of what God as a Father is like. Looking back to the Old Testament in light of the

---

[5]See George A. F. Knight, *A Christian Theology of the Old Testament* (Richmond, Va.: John Knox, 1959), pp. 169-74; cf. Allan Coppedge, *Portraits of God* (Downers Grove: InterVarsity Press, 2001), pp. 252-57.

New, we are able to see that God's fatherhood paints a much fuller picture of concern and care on the part of God for his people.

Familial language directly introduces God's relationship to his people. This is shared life, which is best understood as being passed from parent to child. When God is described as Father or the king is described as a son, this emphasizes a close relationship. Thus Jesus' speaks of coming into a relationship with God the Father as a new birth (Jn 3), and growing up in the family of God is a life of shared relationships. God shares his life with Israel through personal relationships with a few individuals (e.g., Moses, Joshua, David). These relationships are illustrative of the sort of life he wants with all. Of course this shared life becomes far richer once the shared life of the Trinity is properly understood. So the language of God as Father is valuable for a full-orbed understanding of Jewish monotheism.[6]

The Spirit of God. The Hebrew word for spirit, *rûah*, may be translated "spirit," "breath" or "wind." Breath was used very early when speaking of God's Spirit. When God created Adam out of the dust, he "breathed into his nostrils the breath of life" (Gen 2:7). This may well be a double reference, not only to the breath of life but also the Spirit of God. The value of "breath" is that it cannot exist apart from a personal being, yet it may be distinguished from its source. So the very nature of the term may suggest why it was chosen to express the idea of "Spirit."[7]

This distinction between God and *rûah* is seen in the opening verses of the Bible, where God's role as Creator is described. First, God "created the heavens and the earth," and then "the Spirit of God" moves over the face of the waters (Gen 1:1-2). Clearly, God's and the Spirit's work in creation are closely associated, but there is a distinction between the two as well.

In relation to people in the Old Testament, the work of the Spirit is described variously. Sometimes the people are said to "have the Spirit of God." Other times they are "filled" with the Spirit of God, and other occasions the Spirit "comes upon them." All of these describe how God through his Spirit guides a person's will and therefore his or her life. The two most prominent

---

[6]For further discussion of the theological implications of the role of God as Father in the Old Testament, see Walter Kasper, *The God of Jesus Christ*, trans. Matthew J. O'Connell (New York: Crossroad, 1999), pp. 130-40.

[7]For discussion of the role of the Spirit regarded as a person, see Arthur Wainwright, *The Trinity in the New Testament* (London: SPCK, 1962), pp. 30-31.

groups of people on whom the Spirit of God rests are leaders and prophets. Significantly, sometimes these figures seem to be controlled by God and sometimes by his Spirit (e.g., David in 1 Sam 16:13, 18). Is this variation an indication of plurality within God?[8]

One of the prerogatives of deity is to give life. The Spirit's life-giving capacity is clear in Genesis 1—2 and elsewhere in Scripture. "For the Spirit of God made me, and the breath of the Almighty gave me life" (Job 33:4). While the Spirit comes upon leaders, he is distinguished from God's working in their lives. Moses is a prime example: "Then the LORD came down in a cloud and spoke to him, and took some of the spirit that was upon him and put it upon the seventy elders; and when the spirit rested upon them, they prophesied" (Num 11:25). Moses himself distinguishes between Yahweh and his Spirit when he says to Joshua, "Would that all the LORD's people were prophets, that the LORD would put his Spirit upon them!" (Num 11:29).

God too makes this distinction regarding the Spirit. When Moses asks for a leader to be designated to take his place, Yahweh responds, "Take Joshua, the son of Nun, a man in whom is the spirit, and lay your hand upon him" (Num 27:18). The same distinction is made with regard to other leaders (Othniel [Judg 3:9-10]; Gideon [Judg 6:34, 36]; Jephthah [Judg 11:27-29]; Samson [Judg 13:24-25]; Saul [1 Sam 10:6-7]; David [1 Sam 16:12-13]) and the prophets (Balaam [Num 24:1-2]; Azariah [2 Chron 15:1-2]; Jahaziel [2 Chron 20:13-14]; Zechariah [2 Chron 24:20]; Micah [Mic 3:8]; Daniel [Dan 5:14, 17-18]). This distinction is very clear in the life of Ezekiel: "He [the Lord] said to me, 'Son of man, stand on your feet, and I will speak with you.' And when he spoke to me, the Spirit entered into me and set me on my feet; and I heard him speaking to me" (Ezek 2:1-2). Elsewhere the Spirit comes and the prophet speaks: "The Spirit of the LORD fell upon me, and he said to me, 'Say, thus says the LORD . . .'" (Ezek 11:5). The Spirit of God comes along with God to enable leaders to lead and prophets to speak. In both cases God's Spirit is distinguished from God.[9]

The early church found two passages of the Old Testament that indicate not only a distinction between God and his Spirit but perhaps of all three persons of the Trinity. The most impressive of these is Isaiah 48:16, where the

---

[8]Allan Coppedge, *Holy Living*, unpublished ms, pp. 336-37.
[9]For theological evaluation of the role of the Spirit in the Old Testament, see Robert Jenson, *Systematic Theology*, 2 vols. (New York: Oxford University Press, 1997-2001), 1:86-88.

promised Messiah is speaking:

> "Draw near to me, hear this:
> from the beginning I have not spoken in secret,
> from the time it came to be I have been there."
> And now the Lord GOD has sent me and his Spirit.

The Lord God (Yahweh Elohim) has sent "me" (the Messiah), and both are distinguished from the Spirit. The early church understood this as a veiled reference to trinitarian thinking by the prophet.

The second passage is Haggai 2:4-7. Yahweh says,

> Work, for I am with you, says the LORD of hosts, according to the promise I made to you when you came out of Egypt. My Spirit abides among you; fear not. For thus says the LORD of hosts: Once again, in a little while, I will shake the heavens and the earth and the sea and the dry land; and I will shake all nations, so that the treasures of all nations shall come in, and I will fill this house with splendor, says the LORD of hosts.

Here the Lord of hosts is clearly distinguished from his Spirit, although both abide with his people. Some have suggested that the reference to "the treasures of all the nations" (v. 7) is a reference to the Messiah. Whether or not all three persons are included, Haggai certainly distinguishes Yahweh from the Spirit.[10]

The word of God. The concept of the word of God is particularly helpful in revealing both the unity and diversity in God. The words a person utters are distinct from the person, yet they also are an extension of who a person is. The Word of the Lord in the Old Testament is God speaking, but sometimes this word appears to have an existence of its own. When the Ten Commandments (Ten Words) are given (Ex 20), the words of God become an extension of God and represent his presence among his people. The word brings revelation from God, but it also symbolizes the very God who is still speaking.

The word is also important because it is a symbol of what it means to be a person. Persons, not things or animals, understand and speak words. Personhood includes rational and verbal capacities. Because a word is an extension of

---

[10]On the Spirit as an indicator of the triune God in the Old Testament see John Oswalt, "The God of Abraham, Isaac, and Jacob: The Trinity in the Old Testament," in *The Trinity: An Essential For Faith in Our Time*, ed. Andrew Stirling (Nappanee, Ill.: Evangel Press, 2002), pp. 21-30; and Leon Wood, *The Spirit of God in the Old Testament* (Grand Rapids: Zondervan, 1976).

a person, every time God speaks, it accentuates his personal nature. Yet there is a distinction between persons and their words, so in some ways the word has its own separate existence. For example, as Samuel grew, "The LORD was with him," "for the LORD revealed himself to Samuel at Shiloh by the word of the LORD" (1 Sam 3:19-21). Here, the Lord and the word are closely related but distinguished. Elsewhere we find that the word of the Lord can be trusted (Ps 119:42) as the source of life (Ps 119:50), light (Ps 119:105) and understanding (Ps 119:169).

A possible connection between the word of God and the second person of the Trinity follows the messianic passage of Isaiah 9:2-7. This passage describes the Messiah in these terms. "For to us a child is born, / to us a son is given" (Is 9:6). Immediately following this is a picture of God sending his word against his people. "The Lord has sent a word against Jacob" (Is 9:8). The passage may be interpreted as the word of God having a distinct existence apart from Yahweh. This does not mean that there is a full-blown concept of the personhood of the Word explicit in the Old Testament. But it sometimes expresses a reality that is present with God, just as one person is present with another (2 Kings 3:12).[11]

References to the word of God in the Old Testament prepare the way for people to understand something distinct within the Godhead. This distinction is more fully developed in the New Testament. John, for example, identifies Jesus as both the Word of God and one who was with God (Jn 1:1). He thus uses *Word* to show both a unity and diversity in God.

Wisdom of God. Wisdom in its proper sense belongs to God alone (Job 12:13; Is 31:2; Dan 2:22-23). His wisdom is particularly related to the practical dimensions of knowledge. Certain things are produced by God's creative wisdom, such as the universe (Prov 3:19-20; 8:22-31; Jer 10:12) and human persons (Job 10:8-12; Ps 104:24; Prov 22:2). Wisdom, like a word, is related to understanding, counsel and knowledge, particularly focusing on a practical understanding of truth, reality and the world.

In terms of wisdom providing veiled intimations of plurality in God, Isaiah connects it with both the Spirit of the Lord and the coming Messiah. In a great messianic passage he talks about both the Spirit of the Lord and Spirit

---

[11]On the Word and the Spirit see Boris Bobrinskoy, *The Mystery of the Trinity* (Crestwood, N.Y.: St. Vladimir's Seminary Press, 1999), pp. 21-36; and William J. Hill, *The Three-Personed God* (Washington, D.C.: Catholic University of America Press, 1982), p. 5.

of wisdom resting upon the Messiah (Is 11:2).

The personification of wisdom in Proverbs (1:20-23; 8:1-36; 9:1-6) led many in the early church to identify it as a separate entity within God. This interpretation became controversial when the Arians used the same passages, which speak of the creation of wisdom, as evidence that Christ was created (Prov 8:22). Even though the wisdom passages probably should be understood as a literary device of personification rather than as designating a separate person (i.e., hypostasis), when viewed parallel to the Word of God, it may indeed suggest plurality in God.[12]

The angel of Yahweh. The "angel of the Lord" (*mal'ak YHWH*) at first appears as a messenger or representative of Yahweh. The tantalizing part of this data is that sometimes the angel of Yahweh and Yahweh himself seem interchangeable. So, for example, "the angel of the LORD appeared" to Moses in a flame of fire, but then, "When the LORD saw that he turned aside to see, God called to him out of the bush" (Ex 3:2-4). When the angel appears to Hagar, the angel speaks repeatedly but is distinguished from the Lord. Yet Hagar concludes the encounter by saying, "Have I really seen God and remained alive after seeing him?" (Gen 16:13; cf. Gen 21:17-19).

This same pattern is repeated elsewhere. God speaks to Abraham about sacrificing Isaac. But then the angel of the Lord speaks and restrains him (Gen 22:1-19). The passage at the same time identifies the angel with God and distinguishes the two. "The angel of the LORD called to him from heaven, and said, . . . 'Now I know that you fear God, since you have not withheld your son, your only son from me'" (v. 12). In verses 15-16, the angel of the Lord speaks as the Lord.

This same phenomenon is repeated on multiple occasions. Sometimes the angel appears to be identified with God (e.g., speaking as God) and yet sometimes he is clearly distinct from God. We see this in the story of his relationship to Jacob (Gen 31:11; 48:15-16), to Moses (Ex 2—6), to Balaam (Num 22:31-35), to Israel (Ex 14:19; 23:20-21; 32:34—33:14; Judg 1:4), to Gideon (Judg 6:11-23), to Manoa and his wife (Judg 13:3-22) and to Zechariah (Zech 1:1—6:8).

The close identification of the Lord with the angel of the Lord suggested

---

[12]For the possible connections between wisdom and Christ or the Spirit see Bobrinskoy, *The Mystery of the Trinity*, pp. 38-51.

to many in the early church that the angel of the Lord might be a preincarnate appearance of the second person of the Trinity. The angel of the Lord is closely identified with and at the same distinguishable from God (Judg 6:11-14; 13:21-22). God refers to the angel (Ex 23:23; 32—34) and speaks to him (2 Sam 24:16; 1 Chron 21:27), and the angel also speaks to the Lord (Zech 1:12).

So it seems legitimate to regard the angel of the Lord as a hint of plurality within God. Patristic, medieval and Reformation commentaries on these passages (using the order of being) identify these references to the angel as preincarnate references to the second person of the Trinity. It should be noted, however, that the New Testament does not explicitly identify the Son of God with the angel of the Lord.

A man of God. Closely related to the angel of the Lord are three places where God is explicitly making himself known, and he is simply called "a man." Although this man is not referred to as the angel of the Lord, many believe such passages are additional references to the angel.

This phenomenon first appears in the story of Jacob wrestling with a man until daybreak (Gen 32:24-30). The man refuses to tell Jacob his name but instead blesses Jacob. Jacob believes he was wrestling with God, saying, "I have seen God face to face" (Gen 32:30).

The second occurrence comes just as Joshua is ready to lead the people of Israel in the conquest of Canaan. There Joshua meets "a man" with his sword drawn. When Joshua asks if the man is for Israel or for its adversaries, the man responds that he has been sent as the commander of the army of the Lord. As a result, Joshua falls to the earth, worships the "man" and declares his submission to his leadership. Then the commander of the Lord's army instructs Joshua to take off his shoes, "for the place where you stand is holy" (Josh 5:15). This statement is identical to that given in Moses' encounter with God on Mount Sinai (Ex 3:5). Joshua's response is appropriate only to deity: worship and submission.

The third place this "man" appears is in the vision of a new temple God gives Ezekiel. In that experience Ezekiel says that "the hand of the Lord was upon me" and that God brought him "in the visions . . . into the land of Israel" (Ezek 40:1-2). Then a man, whose appearance was like bronze, comes to Ezekiel and gives him a vision of the temple, which Ezekiel is to declare to all of Israel (vv. 3-4). The man also reveals the measurements and dimensions of the new temple (Ezek 40—42). Then he brings Ezekiel to a gate where Ezekiel sees the glory of the God of Israel returning from the East. When Ezekiel falls down to worship, the Spirit of God lifts him up so that he may behold the glory of the Lord filling the temple. Finally, with the man still standing beside him, Ezekiel hears God speak to him out of the temple (Ezek 43:1-6). If the "man" is the preincarnate second person of the Trinity, then this is a trinitarian manifestation of God's return to his temple. In this revelation sometimes the Lord is clearly speaking (Ezek 43:6-7; 44:5, 9) and sometimes it appears to be the "man" speaking (Ezek 43:18; 44:1-3), which is very suggestive. It appears as though the one God is himself giving revelation in two ways (as the Lord and as the man), but the persons are certainly distinct.

In all three of these places where a "man" of God appears, there is a clear manifestation of God through him. Whether or not this man is identified with the angel of the Lord, his appearances strongly suggests a preincarnate revelation of the second person of the Trinity.[13]

Other intimations of plurality. *Theophanies.* While the appearance of God in human form by itself would not be significant evidence for plurality within God, God's coming to Abraham as three men certainly is. The text says, "The LORD appeared to him," but Abraham beheld "three men . . . in front of him" (Gen 18:1-2). But from among the "men" the Lord speaks to Abraham and Sarah (vv. 10, 13-15). It is possible that Yahweh appears with two angels, but patristic, medieval and Reformation exegetes took the number three as a veiled reference to the triune God. The interchange between the "men" and the "Lord" is a very strong suggestion that the Lord manifests himself visually in a threefold way (Gen 18:16-17). When the story shifts to Lot in Sodom, the men are described as two angels (Gen 19).

A dialogue between God and his Son. The messianic Psalm 2 is about the Lord and his anointed (v. 2). When the Messiah describes the declaration of Yahweh, he states:

> He said to me, "You are my Son,
> today I have begotten you.
> Ask of me and I will make the nations your heritage,
> and the ends of the earth your possession." (Ps 2:7-8)

Here the Messiah seems to be described as the Son of God, begotten of

---

[13]Oswalt, "God of Abraham," pp. 25-27.

God, who is in conversation with Yahweh (v. 6). The New Testament writers, looking back on this passage, certainly interpreted it as the Father conversing with the Son (Acts 13:33; Heb 1:5).

Repetition of the divine name. Since the name of God is an alternative way of describing his personal being, it always carries particular significance in the Old Testament. The adjective most closely associated with the name of God is *holy.* While the Old Testament refers five times to God's "glorious name" and four to his "great name," all others (twenty-three times) are to his "holy name." So when Isaiah reports that the seraphim called out to God, "Holy, holy, holy is the LORD of hosts; the whole earth is full of his glory" (Is 6:3), the threefold reference is very significant. Is this more than the Hebrew way of using the superlative to accent God's holiness? The early church believed it referred to the triunity of God in part because of the similar vision at the end of the New Testament, where the seraphim cry, "Holy, holy, holy is the Lord God Almighty, who was who is and is to come" (Rev 4:8). The trinitarian references that surround the vision in Revelation (Rev 1—4) reinforce their conclusion. Isaiah probably did not understand the full implications of what he saw, but it may well be a hint of what was to be revealed more fully later.

The same could be said about the Aaronic blessing in which the priests pronounced "the name" of God in blessing over his people: "The LORD bless you and keep you: The LORD make his face to shine upon you, and be gracious to you: The LORD lift up his countenance upon you and give you peace. So shall they put my name upon the people of Israel, and I will bless them" (Num 6:24-27). Is the threefold reference to the Lord just a reminder that God is doing all of these things, or does it suggest that God has a threefold nature? Israel understood it in the first way, but practical exegetes throughout church history have seen this as one more hint about God's nature that would be fully revealed at a later time.

The plurality of the divine name. The chief Hebrew word for God in the Old Testament is *Elohim,* which is plural. This plurality is a little unusual in the light of a strong declaration of monotheism within Israel (Deut 6:4) and is usually explained in terms of a qualitative plural, a plural of intensity or a plural of majesty. Most contemporary scholars opt for a plural of majesty since the word is most often used with a singular verb (e.g., Gen 1:1). While this certainly may have been the understanding of many in the Old Testament, the possibility of Elohim suggesting something more about the plurality of God is enhanced with the observation that sometimes God speaks with a plural of deliberation: God expresses his decisions with a plural verb.

> Then God [Elohim] said, "Let us make man in our own image, after our like-ness." (Gen 1:26)

> Then the LORD God [Yahweh Elohim] said, "Behold, the man has become like one of us, knowing good and evil." (Gen 3:22)

> And the LORD [Yahweh] said, . . . "Come, let us go down, and there confuse their language." (Gen 11:6-7)

In these illustrations both Elohim and Yahweh are used with a plural verb. There are three possible explanations: (1) this suggest some holdover from a polytheistic age prior to biblical revelation, (2) God is deliberating with the angels as the Lord of hosts, or (3) it indicates a plurality within the Godhead. It is certainly not difficult to see why the exegetes of the patristic, medieval and Reformation periods, trying to think in holistic trinitarian categories, saw verses such as these as hinting at the triunity in God. Their conviction was, whether or not Elohim or the plural verbs are clear indications of the Trinity, Christians certainly know that the Creator is a triune God.[14]

Conclusion. Our review of the Old Testament materials indicates that there are a number of ways that the monotheistic God reveals plurality within his own nature. These include the introduction of God as Father, the Spirit of God, the word of God, the wisdom of God, the angel of the Lord and the man of God. Thus there is strong evidence in these cases for a prefiguring of a trin-itarian understanding of God. Several other texts that hint at God's plurality are either not as extensive or the evidence is not as compelling. These include the appearance of God in certain theophanies, the dialogue between God and his Son in Psalm 2, the repetition of the divine name, and the plural character of the name *Elohim*.

Reading the Old Testament material via the order of knowing gives us a progressive understanding of the plurality within the one God. But when we read Old Testament in light of the order of being, where revelation is com-

---

[14]R. A. Johnson understands the plurality of *Elohim* as a part of a larger concept he feels is indicative of plurality within the one God. He believes the Hebrews had a concept of "extension of personality" or "collective personality": "We must be prepared to recognize for the Godhead just such a fluidity of reference from the one to the many or from the many to the one as we have already noticed in the case of man" (cited in Wainwright, *Trinity in the New Testament*, p. 20. For Wainwright's own inter-pretation of God speaking of himself in the plural, see ibid., pp. 23-29).

plete, we can see more fully what was intimated at an earlier stage of revelation. While it is necessary to avoid reading too much into the earlier text, we also must be careful to avoid the opposite error of not reading enough into it. In light of the order of being, it is not difficult to see that God was preparing Israel to understand his triune nature. The promise of the coming Messiah, who would also be God's Son, God's Word and God's Wisdom, certainly prepared the way for understanding the incarnation and the proper interpretation of the person of Jesus. Further, the extensive work of God through his Spirit in the Old Testament clearly opens the way for interpreting Pentecost and the full revelation of how God works through his Spirit.

So beginning in the Old Testament and extending into the New, the revelation of Father, Son and Spirit gives us the full data that the church has sought to understand, appropriate and articulate as it follows the triune God.

II. FROM BIBLICAL MATERIALS TO THEOLOGICAL FORMULATION

There is no forward movement without reviewing the biblical data that underlies the doctrine of the Trinity. So far we observed that the coming of Jesus in the incarnation and the expanded revelation of the Spirit at Pentecost forced the New Testament church to understand God more fully. Intimations from the Old Testament of plurality within the monotheistic God become much more explicit in the New Testament materials. Because Yahweh, the God of Israel, makes himself known through Jesus and his Spirit in the New Testament, there is a continuity between the Testaments. The revelation beginning in the Old Testament expands to include the New Testament so that God's plans and purposes that were "veiled" or "mysterious" in the Old Testament, now become unveiled.[15]

The triune nature of God is the most important part of this unfolding revelation. But now that the church has full access to all the supranatural revelation of God about himself and can thereby shift from the order of knowing to the order of being, it is in a position to put all the pieces of this revelation together to give a more coherent and unified understanding of what God is like. The early church leaders could synthesize the total revelation to see how it goes together, how its unity is expressed more fully. This in turn helped them

---

[15]Ralph del Colle describes this biblical presentation as "primary trinitarianism" ("The Triune God," in *The Cambridge Companion to Christian Doctrine*, ed. Colin Gunton [Cambridge: Cambridge University Press, 1997], p. 123).

see the implications of the trinitarian data given in Scripture.

The process is like putting together a giant puzzle, with some parts of the puzzle being supplied by Old Testament materials and significantly more coming from the New Testament. The theological task of the church is to see how these multiple parts (Old and New Testamant data) can be assembled into a whole so that its unity and coherence are spelled out and its implications can be seen more clearly. The last pieces of the puzzle (i.e., the theological ones) complete the picture of what God is like and what he is doing. Then we will have a holistic doctrine that allows the church's proclamation to be more complete and its implications spelled out more fully. The parts are put together to form a whole, which gives the individual parts far more significance, but the whole is, in a sense, greater than the sum of the parts, carrying a theological weight that the parts alone could never handle.[16]

So the steps in the development of trinitarian thinking are (1) implicit statements about God's character in the Old Testament, (2) more explicit statements about God in the New Testament, and (3) further explication of God's character as the church reflects on Scripture and pieces together its wholeness, coherence and implications for the life and ministry of the church.[17]

Theologically this movement is from *the order of knowing*, where Old Testament materials lead to New Testament revelation, to *the order of being*, which helps spell out the wholeness, unity and coherence of this data. All of this has enormous implications for our understanding of God. The Old Testament starts this process by spelling out five key characteristics of God.

Theological Themes from the Old Testament

Monotheism. In a polytheistic world, Israel claimed that there is only one God. This unique picture of God—centering on the essential oneness of God's being—differed greatly from all other ancient religions.

Supranatural being. The one God, the Creator of all that is, transcends space and time, and unlike the gods of polytheism, he is not a part of the natural world. Nevertheless, Israel believed that this supranatural God relates to and enters into the world he has made. While Israel's story begins

---

[16]T. F. Torrance, *The Christian Doctrine of God* (Edinburgh: T & T Clark, 1996), pp. 35-37.
[17]Thomas Oden, *The Living God* (San Francisco: Harper & Row, 1987), pp. 189, 209.

with a transcendent, supranatural view of God, it also allows for his immanence.[18]

The roles of God. In describing how the transcendent God relates to our world, the Old Testament uses a variety of metaphors. God is described as Creator, King, Judge, Redeemer, Father, Shepherd, Teacher, Husband, Physician and so forth. Each of these roles gives us insight into the way God works and how people relate to him.

The personal nature of God. This supranatural God, who makes himself known in multiple ways, is personal. He is not a force or raw power, as in some contemporary thinking. Neither is he an element of nature, as in ancient polytheism. Rather, he is personal and therefore enters into personal relationships with those created in his image.

The holiness of God. Holiness is central to God's identity. Holiness characterizes all of God's being and activity: his personal nature, his transcendence (separateness), his immanence (roles), and the character traits that describe who he is and his relationships to others.

Theological Expansion by the New Testament

When the New Testament was complete, people had an abundance of new information about the triune God. These materials were an elaboration of the God who had already made himself known through the Old Testament. They are like one further ring in an expanding set of circles in which God reveals more about himself, affecting the way we understand the five Old Testament themes about God. With the New Testament data the church had all the revelation necessary to fully develop its doctrine of the Trinity. Thus the five Old Testament themes were modified as follows:

Monotheism plus Son and Spirit. The monotheism of Israel is significantly modified when Jesus and the Spirit are identified with God in the New Testament. That the Son and the Spirit share in the divine nature is the first challenge to Israel's monotheism.

Supranatural being of the Son and Spirit. The New Testament teaching about the preexistence of the Son and the identification of the Holy Spirit

---

[18]In many works the terms *supranatural* and *supernatural* are used synonymously. I am using the term *supranatural* to indicate God as above and beyond the natural world, i.e., he is outside of the world of space and time. This is to avoid possible misunderstanding. *Supernatural,* for some, may carry the connotation of being just larger than natural, like Superman.

with the Spirit of God in the Old Testament identified the supranatural nature of both persons. This complements the divine nature of the Son and the Spirit in expanded monotheism.

Roles of God paralleled by the Son and Spirit. The roles of God are now attributed to Jesus and the Spirit. For example, one of the prerogatives of the divine role of God as Creator is that he gives life, and in the New Testament the Son and the Spirit have this power. Both Jesus and the Spirit are viewed as working just as God works in his various roles.[19]

Personal nature of the Son and the Spirit. Alongside the personal nature of God, the personal character of Jesus and the Spirit is described in such a way as to make the concept of personhood more concrete. Jesus in particular provides the basis for understanding more fully both divine and human personhood. The personal nature of the Spirit clarifies that he is not simply an emanation or force from God.

Holiness revealed in the Son and the Holy Spirit. The nature of moral holiness is now known concretely in Jesus as the Holy One of God, and in the Spirit of God, the *Holy* Spirit. Jesus gives a pictorial vision of what holiness looks like in a divine as well as a human person, and the Holy Spirit's character and work illustrate the way holiness conditions the character and work of persons, first divine and then human. Love, one component of moral holiness, is increasingly emphasized, suggesting that it is more central than other aspects of holiness.

Theological Development by the Early Church

The early church picked up the theological task of correlating all the data from the Old and New Testaments, and began to spell out how the New Testament materials affected the Old Testament data, and then how both fit coherently into one total revelation of God. Thus the early church's concept of the Trinity becomes essential for understanding God, because the whole picture provides an interpretive key to fully understanding the five themes revealed about God.

Trinitarian monotheism. The Trinity defines what kind of monotheism the Scripture has revealed. There are three persons in one God. Trinitarian theol-

---

[19]Within some roles the language varies when applied to Son and Spirit even though it comes within the same metaphor system. So when God is working as Father, the second person of the Trinity is described as Son (still using family language) and the Spirit works as the agent of the new birth.

ogy is an unfolding of this point; it is a holistic way to understand the biblical materials about one God as three persons.

The triune supranatural being. The relationships of the three persons within the triune God helps explain both his transcendence and his immanence. He is separate from the creation in his ontological existence, but he enters space and time to relate to human persons through the Son and the Spirit.

Three persons in each role of God. The roles of God, which function in both Testaments, provide the basic data for trinitarian thinking because the second and third persons work in a similar, complementary way (i.e., in the same roles) as the first person. A trinitarian understanding of these roles provides a holistic picture of God himself and of other aspects of Christian theology that relate to these roles.

Three persons in one Godhead. The personal nature of God is fleshed out through trinitarian theology and is enhanced by the view of God in three persons, a concept that lays the foundation for the whole concept of personhood and personal relationships.

A holy, loving, triune God. The holiness of God becomes the key to defining (1) how the three persons relate within the Godhead, (2) God's purposes for his people in the world and (3) how all three persons work to accomplish those purposes. Love is the chief way the three persons relate to each other and the way God relates to his creation.

Obviously, the biblical data discussed in chapters one and two reveals that the doctrine of the Trinity is not related to a few isolated texts. Nor is the concept of a triune God an extracanonical way of thinking. The data widely spread throughout Scripture demands that what is implicit in the Old and New Testaments should be made more explicit. This was accomplished as the church shifted from the order of knowing (progressive revelation) to the order of being (completed revelation), with the subsequent implications.

There is also a reciprocity between the Old Testament, the New Testament and the early church's theological formulation, so that they assist and illuminate one another. Just as the Old Testament informs the New Testament, so the New Testament helps better interpret what is implicit in the Old.[20] And the early church's theological formulation of all the biblical materials under

---

[20]Oden describes this correlation of biblical texts as the principle of the analogy of faith, by which one passage of Scripture is understood in relationship to what is known of other passages (*Living God,* p. 192).

certain rubrics, such as the doctrine of the Trinity, provides a better under-standing of the depths of what has been revealed in both Testaments. So the doctrine of the Trinity becomes a valuable interpretive tool. The doctrinal for-mulation of the church does not replace the authoritative status of biblical rev-elation but complements it while remaining under its final authority.

But why was a more fully developed doctrine of the Trinity not spelled out in the New Testament? Part of the answer is that only with the completion of God's progressive revelation do we see the wholeness of what God is making known. God first unfolds data about himself, and then when all the materials are available, his people are in a position to see and understand who he is more fully. What God has said becomes obvious over a period of time as the church grows in understanding the total revelation. The same is true of Christology, ecclesiology and other doctrines in the New Testament.

THE DEVELOPMENT OF
THE DOCTRINE OF THE TRINITY

No Christian doctrine can be developed without a widespread biblical foundation. The purpose of chapters one and two was to indicate that the data available regarding the Trinity is much more extensive than is sometimes thought. In this chapter we now move to the theological development of this biblical foundation. While our focus is primarily on the doctrine of the Trinity, its important to carefully examine the method used in shifting from the biblical data to doctrinal formulation, because the church repeatedly needs to make this transition. While discussing the development of the doctrine we will also discuss the faulty theology that forced the church to spell out its trinitarianism and note the key figures in the early church who helped craft the doctrine of the Trinity. In this process, we will identify the key terms used to describe the biblically based trinitarian reality. These terms are foundational for the way the doctrine of the Trinity affects the doctrine of God throughout the rest of this study. Finally, we will examine how different branches of the Christian church emphasize different aspects of the Trinity.

I. MOTIVATION FOR SPELLING OUT THE DOCTRINE OF THE TRINITY

Historical Context

In practical terms, everyday ministry forces the church to articulate more clearly the truths seen in Scripture. This is particularly important when non-scriptural views (i.e., heresy) have a negative impact on the life and ministry of the church. Since most heresy begins with only a partial truth, the church's responsibility is to utilize all that God has revealed to state the whole truth.

This is what happened in the third and fourth centuries when incorrect thinking about Jesus, the Spirit and God began to influence the church. While the church had intuited the meaning of the Scriptures, now it had to spell out in more detail what biblical revelation says about God.

To refute heresy and strengthen its own ministry, the church digested the biblical materials and formulated the doctrine of the triune God through the Council of Nicea (A.D. 325) and the Council of Constantinople (A.D. 381). The church tackled this task so fully in the fourth century that its doctrinal definition has remained the standard summary of the Trinity for the Christian church across the ages. The church has affirmed these councils for so long because they accurately and succinctly summarize all the scriptural data and help us understand its implications for the life of the church. It is to this historical formation of the doctrine of the Trinity that we now turn our attention.

Two Key Questions

The two theological issues that demanded the church's attention in the third and fourth centuries were the degree to which Jesus and the Holy Spirit are divine. Since the church grew out of a Jewish context, it was monotheistic. But then how were they to explain the incarnation? Since the Gospel stories indicate that there is a supranatural dimension to the birth of Jesus (Mt 1:18, 20; Lk 1:35; Jn 1:14), he is in some way a divine person. While the full implications of this were implicit during Jesus' lifetime, his death and resurrection made his position as the divine Son of God even more clear.

Since the Gospels were written after the resurrection, the four Evangelists had a perspective that allowed them to "theologize," that is, they chose materials, provided information and then interpreted what God had been doing through Jesus. The apostolic letters and writings to the early church further spelled out the implications of the biblical narrative.

A similar phenomenon happened with the fuller work and revelation of the Spirit at Pentecost. Jesus prepared the way for this (Jn 14—16), but when the Spirit descended on the 120 believers in the upper room, his person and work became much more clear. The book of Acts details how the Spirit operates, and the Epistles give further explanation of his activity. In their descriptions of who Jesus and the Spirit are, the New Testament writers reveal the divinity of both. But how do these divine persons fit with the monotheistic presuppositions that the church inherited from Judaism?[1] This demanded a rethinking of their understanding of God, and their conclusions affect the rest of their theology.

Three books of the New Testament in particular point to the fact that the early church was fully aware of the theological task of trying to explain Jesus' and the Spirit's relationship to Yahweh. The Gospel of John is the most theologically oriented of all the Gospels. Traditionally assigned to the apostle John, who wrote toward the end of the first century, it provides theological perspective on the more historically oriented Synoptic Gospels. In John we find evidence of serious reflection on the nature of all three persons of the Trinity.

The book of Romans is the most systematic of the canonical epistles, spelling out the significance of the gospel for soteriological concerns. The theology of the first half of Romans is applied to the Christian life in the second half. While a full systematic theology is only developed later in the church, this book systematically unfolds the various themes related to the gospel (God, sin, salvation, faith, sanctification, salvation and the Jews, the Christian life), beginning with a trinitarian introduction to the whole.

Finally, Hebrews, more than any other New Testament book, shows the continuity of God's work from the Old to the New Testament. Its theological focus is more on the person and the divinity of Jesus than the Holy Spirit. Nonetheless, the author attempts to explain the connections between the Old and New Testaments and the progressive revelation of God, which has come to fruition in the divine-human person of Jesus.

This is not to say that other New Testament books are not theologically oriented, but John, Romans and Hebrews in particular helped the early church to spell out the relationships between the Old and New Testaments, and then to develop this data theologically. So the model for the theological task of the church is laid down within biblical revelation itself.

II. HISTORICAL ISSUES BEHIND THE DOCTRINE OF THE TRINITY

A variety of nonbiblical teachings about Jesus challenged the church to artic-

---

[1]Cf. the articulation of this by Arthur Wainwright, *The Trinity in the New Testament* (London: SPCK, 1962), pp. 3-5. Wainwright argues that while a doctrine of the Trinity is not spelled out in the New Testament, the problem of the Trinity—explaining the relationship of Jesus the Son to the Father—is certainly in the minds of the New Testament writers. So while there is no formal statement about the doctrine of the Trinity, the New Testament writers are certainly addressing the problem. "You will be misleading to say that trinitarian theology is entirely post-biblical" (pp. 4-5).

ulate the doctrine of the Trinity.[2] Committed to a monotheistic view of God, Christians had to balance the unity of God with the particularities of the Father, Son and Holy Spirit. How we speak about God is shaped by whether we begin with the unity or the diversity within the Godhead. Some, following the lead of progressive revelation, believed we should begin by emphasizing the oneness of God's being. Others wanted to shift to the order of being, which would emphasize all three persons in relationship as constituting one God. Whether we discuss the Trinity in terms of the one or the three is a very important issue.

Trinitarian thinking faces two theological dangers. The first is the danger of tritheism. Some feared that focusing on three divine persons would move the church back to polytheism (or tritheism). So in the historical discussions, when too much emphasis was placed on the three persons, a red flag was raised. Fortunately, throughout most of church history the church's foundation in Old Testament monotheism has prevented it from embracing tritheism. Because the foundation of monotheism is so strong, it has created the greater number of theological problems, that is, too much emphasis on the oneness of God. The theological task has always been to find a balance between unity and diversity in the Godhead since both are thoroughly documented in Scripture.

Historically, three nonbiblical ideas about Jesus have their roots in the overemphasis on the unity of God: adoptionism, modalism and Arianism. These three are included under the umbrella of monarchianism. "Monarch," in this context, refers to one *archē* (origin or source), so this designation, monarchianism, places the accent on God's oneness. Let's look at each.

Adoptionism

Adoptionism is sometimes referred to as "dynamic monarchianism." Christ is described as the "new man" on whom the Spirit of God descended. Adoptionists do not see Jesus as divine from his conception, but rather he was "adopted" by the Father at his baptism.

---

[2]This historical section is heavily indebted to the outline of materials by J. N. D. Kelly, *Early Christian Doctrines* (London: Adam & Charles Black, 1965). Though this book is not primarily a historical theology, it is important to provide some historical introduction of terms and ideas that are essential background for the theology of the Trinity. For those who would like to pursue the historical debate on the Trinity in further detail, see the valuable secondary literature in the footnotes.

In this view, Jesus represents God, but God's monarchia (one origin) is preserved. This theory is often attributed to Theodotus in about A.D. 190. His view was that prior to Jesus' baptism he was not the Son of God but an ordinary man who lived a virtuous life. But at his baptism, when the Spirit descended on Jesus, he was adopted as God's Son. Then Jesus began to work miracles, but without becoming divine. Others following this lead suggested that Jesus was deified at his resurrection.

Paul of Samosata in the third century was another well-known proponent of adoptionist thinking. He proposed a theory that denied any personality or subsistence to the Word of God. A thinly veiled unitarian, Paul thought that "the Son" and "the Spirit" were merely names for the inspired man Jesus Christ and the grace of God that was poured upon the apostles. He was condemned by the Council of Antioch in A.D. 268.[3]

The church responded to adoptionism by pointing out that it focused on only a few texts of Scripture and did not take into account the larger biblical picture. In particular it did not factor in the texts that speak of the eternal relationship of Jesus to the Father (e.g., Jn 1:1-18; Phil 2:5-11). Nor did it take seriously enough texts on the birth narratives and the incarnation, which describe Jesus' divinity before his baptism (e.g., Mt 1:20-23; Lk 1:35; Jn 1:1-3; Phil 2:5-11; Col 1:15-19; Heb 1:1-5). So adoptionist Christology was deemed biblically inadequate and unacceptable.[4]

Modalism

The second form of monarchianism the church countered is sometimes called "modalistic monarchianism." Frequently connected with Sabellius of Ptolemais, it is also known as Sabellianism. Modalism so strongly emphasized the oneness *(monarchia)* of God that the Father, Son and Spirit were understood as merely three different ways of viewing the same God. God revealed himself as Father in the Old Testament, as Son in the Gospels and as the Spirit in Acts. To put it another way, the three persons describe (1) God in himself, (2)

---

[3]For references to monarchianism see J. N. D. Kelly, *Early Christian Doctrines* (London: Adam & Charles Black, 1965), pp. 115-18; Bernard Lonergan, *The Way to Nicea* (Philadelphia: Westminster Press, 1976), pp. 36-37; Thomas Oden, *The Living God* (San Francisco: Harper & Row, 1987), p. 12; and Jaroslav Pelikan, *The Emergence of the Catholic Tradition (100-600)*, The Christian Tradition: A History of the Development of Doctrine (Chicago: University of Chicago Press, 1971), 1:175-78.

[4]Ignatius *Trallians* XI, Ante-Nicene Fathers, ed. Philip Schaff and Alexander Roberts (Peabody, Mass.: Hendrickson, 1994), 1:71; and Oden, *Living God*, p. 212; Kelly, *Early Christian Doctrines*, pp. 115-19.

God revealed and (3) God active in other persons. The distinctions are not ontologically real but are our perceptions of God and his relationship to us. This
resulted in a trinity of one personal God with three different identities. God
is not three persons, he is one person who plays three different roles. It fails to
distinguish adequately the three divine persons of the Bible.

Sabellianism regards the Godhead as a monad that is expressed in three operations: God first projects himself as Father, then as the Son and finally as the
Spirit. As Creator and Lawgiver the one God is called the Father; in regard to
redemption he is the Son; and when he inspires and bestows grace on others,
he is called Spirit.[5]

The church's response was that modalism does not adequately take into account the biblical materials about the distinctness and interrelations of the
persons of the Trinity. The monarchy or oneness of God is overemphasized.
Communication between the Father and Son before the creation of the world
(Jn 1:1-4) and while Jesus was on the earth indicates a clear distinction between the persons within God. If the Father, Son and Spirit are only three fac-
ets or modes of the one God, church theologians wondered why the Scripture
presented God as addressing himself.

The early church was fully aware that God worked in different roles. But
they did not believe that the Father, Son and Spirit were roles that a unitary
God played in relation to the world. Thus they felt that modalism inadequately explained all the biblical materials describing the distinctions of God.

Arianism

The most significant challenge to trinitarian thought came from a presbyter
named Arius who began to publish his views in Alexandria in A.D. 318. His
fundamental presupposition was the unique transcendence of a monotheistic
God who was the unoriginate source of all reality. Thus Arius shares with dynamic monarchianism (adoptionism) and modalistic monarchianism (modalism) an overemphasis on the oneness *(monarchia)* of God. But his way of ac-
counting for the role of Jesus and the Spirit was somewhat different.
Beginning with the transcendent and the individual nature of God, he was
convinced that the essence *(ousia)* of God could not be shared or communi-

---

[5]Kelly, *Early Christian Doctrines*, pp. 119-23; Oden, *Living God*, p. 213; Lonergan, *Way to Nicea*, pp.
38-39; Pelikan, *Emergence of the Catholic Tradition*, p. 179; Boris Bobrinskoy, *The Mystery of the Trinity*
(Crestwood, N.Y.: St. Vladimir's Seminary Press, 1999), pp. 217-20.

cated to another without undermining monotheism. Therefore, everything (including the Son and the Spirit) other than God must have come into existence by an act of creation. So the heart of his thinking was that Jesus and the Spirit were created beings.

Arian thought may be capsulized in four summary statements. First, the Father created the Son out of nothing by fiat. The use of the term *beget* ("the only begotten Son" [Jn 1:18 KJV]) really means to "make." The Son is not self-existent but is God's perfect creature above all others. Second, the Son must have had a beginning if he was created. The standard Arian description is "there was when he was not." To have the Son coeternal with the Father would be to undermine the monarchia of the Father. Third, because the Son does not share the Father's essence, he has no direct knowledge of or communion with the Father. Jesus may be called the Word and Wisdom, but he is distinct from the word or wisdom that comes from the Father. He participates in the communication of God's word and wisdom, but he is still a creature, alien from and dissimilar to the Father's essence. Fourth, as a created being, the Son is liable both to change and even to the possibility of sin.

Why then should the Son be called God or the Son of God? The answer of the Arians was that these were courtesy titles. "Even if he is called God, he is not God truly . . . he is called God in name only."[6] So when Arius speaks of a Holy Triad, he envisions the three as having entirely different essences and not sharing the same basic nature. The effective result is to make the Son a demigod. Even though he transcends other creatures, he is no more than a creature in relationship to the Father. The same things would be said of the Spirit.[7] The Arian explanation of Jesus as a created being is called subordinationism. Basically they argued that Jesus, and later the Spirit, are subordinate to God the Father in their essences.[8]

The threat of Arianism forced the church to spell out in unambiguous terms what the Scripture taught regarding the person of Jesus and the triune God. The church did not create something new; it synthesized all of the bib-

---

[6]Bertrand DeMargerie, *Christian Trinity and History* (Petersham, Mass.: St. Bebe's, 1982), pp. 87, 89; see also Pelikan, *Emergence of the Catholic Tradition*, pp. 191-200; Lonergan, *Way to Nicea*, pp. 68-87.
[7]Kelly, *Early Christian Doctrines*, pp. 226-30.
[8]On Arianism as a form of subordinationism, see G. L. Prestige, *God in Patristic Thought* (London: SPCK, 1952), pp. 146-56; and T. F. Torrance, *The Christian Doctrine of God* (Edinburgh: T & T Clark, 1996), pp. 13-18.

lical materials about the person of Jesus, helping Christians comprehend what had been part of their proclamation from the time of the New Testament church. We will now turn our attention to the theological formulation of the doctrine of the Trinity.

III. THE CHURCH'S RESPONSE TO INADEQUATE THEOLOGY

Scripture, Theology and Creed: Developing Conceptual Tools

The theological issues raised by deviations from apostolic proclamation required the church to spell out what it did and did not believe about the person of Jesus, and what this meant for its understanding of God. Just as it had responded to adoptionism and modalism, the church's response to Arianism was that it used Scripture selectively and did not take into account all the biblical data about the Father, the Son and the Spirit. Immersed in Scripture, the early church fathers worked together to develop a holistic understanding of God, and a concise version of this was set down at the councils of Nicea and Constantinople.

The fruits of their labor is known as the Nicene Creed (or the Nicene-Constantinopolitan Creed), which is the distillation of essential biblical truths about the three persons of the Trinity and their relationship to one another, and it still serves as a shorthand way of distinguishing the orthodox position of the church from Arianism and other distorted views of God. The creedal summary was designed not as a substitute for Scripture but as a brief capsulization of essential biblical truth about who Jesus is, and therefore who the Father and the Spirit are. The early church leaders believed they were defending biblical faith against distortion, and therefore they made use of more precise language than that found in the New Testament. This exact creedal language made it more difficult for heretical groups to sound biblical while in reality circumventing the heart of biblical truth. The church fathers did not see their work as the invention of new doctrine but as a synthesis of the apostolic teaching from the New Testament, which had been proclaimed within the church from the beginning.

The Nicene Creed attempts to hold together the threeness and the oneness of God and thus preserve the biblical data on both. The Nicene Fathers "believe in one God," who is defined as "the Father, the Almighty," the "one Lord Jesus Christ, the only Son of God," and "the Holy Spirit, the Lord, the giver of life." There is a balance that starts with the oneness of God, but God is defined in terms of three persons.

The threeness of the persons is held together in the oneness of God. The creed states that the Father and the Son are of the same essence *(homoousios)*. This statement speaks directly to the Arians, who thought Jesus, a created being, did not share the same essence with God. *Homoousios* is reinforced by declaring that Jesus is "the only Son of God, eternally begotten of the Father, Light from Light, true God from true God, begotten, not made, of one Being *[homoousios]* with the Father."[9] This sharing of the same essence was extended to the divine nature of the Holy Spirit before the completion of the final draft of the Nicene Creed. Instead of using the term *homoousios*, the fathers described the Spirit as "the Lord, the giver of life," an alternative way of making the same point, but still a clear indication of the full divinity of the Spirit. The result was that both the Son and the Spirit were given fully divine status in the creed, and the theological term that best describes this is *homoousios*. This allowed the church to maintain the oneness of God while at the same time indicating God eternally exists as three different persons.[10]

After the crafting of the *homoousios* in the Nicene Creed, the next key theological development was the historic formula describing the Trinity in terms of *one essence* and *three persons*. The problem of differentiating the three within the one God was accomplished by distinguishing the persons according to their relations to one another. So the Father is understood as unoriginate, the Son is eternally begotten and the Spirit eternally proceeds from the Father and is sent by the Son. This of course distinguishes the relations of the persons of the Trinity in terms of the being (i.e., ontology) of the Godhead. The persons of the Trinity can also be distinguished by their functional relationship to creation, describing the Trinity in its relations to God's plan *(economia)* for the world. Here the Father is more fully identified with the work of creation, the Son with the provision of redemption and the Spirit with the application and consummation of redemption.

The third key theological tool used by the early church to balance the

---

[9]How *homoousios* fits with the overall doctrine of the Trinity will be addressed in chap. 4. Cf. Torrance, *Christian Doctrine of God,* pp. 80-81.

[10]For an excellent discussion of the development of the *homoousios* and its theological implications for the doctrine of the Trinity, see Walter Kasper, *The God of Jesus Christ,* trans. Matthew J. O'Connell (New York: Crossroad, 1999), pp. 258-63.

three in one is the concept of shared existence, which centers around the use of the term *perichoresis* or coinherence. This concept means each member of the Trinity shares fully in the life of the other two; each permeates and participates in the existence of the others; each coinheres in the life of the others.[11]

These major components—the term *homoousios;* the formula *one essence, three persons;* and the concept of perichoresis—made it possible to establish an orthodox doctrine of the Trinity. With these conceptual tools the church felt that it had distilled scriptural truth, both Old and New Testaments, about God. This allowed the church to defend itself against distorted views. Though the theologians of the early church made generous use of Greek terms and ideas to articulate the theology of the gospel, they did not use them blindly but reshaped them in light of Scripture. The use of words such as *being, Word, act* and so forth came to mean something quite different than in Platonic, Aristotelian or Stoic thought. As used in the church, they are rather un-Greek. As T. F. Torrance puts it, "Far from Nicene theology resulting from a Hellenization of biblical Christianity, there took place in it a Christian recasting of familiar Hellenistic thought-forms in order to make them vehicles for the saving truth of the Gospel."[12]

In the end, the Nicene Creed became a test of orthodoxy, specifically but not exclusively directed toward the Arian threat. Its wording makes it possible to distinguish competing and unorthodox views about God. It identifies the church's consensual understanding of what the Scripture teaches about God the Father, God the Son and God the Holy Spirit.[13]

Key Church Leaders Develop an Orthodox Doctrine of the Trinity

For a better grasp of the orthodox view of the triune God, it will be helpful to know the key figures who helped synthesize the biblical materials and formulate them in the great creeds of the church. Two things should be noted about these early leaders of the church. First, they lived with the Scripture and continually grappled with the breadth of the biblical text. The point is illustrated by Origen's conviction that to be a serious theologian the Scrip-

---

[11]For the development of the concept of *perichoresis,* see G. L. Prestige, *God in Patristic Thought* (London: SPCK, 1956), pp. 282-300.

[12]Torrance, *Christian Doctrine of God,* pp. 127-28.

[13]Oden, *Living God,* pp. 213-15.

tures call for long study, meditation and prayer and hard labor.[14] These writers tirelessly labored to come to grips with the unity, coherence and implications of Scripture.

Second, all of these leaders were concerned with the pastoral and practical implications of theology for the lives of everyone in the church. Most of them were bishops, and during this period of the church bishops were not primarily administrators but pastoral overseers of one or more congregations. They were *not* ivory-tower theologians splitting hairs for academic purposes. They were driven by the practical needs of the spiritual lives of their flock. In particular, their concern for the salvation of people was paramount. For example, Athanasius, a key player in the development of orthodox trinitarian thought, believed that if the Arian view of God were right, salvation would be undercut. So the practical aspect of theological ideas is in the forefront of the whole discussion.

No single person's theology controls the church. Thus the development of the great traditions of the church, found in the General Councils, has always been consensual. Thus the creedal statements of the church are a social affair, a very appropriate reflection of the common mind of the triune God whom the church leaders are trying to describe. While we cannot identify every person who contributed to the development of the doctrine of the Trinity, we will highlight several who made significant contributions.

Irenaeus. Irenaeus best represents the thought of the second century. He is a key figure in the church's move from New Testament data to its more explicit trinitarian formulations. His trinitarian focus is seen in his use of what he calls the church's "Threefold Rule of Faith." First comes the identification of "God the Father, uncreated, uncontained, invisible, one God, the Creator of the universe." Next, the Son is "the Word of God, the Son of God, Jesus Christ our Lord." Third he extols "the Holy Spirit, through whom the prophets have prophesied and the prophets have learned the things concerning God."[15]

The historical significance of Irenaeus's (and also the Latin writer Tertullian's[16]) use of the rule of faith is that he, along with the Apologists, a group of

---

[14]Thomas F. Torrance, *The Trinitarian Faith* (Edinburgh: T & T Clark, 1995), p. 38.

[15]Irenaeus *Against Heresies* 1.10, Ante-Nicene Fathers, ed. Philip Schaff and Alexander Roberts (Peabody, Mass.: Hendrickson, 1994), 1:330.

[16]For more information on Tertullian, see below.

early theologians who defended the faith in the second century, used a trinitarian understanding of God for both baptismal formula and in public worship. As Walter Kasper says, it is a

> concise normative summary of the entire faith which the Church has received
> from the Apostles. It all the more significant, then, that these summaries are
> thoroughly trinitarian in character. This fact tells us that in their teaching on the
> Trinity the early theologians of the Church were expounding not only their pri-
> vate reflections and speculations but the common, public faith of the Church
> that was binding on all.[17]

Irenaeus inherited this use of the rule of faith from the Apologists, but
he made more direct use of it. He looked at the triune nature of God from
two directions.[18] First, he identified God as God makes himself known in
relationship to the universe—the economic Trinity. But Irenaeus also described God as God exists in his own intrinsic being—the ontological
Trinity. In the ontological view the focus is on the Father, who from all
eternity contains within himself his Word and his Wisdom, that is, the
Son and the Spirit, whom Irenaeus identifies with God's work in creation,
redemption and revelation, speaking of the Son and the Spirit as the Father's two "hands."

While we should not read too much into Irenaeus, his reference to the
Word and Wisdom coexisting with the Father for all eternity suggests the
eternal generation of the Son and perhaps eternal procession of the Spirit. He
clearly sees all three as divine and constituting who God is. So he states, "His
Word and his Wisdom, his Son and his Spirit, are always by Him." The Son
is fully divine. "The Father is God, and the Son is God, whatever is begotten
of God is God."[19] Although he does not refer explicitly to the Spirit as God,
the Spirit clearly is divine in Irenaeus's eyes, for he understands the Spirit as
welling up from within God's being. Thus we have in Irenaeus the most explicit trinitarian thinking of the second century.[20] Yet this is not a fully developed concept of three equal persons. It is more of a focus on the Father as a
single person who has a mind and wisdom. Nevertheless, Irenaeus also high-

---

[17]Kasper, *The God of Jesus Christ*, p. 251; cf. DeMargerie, *Trinity in History*, pp. 68-69.
[18]William G. Rusch, ed., *The Trinitarian Controversy* (Philadelphia: Fortress Press, 1980), pp. 6-7.
[19]Kelly, *Early Christian Doctrines*, p. 107.
[20]For significant evaluation of the theological contribution of Irenaeus, see Torrance, *Christian Doctrine of God*, pp. 75-80.

lights the economic way of looking at the Trinity in terms of all three persons related to creation.[21]

Tertullian. From North Africa, Tertullian (c. 160-c. 220), working in Latin, built on Irenaeus's dual approach to the Trinity. But when discussing how God exists in his own eternal being (ontologically), Tertullian followed a different path than Irenaeus, equating both the Word and the Wisdom of God with the Son of God. God possesses within himself the Word, his reason, in such a way that this reason or Word is "another" or a "second" in himself. The identification of the Word with the Son is connected with the work of creation. The specialized meaning of God as the Father of the Son arose at creation. Now the Word or Son is a "person" *(persona)*, "a second in addition to the Father." The Spirit then becomes the "representative" or "deputy" of the Son. The Spirit issues from the Father by way of the Son, being "a third from the Father and the Son." The Spirit like the Son is a "person" so that the Godhead is a "Trinity" *(trinitas;* Tertullian is the first to use this term). Tertullian held the three and the one together this way: "We believe in only One God, . . . that the One and only God also has a Son, his Word, Who was issued out of himself, . . . which Son then sent, according to his promise, the Holy Spirit, the Paraclete, out of the Father."[22]

Tertullian's second approach to the Trinity discussed God as he reveals himself in the process of creation and redemption. Here Tertullian built on Irenaeus's concept of "economy" (Greek: *oikonomia,* Latin: *dispensatio).* The meaning of this term in both languages changed from "the divine plan," or God's secret purpose, to indicating the goal of the divine purpose as seen in the incarnation. Originally, the notion of economy included elements of distribution, organization and the arrangement of the number of factors in some regular order, but came to be used to distinguish God's redemptive plan as worked out through the Son and the Spirit. For Tertullian the three persons of the economic Trinity were not incompatible with God's basic unity. He used the images of the unity between root and shoot, the source and a river, and the sun and its light. So he said the Father, Son and Spirit are one in substance. They are not divided but "extended." So he spoke of the Son as being "of one substance" with the Father. This means they share the same divine na-

---

[21]DeMargerie, *Christian Trinity in History,* pp. 68-72; Bobrinskoy, *Mystery of the Trinity,* pp. 204-11.

[22]Cf. Jürgen Moltmann's appreciation of the foundational contribution of Tertullian in *The Trinity and the Kingdom* (Minneapolis: Fortress, 1993), pp. 137-39.

ture or essence, which helps maintain the unity of God. For the distinctive persons of the Trinity the use of the terms *prosopon* and *persona* were used to talk about the otherness or independent subsistence of the Three.[23]

The church is indebted to Tertullian for creating new theological language to help express the trinitarian faith. He was the first to use the term *Trinity (trinitas)* and the trinitarian formula "three persons, one substance" *(tres peronae, una substantia)*. The church is also indebted to him for the expressions "God of God" and "Light of Light" that found their way into the creeds.[24]

Origen. The Eastern church was influenced by the catechetical school at Alexandria, led by two significant thinkers, Clement (155-220) and Origen (185-254), the more influential of the two. Origen's trinitarianism is characterized by two significant components. First, he focused on the threeness of the triune God. The Father, the Son and the Holy Spirit are three hypostases. Each is a distinct person from all eternity and not, as Tertullian had suggested, only manifested in the economy of God. This is connected with his conviction that the Father begets the Son by an eternal act; therefore there is never a time when the Son was not. Eternal generation of the Son is foundational. Originally the terms *hypostasis* and *ousia* were synonymous and had the meaning of "essence" or "real existence," that is, what a thing really is. But in Origen *hypostasis* carried more of a sense of individual subsistence, so the distinction between the persons was now identified with *hypostasis*. This is important for the future development for trinitarian thought.[25]

Although each member of the Trinity is his own person, the unity of the three is maintained because the Son, as the Father's offspring, is eternally poured forth from the Father's being and therefore is an extension of his Godhead. Origen describes the Son as a "pure effluence of the Glory of the Almighty." This, Origen says, "suggests a community of substance between the Father and the Son. For an effluence would appear to be *homoousios* [of one substance with] that body of which it is an effluence or vapor." Here we see the use of *homoousios* as a way to describe the oneness of God along with a focus on the three hypostases of God. This is how Origen contributed to the de-

---

[23]For the development of the use of the Latin terms *persona* and *prosopon*, see Prestige, *God in Patristic Thought*, pp. 157-62.
[24]See DeMargerie, *Christian Trinity in History*, p. 85; and Kelly, *Early Christian Doctrines*, pp. 110-15.
[25]See Veli-Matti Kärkkäinen, *The Doctrine of God: A Global Introduction* (Grand Rapids: Baker Academic, 2004), pp. 73-74.

velopment of trinitarian thought. He spoke of the three persons in terms of separate hypostases, while maintaining the unity of God by focusing on the unoriginate Godhead concentrated in the Father, who is described as "the fountainhead of deity."

But Origen's trinitarianism is also strongly subordinationist.[26] In the strict sense God is found in the Father alone *(autotheos)*, because the Father alone is ungenerated. While the Son is begotten by an eternal act of God, his deity is derivative; thus he is a "secondary God," while the Holy Spirit is "the most honorable of all the beings brought into existence through the Word." The ultimate ground of the Spirit's being is the Father, but it is mediated to him by the Son. The influence of Platonic thought on Origen is profound. In addition to the Word and the Spirit, there are other spiritual beings who are coeternal with the Father. This basically undermines the idea of a transcendent God who creates a contingent order. The Son and the Spirit are transcended by the Father, and they in turn transcend the realm of inferior beings. Origen seems to be describing the Platonic chain of being that ends with the world.[27]

Athanasius. Athanasius (296-373) attended the Council of Nicea in the entourage of Bishop Alexander of Alexandria. While not a member of the council, he was certainly a part of the team that put together the first version of the Nicene Creed. On the death of his mentor Alexander, he was elected to replace him as bishop in A.D. 328, and from that leadership position Athanasius became the champion of Nicene orthodoxy for the next half-century. The role cost him dearly, as he was sent into exile five times for his views. Nevertheless, he continued to lead the Nicene party until the orthodox understanding of the Trinity prevailed.[28]

The Nicene Creed was a response to the Arian view that the Son is a creature rather than fully God. Thus Athanasius strongly promoted the Nicene position in opposition to Arius and those who followed him. First, Athanasius felt Arianism undermined the doctrine of God. In practice it reintroduced polytheism by setting forth a divine Triad that is neither eternal nor fully God.

---

[26]For further discussion of subordinationism and its origins see Prestige, *God in Patristic Thought,* pp. 131-38.

[27]See Kelly, *Early Christian Doctrines,* pp. 128-132; Lonergan, *Way to Nicea,* pp. 56-67; and Bobrinskoy, *Mystery of the Trinity,* pp. 211-15.

[28]For the story of Athanasius's remarkable perseverance in establishing the orthodox view of the Trinity, see Roger E. Olson, *The Story of Christian Theology* (Downers Grove: InterVarsity Press, 1999), pp. 161-72.

Second, the Arian view completely undercut the liturgical practice of the church in baptizing people in the name of the three persons of the Trinity. Third, Arianism undermined the whole concept of salvation, since it provided a picture of a mediator who was not fully divine and therefore could not mediate between God and humanity.[29]

The Nicene Creed clearly states that the Son was "begotten not made," explicitly countering the claim that Jesus was a creature. It also insists that the Son shares the same substance *(homoousios)* as the Father. This consubstantiality with the Father was the creed's clearest statement of the divinity of Jesus and was the heart of its case that he is as divine as the Father. This became the centerpiece of Nicene theology, which was debated for the next half-century. All of this came out of the conviction that the Son shares completely in the divine nature of his Father.[30] The council used the *consubstantiality* (Latin) or *homoousios* (Greek) of the Son to express the unity of the Godhead. Furthermore, to the Western wing of the church this was a comparable translation of the formula *unius substantiae*, which they had received from Tertullian.

The debate within the church in the middle of the fourth century included not only the Arians and the Nicenes but also a third fairly sizable group who rallied around the leadership of Basil of Ancyra. The latter group proposed a compromise formula that the Son was "of like substance" *(homoiousios)* with the Father. Whereas the Nicene's *homoousios* indicated that the Son is of identical substance *(ousia)* with the Father (preserving the divinity of the Son), this third party was attempting to preserve the distinctness of the three persons of the Trinity.[31]

In sorting through both theological and political issues during this time, Athanasius's thinking became the classic exposition of Nicene theology. Athanasius carried a significant pastoral concern for the spiritual lives of his people. His key concern was the demands of redemption, believing that it would be undermined if the Mediator were not fully divine. If Christ were not both divine and human, how could he mediate between God and human persons?[32] Without divinity, Christ could never impart divine life to humankind.

---

[29]Kelly, *Early Christian Doctrines*, p. 233.

[30]Thomas F. Torrance, *The Mediation of Christ* (Colorado Springs: Helmers & Howard, 1992), pp. 111-12, 122-25.

[31]For the development of the concept of *homoiousios*, see Prestige, *God in Patristic Thought*, pp. 197-218.

[32]Athanasius, *On the Incarnation* (Crestwood, N.Y.: St. Vladimir's Seminary Press, 1996), p. 64.

The tools for asserting the divinity of Christ were two. The first was Athanasius's strong articulation of *homoousios*. That Christ is *homoousios* (of the same substance) with the Father means that he shares the identical essence *(ousia)* of the Godhead. This signified that what Jesus revealed about God to the world is exactly what God is like in himself. This connected the Trinity seen in redemption with the internal relationships of the Trinity. With *homoousios*, Jesus' divinity is guaranteed and therefore his ability to mediate between God and humans is secured. Without this crucial ingredient, the gospel loses its force and Christ is unable to effectively serve as high priest between God and humanity.[33]

Since the Son is *homoousios* with the Father and shares the same *ousia* with God, the unity of God in his being is coupled with the unity of his work through the concept of coinherence (or perichoresis). While the actual term *coinherence* was not used by Athanasius, the concept is certainly there. The concept of coinherent relationships within the one God (i.e., the mutual indwelling of each person with the other) means that when one member of the Trinity acts, the whole Godhead is involved. So because Christ is *homoousios* with the Father and shares his divinity, when Christ comes in redemptive work through the incarnation and the atonement, the whole Godhead is involved with him in this redeeming work. The shared *ousia* of the three persons of the Trinity does not make it necessary for Athanasius to see the Father as the *archē* or origin of the other members of the Trinity. There is a mutual indwelling, one with the other: the Son being Son of the Father, but the Father being Father of the Son in such a way that their mutual relationships are what constitutes their *ousia*. This allows Athanasius to avoid any subordination between the members of the Trinity.[34]

Athanasius's second way of dealing with the eternity of the Son relates to the Father's generation of the Son. Since the Son must eternally exist alongside the Father, Athanasius explains the relationship in terms of the eternal generation of the Son. By being the Father's offspring, the Son must be distinct from the Father. But because his generation is eternal, he must share the same nature as the Father. Athanasius's basic position is that the divine *ousia*—infinite, simple and indivisible—is at once Father and Son. His favorite anal-

[33]Torrance, *Trinitarian Faith,* p. 3.
[34]T. F. Torrance, "Athanasius: A Study in the Foundations of Classical Theology," in *Theology in Reconciliation* (Grand Rapids: Eerdmans, 1975), p. 252; Torrance, *Trinitarian Faith,* pp. 311-13.

ogy of this phenomenon is that of the light and its brightness, a figure of speech that allows two things to be distinguished when they are really one and the same substance.[35]

After a great deal of debate in the middle decades of the fourth century, the final establishment of Nicene theology came about through two major developments: first, a large number of the *homoiousian* faction was won over to the Nicene position, and second, the divinity of the Holy Spirit was further developed. Athanasius was largely responsible for the first, and he contributed significantly to the second.

The ground was laid for the conversion of the *homoiousian* party by Athanasius's statesmanlike approach in which he stated that the important thing was not just the terms they were using but the meaning signified by them. He made the case that both parties wanted to secure the full divinity of Jesus against the Arians, and at an Alexandrian council in 362 his efforts carried the day. At that time it was formally recognized that it was not the language but the meaning underlying it that counted, and the meaning behind *homoousios* was that Jesus was fully of the essence of God. The result of this mutual understanding was that the *homoousios* position prevailed as the standard formula of orthodoxy.

The council also sorted through the thorny issue of the difference between the language of *ousia* and *hypostasis*. In some branches of the church, both of these meant "essence" or "basic nature." So in an earlier part of the debate, when three hypostases were referred to, it sounded to some as though they were talking about three *ousia*, that is, three divine beings.[36] But the Council of Alexandria more clearly defined *hypostasis* as referring to a person. Thus they made the case that three persons *(hypostases)* could exist consubstantially *(homoousios)* within the Godhead. This made possible then the formula that became the badge of orthodoxy, *one ousia, three hypostases*.[37]

Also critical to the establishment of Nicene orthodoxy was the recognition of the full deity of the Spirit. This issue got little attention at the Council of Nicea. The first version of the creed simply declares, "I believe in one Holy Spirit." But in the debate over the role of the Son, it became clear that the role of the Spirit would have to be included in the discussion. Arius deemed the

---

[35]Kelly, *Early Christian Doctrines*, pp. 247, 245.
[36]For the development of the term *hypostasis*, see Prestige, *God in Patristic Thought*, pp. 162-78.
[37]Torrance, *Trinitarian Faith*, pp. 310-12.

Spirit a hypostasis, who was utterly unlike the nature of the Son but like the Son a creature. Later Arius regarded the Spirit as the noblest of the creatures produced by the Father, but still not fully divine.

Athanasius again led the way in expounding a theology of the Spirit as fully divine, consubstantial with the Father and the Son. First, his reasoning was that the Spirit, who comes from God, bestows sanctification and life, and he could not do that without being fully God. Then, since the Trinity is eternal, homogenous and indivisible, and since the Spirit is a member of it, he must therefore be consubstantial with the Father and the Son. Third, the close relationship between the Spirit and the Son indicates that he belongs in essence to the Son exactly as the Son does to the Father. We see this indivisibility in the coactivity of Son and Spirit in inspiring the prophets and in the incarnation. Finally, Athanasius deduced the Spirit's divinity from the fact that he makes us all partakers of God. If the Spirit were not fully divine, we would have no participation in God through him. Accordingly, Athanasius reasoned that the Spirit belongs to the Word and to the Father by sharing with them the same substance *(homoousios)*.

This means that for Athanasius the Trinity was a triad of persons who share one identical and indivisible substance or essence *(homoousios)*. All three persons share in one and the same activity, however, so that "the Father accomplishes all things through the Word in the Spirit."[38] Whatever the Father does, he effects through his Word and whatever the Word does, he carries out through the Spirit.[39]

The Cappadocian Fathers. While Athanasius set the stage for understanding the full divinity of Christ through the consubstantiality of the Son, the Cappadocians settled the issue. The theological contribution of the Cappadocian Fathers built on the soteriological and ontological convictions of Athanasius, but they added some concern for the Christian way of life after redemption. So with them spiritual and moral issues are of special interest under the power of divine energies and the sanctifying and deifying work of the Holy Spirit.[40]

The Cappadocian Fathers are Basil the Great, bishop of Caesarea, his

---

[38]Kelly, *Early Christian Doctrines*, p. 258.
[39]Pelikan, *The Emergence of the Catholic Tradition*, pp. 203-10; DeMargerie, *Christian Trinity in History*, pp. 90-92; Lonergan, *Way to Nicea*, pp. 88-104; Torrance, *Trinitarian Faith*, pp. 47-64.
[40]Torrance, *Trinitarian Faith*, p. 113.

younger brother Gregory of Nyssa, and his close friend Gregory of Nazianzus. Basil was the theological mentor of the two Gregories, who in turn expanded on his teaching and brought out its full implications. Part of this was possible because of their close personal relationships. Two of them are brothers, and there is at least the possibility that Gregory of Nazianzus married a sister of the other two. In any case, their close relationships made possible some theological dialogue and interaction that expresses itself in a similarity of thought. They are a concrete of illustration of how persons made in the image of a triune God can reflect the intellectual dimension of this image by sharing a great deal of common thought.

On the issue of the divinity of the Holy Spirit, Gregory of Nazianzus reported in A.D. 380 that some considered the Holy Spirit to be a force, some a creature and others fully God. Still another group declined to commit themselves, expressing the view that Scripture was not clear on the issue. While the Nicene (homoousian) party represented those promoting the full deity of the Spirit, those opposed to his deity fit into two categories. One group was the Arians and the other was the Macedonians or Pneumatomachians ("Spirit Fighters").

Basil took the lead for the Cappadocians in promoting the full Athanasian position of the consubstantiality of the Spirit. In his treatise *On the Holy Spirit* (A.D. 375) he urged that the Spirit must be a part of the same glory, honor and worship as the Father and the Son. Although he nowhere calls the Spirit "God," he does confirm the Spirit's consubstantiality by saying, "We glorify the Spirit with the Father and the Son because we believe he is not alien to the divine nature."[41] Basing his thinking on the challenge of Jesus to make disciples by baptizing them in the name of the Father, Son and the Holy Spirit, he marshaled arguments from worship for the "godly conumbering" of the Holy Spirit with the Father and the Son in conjoint worship, adoration and invocation of the holy Trinity. Rather than being alien in nature, Basil declared the Spirit to be an ineffable mode of existence as a hypostasis in the indivisible fellowship of the triune God. At the same time he connected the Holy Spirit with the Father and the Son because of the Spirit's role as Creator and cause of all existence. This means that the persons are to be seen as belonging inseparably together while being distinguished from one another. Basil insisted that

---

[41]Basil the Great, cited in Kelly, *Early Christian Doctrines,* pp. 260-61.

"the relation of the Spirit to the Son is the same as that of the Son to the Father. And if the Spirit is coordinate with the Son, and the Son with the Father, it follows that the Spirit is also coordinate with the Father."[42]

Gregory of Nyssa built on Basil's teaching by emphasizing the oneness of the nature shared by the three persons. He concluded that the activity of the Spirit is identical with that of the Father; and since the Son is identified in the same way, there must be no difference in the nature of the three persons. Act and being must go together in the triune God. Gregory of Nazianzus is even more explicit. "Is the Spirit God? Yes indeed. And is he consubstantial? Of course, since he is God."[43]

The concept of the consubstantiality of the Spirit with the Father and the Son was the first way the Cappadocians addressed questions of the unity of the triune God. This was complemented by their concern for the issue of the distinctness or threeness of the persons, which they treated in terms of the persons' mode of origin. Whereas the Son issues from God by way of generation (he is eternally begotten), the Spirit "proceeds from the Father," and like the Son's begottenness the Spirit's procession is eternal. This means that the Father is the cause (not in a temporal sense) and the other two are caused, one is begotten and the other proceeds. This led to another way they established the unity of God, that is, by anchoring it in the person of the Father as the one principle of origin *(archē)* and cause of the Son and the Spirit. Because there is no temporal beginning, the Son and Spirit are eternally caused by the Father. They are not ontologically subordinate to the Father, but logically—in terms of their internal relationships—the Son and the Spirit are begotten and proceed from the Father. Because of the Cappadocians concept of *ousia*, they were led to say that the Son and the Spirit owe their being to the person (hypostasis) of the Father. This is a slight variation from the earlier Athanasian focus on the Son and the Spirit receiving the *ousia* of the Father. It later became the basis for the Eastern church's understanding of the doctrine of the procession of the Spirit as from the Father *through* the Son rather than from the Father *and* the Son.

In order to address more specifically the potential problem of subordinationism by emphasizing the relations of the Trinity, Gregory of Nazianzus proposed

---

[42]Basil the Great, cited in Torrance, *Trinitarian Faith,* pp. 314-15.
[43]Gregory of Nazianzus, cited in Kelly, *Early Christian Doctrines,* p. 261. See Torrance, *Trinitarian Faith,* p. 320.

that the Father, Son and Holy Spirit should be thought of as eternally and sub-sistently existing as God and therefore beyond time, origin and cause. These re-lations between the divine persons refer to what the Father, Son and Spirit are in themselves in their distinctive personal natures and in their reciprocal rela-tionships with one another.[44] If this is to be understood as further explication of the *ousia* of God, it means that Gregory has taken Athanasius's concept of the divine *ousia* and turned it into a more dynamic form. In the Godhead all are mu-tually interpenetrating each other out of their perichoretic shared existence.[45]

One of the analogies the Cappadocian Fathers used to illustrate the rela-tions of the three persons is a torch that was first used to light another torch and then through it to a third. The Cappadocians were wrestling with the question of how to keep the Spirit closely tied to the Father but also being true to the biblical materials that relate the Spirit to the Son. Following their anal-ysis, the Eastern church's position came to be stated in terms of the procession of the Holy Spirit "out of the Father through the Son."[46]

The triumph of Nicene theology and the fuller development of an orthodox position of the Trinity came to fruition at the Council of Constantinople in 381. Here the full divinity of the Spirit as well as the Son was affirmed, and the article of the creed on the Holy Spirit expanded to make it more complete. The Cappadocian Fathers promoted the formula "one ousia in three hy-postases," which was already stated by the Council of Alexandria (362). Their focus is often on the three hypostases in order to give a full separate existence to the Father and to the Son and to the Spirit. But because the Father is the fountainhead of all divinity and because they are committed to the *homoousios* of the Son and the Spirit, they hold the three together in unity. The heart of their position is that there is one God who simultaneously exists in three modes of being or hypostases.

Gregory of Nyssa described how the persons of the triune God are insepa-rably interrelated. All that is seen in the Father is seen in the Son, and all that is the Son's is the Father's since the Son dwells in the Father and likewise has the Father in himself. Therefore the person (hypostasis) of the Son is, as it

---

[44]For further discussion of how the Cappadocians developed the concept of "relation" as the key to un-derstanding the ontological Trinity, see Catherine M. LaCugna, *God for Us* (San Francisco: Harper, 1991), pp. 55-66.

[45]Torrance, *Trinitarian Faith*, pp. 317-22.

[46]Kelly, *Early Christian Doctrines*, p. 263.

were, the form and the face of the knowledge of the Father, and the person (hypostasis) of the Father is known in the form of the Son, while the particularities contemplated in them are due to the clear distinction of their persons.[47]

Basil's approach treated *ousia* as the general or universal principle of God and the *hypostases* as the particulars. Treating *ousia* as a more abstract and generic category had the effect of modifying the earlier concept of *ousia* and made it more like the discussion of *physis* or the common nature of the three divine persons. The approach shifted the understanding of *ousia* from what derives from the intrinsic relations of the three persons to identifying clearly the equality between the persons.[48]

It was the use of *hypostasis*, then, that became the basis for differentiating the particularities of Father, Son and Holy Spirit. To help explain how this is possible the Cappadocians used the language of coinherence (Latin) or *perichoresis* (Greek). This "shared life" of the three persons means that they share an identical nature in the three hypostases. The concept of *perichoresis* also makes possible the exclusion of all ontological subordinationism. Although the Son is begotten of the Father and the Spirit proceeds from him as the fountainhead of the Godhead, because they perichoretically share life, they all are equally of the same *ousia;* in other words, they are consubstantial. Their distinctness is sometimes described in terms of paternity, sonship and sanctifying power. Alternatively, it may be categorized as ingenerateness, generateness and mission. This means that the distinction of the persons is grounded in their origin and mutual relations. So the Cappadocians have taken the concept of *hypostasis* to a higher level than Athanasius. They are more emphatic about the three hypostases that share one and the same nature, so there is a strong emphasis on the threeness within the Godhead. We will see this carry significant implications for some branches of the church in the future.[49]

Augustine. The greatest theological influence on the Western church came through Augustine (354-430), even though his work was not completed until after the establishment of the Nicene Creed (381). During the first part of the fifth century Augustine devoted nearly thirty years to his own study on the Trinity. The fruits of his labor are recorded in his major work, *de Trinitate.* The only other writer he refers to is Hilary; apparently his lack of a working knowl-

---

[47]Gregory of Nyssa and Basil the Great *Epistles* 38.8, cited in Torrance, *Trinitarian Faith,* p. 316.
[48]Torrance, *Trinitarian Faith,* pp. 316-17.
[49]DeMargerie, *Christian Trinity in History,* pp. 110; and Bobrinskoy, *Mystery of the Trinity,* pp. 233-49.

edge of Greek did not give him serious access to the works of Athanasius or the Cappadocians.

In tackling the issue of the Trinity, Augustine focuses on Scripture. So books one to seven of *de Trinitate* deal primarily with scriptural exegesis. In books eight to fifteen Augustine reasons his way forward from what he believes to be a scriptural rather than a philosophical base, but the latter books also include analogies from experience. Augustine affirms with the tradition of the catholic church and the Nicene Creed that the one God is triune, and that the Father, Son and Holy Spirit are coessential—distinct and yet numerically one in substance. Four key areas will help us capture the essence of Augustine's contribution to the doctrine of the Trinity.

First, Augustine strongly emphasizes the unity and equality of the Trinity (see esp. bks. 1, 2, 4). This unity of the Trinity is accented with his affirmation of the *homoousios* of the Father and the Son against the Arians (bks. 4.21, 10.8). At the same time, he emphasizes the double procession of the Spirit (bk. 4.20.29). The background of all of Augustine's exposition is his concept of God as absolute being, simple and indivisible. Unlike the fathers of the East, who made God the Father the beginning point of discussion, Augustine starts with the divine nature. It appears that he stresses the role of God as sovereign monarch with an emphasis on his unified, simple, immutable essence. So subordinationism of any kind (like Arianism) is rigorously excluded.

This focus on the unity or oneness of God implies several things. First, it means Augustine conceives of the Father, Son and Spirit not as three separate individuals, like three human beings all sharing humanity. Rather, each of the divine persons is identified with the others and with the divine essence itself. This is possible because the three persons coinhere. Thus the concept of *perichoresis* makes it possible to focus on their shared life and unity. Second, this means that whatever belongs to the essence of God's nature should be expressed in the singular, since the focus is on one God. So God is eternal, infinite, omniscient, the one who creates and so on. Third, the triune God has a single will and therefore a single, indivisible action. His work is inseparable. So that even as the Trinity relates to the created order, the three persons act inseparably as one principle. Fourth, Augustine's focus on the unity of God makes it difficult to distinguish the three persons. He asserts that each person possesses the divine nature in a particular manner; therefore, in the external operation of the Godhead it is proper to attribute to each of them that function which is appropriated to him by virtue of his origin.[50]

The distinction between the three persons of the Trinity leads to the second major issue for understanding Augustine's contribution to the doctrine of Trinity. Augustine grounds these distinctions in the mutual relations of the persons within the Godhead. So the difference comes because the Father begets, the Son is begotten and the Spirit is bestowed by them as a common gift. Whereas the Cappadocians had distinguished the persons of the Trinity by means of paternity, sonship and sanctifying power (Basil), or ingenerateness, generateness and mission/procession (the Gregories), Augustine's language distinguishes them by begetting, begotten and breathed/spirated/proceeding.

However, because he begins with the unity of the Trinity, Augustine's method of distinguishing the three tends to minimize the persons within the Trinity. It is clear that Augustine is not comfortable with the Greek use of the term *hypostasis* for "person" (bk. 5.8.10). What is the meaning of the three? Augustine responds that we use this language because of the poverty of speech. We speak of "three persons, in that it might be spoken, but that it might not be left unspoken" (bk. 5.9). Augustine did not feel the three persons are described this way in Scripture (bk. 7.4.8). But since they are not the same, they are called three "persons." So he went along with the contemporary usage, possibly hoping to avoid the implication of modalism, but at the same time downplaying the use of persons to describe the Trinity.

On the positive side, Augustine attempts to describe the three members of the Trinity in terms of subsistent relations. To do so he uses the Aristotelian categories of substance, accident and relations. He ruled out accident (because of its reference to that which is not essential) for any discussion of God, and he had already used substance in his discussion of the unity of God. Augustine used relation (how one entity is seen in connection to another) when speaking about the members of the Trinity in a relationship of begetting, begotten, and proceeding. Unfortunately, because he did not tie relation to a clearer concept of personhood, this does not bear the fruit that it might have.

Augustine's third contribution to the doctrine of Trinity is his explanation of the procession of the Spirit. He describes the Spirit as the mutual love be-

---

[50]Jenson's evaluation is that Augustine "was mostly blind to Athanasius' and the Cappadocians' specific achievement, and when he saw it rejected it. Thus the Cappadocian ways of distinguishing Father, Son, and Spirit in the deity itself, without falling into tritheism, were hidden from him" (*Systematic Theology*, vol. 1, *The Triune God* [Oxford: Oxford University Press, 1997], p. 111).

tween the Father and the Son: "Holy Spirit is something common both to the Father and the Son" (bk. 6.5). This communion is consubstantial and coeternal, or it could not bind the Father and the Son together. It could be called "friendship," but he maintains that it is more aptly described as "love."

The analogy that he uses is that of the Father as the lover, the Son as the beloved and the Spirit as the love that joins the two together. The positive side of this is that it reinforces the concept of relations within the Trinity. The negative side is that it seems to reduce the Spirit to a mere connection between the Father and Son without giving the Spirit the same status of personhood. This approach appears to be related to Augustine's discomfort with the concept of personhood within the Trinity. A corollary to this perspective on the Spirit as love between the Father and the Son is that Augustine implies more clearly than anyone else among the Western fathers the double procession of the Spirit from the Father *and* the Son *(filioque)* (bk. 9.2).

The last area where Augustine contributes significantly to trinitarian theology is through his analogies of the Trinity. His conviction is that some things in this world tell us certain things about God, although he is fully aware of the limitations of all analogies. Augustine sees "vestiges" of the Trinity throughout creation. If we look carefully, we can find these faint hints of the triune God who created the world. The most significant vestige of the Trinity is found in human persons, who are made in the image of the triune God (Gen 1:26-27). God said, after all, "Let us [the triune God] make man in our image, after our likeness." Thus Augustine believes that we can see the triune nature of God within a single individual. Since he tends to define a person as "an individual substance of a rational nature," he is inclined to look for reflections of the image within the intellect.[51]

Augustine sees these reflections of the Trinity in three different ways. The first is the trinity of mind, knowledge and love (bk. 9). He argued that the mind has knowledge of itself and love of itself. The second is the trinity of memory, understanding and will (bk. 10). The third views the mind as memory, understanding and love (bk. 14.8.10.12). It is apparent that love and will are sometimes interchangeable in his thinking.

Augustine's analogies have had significant effect on Christian thought, es-

---

[51]This definition of personhood actually postdated Augustine, coming from Boethius, who lived A.D. 480-524/25.

pecially in the Western church. His thought is the basis for a "psychological" understanding of the Trinity. So instead of defining the Trinity as the relationships of three persons, the Trinity is understood as a mental process within the intellect of a single individual.[52] The problem here seems to be not understanding what the image of God in persons entails. In Scripture this image includes the social or relational image of God, where three persons of the Trinity have created men and women in their (the Trinity's) own image, so that human persons must relate to other human beings in order to reflect the image of the triune God. Because men and women are social, just as the triune God is, God places people in families (Gen 1—2).

Augustine rejects marriage as an analogy of the Trinity because he was concerned about the sexual overtones that it might suggest (bk. 12.5). While this protects God from questions of sexuality, it missed a valuable analogy of persons in close, intimate relationship that might well have been an alternative to his psychological analogies.[53]

The impact of Augustine's analogies is twofold. First, internal analogies of the human psyche focus on the individual as reflecting the triune God, not three persons in relationship to one another. This is accented when Augustine looks to the intellect as the basis for understanding the image of God. Thus he emphasized the rational components that make up the intellect rather than the totality of persons who relate to other persons.

Second, Augustine's analogy of the Holy Spirit as the love bond between the Father and the Son seems to depersonalize the Spirit. Some believe this lack of attention to the Spirit accounts for the poorly developed pneumatology in the Western church. Again, the tendency is to downplay the distinctness of the persons in the Trinity and to focus more heavily on the monarchy of God.

In this introduction to the key figures in the development of the doctrine of the Trinity, we have discussed the advantages and disadvantages of beginning either with the unity or with the diversity of God. Augustine began with God's oneness, and accordingly, the three persons of the Godhead received less attention.[54]

---

[52]For further discussion of the interior or psychological approach to the Trinity by Augustine, see LaCugna, *God for Us*, pp. 93-104.

[53]Kelly, *Early Christian Doctrines*, pp. 271-79; DeMargerie, *Christian Trinity in History*, pp. 110-21.

[54]For the impact of Augustine's trinitarian approach on spirituality in the West see James M. Houston, "Spirituality and the Doctrine of the Trinity," in *Christ in Our Place*, ed. Trevor Hart and Daniel Thimell (Exeter, U.K.: Paternoster, 1989), pp. 53-87.

Procession of the Spirit

Between the development of the first Nicene Creed in 325 and its final version at Constantinople in 381 came the recognition that for a full-orbed doctrine of the Trinity there must be a fuller explanation of the role of the Holy Spirit. The first version simply said, "I believe in the Holy Spirit." The final and expanded version stated belief "in the Holy Spirit, the Lord and giver of life, who proceeds from the Father, who with the Father and the Son together is worshipped and glorified, who spoke by the prophets." The primary focus was to identify the Spirit as divine by giving him the title "Giver of Life." At the same time his relationship with the Father and the Son is described as one that "proceeds from the Father, who with the Father and the Son together is worshipped and glorified." So the original Nicene Creed had the Spirit proceeding from the Father alone.

Later in the Western Church this dimension of the Creed was altered to describe the Spirit "who proceeds from the Father and the Son *(filioque)*." This appeared first in the Latin versions of the Creed and was added officially by Spanish bishops meeting at Toledo in 589. In the West this version of the Nicene Creed became popular and was officially endorsed in 1017. However, the Eastern branch of the church objected to the adding of a clause to an ecumenically established creed, and this became a major point of theological contention that contributed to the separation of the Eastern church from the West in 1054.[55]

The West was apparently concerned that in the fight against Arianism the Son must be given equal status with the Father in sending the Spirit. To the East, the adding of the *filioque* clause seemed as though the Spirit was subordinated to the other two persons and was given a lesser place. Their counterformula, borrowed from Gregory of Nazianzus, was that the Spirit proceeds from the Father through the Son.[56] Both had legitimate concerns theologically and the issue has never been resolved between the two branches of the church. Protestants in the Western tradition have adopted the Western version of the Nicene Creed.

The growing interest in the Trinity toward the end of the twentieth century

---

[55]Wayne Grudem, *Systematic Theology* (Grand Rapids: Zondervan, 1994), p. 246. For a review of this controversy see Kasper, *The God of Jesus Christ*, pp. 214-22.

[56]For the theological background and implications of this debate see Roger Olson, *The Story of Christian Theology* (Downers Grove: InterVarsity Press, 1999), pp. 307-10.

has also led to a growing consensus among many scholars that the Western church acted precipitously in changing an ecumenically received creed, but that has not addressed the underlying theological issues or what should be done now. T. F. Torrance has suggested that taking more seriously the concept of perichoresis and the interpenetration of the three persons of the Trinity may take us behind the controversy to see the Spirit proceeding from the Father and the Son, because the Spirit shares perichoretically the same basic interrelatedness of the triunity of God. This would not make him any more subordinate than either of the other two members in relation to the others.

> In proceeding from the Being of the Father, however, the Holy Spirit proceeds from the one Being which belongs to the Son and to the Spirit as well as to the Father. . . . Thus the procession of the Spirit cannot be thought of in any partitive way, but only in a holistic way "as whole from the whole," that is as proceeding from the wholly coherent relations of the three divine persons within the indivisible Being of the One God who is Trinity in unity and unity in Trinity.[57]

One of the more helpful suggestions in our day comes from Thomas Smail who suggests two changes in the Creed. He proposes that the Spirit proceeds from the Father through the Son, as in the Eastern theology, but he adds a second change that would state that the Son is begotten by the Father through the Spirit. This puts all three persons of the Trinity in a fuller interactive relationship with each other, not dissimilar to that perichoretic sharing of nature proposed by Torrance.[58]

Two Approaches to the Trinity

In our overview we have seen that the two branches of the church have approached the Trinity from different directions.[59] Some begin with God's unity and then try to account for the three persons; others begin with the three persons and then move on to God's unity. The challenge is to hold both components together. Though everyone attempts to maintain a balance, the fact is that the starting point often seems to be determinative.

Historical development of the different approaches to the Trinity. Up to

---

[57]Torrance, *Christian Doctrine of God*, pp. 190-91.

[58]Thomas Smail, "The Holy Spirit in the Trinity," in *Nicene Christianity*, ed. Christopher Seitz (Grand Rapids: Brazos Press, 2001), pp. 164-65.

[59]Karl Rahner, *The Trinity*, trans. Joseph Donceel (New York: Crossroad, 1997), pp. 58.

this point we have seen a group within the church that wanted to preserve the monotheism of the God who made himself known in the Old Testament. This overemphasis on the monarchia of God led to certain heretical positions: adoptionism, modalism and Arianism. All three in their distinct ways were trying to preserve the oneness of God and account for the distinction of the Son and the Spirit in relationship to God in other ways.

In very general terms the Eastern church, led by Athanasius and the Cappadocians, emphasized the three persons, basing their thinking on the New Testament accounts of the three. They solved the unity problem with the concept of *homoousios*. The unity of the three persons was made clear through the concept of *perichoresis*, which revealed how the three distinct persons could share the same essence. In their understanding, the economic Trinity revealed in Scripture is continuous with the ontological Trinity; that is, God in his inner being has the same threeness as in his relations to creation. Thus the church in the East, which helped establish the Niceno-Constantinopolitan understanding of the Trinity, took a different approach to the Trinity than did the church in the West.

The Western church has been influenced more by Augustine's theology of God.[60] Apparently he was not comfortable with the concept of persons within the Godhead, thus he emphasized God's unity over his diversity. While the difference between the Eastern and Western approaches can be overstated, these two approaches seem to have had a significant influence throughout the history of the church.[61]

In the West, Augustine's emphasis on the unity of God was reinforced by Boethius's definition of a person as an "individual substance of a rational nature." Thus, throughout the Middle Ages, theologians like Aquinas focused on the unity and rationality of God, beginning their theologies with his being and existence. So in the West an examination of the existence and the being

---

[60]For an overview of Augustine's impact on the Western church, see Robert Jenson, *Triune Identity* (Philadelphia: Fortress Press, 1982), pp. 131-38. See pp. 144-50 on the general distinctions between the Eastern and Western churches.

[61]Colin Gunton, "Augustine, the Trinity and the Theological Crisis of the West," in *The Promise of Trinitarian Theology* (Edinburgh: T & T Clark, 1991), pp. 31-55; and Moltmann, *Trinity and the Kingdom*, pp. 16-17. For an alternative evaluation of Augustine, see the discussion in Kärkkäinen, *Doctrine of God*, pp. 79-80; and Kasper, *God of Jesus Christ*, pp. 296-97. Michael Barnes, "Augustine in Contemporary Trinitarian Theology," *Theological Studies* 56 (1995): pp. 237-50, notes that whether or not this is true, "A belief in the existence of this Greek/Latin paradigm is a unique property of modern trinitarian theology."

of the one God is foundational. The discussion of the triuneness of God is secondary.[62]

This pattern was followed not only by the scholastics of Roman Catholicism but also by the Reformers. This approach crossed over into contemporary thought through the influence of Descartes, who looked within himself to find a basis for assured knowledge. Descartes' lead was followed by Kant and the Enlightenment thinkers, for whom the individual and intellect were central to all knowing.

In his pioneering work in the twentieth century, Karl Barth reopened discussion of the Trinity. But when Barth described three persons, he spoke of three "modes of existence." This naturally leads to an understanding of one God in a threefold repetition. Jürgen Moltmann describes Barth's position as "nothing other than Christian monotheism."[63] Barth's reluctance to affirm the three "persons" of the Trinity meant he too emphasized the oneness of God. Others who have followed Barth by focusing primarily on the unity of the Trinity include the Roman Catholic Bernard Lonergan and among the Protestants Emil Brunner, Wayne Grudem, Thomas Oden, Louis Berkhof, John Feinberg and John Frame.

The effect of this approach to the Trinity may be seen in the teaching structure of the Roman Catholic Church (and some would say other state churches) where there is far less emphasis on the role and activity of the Spirit. Because of the deemphasis on the persons of the triune God, the place of the Spirit seems to be reduced. Often the result is that people relate to God in a general kind of way as a personal being.

Alternatively, following Athanasius and the Cappadocian Fathers, some theologians focus on the diversity within the Godhead, placing the accent on the distinction of the three persons.[64] One such figure from the East is Gregory Palamas (1293-1381). But representatives of this viewpoint have not been limited to the East. In the West it is seen clearly in Richard of St. Victor's (d. 1173) significant analogy of interpersonal love.[65] This same perspective

---

[62]LaCugna, *God for Us*, pp. 43-44, 96-97; Wolfhart Pannenberg, *Systematic Theology*, 3 vols., trans. Geoffrey W. Bromiley (Grand Rapids: Eerdmans, 1991-97), 1:287-89.

[63]Moltmann, *Trinity and the Kingdom*, pp. 63, 139-44.

[64]The first to call attention to this distinction between the East and the West was Theodore de Regnon, *Etudes de Theologie Positive sur la Sainte Trinite* (Paris, 1892), 1:433.

[65]See Pannenberg's evaluation of the positive contribution of Richard in his *Systematic Theology*, 1:286-87.

may be seen in the work of William of St. Thierry (1085-1148) and Jan van Ruysbroeck (1293-1381).[66] It also appears among those segments of the Western church that champion the role of the Spirit, which, of course, come out of a clearer understanding of the different roles of the Trinity. Some of this appears in John Wesley and John Fletcher, who were part of the eighteenth-century revival movement in Britain. Its contemporary form finds expression in the work of Karl Rahner, a Roman Catholic, and in the work of Protestants Jürgen Moltmann and Wolfhart Pannenberg.[67] The latter are students of Karl Barth, but they pay more attention to the persons of the Trinity and not just the monarchy of God. Still more recent expressions of this revived interest come from T. F. Torrance (Church of Scotland), John Zizioulas (Orthodox), Walter Kasper and Catherine LaCugna (Roman Catholic), Colin Gunton (United Reformed Church), and Robert Jenson (Lutheran).[68]

The churches related to Eastern Orthodoxy generally take this approach to the Trinity, and in the West some free churches (as opposed to state churches) have begun to be open to the working of the Spirit, which comes out of a greater understanding of persons of the Trinity. Where voluntary societies within larger churches appear, like the Pietists among the Lutherans and the Methodist societies among the Anglicans, the same may be detected.[69]

While drawing a distinction between those who begin with the unity of God and those who begin with the three persons of the Trinity carries the risk of painting with too broad a brush, there are some indicators that the contemporary church reflects the two different approaches, and each approach seems to entail certain theological and practical implications.[70]

---

[66]William of St. Thierry, *The Enigma of Faith*, ed. J. D. Anderson (Kalamazoo, Mich.: Cistercian Publications, 1974); and J. Ruysbroeck, *The Spiritual Espousals and Other Works*, ed. J. A. Wiseman (New York: Paulist Press, 1985); Louis Dupré, *The Common Life: The Origins of Trinitarian Mysticism and Its Development by Jan Ruysbroeck* (New York: Crossroad, 1984).

[67]In spite of Rahner's fresh emphasis on the threeness of God, Moltmann identifies his view as very similar to that of Barth and refers to it as Rahner's idealistic modalism, which he feels is only another form of Christian monotheism (Moltmann, *Trinity and the Kingdom*, pp. 144-48).

[68]See Jenson's call for correction of the Western tradition's dysfunctional use of the doctrine of the Trinity in both piety and theology in his *Systematic Theology*, 1:110-14.

[69]For an alternative evaluation of this difference of approach between East and West see David Bentley Hart, *The Beauty of the Infinite* (Grand Rapids: Eerdmans, 2003), pp. 169-75.

[70]Gunton, *Promise of Trinitarian Theology*, pp. 31-57; Kasper, *God of Jesus Christ*, pp. 261-63; LaCugna, *God for Us*, pp. 21-205. For further evaluation of contemporary interest in the Trinity see Stanley Grenz, *Rediscovering the Triune God: The Trinity in Contemporary Theology* (Minneapolis: Fortress Press, 2004).

4

THE TRIUNE GOD IN
RELATION TO CREATION

I. KEY TERMS

In our review we have seen how the discussion of the Trinity was shaped by a refining of language. The Eastern church worked in Greek and the Western church worked in Latin, which complicated their communication and the clarification of terms. A major step forward was realized at the Council of Alexandria (362) when Athanasius took the creative step of proposing that they debate not only terms but the actual meaning behind the terms. Once the vast majority agreed on the meaning of a particular matter, they could choose among the best terms to express that meaning. The discussions continued through the fifth century, with some persons holding reservations about one term or another because of their connotations. In the final analysis, however, the church united behind certain language and defined the terms to carry specific meaning. The result was not, as some suggest, that the terms of Greek and Latin metaphysics shaped Christian theology, but rather the church's theology reshaped key words of both Greek and Latin. The church influenced the culture rather than vice versa.[1]

By the time of the church's Fifth Ecumenical Council in Constantinople (A.D. 553), it confessed three hypostases (or persons) within the one nature (or essence) of the consubstantial Trinity. Or to phrase it slightly differently, they were committed to three consubstantial subsistences (hypostases/persons) in

---

[1]Torrance believes this was one of the most significant features of Nicene theology, "not the Hellenizing of Christianity, but the Christianizing of Hellenism" (T. F. Torrance, *The Trinitarian Faith* [Edinburgh: T &T Clark, 1998], p. 68).

single divinity or divine substance (*ousia*/essence).[2] Table 4.1 will perhaps help keep the English, Greek and Latin terms in perspective.

Table 4.1. Key Terms of Trinitarian Theology

English	Greek	Latin
essence substance	*ousia*	*essentia* *substantia*
person	*hypostasis* *prosopon*	*persona*
same essence consubstantial	*homoousios*	*consubstantia*
coinherence	*perichoresis*	*circuminsessio*
mode of existence of God		*subsistentia in divina essentia*
three persons, one essence	three *hypostases,* one *ousia*	three *personae,* one *essentia*

II. TWO APPROACHES TO THE TRINITY

Our theological discussion of the Trinity must begin with the recognition that we approach the triune God from two perspectives. One is in terms of how God has made himself known to the created world. From this perspective, which is termed the economic Trinity (economy = plan, order), we know God as revealed through his relationship to creation, particularly in Israel, in the incarnation and at Pentecost. We come to know the triune God—how God relates to us in our world—through the unfolding story of progressive revelation. Here the Trinity is understood according to function.

But once we understand the working of the economic Trinity, we immediately wonder how the persons relate to each other. This internal relationship of God is called the ontological Trinity (*ontos* = being). The ontological Trinity refers to the inner relationships of three persons within the being of the one God. This may be described as the Trinity understood according to essential nature.

Whether we describe the Trinity in terms of how God relates to the world *(pro nobis)* or how he relates to himself *(in se)*, we are relating to the same God. This assumes that there is a coherence between what God does in relationship to the world and in relationship to his own being. This presupposes that what

---

[2]For the development of the terms *hypostasis* and *ousia* see G. L. Prestige, *God in Patristic Thought* (London: SPCK, 1956), pp. 179-96.

God has revealed about himself through his actions toward creation also gives us an accurate (although not exhaustive) understanding of who he is within himself. Therefore, we are beginning with the premise that there is one Trinity, not two, and that God is the same in his own inner being as he is in his actions toward us. Though different terms are used (economic Trinity and ontological Trinity), we need to remind ourselves that we are dealing with one God.[3]

Having declared our conviction that God is consistent in his action and being, we must also acknowledge that we begin knowing God through the economic Trinity. This means that the God who made himself known as Yahweh in the Old Testament has unfolded a clearer picture of himself as Father, Son and Spirit in the New Testament. So the description of God as the economic Trinity, God making himself known to us in our world, is our key to knowing him. This is what dominates the biblical materials. Once we come to the end of this data (i.e., when we have all that God has revealed to us in Scripture), we are in a position to see how all of the evidence fits together to tell us who God is in himself, that is, the ontological Trinity. So once we have the revelation that describes the economic Trinity, we still have the theological task of articulating what this implies about God in himself. Regarding this, T. F. Torrance says, "what God is toward us in the Word and Activity of Christ and the Spirit he is in his ultimate being or *ousia*."[4]

This movement from observing what God reveals about himself in Scripture (primarily about the economic Trinity) to knowing God as he existed before the creation of the world and in himself (the ontological Trinity) is the shift from the order of knowing (progressive revelation) to the order of being (a holistic view).[5] When we see the unity and coherence of the biblical data, which gives a whole picture of God as he is apart from creation in the order of being, we are in a better position to understand more fully what he is saying via the order of knowing. So there is a mutual relationship between the order of knowing and the order of being, each illuminating the other.[6] The parts make possible a knowledge of the whole, and, in turn, the whole illuminates the parts.

---

[3]T. F. Torrance, *The Christian Doctrine of God* (Edinburgh: T &T Clark, 1996), p. 7.
[4]Ibid., p. 129.
[5]The Latin for order of knowing is *ordo congnoscendi* and for order of being o*rdo essendi* (ibid., p. 136).
[6]For further discussion on the relationship of the order of knowing (the epistemological order) to the order of being (the ontological order), see David Coffey, *Deus Trinitas: The Doctrine of the Triune God* (Oxford: Oxford University Press, 1999), pp. 15-16.

We will begin our discussion of the Trinity with a focus on the economic Trinity: what the Scripture says about the three members of the Trinity and how they relate to creation. This data will lead us to a discussion of the ontological Trinity, bearing in mind that these two continually inform one another, and each assists in the full understanding of the triune God.

The consistency between the economic and the ontological (immanent) Trinity has been most clearly articulated by Karl Rahner in his famous axiom, "The economic Trinity is the immanent Trinity, and the immanent Trinity is the economic Trinity."[7] This statement is so significant that it is now called "Rahner's Rule." It reminds the church that the God who has made himself known in creation, redemption and sanctification is not different from who God is in himself, which helps preserve the essential connection between God and salvation, and sets the stage for reconnecting the doctrine of the Trinity with the rest of Christian theology.[8]

It is probably better to see Rahner's insight as a methodological one, so the economic Trinity is understood as revealing the ontological Trinity.[9] To take his rule in an ontological way might blur the distinction between the being of God and the doing of God. If that should happen the focus is on what God does in relation to creation and leads to a functional understanding of the Trinity. The result would be not enough attention given to the relationship of the triune God within himself.[10] Both how God relates to us and what he is in himself are properly held in balance if the first (economic Trinity) leads to understanding the second (ontological Trinity).

III. THE ECONOMIC TRINITY: *OPERA AD EXTRA*

The church has always understood that God unfolds revelation about himself in the Old and New Testaments. When we have this data fully in hand, it is clear that he works as Father, Son and Holy Spirit in areas like creation, redemption and sanctification. This is how God relates to our world; these actions are the external operations of the Trinity, captured in the phrase *opera ad extra.*

---

[7]Karl Rahner, *The Trinity*, trans. Joseph Donceel (New York: Crossroad, 1997), p. 22.

[8]For discussion of the value and limitations of Rahner's axiom, see Walter Kasper, *The God of Jesus Christ*, trans. Matthew J. O'Connell (New York: Crossroad, 1999), pp. 273-77.

[9]For a qualified use of Rahner's rule see David Bentley Hart, *The Beauty of the Infinite* (Grand Rapids: Eerdmans, 2003), pp. 155-75, 179-80.

[10]Jürgen Moltmann, *Trinity and the Kingdom* (Minneapolis: Fortress, 1993), pp. 137-39.

The progressive unfolding of this data reveals God's plan, or the economy of God: the economic Trinity. Unfortunately, today the term *economic* carries commercial overtones that certainly were not part of its original use. To avoid the contemporary implications of the term *economic*, other terms have been suggested. Some have proposed using *evangelical* Trinity, because the focus of all three persons of the Trinity is on bringing the gospel of salvation to our world. Others suggest the *revealed* Trinity because God reveals himself as Father, Son and Spirit. Still others argue that we should use *operational* Trinity because each member of the Trinity operates in relationship to creation. All of the terms have their advantages and disadvantages, but because of its long history I will continue to use *economic* Trinity.

Because Scripture highlights the three persons of the Trinity, with a particular focus on the incarnation and Pentecost, I will begin from this perspective. Then I will move from the economic Trinity to the unity they share within the Godhead. In other words we begin with the diversity and move toward the unity of the Trinity.

A Difference in Threeness:
Diversity in Both Revelation and Redemption

Every act of God is trinitarian, but those acts are distributed in a personal and dynamic way. Scripture indicates that particular members of the Trinity are closely connected with certain activities in relationship to our world. This does not mean that the other members are not also involved, but each of the three has a locus of work and responsibility. This means there is diversity in their functions, but certainly not an absolute division of labor. This diversity relates to two major areas: revelation and redemption. We will examine each of these in turn, both from the perspective of how God is relating to us, and then the reverse, how we relate to God.

The economic Trinity and revelation. From God to us. A shorthand résumé of how God works in revelation is *from the Father through the Son by the Spirit.* Revelation is usually divided into two categories. The first is general revelation, which is found through creation. The created world makes it possible for God to speak to his creatures from the physical creation, from reason, from conscience and from a variety of experiences. These experiences are further subdivided in terms of our experience of the physical creation, animals and people, including personal, familial and social/cultural/political relationships.

The fact that the Father is especially connected with creation means that he is speaking to us through the creative order and its various dimensions (see Ps 19:1-6; Acts 13:24-29; Rom 1—2).

The Father also speaks to us through special revelation—words and events. This is seen particularly in his direct speech to Israel and the events by which he made himself known. Through accurate recording and interpretation, the events were translated into words, and thus God's special revelation comes to us first in the Old Testament and then in the New. So God as Father has revealed himself to us through general revelation and special revelation, the second being the control and interpreter of the first.

But the Father speaks *through the Son*. And just as the Father speaks through word and event, so the Son comes to us as both word and event (or model). He is described as the living Word (Jn 1:1-4), who speaks what is given to him by the Father. His words are the heart of God's communication in the Gospels, and his life modeled or illustrated most things that he verbalized. So there is a match between his life and his speech. His incarnation was a living model of what God wants us to understand, and his words are a more exact description of what God wants us to hear. Both his life and words then become part of God's special revelation to his people.[11]

Though the Father speaks through the Son, he also speaks *by the Spirit*. The Spirit's role in special revelation is to oversee the record of that revelation in Scripture. So he is often described as the one who actually is responsible for what God has said in Scripture. But he also witnesses to the hearts of individuals that the Scripture is true. This classic Reformation doctrine declares that the word given by God in Scripture is witnessed to by the Spirit as the truth. So there is a double witness to individuals, externally in Scripture and internally by the Spirit.[12]

The Spirit further witnesses to general revelation as interpreted through the lens of Scripture. This means that in light of special revelation the Spirit assists God's people to interpret what God is saying through general revelation (creation, reason, conscience and experience).

---

[11]This revelation of God may also be described as coming both by word and by being. It is possible because of the *homoousios*—the identity of the Son with the Father—so that there is a full correlation between what the Father reveals through the Son and what God really is in himself, in his own being (Torrance, *Christian Doctrine of God*, p. 143).

[12]John Calvin *Institutes of the Christian Religion* 1.7 (Philadelphia: Presbyterian Board of Christian Education, 1813), pp. 85-92.

The sum is that God the Father has spoken through the Son and by the Spirit so that all three members of the Trinity are involved in revelation, but each has a slightly different function in this revelatory work. This is true with regard to the total revelation of God to us, but it is particularly true of revelation of the triune God about himself. As T. F. Torrance says, "As God may be known only through himself, through his self-revelation, so the Holy Trinity may be known only through the Trinity, in God's trinitarian self-revelation of himself."[13] This is summarized in table 4.2.

Table 4.2. From God to Us

from the Father	• creation: general revelation • word and event: special revelation
through the Son	• living Word • word (speech) • model (illustration)
by the Spirit	• records revelation of word and event/model in Scripture • witnesses to Scripture as truth • witnesses to general revelation as interpreted by Scripture • applies the Word

The presupposition behind this connection between the economic Trinity and revelation is that God alone makes himself known. According to Scripture, he makes himself known through the Son and the Spirit. Because of the triune nature of God in revelation, we know that we are getting an accurate description of what God is really like. Thus God is never to be thought of as something different from what he has made known about himself in the person of Jesus and revealed to us by the Spirit. He is exactly as the Son and the Spirit have made him known. This gives us confidence that we can actually know God as he is, not as hidden and obscure but as self-revealing. He has made himself known to us so that we might enter into relationship with him as Father, Son and Spirit.

From us to God: Response to revelation. The Trinity not only speaks to us in revelation, but God also expects a response from us. This is part of the twofold nature of theology mentioned in the introduction. Again, all three persons of the Trinity are involved. The formula that best helps us to understand how this

---

[13]Torrance, *Christian Doctrine of God,* p. 74.

works is that we respond *by the Spirit through the Son to the Father.*[14]

God is first involved in our response to his revelation *by the Spirit.* This begins when the Spirit helps us receive revelation from both Scripture and nature. The Spirit opens our spirits so that we can understand and be receptive to the truth; he helps us understand what God is saying. Then the Spirit witnesses to this revelation as truth. Finally, the Spirit empowers us to respond positively to the revelation we have received from God, bringing an enabling grace that allows us to be receptive, to trust and then to respond appropriately (e.g., obedience, love, thanksgiving, etc.).

This assistance from God comes by the Spirit *through the Son.* God's revelation concentrates on the person of Jesus, and his primary design is for us to come to know about the Son so that we may actually come to know the Son. First comes knowledge *about* the person of Jesus, and second a personal and direct knowledge (experience) *of* Jesus. After the incarnation, knowledge of God is mediated through the Son. There is no saving knowledge of God apart from Jesus (Jn 1:18; 14:6).

Then the work of God by the Spirit through the Son leads us *to the Father.* This means that the Spirit leads us to the Son, and the Son leads us to the Father (Jn 14:9). Our response to revelation is not just a passive receptivity but also a positive response that brings us into relationship with all three members of the Trinity. So by the Spirit through the Son we come to know the Father, and in knowing the Father we know the Son and the Spirit. Table 4.3 summarizes this process.

Table 4.3. From Us to God: Response to Revelation

by the Spirit	• We receive revelation from Scripture and general revelation • Spirit witnesses to it as truth • Spirit enables us to respond positively
through the Son	• come to know the Son
to the Father	• know the Father

The economic Trinity and redemption. The persons of the Trinity not only relate to the created world in terms of revelation but also in terms of redemp-

---

[14]See Wolfhart Pannenberg, *Systematic Theology,* 3 vols., trans. Geoffrey W. Bromiley (Grand Rapids: Eerdmans, 1991-1997), 1:331.

tion. This refers to what God is doing in remaking his relationship with people. In parallel to the relations between the economic Trinity and revelation, the discussion of the economic Trinity and redemption is divided into two parts: from the triune God to us and from us to the triune God.

From God to us. Just as the economic Trinity relates to us through revelation, God also relates to us in redemption, that is, *from the Father through the Son by the Spirit.* Each person of the Trinity is particularly identified with some function in the process. The other two members, though, serve in a complementary, perichoretic way.[15]

We first see this with the Father. Redemption begins *from the Father* and is particularly related to the creation of the world according to God's purposes. The Scriptures closely connect the work of the Father with creation. Central to the Father's purpose for creation is his desire that human persons reflect his image (Gen 1:26-27). While Scripture clearly indicates that the Son and the Spirit have a part in creation, including God's purposes, the Father seems to be the "representative person" in the biblical picture of how God relates to us (see fig. 4.1).

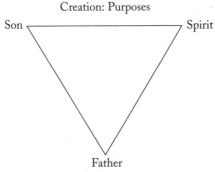

Creation: Purposes

Figure 4.1. From the Father

Unfortunately, God's purposes for his people have been interrupted by the entrance of sin (Gen 3). Sin has produced a situation in which women and men are not truly reflecting God's image. So God's purpose in redemption is to restore people so they might ultimately reflect his original design for them

---

[15]In more contemporary language, we might describe one member in each function as the "point person." This is why we use the point of a triangle as a symbolic emphasis of the functions of the various members of the Trinity.

at creation. This work by the Father to accomplish his purposes in spite of sin is done through the Son by the Spirit.

The creation of the universe and of people to reflect God's likeness is accomplished by the Father *through the Son*. Redemption is provided through Jesus' incarnation, life, death and resurrection. Jesus illustrates what people made in the image of God are supposed to be like, and his teaching spells this out. His death and resurrection are an integral part of this redemption. Christ makes redeeming grace available to restore people to a right relationship with God and thus manifest the image that he originally designed for them at creation. The second person of the Trinity is the incarnate one who lives a sinless life and who dies and is raised from the dead to provide for God's redeeming work among people. The Son functions uniquely in redemption; he participates in redemption in a way that neither the Father nor the Spirit do. This does not mean that the Father and the Spirit are not intimately involved in this process, but it is obvious that the Son carries a distinct role in this capacity (see fig. 4.2).

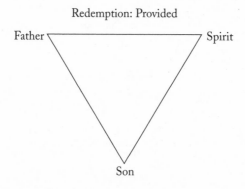

Figure 4.2. Through the Son

The Father is the key person in creating and establishing his purposes for us in the world. The Son is responsible for providing redemption. But the Spirit is primarily responsible for the actualization of this redemption. So the formula is *from the Father through the Son by the Spirit*. The Spirit's work is sometimes described in terms of sanctification, or the application of redemption or the consummation of God's work (see fig. 4.3). The Spirit actually applies the redeeming grace provided through the Son in the individual lives of people. He is the agent of the new birth that begins to regenerate people and make them again like God. The Spirit is also the one who restores human persons to a right relationship with God. So the Spirit is (1) the personal presence of the triune God working in individuals to bring them into a right relationship with the Godhead, and (2) the one who subjectively transforms people on the basis of the redemption the Son provided so that they then can fulfill God's purposes to be a holy people, reflecting fully the image of the triune God.

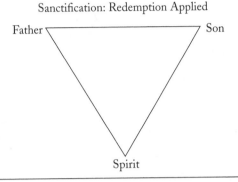

Sanctification: Redemption Applied

Figure 4.3. By the Spirit

From us to God. God has worked from himself to us to make redemption available, and we respond in a parallel way, captured succinctly in Ephesians 2:18, which speaks of how we relate to God through Jesus in the Spirit: "For through him [the Son] we both have access in one Spirit to the Father."

1. In redemption the Trinity works in us *by the Spirit through the Son to the Father.* This means that the Spirit draws us to God when we receive his revelation. The Spirit also enables us by grace to respond in faith to the Son. So the work of God the Spirit in us first enables us to receive revelation and then empowers us to respond by faith. By the Spirit we are drawn through faith in the Son to the Father. As we trust in the Son and his work for us, we enter into a relationship with him, and through this relationship with the Son we then come to the Father. In this process the Spirit applies the grace that makes it possible to come into a relationship with the Son and through him have a personal knowledge of the Father (see fig. 4.4).

2. This trinitarian mode of working expresses itself in a variety of ways in our experiences of knowing him and appropriating his grace. This happens in our presalvation experience when we are drawn by the Spirit through the prevenient grace provided by the Son toward the Father. It happens in our

salvation when the Spirit becomes the agent for the new birth, which brings the Son's saving grace so a relationship is established with the Father and we are renewed in the image of the triune God.

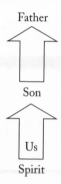

Figure 4.4. By the Spirit *through the Son* to the Father

But God continues to work after our experience of initial redemption. We experience the witness of God's Spirit, who reassures us of the Son's saving grace, which in turn gives us assurance of our relationship to God the Father. This fosters growth in the image and likeness of God (progressive sanctification) by living in the Spirit, and growth in the grace that the Son has provided and in a deepening relationship with the Father (and the whole Godhead). Full sanctification may be described as the infilling or the baptism of the Spirit, where purification from sin is made possible by the grace of the Son so that one is able to experience the fullness of God and to love unconditionally as the Father does. Then it becomes possible to go on in maturity, in further growth after full sanctification. This consists of walking in the fullness of the Spirit and growing in grace toward mature likeness of Jesus, which leads to a deeper knowledge of the Father and a greater likeness of the whole triune Godhead. Table 4.4 shows the multiple ways the triune God works in us.[16]

Unity and the Economic Trinity

The economic Trinity as revealed throughout Scripture emphasizes the diversity of the three members of the triune God in relationship to creation. But is the unity of God addressed? Do we see God as one in terms of his relationship

---

[16]Further elaboration of the activity of the economic Trinity will come in chap. 9, which discusses how all three members of the Trinity work in each of the various roles of God.

Table 4.4. The Triune God and Our Life in Him

Our life	by the Spirit	through the Son	to the Father
presalvation	drawing/convicting	prevenient grace	toward the Father
salvation	agent of new birth	saving grace	relationship established with the Father, renewal of image of God
assurance	witness of Spirit	reassurance of saving grace	assurance of relationship
progressive sanctification	living with Spirit	growth in grace	deepening relationship
full sanctification	infilling/baptism of Spirit	full lordship purification from sin	fullness of God perfect love
maturity	walking in fullness of Spirit	growth in maturity	deeper knowledge of the Father, greater likeness to the Father

to us in revelation and redemption? Several factors in Scripture help us see unity within the Trinity's economic activity.

Grounded in monotheism. First, the entire unfolding of God's plan (economy) begins with God's self-revelation in the Old Testament. Here God emphatically declares to Israel that there is only one God and that Yahweh is that God. Whereas in polytheism, pagans constantly struggle to balance their relationship with many gods, Israel knows that there is only one God, and all of their attention is focused on him. This declaration of monotheism is spelled out at Mount Sinai and reiterated throughout the history of Israel in the great Shema. "Hear, O Israel: The LORD our God is One LORD" (Deut 6:4). This is reinforced by the first commandment that Israel shall have no other gods before Yahweh (Ex 20:3); he alone is the One with whom they have to do.[17]

This one God is clearly the Creator of all the universe and the one who reveals his purposes and plans to his people. Further, he is the one who has begun to provide a solution to the problem of sin by establishing a covenant with his people, drawing them back into relationship with himself that he might transform them once again into the likeness of his own image.

---

[17]Yehezkel Kaufmann, *The Religion of Israel* (Chicago: University of Chicago Press, 1960), chap. 3.

The strong monotheism of the Old Testament had to be addressed when Jesus and the Spirit appear in the New Testament. How do we account for their divinity in the light of this monotheistic declaration to the people of Israel? This focus on the one God undergirds the whole discussion of the Trinity. When we acknowledge the three persons within the Godhead, we are continually reminded that there is only one God who relates to his people. It is as though the triune God gave Israel time to comprehend that there is only one God, and then, in the New Testament, he begins to explain more fully what his oneness entailed. So the unfolding of the second and third persons of the Trinity in the New Testament must be understood in the context of Old Testament monotheism, and that monotheism must now be understood against the background of the Trinity.

In light of the New Testament revelation, we normally identify the work of Yahweh in the Old Testament primarily with that of God the Father. This is because when Jesus refers to Yahweh, he refers to him as his Father (e.g., Jn 20:17). Rarely does Jesus refer just to God. A case could be made, however, that Yahweh in the Old Testament may well be a picture of an undifferentiated Trinity.[18] Nevertheless, the New Testament references to God that are not otherwise spelled out normally refer to God the Father (cf. 2 Cor 13:14). So the New Testament church along with the early church tended to identify Yahweh of the Old Testament with God the Father. The effect of this is a further grounding of the unity of the Godhead in the monotheism of the Old Testament.

The roles of God. In the Old Testament Yahweh makes himself known in eight major roles (Creator, King, Personal Revealer, Priest, Judge, Father, Redeemer and Shepherd) and a number of minor roles (Physician, Warrior, Teacher, Prophet, Friend, Husband and Bridegroom). We will discuss these roles at some length in chapter nine. At this point it is sufficient to note that God makes himself known through these roles, which by analogy tell us the way God works in relationship to his creation. They are figures of speech borrowed from our world to draw comparisons with who God is and how we relate to him.[19]

The key thing for our purposes at this point is to notice that when Jesus

---

[18]See the references to the implicit plurality of God in the Old Testament in the discussion of the Messiah, the Spirit, the Wisdom and the Word of God in chap. 2. See also Peter Toon, *Our Triune God: A Biblical Portrait of the Trinity* (Wheaton, Ill.: Victor Books, 1996).

[19]Allan Coppedge, *Portraits of God* (Downers Grove: InterVarsity Press, 2001), pp. 26-33.

and the Spirit appear in the New Testament, they do the same kinds of work that the Father does in the Old Testament. This means that they function in all of the same roles as Yahweh does. For example, while God as Creator gives life in the Old Testament, the New Testament speaks of the Son as giving life (Jn 1:4), while the Spirit is also described as having the same capacity (2 Cor 3:6). The value of understanding these roles is that they provide part of the data that point to the divinity of both the Son and the Spirit.[20] The roles strengthen the unity of the economic Trinity by indicating that Father, Son and Spirit work in a similar way.[21] They do the same things in relationship to the world even when the emphasis is different. They all are involved in the same divine activities toward creation. So in the unfolding economy of God we find the Father, the Son and the Spirit functioning in the same roles. The unity of the Godhead is seen in the similar work of the members of the Trinity.

The external operations of the Trinity are indivisible. Additionally, the unity of the economic Trinity is boosted in the New Testament by the fact that all members of the Trinity share in the role that distinguishes each individual member. So the New Testament makes clear that while the Father is primarily responsible for creation, both Jesus (Jn 1:3; Col 1:16; Heb 1:1-3) and the Spirit (2 Cor 3:3, 6) are involved in bringing creation into existence. In the same way, while the Son carries a special responsibility in redemption, the Father sends the Son into the world and the Spirit conceives him in the incarnation. Both witness to him at his baptism, and sometimes the resurrection is attributed to the Father (Acts 2:32-33) and at other times to the Spirit (Rom 1:4). The redeeming work of God is clearly the work of all three, even though the Son is primarily the Redeemer. The unified work of the three persons can especially be seen in Hebrews 9:14 and Ephesians 2:18, where they all contribute to our redemption.

In like manner, both the Father and the Son share in the work of the Spirit in sanctification (Rom 15:16). The Father sends the Spirit at Pentecost at the request and with the assistance of the Son (Acts 2:33). So the Spirit's work in

---

[20]Ibid., pp. 366-71.

[21]Within some of the language of each role there will be variations of how each member functions. So in the family language, the first person functions as Father and the second as Son. The Spirit does not have a family title in the same way but functions within the family context, e.g., agent of new birth. This variation within each role protects us from assuming Jesus acts exactly like the Father. Rather, he relates as Son to Father within this family role language.

the world is clearly understood in terms of a joint work with the Father and the Son (Jn 14).

So while each member of the Trinity is identified with a special work in the economy of God, all three persons are involved in each of these three major activities of God: creation, redemption and sanctification. This accounts for the classic Latin phrase *opera ad extra sunt indivisa:* "the external operations of the Trinity are undivided."

The unity in the work of the economic Trinity is best captured by the early church's concept of mutual indwelling or perichoresis. Reflecting the teaching of John 14:10-11, 20 and John 17:21, perichoresis points to the inner penetration of each member of the Trinity with the others, so that each shares the life and the activity of the other two. Of course, perichoresis is also closely tied to the concept of *homoousios* in which the members of the Trinity share the same essence. *Homoousios* is grounded in the monotheism of God. All three persons of the Trinity share the same being because there is one God, and out of this shared existence (perichoresis) each one is involved in the activities of the others in relationship to the created world. The early church grasped the unity of the persons but did not blur the distinctions. Thus they said that everything which could be said of the Father could be said of the Son and Spirit, except that the Father is not the Son or Spirit. And the same is true of the Son and Spirit. They can be distinguished only by their persons and unique relationships to each other, but cannot be distinguished by their attributes, authority, roles or external actions toward creation. The persons are one in being.

5

THE TRIUNE GOD WITHIN HIMSELF

I. HOW THE ECONOMIC TRINITY REVEALS THE ONTOLOGICAL TRINITY

We began with the economic Trinity because this is the way God reveals himself in Scripture. From the scriptural data, we have every reason to believe that the economic Trinity is the same as the ontological Trinity.[1] This means that the question of how God relates *within himself* should certainly be consistent with what he has made known *about himself* in his relationship to the world. The central fact about their being is that all three persons share the same divine essence *(homoousios)*.[2] We discover this in part from the data about how God reveals himself to us in the economic Trinity. On the basis of Jesus' own teaching we are given explicit warrant to move from the economic Trinity to the ontological Trinity. That is, we can look at how the triune God has revealed himself in relationship to creation and from this we are able to grasp in a true way some of what God is actually like in himself. This task begins with Scripture and draws out its theological implications. It involves a shift from the order of knowing to the order of being. This involves a corresponding shift from biblical theology that unfolds the way God has made himself progressively known in Scripture to systematic theology, which develops a holistic picture of God. So we will shift from an economic to an ontological description of the Trinity, piecing the

---

[1]An example of the contrary position is Royce Gordon Gruenler, *The Trinity in the Gospel of John* (Eugene, Ore.: Wipf & Stock, 1986), p. xvii. Gruenler argues that in the economy of redemption the Son and of the Spirit have "modes of operation" reflected in their subordination to the Father that are not the same as the way the ontological Trinity works in "modes of being."

[2]The significance of *homoousios* in this connection between the two understandings of the Trinity is why T. F. Torrance can say, "The *homoousion* is the ontological/epistemological lynch pin of Christian theology" (*The Christian Doctrine of God*, [Edinburgh: T &T Clark, 1996], pp. 92-98).

biblical data into a whole and drawing inferences about the nature of God in himself.[3]

Figure 5.1 illustrates the shift from the economic to the ontological Trinity. In the economic Trinity the Son is primary; that is, he is the person through whom we know the most about the other two. The way to understand the Father and Spirit is through our understanding of the Son.

However, we do not wish to overstate this case. Since the external relationships of the Trinity are undivided, we know something about economic Trinity both from our understanding of the Father and the Spirit as well as the Son. Nevertheless, the clearest indication that we have of the three persons of the Trinity comes in our understanding of the Son as he is made known to us through the incarnation. Once the Son is fully revealed and helps us understand more clearly the Father and the Spirit, then we are in a position to discuss the ontological Trinity, what God is within himself, and here we get a picture of the role of the Father who begets the Son and breathes the Spirit, so the second and third persons of the Trinity have their ontological "origin" in the Father (see fig. 5.1).

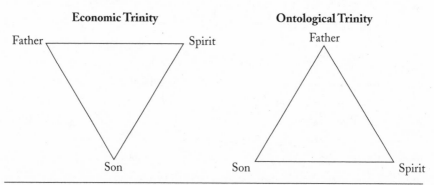

Figure 5.1. Differences in the economic and ontological Trinity

The complementary nature of the two perspectives might be described like this: In terms of our knowing God (our epistemology) we begin with Jesus and

[3]For an alternative approach see the work of David Coffey, who believes the biblical doctrine of the Trinity is not to be identified with the economic Trinity. The biblical doctrine should lead us to an understanding of the ontological/immanent Trinity and that understanding of the Trinity should then help us understand the economic Trinity. The value of Coffey's work is to remind us of the reciprocity of the two (*Deus Trinitas: The Doctrine of the Triune God* [New York: Oxford University Press, 1999], p. 16).

the economic Trinity. However, with the being of God (our ontology) we focus on the role of the Father and the ontological Trinity.

The following is an example of how the economic Trinity helps us understand the ontological Trinity. In the economic activity of God, the Father is described as the head of Christ (1 Cor 11:3). This seen when it is repeatedly said that the Son is sent by the Father (e.g., Jn 20:21), demonstrating the Father's direction over the Son. Likewise, the Spirit is sent from the Father through the Son in such a way that he does not speak for himself but calls attention to what has been said by the Father through the Son (Jn 16:13-15). So when we think of the Trinity in economic terms, it seems that the Son sees himself under the direction of the Father, even though they are in intimate communion. In the same way the Spirit, who does not speak on his own, is pictured as being under the direction of the Father and the Son. Again, in spite of intimate relationships (sometimes he is described as Spirit of the Father and sometimes as Spirit of the Son), he does not act independently but under their direction.

If the being (ontology) and function (economy) of the Trinity are the same reality, then the functional descriptions suggest that there is a similar ordering in the being of the Trinity. While there is no subordination (i.e., that the Son or the Spirit is inferior or less fully divine than the Father), there is an order in social relationships, even within the Godhead. We are now in a position to more fully understand the internal work of the triune God, so we turn our attention to the ontological Trinity.

II. THE ONTOLOGICAL TRINITY: *OPERA AD INTRA*

Beginning with the relationships of the triune God to the created order, we are able to infer some things about God's relationships within himself. This internal working of the Trinity *(opera ad intra)* centers on the very essence of God. Some authors call this the "immanent Trinity" because of the close interrelationships between the persons of the Trinity. A few prefer to describe this as the "social Trinity," to accent the social relationships that are taking place within the triune God. Still others prefer "relational Trinity" because this is how the three persons relate to themselves. Each term has its strengths and weaknesses, but we will use the traditional "ontological Trinity" to talk about the *opera ad intra*.

Several questions press to the forefront when discussing the ontological

Trinity. One is how to account for the distinctness of the persons within one God. Another has to do with the unity that brings them together. A third is how the three relate to each other within the Godhead.

Distinctness of Persons

The distinctness of the persons may be understood in terms of the personal identities of the three members of the Trinity. The key way in which the persons of the Trinity are distinguished in their being is that the Father is the fountainhead of divinity *(fons totius divinitas)*. Sometimes this is described in terms of the Father being the source of divinity, as long as *source* is not understood in a temporal sense. It comes from the fact that we cannot have a son without a father, and along with the human analogy, the Father is the source or origin of a Son. So the distinction between Father and Son is that the Father begets the Son and the Son is begotten of the Father. The early church was careful to identify this as an *eternal* begetting so there would be no confusion between divine relationships and the analogous human relationships, where a father begets a son in time. In the case of the divine Father and Son, there was no time when the Son did not exist.

If the Father is the fountainhead of divinity in terms of begetting the Son, his role in relationship to the Spirit is that the Spirit proceeds from the Father through the Son. Accordingly, the Spirit is described as breathed or spirated. The classic distinction between the Son and the Spirit is that one is begotten and the other is breathed. The persons are distinguished in that they are noninterchangeable, neither confused nor fused, but have unique and permanent names and unique relationships.

The early church leaders were fully aware that they were working with analogies that did not fully explain all of the mystery of the Trinity. They were trying to be faithful to the biblical data that describes the relationship of Son to Father, and Spirit to Father, by using the terms *begotten* and *breathed*. When they had gone that far, they realized they could not go much further. They were conscious that these analogies are imperfect and that there is much that is wrapped in mystery. But the appeal to mystery should not obscure the real gains made. The result was that they had a concept of the Son being eternally begotten by the Father and the Spirit eternally breathed by him. *Begetting* and *breathing* are valuable terms because they convey both oneness and separateness, and both are tied to the central concept of life. They show intimate connection between triune persons while preserving their distinctness. They are imperfect terms, but they also are valuable personal terms that helped the church move forward a major step in understanding the internal relations of the Trinity.[4]

Equality and Oneness: Unity of the Trinity

Having looked at how the internal relations of the Trinity are distinguished in terms of personal identities, we now give our attention to the unity within the Godhead.

One essence. The debate in the early church was first over the divinity of Christ and then over the divinity of the Spirit. This discussion led to the holistic view that the biblical data presents the three persons as sharing the same essence or substance. The development of the term *homoousios* was the shorthand form of saying that all three persons are of the same nature. They are not merely *like* each other *(homoiousios)* but they are of the *same essence (homoousios)*. Thus the three members of the Trinity equally share in the divine being.

What is this one nature *(ousia)* shared by the persons of the Trinity? The most pervasive biblical answer to this question is that the essence of God is most aptly described as his holiness. We will treat this data more fully in chapter six, but an introductory word will help set the context for our present purposes. God reveals his holiness as he establishes a people who belong to him (Lev 11:44-45), and he continues to do the same through Scripture to the end of the New Testament (1 Pet 1:14-16). When visions of God's being are given in both Testaments, heavenly creatures declare his holiness (Is 6:3; Rev 4:8). Further, the biblical titles for God and the three persons of the Trinity are "the Holy One of Israel," "Holy Father," "the Holy One of God" and, of course, "the Holy Spirit." No other term is used so pervasively for God than his holiness. While other terms have been suggested (e.g., good, sovereign), in Scripture none carry the weight or the pervasiveness that holiness does in describing the essence of the divine nature.

In addition to seeing the essence of God in his holiness as the foundation of his unity, the church has historically taken two approaches to describing the unity of this holy God. The Western church tends to ground God's unity in

---

[4]Vladimir Lossky, *The Mystical Theology of the Eastern Church* (Crestwood, N.Y.: St. Vladimir's Press, 1998), pp. 23-43.

the substance of God. This means that the ontological principle of God's unity is not found in the persons but in the one substance or being of God.

Alternatively, the Eastern church grounded the unity of God in the person of the Father. Here the Father is the "cause" of both the generation of the Son and the breathing of the Spirit. So the ontological principle of unity is traced back to a person. This results in a heightened focus on the persons of the Trinity, and so the unity of God is closely tied to the three. The three persons, who coinhere and share a relational life, are not simply used to explain God's diversity but also provide the explanation for his unity. Of the two options, this seems more satisfactory.[5]

Recently a third means of describing the unity of God has been set forward by T. F. Torrance, who points out that some of the Eastern fathers—Athanasius, Gregory of Nazianzus and Didymus the Blind—questioned the widespread Eastern notion of finding the unity of God in the Father. Their reservations were related to the fear that making the Father the "cause" of the others might lead to subordinationism. They suggested that God's unity was better found in his triunity, centered in his perichoresis. Here the monarchy of God is not limited to the Father. The Son and Spirit do not derive their being from the Father but have their being in triunity: Trinity in unity, unity in Trinity. So the persons derive only their personhood, their personal differences as Father, Son and Spirit, from the other persons, but not their oneness and being. Their unity comes in a mutual perichoretic sharing of life and existence together.[6]

Holiness/love and persons. Because the Bible describes God as holy in essence, then the three persons too must be understood as holy. This means holiness is not a "thing" but rather is personally based and therefore expressed in personal categories. In Scripture, holiness is described as personal in several ways, but the chief expression is love. Thus the holy God's steadfast love *(hesed)* is central to the Old Testament, and the triune God is described twice in the New Testament as love (1 Jn 4:7, 16).[7]

---

[5]John D. Zizioulas, *Being as Communion* (Crestwood, N.Y.: St. Vladimir's Seminary Press, 1995), pp. 40-41, 88-89.

[6]See T. F. Torrance, *Trinitarian Perspectives* (Edinburgh: T & T Clark, 1999), and *The Christian Doctrine of God.*

[7]Zizioulas describes love as the supreme ontological predicate of God, that which constitutes his being (*Being as Communion,* p. 46). We will return to how holiness, personhood, love and other personal qualities are interrelated in chap. 6.

Another factor in understanding the *ousia*, and therefore the *homoousios*, of the triune God is that this term is not defined primarily by Greek philosophy but by Hebrew thought. God, from the Hebrew perspective, is not a static but a living and therefore personal being. God's revelation of himself to Moses at Sinai—"I AM WHO I AM" (Ex 3:14)—reveals that in essence he is personal. This gets clearer when we understand that the Son and the Spirit share this *ousia* of God—they are of the same substance *(homoousios)*. So we have a personal and triune God sharing the essence of his being in holiness and love in an intrapersonal and conjunctive way.[8]

Equality in attributes of deity. The unity of the Trinity is further seen in the fact that the three members share the attributes of deity. These attributes may be grouped under the following four headings.

Personal attributes. The personal attributes include the concepts of reason, imagination, emotions and will that are expressed in life, sociality, freedom, morality, creativity and responsibility.[9] Whether we are describing the Trinity economically or ontologically, Scripture demonstrates that all persons of the Trinity perichoretically share these personal attributes.

Moral attributes. Moral attributes require other persons for expression, and here the holiness of God is expressed first of all in self-giving love. Then holiness through love is seen in grace, goodness, truth, faithfulness, righteousness and purity.

Relative attributes. The relative attributes depend on the relationship of God to his creation for their expression. These include his omnipotence, omnipresence, omniscience and wisdom. These are shared as well by the persons of the Trinity.

Absolute attributes. The absolute attributes of God hold true apart from any relationship to creation, and they too are shared by all three persons. They in-

---

[8]Torrance, *Christian Doctrine of God,* pp. 116-25. Torrance puts it this way: "The being of God is to be understood as essentially personal, dynamic and relational being. The real meaning of the being or I AM of God becomes clear in the two-way fellowship he freely establishes with his people as their Lord and Savior. The being of God is again the Spirit, therefore, as living and dynamic being, fellowship-creating for communion-constituted being, but if it is communion-constituted being toward us it is surely to be understood also as an ever-living, ever-dynamic communion in the Godhead. By his very Nature he is a communion in himself" (ibid., p. 124). Torrance uses his brother's description of God's being as "his Being-In-Communion" (see J. B. Torrance, "Contemplating the Trinitarian Mystery of Christ," in *Alive to God,* ed. J. I. Packer and L. Wilkinson [Downers Grove: InterVarsity Press, 1992], p. 141).

[9]These will be discussed more fully in chap. 7.

clude the simplicity of God, his infinity, including his eternity and immensity, his constancy, his aseity and his perfection.[10]

The members of the Trinity share in all four categories of attributes. The unity of the Godhead is found in that all three persons fully share in all classes of attributes and in each one of the attributes. This is the heart of the argument against ontological subordination within the triune God. The Father, Son and Spirit are fully God, and by sharing fully the attributes of God no one person is less divine or of less value than the others.

Each exists in the others. The unity of the Trinity is also established in terms of each person sharing the common essence and life of the others. The corollary to *homoousios* (same essence) is perichoresis (coinherence), which means that each member permeates and completely conditions the other two. This accounts for how they share God's holiness, and out of this holiness how they share the personal, moral, relative and absolute attributes. The concept of *perichoresis* accents the mutuality of the persons of the Trinity in self-giving love to one another out of their holy nature.[11]

Perichoresis is often described in terms of light. This is one of the most pervasive analogies used by the early church in describing the Trinity. In fact, it is the only physical analogy that was used in the Nicene Creed, where the Son is described as "God from God, Light from Light." The church fathers also used the source of light, a ray of the light, and the illumination of light to depict the three members of the Trinity. Within the providence of God, a better understanding of the physical qualities of light has enhanced the analogy in our own day, describing the interpenetration of the life of the Trinity. A beam of light shining through a prism breaks it into different colored rays, like that of a rainbow. But a normal beam of light mixes the colors together. The single beam of light is analogous to the shared existence of the members of the Trinity united in coinherence. The distinctive functions of the economic Trinity are analogous to light shining through a prism. But these functional distinctions do not prevent each member of the Trinity from continuing to share through mutual permeation the common divine life of the others.

The concepts of *homoousios* and *perichoresis* together make it possible to understand the unity of the persons of the Trinity. The three perichoretically

---

[10]The relative and absolute attributes will be discussed more fully in chap. 8.
[11]For the theological role played by *perichoresis*, see Torrance, *Christian Doctrine of God*, p. 102. For further introduction to the concept of *perichoresis*, see Torrance's discussion in ibid., pp. 168-73.

share the same essence (as in the holiness of God). This sharing of holy being is a personal and mutual self-giving between the persons of the Trinity and is expressed in holy love. And this is reinforced by the unity of shared attributes.[12]

Diversity in Trinity: Difference in Threeness

We have discussed the distinctness of persons in terms of their personal identities and unique relationships. This was complemented by a focus on the unity of the Trinity centering in God's holiness, which is expressed in self-giving love and the mutually shared attributes. Having seen all of these as aspects of the ontological Trinity, we return now to how the persons of the Trinity relate to one another. If they are distinctly three but share a common essence, how do we conceive of the internal operations of the Trinity or the *opera ad intra?*[13]

How the three persons relate in the ontological Trinity. In identifying the distinctness of the persons of the Trinity, we may say that the Father begets the Son and breathes the Spirit. The language used is familial. Though the Father's breathing the Spirit is not as direct, the relations of Father and Son place family language at the center of our understanding of the Trinity.[14] Thus the relationships among the persons of the Trinity are best described in terms of self-giving love. If love is an expression of holiness, the ousia of God, then it is natural to see holiness in a shared life where there is also a mutual self-giving to one another in love. So the distinctness of the persons in terms of their personal identities assists in understanding how they relate in other-oriented love.[15]

This is a new way of understanding all reality. It is based on person-to-person relationships growing out of holy, self-giving love that is expressed in terms of mutual giving and receiving. As Walter Kasper notes, "The ultimate reality . . . is the person who is fully conceivable only in the relationality of giving and receiving."[16] If this is an accurate understanding of the triune God, it sets the stage

---

[12]For their own perichoresis as a movement/communion of love within the triune God, see ibid., p. 171.

[13]For discussion of the use of the language of "three persons," see Walter Kasper, *The God of Jesus Christ,* trans. Matthew J. O'Connell (New York: Crossroad, 1984), pp. 285-90.

[14]It is likely that the Spirit is not referred to as Mother so that the persons of the Trinity will be understood to transcend gender.

[15]See Richard of St. Victor, *The Twelve Patriarchs, the Mystical Ark, Book Three of the Trinity,* trans. Grover A. Zinn (New York: Paulist Press, 1979), p. 9.

[16]Kasper, *God of Jesus Christ,* p. 310.

for an appropriate understanding of the way human persons should relate as well.

Earlier we saw the distinctness of the three persons in terms what had been revealed by the economic Trinity. We observed the Father is the head, the Son is the one sent by the Father and the Spirit proceeds from the Father through the Son. The content of the Father's headship (1 Cor 11) is defined by love (1 Cor 13). Headship within the Trinity is not governed by God as King but by God as Father (of the Son). So the Father sends the Son and then the Spirit into the world as an expression of their threefold self-giving relationships to one another in love. The other-oriented love of the ontological Trinity expresses itself in the sending of the Son and the Spirit in the economic Trinity. So while there is a functional distinction within the economic activity of the Father sending the Son and the Spirit, this external act arises from an eternal, mutual self-giving within God. This onto-relational context of holiness in mutual self-giving love sets an entirely different context for understanding the functional roles of the Trinity. There is a possibility of both equality and mutual self-giving among persons while their appropriate external functioning with one another is ordered in a complementary way. So that all the external acts of God arise from one eternal nature and character of the Godhead. These acts arise out of the holy love of Father for Son and Spirit.

Holiness expressed through love. Holiness, representing the essence *(ousia)* of the Trinity, is first and primarily expressed through love (emphasizing the relationships between the three persons of the Trinity). This combination of holiness and love is expressed internally within the triune God through the five other aspects of God's moral character. So in addition to the unconditional love *(agapē)* and permanent commitment of the three members to each other, their relationship is characterized by grace, goodness, truth, righteousness and purity. Grace overlaps with love in its self-giving character, but it also involves favoring and empowering others. In addition to this enabling grace, holiness as expressed through love shows up in the goodness of God in caring and selflessly sharing with the other members. This is complemented by truth in personal communication, which is always accompanied by personal faithfulness in relationships.[17] Holiness expressed through love also is characterized by righteousness, that is, right relationships, and by purity from self-centeredness, which grows out of God's self-giving love.

---

[17]Truth and faithfulness express two sides of the same coin in Hebrew.

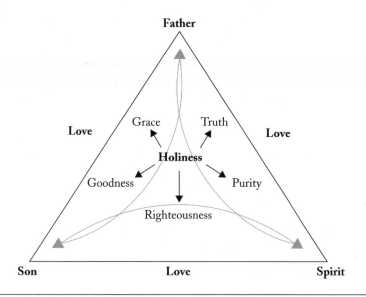

Figure 5.2.

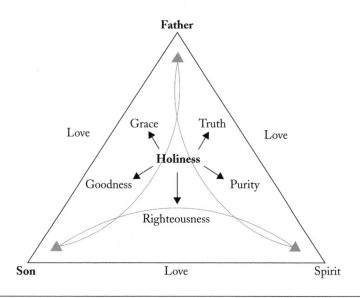

Figure 5.3.

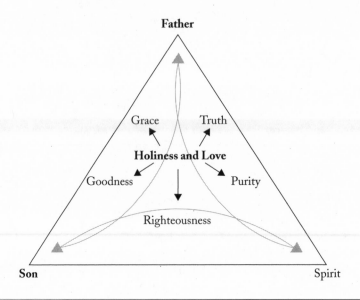

Figure 5.4.

Figures 5.2 through 5.4 are three ways to picture God's holiness expressed through love.

Holiness and love in unconditional commitment are expressed through

- empowering grace
- caring goodness
- truth in communication
- rightness in relationships
- purity from self-centeredness.

This is the familial character of the Godhead. The Father, the head, begets the Son and breathes the Spirit, but he does so as a loving Father, not as a sovereign King. The emphasis is not on kingship but paternity. The family relationships are not expressed in terms of authority and submission but in terms of self-giving love, empowering grace, caring goodness, truthful communication, righteous relationships and purity from self-centeredness. These characteristics express how the triune God relates internally within himself prior to expressing them to other persons. But they do set the stage for an even clearer understanding of how the Trinity relates to persons in the created world, and subsequently how this then becomes a pattern for person-to-person relationships.

The Ontological Trinity and Economic Trinity

We have approached the Trinity by beginning with the data we have in Scripture, which reveals that the Trinity works in relation to creation, particularly in revelation and redemption. While all three members of the Trinity are involved in God's revelation to people, special emphasis is given to the Father in creation, the Son in redemption and the Spirit in sanctification. Starting with this data, we have inferred how the persons of the Trinity relate to one another in their own being. So the *opera ad extra* assists us in understanding the *opera ad intra*. The rule of thumb in connecting these two is that there is no essential difference between the economic and ontological Trinity. What God reveals about himself in relationship to the world is also true about who he is in himself. We do not have two trinities, we have one Trinity understood from two different perspectives. There is a coherence between the two. The triune God who makes himself known in his acts and words is the same triune God in his being. Act and being are one in God.

Based on our understanding of the economic Trinity, we see more clearly how the ontological Trinity works. And our understanding of the ontological Trinity further illuminates our understanding of how the Trinity works in relation to creation. So there is a reciprocal understanding of these two approaches to the Trinity, each assisting in and forming our understanding of the other.[18] It must be added, however, that when the external operations of the Trinity illuminate the internal relations of the Trinity and vice versa, our understanding is enriched but not final. Here we reach the limits of our knowledge and the Trinity retains an element of mystery.

III. THE MYSTERY OF THE TRINITY

Limits of Our Knowledge

When we have correlated all of God's revelation in Scripture with our best un-

---

[18]Cf. Jürgen Moltmann's description of the principle that relates the two understandings of the Trinity: "Statements about the Immanent Trinity must not contradict statements about the Economic Trinity. Statements about the Economic Trinity must correspond to doxological statements about the Immanent Trinity" (*Trinity and the Kingdom* [Minneapolis: Fortress, 1993], p. 154; see also pp. 158-61).

derstanding of how it fits together in our theology, we are fully aware that we do not comprehend everything there is to know about God. We have enough knowledge to know that God is bigger than our understanding of him. If Scripture is true, we can understand all that we need to know to relate to God. So we have adequate knowledge, but we do not have comprehensive knowledge of God. We understand only in part.

The Eastern tradition of the church says we know God through his energies (activities/revelation), but in his essence God is unknowable. This is known formally as *apophatic theology*. It means that we know the way God works, but in his inner being he cannot be fully known.[19]

This tradition reminds us that we do not have exhaustive knowledge about God. The case can be overstated, however, as though we know nothing about the essence of God.[20] The concept of revelation redresses the imbalance of a purely apophatic theology. What is clear from Scripture is that God has made himself known, and in the process he has revealed a great many things about himself. What we have is *true knowledge*, but not *exhaustive knowledge*. The case we are making is that by means of revelation (Scripture) and our attempts at finding its unity and coherence (theology), we can have a true knowledge of God without having an exhaustive knowledge of God. In other words we have truth without having all the truth.

Thus, in spite of all of our understanding of Scripture and our knowledge of how it fits together in theology, there is still an element of mystery. There will always be some things we cannot comprehend about God. From revelation, we know that the proper response to this mystery is twofold. The first is trust. God asks for this response in all contexts. The second is worship, which includes thanksgiving for who God is and for what he is doing. We must respond to the mystery of God in both trust and worship.[21] Athanasius captures the appropriate response: "Thus far human knowledge goes. Here the cherubim spread the covering of their wings."[22]

---

[19]Lossky, *Mystical Theology*, pp. 23-43; Boris Bobrinskoy, *The Mystery of the Trinity* (Crestwood, N.Y.: St. Vladimir's Seminary Press, 1999), pp. 303-16.

[20]For the unknowability of the ontological Trinity through the development of the *via negativa* of pseudo-Dionysius, finally leading to the theology of Gregory Palamas, see Catherine LaCugna, *God for Us* (San Francisco: Harper, 1991), pp. 44, 181-98.

[21]For a valuable discussion of the concept of mystery in the tradition of the church, see Kasper, *God of Jesus Christ*, pp. 267-71.

[22]Athanasius, cited in Torrance, *Christian Doctrine of God*, p. 81.

Mystery helps us live with the limitations of our theology. Sometimes we gain knowledge from a trusted and authoritative source (revelation) without having a full explanation, which we usually desire. We sometimes have knowledge of *what* exists without being able to fully explain *why* or *how* it exists. And in Christian theology we clearly understand that God *is* triune without fully knowing *how* he is so. The concept of mystery assists us with the willingness to live with partial but true knowledge. It means we do not need to know everything (exhaustive knowledge) before we can accept some things as true knowledge.

In this chapter we have been exploring as far as we can the limits of our knowledge of the triune God. Through the light of revelation and our inferences about it, we can understand a great deal about the triune God. He is three persons who have a common essence *(homoousios)* and a shared life (perichoresis). That this is what God is like is made known to us; *how* he is what he is we do not fully understand. What is clear and supremely important is that we know enough to relate to this triune God. Our proper response is to take advantage of what we do know instead of complaining about what we do not know. Since we do want to take advantage of all we can know, are there any parallels that may assist us for living with this mystery?

Parallel Mysteries

Some mysteries that are part of our experience are analogous to the mystery of the triune God. The first comes from our personal relations. If we consider the people we know best and with whom we have had the longest acquaintance, we certainly can say that we have some significant and true knowledge of them without having exhaustive knowledge about them. Can anyone claim to know everything there is to know about another person? Do we not intuitively understand that there are depths to a person that may not be fathomed by another? While the answer is obvious, this does not prevent us from relating to them as best we can in light of the knowledge we have. Further, the people we know best, usually those within our own family, are the people we enjoy most and continue to relate to most often. The lack of exhaustive knowledge obviously does not prevent us from close relationships of delight in another person.

The parallel in our relationship to God is obvious. The fact that we do not fully understand his trinitarian nature does not mean we cannot enjoy him and personally relate to him. Lack of exhaustive knowledge does not mean that we lack true knowledge. We have enough knowledge to provide a firm foundation for a close personal relationship with God.

A second parallel mystery is love. Observe the many books, songs and poems that have been written either to explain or express romantic love. But who would say they have an exhaustive understanding of this kind of love? Yet we intuitively know some things about romantic love, some things about the way it works, some things about the way it expresses itself. What man or woman would want to be excluded from experiencing romantic love simply because he or she did not have exhaustive knowledge about it? We certainly know enough to realize that we wish to experience it. We know enough to enjoy it, even if we cannot explain how it works or why it works as it does.

The analogy is obvious. We understand God partially but not exhaustively. We understand him sufficiently to accept the reality of his triune being and to enjoy a personal relationship with him. This does not mean we have exhausted who he is or have a full understanding of how or why he is triune. But we know enough to know, love and enjoy him.

Mystery helps us understand the limits of our knowledge, but it does not prevent us from enjoying that which we do not fully comprehend. This is especially true in personal relationships. Even rudimentary knowledge leads to relationships, and growing personal knowledge leads to deeper and richer relationships. Thus even though we never have exhaustive knowledge of another person, we still can cultivate rich relationships. We would do well to follow the example of the early church, recognizing that we know all that we need to relate to God in an intimate, personal way, and when we come up against our limited knowledge of him, we revel in the mystery while continuing to trust and worship him.

Analogies of Trinity

Throughout the history of the church several helpful illustrations of the Trinity have emerged. Some of these illustrate the mystery of how three persons make up one Godhead. They have largely consisted of analogies. An analogy compares two things that are alike in some ways but not in every way. This means no analogy is perfect, and some are more limited than others. But analogies help us learn and give us some tools to conceptualize things we do not fully comprehend.

Analogies are not proofs of the doctrine of the Trinity. They are illustra-

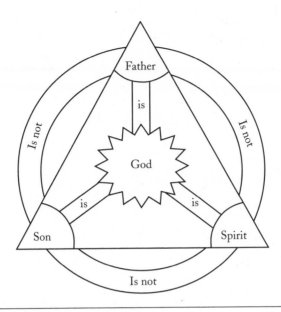

Figure 5.5.

tions from our world that point to the Trinity in the supranatural world.[23] We need to keep reminding ourselves that analogy means similar in some ways but not in every way. Several analogies, verbal and pictorial, have been helpful.

Pictorial analogies. The purpose of figure 5.5 is to indicate that the Father is God, the Son is God and the Spirit is God, but the Father is not the Spirit, the Spirit is not the Son, the Son is not the Father. It is an attempt at diagramming the unity of God as well as indicating the distinctness of the persons. The equilateral triangle that forms the heart of the diagram has become a frequent symbol of the Trinity by indicating the equality, distinctness and unity of the three persons in the Godhead.

The middle of the three ellipses (fig. 5.6) suggests the inner, connected life of the three persons. This is the perichoretic existence of the Trinity. The outside of the ellipses suggests the distinctness of the persons.

Numeric analogies. When the early church summarized the Trinity in the phrase "three persons, one essence," it was not thinking primarily in numerical terms. Yet as soon as the Trinity—three in one—is mentioned, it is difficult

[23]Kasper, *God of Jesus Christ*, p. 268.

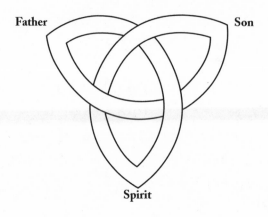

Figure 5.6.

not to think of numbers: how does 1 + 1 + 1 = 1? Perhaps we should move from addition to multiplication: 1 x 1 x 1 = 1. This obviously is much more satisfying. We could do the same with division: 3 ÷ 3 = 1.

Nothing is proved by the use of these numeric variations, but the use of multiplication and division makes it possible to comprehend how three and one fit together in a way that addition does not. There are alternate ways of comprehending reality when it comes to understanding the triune nature of God.

Analogies from creation. One of the analogies used in the early church was that of water, frequently described in a threefold manner: its source, its flow and its collection together. Though there are variations on this, it might well be described as a spring, stream and a lake. The key is that the same substance takes three different forms.

In our discussion of perichoresis we saw that light has been regularly used as a symbol of the Trinity. The early church used the analogy of the source of light, a ray of light and its illumination of something. But a contemporary understanding of light might be even more helpful. A single beam has multiple rays that create different colors, and running a beam of light through a prism separates the colors. The unified rays in a beam of light serves as an illustration of the inner penetration or perichoresis of the members of the Trinity.[24]

---

[24]The early church used a variation of this: one torch lights two other torches by the same fire. These may be seen as three separate torches, but when held together in one hand it forms a common fire.

One advantage of this analogy is the connection of light in the Old and New Testaments as a symbol of the presence of God. This is related to the concept of God's holiness as brilliance, which was expressed when the glory of God descended on the mountain, the tabernacle and the temple in the Old Testament (Ex 19; 40; 1 Kings 8). This is seen even more clearly in the New Testament when Jesus says, "I am the light of the world" (Jn 8:12; 9:5). This biblical figure may be one of the most effective analogies we have from the physical world.

Analogies from music. Spatial, verbal and visual analogies have distinct limits. It may be that an audible analogy will help us break out of some of those limitations. The experience of music in this regard seems particularly promising. Three notes sounded individually carry their own distinctness but when played together in a chord are experienced as one sound with three distinct components. A variation of this is three instruments playing the same note but with three distinct sounds that blend together in harmony. An extension of the same analogy would be three melodies intricately woven together in a polyphony of blended sounds within a symphony. The interactivity and multiplicity of the latter has a special attractiveness that draws a person into the experience of these audible sounds.[25]

The disadvantage of these analogies is that they leave out the personal dimension of God, and this is a very serious limitation. Some have attempted to develop personal analogies, which we will examine next.

Personal analogies. We have seen how Augustine attempted to understand the Trinity in terms of a human individual, who of course is made in the image of God. Much of Western theology followed Augustine on this point, looking for God's image within the human psyche rather than in relationships between persons. He suggested the internal, intrapersonal analogy of memory, understanding and will, or alternatively mind, knowledge and love. While this was a positive attempt to connect the Trinity with people, who bear God's image, by looking to the psyche of one person he ruled out interpersonal relationships, which are fundamental to the trinitarian data of Scripture. Augustine's analogies tend to make God more of a single unitary being rather than three persons in relationship.

---

[25]Jeremy Begbie, "Through Music: Sound, Mix," in *Beholding the Glory: Incarnation Through the Arts*, ed. Jeremy Begbie (London: Darton, Longman and Todd, 2000), pp. 138-53.

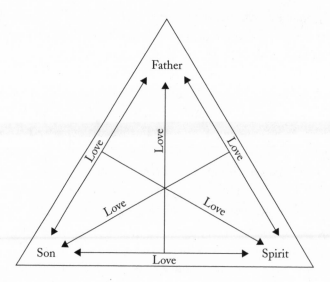

Figure 5.7. Richard of Saint Victor's interpersonal analogy

Augustine offered an alternative that relates persons to one another. It is his description of the Trinity as the lover, the beloved and the love between them. The Father is the lover, the Son the beloved and the Holy Spirit is the love relationship between them. At least in regard to the lover and the loved this analogy lends itself to interpersonal relations; unfortunately, making the Holy Spirit the love connection between the other two seems to depersonalize him. Thus the trifold relationship of the Trinity is not developed. Still, this is better than his psychological analogies.

Better still is the interpersonal analogy suggested by Richard of Saint Victor (see fig. 5.7). He begins with a discussion of reciprocal love between two persons. But he broadens this to suggest that a third dimension of real love comes when two people who love each other in turn love a third. It is in the shared love toward a third that love is fully expressed and enjoyed.

The family would obviously seem to be an analogy closely tied to that of Richard (see fig. 5.8). Here we find a husband and wife mutually loving each other in unconditional, self-giving love. But when a child is born, they both share love for the child and expand their love for each other. When a child comes to a certain age, then the child and husband/father share love for the wife/mother and the wife/mother and child share love for the husband/father. Here is a multifaceted dimension of shared love expressive of shared love between Father, Son and Spirit.

Some have shied away from the family analogy because of a desire to avoid any sexual overtones when discussing the nature of God. All analogies have limitations. Nevertheless, the family (without gender or sexual overtones) may well be the best analogy of the interpersonal workings of God. This would certainly fit with Genesis 1—2, where God made man and woman in his own image, which includes the interpersonal relationships of the family. Sin disrupts this pattern even before the family expands to include children, but the inference may still be drawn that God's intent is for people, who reflect his own social image, to have loving relationships with others with whom they are joined in permanent commitment, communication and self-giving.

The family analogy, of course, readily illustrates multiplicity and unity. Depending on how many children belong to each family unit, families are described in terms of three or more members. This obviously focuses on the family's diversity. But families are also referred to as a unit: one family with several members who are in solidarity (in close parallel to Paul's analogy of one body with multiple members). Unity *and* diversity are the common experience of most family relationships, and this may help us conceive of the triune God.

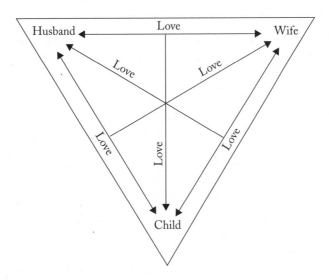

Figure 5.8. Analogy of love within a family

But like all analogies, the family analogy has its limitations.

The mystery remains. It is not difficult to see the limits of every analogy suggested, which brings us back to the mystery of the Trinity. There is no satisfactory explanation of everything that we wish we knew about God. No analogy is perfect, and our knowledge of the essence of God continues to have its limits. But the analogies help us to conceptualize the Trinity and how we may relate to God. This is particularly true of the personal analogies that assist us in understanding the intrapersonal relationships of the triune God. Out of this pattern we may learn how to relate to him and to other persons. While we do not have full knowledge, we have sufficient knowledge for the full development of all our relationships, both divine and human.

So these analogies can help us build a conceptual framework for understanding the Trinity. But all of our attempts to make concrete the abstract discussions of God as three persons in one are limited. Each has it strengths in giving us a fuller appreciation of the unity and diversity within God, but each certainly carries its own limitations. The analogies of light and family are certainly among the strongest, and we should use these to the fullest advantage. But even with these, God is bigger than all our intellectual and conceptual efforts. God indeed is mysterious.

There is, however, good news! With the coming of Jesus and the Spirit, our knowledge of the triune God has opened the way for us to know him accurately if not exhaustively. As a result we are invited into a relationship that allows us to participate in the triune life and love of God. So we return to the expression of the triune God in the person of Jesus, who invites us to relate to him—modeled by his relationship to his disciples—through the Spirit to the Father.

6

THE NATURE OF THE TRIUNE GOD

The traditional approach to understanding God begins with the existence and attributes of God and then moves to a discussion of the triune nature of God. This has been particularly true in the West following the structure of Thomas Aquinas's *Summa Theologica*.[1] We are reversing this order, beginning with the triune God and then moving to God's attributes in the light of his trinitarian nature. Unlike Aquinas, we will not attempt to prove the existence of God with philosophical arguments, but like Scripture we assume the existence of God. The question for Israel and the early church was not, Does God exist? but What is God like? Since the full revelation of God discloses what he is like—triune—we are now ready to understand his nature and attributes.[2]

One thing that is obvious about the triune God is his personal nature. Since he is three persons in one being, his personhood is clearly primary and deserves priority attention. We will discuss the personal being of the triune God through the personal attributes of God, attributes that provide us with the content of the concept of personhood.

Along with personhood two other characteristics of God control the biblical understanding of what he is like: his holiness and his love. Throughout the history of the church, love has been central to understanding the holy Trinity. This is not surprising in light of God's self-description, "I am holy" (Lev

---

[1] Catherine LaCugna describes this discussion of the attributes of God without reference to the Trinity as a fruit of Thomas's theology that has led to the "marginalization of the doctrine of the Trinity" (*God for Us* [San Francisco: Harper, 1991], pp. 150-67; cf. Wolfhart Pannenberg, *Systematic Theology*, 3 vols., trans. Geoffrey W. Bromiley [Grand Rapids: Eerdmans, 1991-97], 1:280-83).

[2] Cf. the similar approach of W. B. Pope, who treats the Trinity before he addresses the attributes of God in *A Compendium of Christian Theology*, 3 vols. (London: Wesleyan-Methodist Book Room, 1880), 1:255-358. See also the contemporary approach of Robert Jenson, who begins with an elaborate discussion of the doctrine of the Trinity and then refuses to identify a separate section on "attributes" (*Systematic Theology*, 2 vols. [New York: Oxford University Press, 1997-2001], 1:223).

11:44-45; 1 Pet 1:15-16) and the apostolic description, "God is love" (1 Jn 4:8, 16). Since both of these relate to God's essence, they should control our understanding of who he is as well as how we conceive his other attributes.

Here's the problem we face: on the one hand we have God's essence, his holiness and love, and on the other his relationality. How do we put these components together? Is this just another form of the older argument between substance and relationality? Or is it possible that beginning with a triune description of God there is a way to transcend the debate between substance and relationality? Is it possible to understand God's holiness and love as relational categories, how he relates within himself even before he relates to the world? Love is obviously a relational category, so it is not difficult to see how this may tie the essence and relationality of God together. I will make the case that holiness is also relational; it describes how God relates within himself as well as to the created order.

I could begin the discussion with God's holiness and love, which are constituent elements of his basic essence, or with his personal attributes. I have chosen to begin with holiness and love, not to place God's relationality in a secondary position but rather to fill out the content of God's relationality by describing the relational nature of holiness and love.

I. HOLINESS AND THE TRIUNE GOD: THE FIRST INDICATOR OF THE BEING *(OUSIA)* OF GOD

One of the keys to holding together the unity and diversity of the triune God is holiness. In chapter five we indicated that holiness constitutes one part of the *ousia* or essence of God. Now we will examine the biblical evidence for the foundational nature of holiness before looking at its rich meaning.[3] Once we understand how holiness relates to the love of God we can see how both affect all of God's attributes. Finally, we will discuss how the economic Trinity has revealed all of this about the ontological Trinity.

Old Testament Unfolding of God's Holiness

Our understanding of God's holiness begins at Mount Sinai, where God tells Israel that he is looking for a holy people (Ex 19:6) because he wants them to

---

[3]For the biblical materials and the concept of holiness, I am relying heavily on my presentation in *Portraits of God* (Downers Grove: InterVarsity Press, 2001), pp. 42-48.

be like himself: "I am the LORD your God; consecrate yourselves therefore, and be holy, for I am holy" (Lev 11:44-45). As God describes the character of the people who are to be his "own possession," he makes clear that he is holy, which he repeats throughout the book of Leviticus (Lev 19:2; 20:7-8, 26; 21:8).

Earlier, at Mount Sinai, God had revealed his name to Moses: "I AM WHO I AM" (Ex 3:14). This is also a revelation of his nature. In Exodus and Leviticus God repeatedly declares, "I am Yahweh," or as in most of our English translations, "I am the LORD." This repetition may well be used to emphasize the Lord as the only God, the One who is the source of all existence.

However, a fuller picture of God emerges as he starts to qualify the "I AM": "I am holy" (Lev 11:44-45). Since his name is so intimately bound up with his nature, the connection of holiness with his name is very significant. It indicates that holiness is the most important thing Israel needs to know about God. Furthermore, in Leviticus 11:44-45 the phrases "I am the LORD" and "I am holy" are used interchangeably. The parallelism is so striking that it is difficult not to see the two as synonymous throughout the book (Lev 19:2-4, 10, 12, 14, 16, 18, 25, 28, 30-31, 34, 36-37; 20:7-8, 24, 26; 21:8, 15, 23; 22:2-3, 8-9, 16, 30-33). The recurrence of these two expressions through the Sinai story strongly indicates that holiness is the chief attribute of God.

This is underlined elsewhere in the Old Testament through the references to the name of God. Leviticus 20:3 provides the first modifier connected with God's name. God pronounces judgment on those who profane his "holy name." So the overall sequence of this revelation is first "I am the LORD," then "I am holy," followed by references to "my holy name." This is certainly the most characteristic adjective connected with the name of God in the Old Testament. There are five references to God's "glorious" name and four references to the "great" name of God, but all the others (23) refer to God's "holy name."

Edmond Jacob points out that the "name" is synonymous with Yahweh. So the name "always expresses the essential nature of a being, manifests the totality of the divine presence." Since "name" in fact refers to the essence of God's being, then holiness seems to be most characteristic of his nature. In Jacob's words, "the relation between holiness and the name reveals the identity of holiness with deity."[4] Given the fact that glory is one of the manifestations of ho-

---

[4]Edmond Jacob, *Theology of the Old Testament* (New York: Harper, 1958), pp. 82, 85, 88.

liness (e.g., Is 6:3), it may be that even the references to his "glorious name" are really only an alternate rendering of "holy name."

In addition to the revelation of his name, at Sinai God gives Israel a concrete representation of his holy character. It comes in the form of the tabernacle pitched in the center of Israel's camp. Within the tabernacle precincts, the place that most clearly represents the personal presence of God among his people is the "most holy place" (Ex 26:33-34). Thus Israel has a visual reminder every day not only of the presence of God but also of his holiness (cf., 1 Kings 8:6-11). By the time of the Sinai events the content of God's holiness includes his relationality (his speaking and presence), his separateness from the world (transcendent source of all), his power (he is the Deliverer), his moral nature (he demands righteousness, love, purity) and his constancy (he is truthful and faithful).

Biblical revelation is progressive in character; it builds on the foundation of what has been made known earlier. Further revelation elaborates our understanding of the character of God without abrogating what has gone before. Thus it is not necessary for God's holiness to receive the same emphasis at all points in Israel's history. The Sinai events were so foundational for Israel that from this time onward God's holiness is a given. At significant points in Israel's history, though, further glimpses into the essential character of God are given. One of these comes with the vision of the prophet Isaiah when he sees the creatures around the throne of God crying, "Holy, holy, holy is the LORD of hosts, the whole earth is full of his glory" (Is 6:3). Though Isaiah sees God as the sovereign King (Is 6:5), God is not described in terms of his sovereignty but rather his holiness, which stands at the very heart of his nature.

This helps explain Israel's reverence for the name of God. God warns Israel about profaning his name by taking it in vain (Ex 20:7). Israel was not to extol the holiness of God's character while failing to reflect that character as a holy people. Ezekiel declares God's judgment on Israel because they took his "holy name" in vain and profaned it among the nations. When they did this, God said he would "vindicate the holiness of my great name" (Ezek 36:20-23).

God's holiness is not only declared at Mount Sinai and reinforced by the prophets, but it is continually reiterated in Israel's worship. Whereas at Mount Sinai God declared himself to be holy, in worship he is declared holy by his people (Ps 22:3). In one short psalm of praise, the people declare that God is holy three different times (Ps 99:3, 5, 9). This statement is complemented by the repeated declarations regarding his holy name (Ps 30:4; 33:21; 97:12; 105:3; 106:47; 111:9). On two occasions the reference to his holy name comes as a general statement that either introduces or summarizes other attributes of God (Ps 103:1; 145:21). Further, worship in Israel is identified with Isaiah's declaration of Yahweh as the "Holy One of Israel" (Ps 71:22; 78:41; 89:18). Holiness is so identified with God's divinity that when God swears by himself, he swears by his own holiness, that is, by his own nature (Ps 89:35; cf. 93:5).

Finally, the holiness of God is repeatedly affirmed by identification of the places that represent the dwelling place of a holy God. This usually is the temple, where the most holy place stands as a symbol of his presence on the earth (Ps 3:4; 5:7; 11:4; 15:1; 24:3; 28:2; 43:3; 46:4; 48:1; 65:4; 68:5, 17; 79:1; 87:1; 93:5; 134:2; 138:2). But sometimes it refers to God in his holy heaven (Ps 20:6; 47:8). What is significant is that the place where Yahweh is worshiped, wherever he is, is a holy place.

God's holiness is revealed when he enters into covenant relationships with Israel and when he is worshiped. This holy God enters into relationships with persons whom he wants to be holy—like himself. This ties the holiness of God to relationality. Thus our understanding of God's holiness is wrapped in relational categories.

New Testament Extension of God's Holiness

By the first century A.D., when the New Testament was written, the holiness of God had been firmly established. As Everett Harrison remarks, "The lesser emphasis in the New Testament is readily accounted for on the assumption that the massive presentation under the old covenant is accepted as an underlying presupposition."[5] Nevertheless, the holiness of God is mentioned at strategic points in the New Testament, and here we find that all three persons of the Trinity are identified as holy.

The holiness of the Father is identified at key places in the New Testament story. In the Lucan birth narrative, Mary exclaims, "He who is mighty has done great things for me, and holy is his name" (Lk 1:49). At the beginning of Jesus' ministry he instructs his disciples to pray to the Father, "Hallowed be thy name" (Mt 6:9), and just before his crucifixion he prays to the "Holy Fa-

---

[5]Everett F. Harrison, "Holiness," in *International Standard Bible Encyclopedia*, 4 vols., ed. Geoffrey W. Bromiley (rev. ed. Grand Rapids: Eerdmans, 1979-1988), 2:725.

ther" (Jn 17:11). Thus the holiness of the Father receives special mention at the incarnation and at the beginning and end of Jesus' ministry. This is particularly significant in light of Jesus' purpose to make the Father known (e.g., Jn 1:18).

The New Testament writers reinforce God's holiness. Peter instructs the early Christians to be holy in all their conduct "since it is written, You shall be holy, for I am holy" (1 Pet 1:15-16). The book of Revelation repeats the vision of Isaiah, where the creatures cry day and night, "Holy, holy, holy is the Lord God Almighty, who was and is and is to come!" (Rev 4:8). It is as though the author is saying that God *has been* holy, *is* holy and *will be* holy. Indeed, God's essence does not change with time; he is the same in the past, the present and the future. The holy God who reveals himself in the Old Testament is still holy at the end of the New Testament.

The New Testament also refers to the second and third persons of the Trinity as holy. In the angel's announcement to Mary, he says, "The child to be born will be called holy, the Son of God" (Lk 1:35). This is not surprising in light of the biblical witness to the divine nature of Christ. Further, at the outset of Jesus' ministry he is recognized as "the Holy One of God" (Mk 1:24), and after a period of time the disciples also come to recognize his holy character. Peter, speaking for the Twelve, professes, "We have believed, and have come to know, that you are the Holy One of God" (Jn 6:69; see also the reference to Jesus as "the Holy and Righteous One" [Acts 3:14]). The leaders of the early church also regularly identify Jesus with the "Holy One" from Psalm 16:10 (Acts 2:27; 13:35). Likewise, they refer to Jesus as God's holy servant (Acts 3:13-14; 4:26, 30).[6]

The Spirit of God is called the "Holy Spirit" three times in the Old Testament (Ps 51:11; Is 63:10-11) and no less than ninety-one times in the New Testament. This is by far the most common expression for God's Spirit, and thus in the New Testament and the church the Spirit of God is almost always referred to as the *Holy* Spirit. Holiness represents the essential nature of the triune God: Father, Son and Spirit. It is the only qualifying adjective so attached to the names of the three.

Emil Brunner astutely observes, "Although in the New Testament the idea

---

[6]"Holy One" is used of Jesus in Mk 1:24; Lk 4:34; Jn 6:69; Acts 2:27; 3:14; 13:15; 1 Jn 2:20; Rev 3:7; see also Lk 1:35; Heb 7:26.

of the holiness of God as a divine attribute is emphasized somewhat less than in the Old Testament, yet it is everywhere presupposed, and it appears at decisive points where the whole revealing and saving work of Christ is gathered up as the revelation of the Name." He concludes, "the whole of the Old Testament is the revelation of the holy God."[7] Otto Procksch agrees: "The holiness of God the Father is everywhere presumed in the New Testament, though seldom stated. It is filled out in Jesus Christ as the holy one of God and in the Holy Spirit."[8]

The fact that the holiness of God is attributed to the Father, the Son and the Spirit is a further indicator of the importance of this term. That all three persons are holy is suggestive of their essential unity, and at the same time that the term itself is relational.

In light of this biblical data many scholars from a wide variety of traditions believe that holiness is the most central concept for understanding the nature and being of God. Geerhardus Vos describes divine holiness as something which

> is not really an attribute to be coordinated with the other attributes distinguished in the divine nature. It is something coextensive with and applicable to everything that can be predicated of God; he is holy in everything that characterizes him and reveals him, holy in his goodness and grace, no less than in his righteousness and wrath.[9]

Walther Eichrodt agrees, stating, "Of all the qualities attributed to the divine nature there is one which in virtue both of the frequency and the emphasis with which it is used, occupies a position of unique importance—namely, that of holiness." Because of this he declares, " 'Holy' is the epitaph deemed fittest to describe the Thou whose nature and operations are summed up in the divine Name; and for this reason it comes to mean that which is distinctively characteristic of God, that which constitutes his nature."[10]

Holiness is at the heart of the picture of God in both Testaments. The-

---

[7]Emil Brunner, *The Christian Doctrine of God,* Dogmatics, trans. Olive Wyon (London: Lutterworth, 1949), 1:157.

[8]Otto Procksch, "ἅγιος," in *Theological Dictionary of the New Testament,* 10 vols., ed. Gerhard Kittel, Gerhard Friedrich and G. W. Bromiley (Grand Rapids: Eerdmans, 1964), 1:101; see also J. Muilenburg, "Holiness," in *The Interpreter's Dictionary of the Bible,* 4 vols., ed. George Buttrick (Nashville: Abingdon, 1962), 2:623; and Skevington Wood, "Holiness," in *Zondervan Pictorial Encyclopedia of the Bible,* 5 vols., ed. Merrill Tenney (Grand Rapids: Zondervan, 1975), 3:180.

[9]Geerhardus Vos, *Biblical Theology* (Carlisle, Penn.: Banner of Truth, 1975), p. 266.

[10]Walther Eichrodt, *Theology of the Old Testament,* trans. J. A. Baker, 2 vols., 6th ed. (Philadelphia: Westminster Press, 1961-1967), 1:270, 274.

odore Vriezen claims holiness is "the central idea of the Old Testament faith in God,"[11] and Everett Harrison says, "It is no exaggeration to state that this element overshadows all others in the character of the deity so far as the Old Testament revelation is concerned."[12] Procksch holds to the same view regarding holiness in the New Testament: "In the New Testament the holiness of God is thought of as his essential attribute in which the Christian must share and for which the heavenly Father prepares him by his instruction." Therefore, "the nature of Christianity is thus centrally determined by the concept of the holy."[13]

In *Faith of the Christian Church*, Gustaf Aulén expresses his conviction that "holiness is the foundation on which the whole conception of God rests." It is not as though these scholars ignore the other attributes of God, but simply that all other characteristics need to be qualified by holiness. Aulén states:

> It gives specific tone to each of the various elements in the idea of God and makes them part of a fuller conception of God. Every statement about God, whether in reference to his love, power, righteousness . . . ceases to be an affirmation about God when it is not projected against the background of his holiness.[14]

So God's righteousness, love and mercy as well as his wrath and jealousy are always understood in Scripture as holy righteousness, holy love, holy mercy, holy wrath and holy jealousy. Holiness qualifies and conditions all the other attributes of God. For this reason P. T. Forsyth writes, "Everything in Christian theology begins and ends with the holiness of God."[15] The holiness of God must be viewed as being at the heart of any truly biblically grounded theology.[16]

What are the implications of God's holiness for a theological understanding of his nature? The extensiveness of the biblical data means that holiness is the first component of the essence, the *ousia*, of God's being. Since all three

---

[11]Theodorus C. Vriezen, *An Outline of Old Testament Theology* (Newton, Mass.: C. T. Bradford, 1970), p. 151.

[12]Harrison, "Holiness," 2:725.

[13]Procksch, "ἅγιος," 1:114, 110 (see also pp. 93, 100). Rudolf Kittel asserts that holiness is not just one side of God's essential being, but "rather it is the comprehensive designation for the total content of the divine being in his relationship to the external world" (quoted in C. A. Beckwith, "Holiness of God," *The New Schaff-Herzog Religious Encyclopedia*, ed. Samuel Macauley Jackson, 13 vols. [Grand Rapids: Baker, 1949-1950], 5:317).

[14]Gustaf Aulén, *The Faith of the Christian Church*, trans. Eric H. Wahlstrom (Philadelphia: Muhlenberg, 1960), p. 103.

[15]P. T. Forsyth, *The Cruciality of the Cross* (Wake Forest: Chanticlear Publishing, 1983), pp. 23-24.

[16]Pope, *A Compendium of Christian Theology*, 1:333.

persons of the Trinity share the same being they all share in his holiness. This is part of the biblical data behind the *homoousios* of the members of the Trinity.

Just as the shift from the Old Testament to the New Testament does not displace the concept of God's holiness but rather augments it, so the shift from monotheism to trinitarian theism does not change the centrality of holiness for understanding God. The Old Testament plus the New Testament provide us with God's order of knowing and sufficient data for us to understand that, in the order of being, one major component of the essence of God is his holiness. Nevertheless, the New Testament's additional revelation allows us to see the holy God under the terms of the new covenant. This expansion of the concept of a holy God is now where we turn our attention.

II. LOVE AND THE HOLY, TRIUNE GOD: THE SECOND INDICATOR OF THE BEING *(OUSIA)* OF GOD

Old Testament Data

The relationship between God's love and God's holiness does not begin in the New Testament.[17] It is also a part of God's self-revelation in the Old Testament, and is closely tied to two key Hebrew words for love: *hesed* and *'āhēb*. We will explore how God's holiness is connected with these two terms as a background for understanding the expansion of the idea of holiness in the New Testament.

Holiness and love (hesed). God's love is related to his holiness in the first passage in Scripture that speaks about the holiness of God. "Who is like thee, O LORD, among the gods? Who is like thee, majestic in holiness. . . . Thou hast led in thy *steadfast love* the people whom thou hast redeemed, thou hast guided them by thy strength to thy holy abode" (Ex 15:11, 13, italics added). In the midst of Israel's experience of deliverance from Egypt, God is identified as "majestic in holiness" and described as the One who leads his people in "steadfast love." The word translated "steadfast love" in the RSV is the Hebrew word *hesed*, which is one of the two major Hebrew words that describes the love of God. It is a covenant term and therefore a relational term whose meaning is one of the richest in Scripture. It refers to God's love but also includes his grace, mercy, faithfulness and goodness, and

---

[17]On the biblical data relating holiness and love, see Coppedge, *Portraits of God* (Downers Grove: InterVarsity Press, 2001), pp. 244-52.

therefore is translated variously as "steadfast love," "faithful love," "loving-kindness" and "mercy." Thus it does not exclusively relate to love but has love at its center, and therefore it is one of the terms that appropriately describes a loving God.[18]

After God calls Israel to be a holy people (Ex 19:6) and spells out for them what this holiness will mean in their lives (Ex 20:1-17), he says he will manifest his steadfast love to thousands of those who respond properly to this standard of holiness (Ex 20:6). The psalmist views this relationship from a human perspective when he exclaims:

Yea, our heart is glad in him
because we trust in his holy name.
Let thy steadfast love, O LORD, be upon us,
even as we hope in thee. (Ps 33:21-22)

It is from the holy name or nature of God that the writer expects to see an expression of God's steadfast love. Isaiah describes the same phenomenon from God's viewpoint when he has "the Holy One of Israel" declare, "My steadfast love shall not depart from you" (Is 54:5, 10). Further, some psalms express the particulars of God's "holy name," of which his steadfast love is one prominent manifestation (e.g., Ps 103:1, 4, 17; 145:8, 21).[19]

The steadfast love of God is related to his trinitarian being not only through his holiness but through his fatherhood. Though *hesed* in the Old Testament is an introductory picture of God as Father, it prepares the way for an expanded trinitarian perspective in the New Testament. The steadfast love of God as an expression of his fatherhood is seen in God's promise to David: "I will be his Father, and he shall be my son. . . . I will not take my steadfast love from him" (2 Sam 7:14-15). In the Isaiah passage that has two of the three

---

[18]On the concept of *hesed* see N. Snaith, *Distinctive Ideas of the Old Testament* (New York: Schocken, 1964), pp. 94-130; P. Toon, "Lovingkindness," *EDT,* ed. Walter Elwell (Grand Rapids: Baker Academic, 1984), pp. 661-62; N. Glueck, *Hesed in the Bible* (Cincinnati: Hebrew Union College Press, 1967); K. D. Sakenfeld, *The Meaning of Hesed in the Hebrew Bible* (Missoula, Mont.: Scholars Press, 1978); R. Laird Harris, "חֶסֶד," in *Theological Wordbook of the Old Testament,* 2 vols., ed. R. Laird Harris, Gleason L. Archer Jr. and Bruce K. Waltke (Chicago: Moody Press), 1:305-7; Procksch, "ἅγιος," 1:696-701.

[19]Wood, "Holiness," 3:183. On love as an expression of holiness see Beckwith, "Holiness of God," 5:318; Muilenburg, "Holiness," 2:622; D. Moody, *The Word of Truth: A Summary of Christian Doctrine Based on Biblical Revelation* (Grand Rapids: Eerdmans, 1981), p. 104; Procksch, "ἅγιος," 1:93; Thomas McComisky, "qādōsh," in *Theological Wordbook of the Old Testament,* 2 vols., ed. R. Laird Harris, Gleason L. Archer Jr. and Bruce K. Waltke (Chicago: Moody Press, 1980), 2:788.

references to the Holy Spirit in the Old Testament, there is repeated reference to the steadfast love of the Lord toward his "sons."

> For thou art our Father,
> although Abraham does not know us
> and Israel does not acknowledge us;
> thou, O LORD, art our Father. (Is 63:16)

Jeremiah, who looks forward to the new covenant, quotes God as saying, "I am a Father to Israel, and Ephraim is my first-born" (Jer 31:9). It is this God who declares, "I have loved you with an everlasting love" (v. 3).[20]

The *hesed* of the Lord, which focuses on his steadfast love but also includes elements of grace, mercy and faithfulness, is best understood as a major expression of the holiness of God. This is based on the Scripture that describe both the holy God and God as the Father expressing steadfast love. These picture the holy God relating in covenant love to his people, revealing the relational nature of both holiness and love.

Holiness and love ('āhēb). The second Hebrew word that describes the love of God is the more common word for love, *'āhēb*. This word is first used in the book of Deuteronomy, when God has Moses review Israel's history. It serves as an interpretive evaluation of the way that God has worked among the Hebrews and the implications of this for the future. In this theological review *'āhēb* is used to describe God's love for Israel (Deut 4:37). God tells Israel that they "are a people holy to the LORD your God" and "a people for his own possession" (Deut 7:6). We are reminded that God has made known that he wants a holy people because he is holy (Lev 11:44-45). Then God explains his motivation for choosing Israel as his own people: "It was not because you were more in number than any other people that the LORD set his love upon you and chose you, for you were the fewest of all peoples; but it is because the LORD loves you" (Deut 7:7-8).

From this passage it is evident that God's love is an expression of his holy character. Therefore, love becomes a manifestation of God's holiness, particularly at the point of the election of Israel. This passage not only relates holiness and love but also parallels God's love *('āhēb)* and his steadfast love *(hesed)*. For those who respond properly to God, "the LORD your God will keep with you the covenant and the steadfast love *[hesed]* which he swore to

---

[20]For the relation between God's steadfast love and his role as Husband see Is 54:5-10 and Hos 2:19.

your fathers to keep; he will love you [*'āhēb*], bless you and multiply you" (Deut 7:12-13; see also v. 9).

When Moses speaks about this One who must be revered as holy, he declares, "He loved his people" (Deut 33:3). Isaiah quotes the Holy One of Israel who promises to redeem his people:

> Because you are precious in My eyes,
> and honored and I love you,
> I give men in return for you,
> peoples in exchange for your life. (Is 43:3-4)

In like manner when God describes himself to Hosea as "God, and not man, the Holy One in your midst" (Hos 11:9), he does so in the context of his love for Israel: "When Israel was a child, I loved him, and out of Egypt I called my son" (Hos 11:1).[21] Other passages also indicate that love was the key motivation for a holy God electing his people (Is 43:4; 63:9; Jer 31:3; Mal 1:2; Hos 11:1, 9).[22] At the same time Deuteronomy makes clear that the Lord set his love not only on Israel and its descendants but also on the sojourner (the non-Israelite [Deut 10:15, 18]). This concern for both Israel and the world stands behind the central New Testament declaration of God's redemption made available for all in Christ: "For God so loved the world that he gave his only Son, that whoever believes in him should not perish but have everlasting life" (Jn 3:16). So the relational nature of holiness and love is highlighted in God's concern for all humankind.

New Testament Data: Explicit

When we move from the Old Testament to the New Testament, the centrality

---

[21]For other Old Testament references to God's love see Deut 23:5; 1 Kings 10:9; 2 Chron 2:11; 9:8; 2 Sam 12:24; Ps 47:4; 146:8; Prov 3:12; 12:9; Is 43:4; 48:14; 63:9; Jer 31:3; Mal 1:2; Hos 3:1; 11:4; 14:4; Zeph 3:17.

[22]On love (*'āhēb*) see Snaith, *Distinctive Ideas of the Old Testament*, pp. 131-42; Richard Alden, "אָהֵב," in *Theological Wordbook of the Old Testament*, 2 vols., ed. R. Laird Harris, Gleason L. Archer Jr. and Bruce K. Waltke (Chicago: Moody Press, 1980), 1:14-15; Ethelbert Stauffer, "ἀγάπη," in *Theological Dictionary of the New Testament*, 10 vols., ed. Gerhard Kittel, Gerhard Friedrich and G. W. Bromiley (Grand Rapids: Eerdmans, 1964), 1:21-25; Gerhard Wallis, "אָהֵב," in *Theological Dictionary of the Old Testament*, 15 vols., ed. G. Botterweck and H. Ringgren (Grand Rapids: Eerdmans, 1974), 1:99-117; D. McCarthy, "Notes on the Love of God in Deuteronomy and the Father-Son Relationship between Yahweh and Israel," *Catholic Biblical Qquarterly* 27 (1965): 144-47; and J. W. Kay, "Man's Love for God in Deuteronomy and the Father/Teacher-Son/Pupil Relationship," *Vetus Testamentum* 22 (1972): 426-35.

of Jesus affects our understanding of love and God's holiness. Here the connection between holiness and *agapē*, a Greek word for love, sets the stage for us.

Holiness and love *(agapē)*. The third biblical word that describes the love of God is the Greek term *agapē*. This is a unique word adopted by the New Testament writers to express the unconditional, self-giving love of God. It is distinct from *eros*, which relates a romantic and physical love, and which must possess its object. It differs further from *phileō*, which better describes friendship, companionship and family love. *Agapē* is a supranatural love that has the special good and concern of the love object as its focus. It has an unconditionality and an other-centeredness about it that is distinct from the other words used for love in Greek. It is particularly used in the New Testament to describe the love of God the Father, Son and Holy Spirit, and the kind of love God implants in the hearts of those who become his spiritual children.[23]

The picture of *agapē* as an expression of God's holy character is seen most clearly in John 17. Here Jesus addresses God as "holy Father." The intimacy of the love relationship between the Father and the Son is seen when Jesus talks about how the Father has loved him (Jn 17:23-24, 26). This love relationship between the Father and the Son must be understood in reference to Jesus' request of the Father to keep his disciples "in thy name" (Jn 17:11). The name of God refers to his nature, described as "holy" in the same verse. Within this holy nature the chief relationship between the first and second members of the Trinity is their love for one another. So through his prayer Jesus reveals that the heart of the holy nature of God is his love for the Son and for those who are becoming the Son's disciples (Jn 17:22, 26).

The centrality of Jesus for tying together the holiness and the love of God becomes clearer when Jesus, the "Holy One of God" (Jn 6:69), reveals the love generated by the economic Trinity. This is the import of the famous text, "For God so loved the world that he gave his only begotten son . . ." (Jn 3:16). Jesus makes known the full love of the Father and the Spirit through his own life in this world (Jn 13:1, 34-35; 14:21; 15:13-14, 16:27).

---

[23]On *agapē* see Stauffer, "ἀγάπη," 1:21-55; W. Harrelson, "The Idea of Agape in the New Testament," *Journal of Religion* 31 (1951): 169-82; Leon Morris, *The Testaments of Love* (Grand Rapids: Eerdmans, 1981); Anders Nygren, *Agape and Eros* (Philadelphia: Westminster Press, 1953); G. Outka, *Agape: An Ethical Analysis* (New Haven: Yale University Press, 1972); C. Spicq, *Agape in the New Testament*, 3 vols. (St. Louis: B. Herder, 1963-66); B. B. Warfield, "The Terminology of Love . . . ," *Princeton Theological Review* 16 (1918): 1-45.

Second, Jesus is not only the expression of the economic Trinity working in the world, he is our way into understanding love within the very being of the Trinity. So that in prayer to the Father, Jesus refers to that "which thou hast given me in thy love for me before the foundation of the world" (Jn 17:24). When we see how the Father loves the Son, this certainly reveals the inner nature of the Trinity (Jn 3:35; 5:20; 10:17; 15:9-10; 17:23, 26).

Finally, Jesus desires that his disciples love as he loves, which is his design for them—to reflect the inner nature of the holy, triune God (Mt 5:42-48; Jn 13:34-35; 21:15-17). There is a parallel here between what God desires in the Old Testament and what Jesus makes even more clear in the New. Under the old covenant the holiness of God (Lev 11:44-45) was to be expressed in persons by love for God (Deut 6:5) and for other people (Lev 19:18). In the New Testament the holiness of Jesus (Lk 1:35; Jn 6:69) is to be expressed in his disciples by love for God and other people (Mt 22:37-40; Mk 12:28-31). So the pattern is that holy people best express the essential nature of God when they love unconditionally as God loves. The holiness of God, though expressed in other moral attributes, finds its fullest expression in love. This is first seen in the Old Testament and then most clearly in the New. This data indicates that the love of God is the second indicator of the being *(ousia)* of God and that this essence is relational in nature.

New Testament Data: Implicit

There is a more implicit component in the New Testament data that strengthens the conviction that love is at the center of the holiness of God. The revelation of the Father-Son relationship between Jesus and his heavenly Father expands our understanding of the triune God. This family language broadens our understanding of what God is like, not only in his relationship to the world but in his inner (ontological) nature. Implicit in this family language we find a much stronger accent on love between the members of the Trinity. We find this expressed in references to Jesus as the "beloved Son" (Mt 3:17) and later as the "son of his love" (Col 1:13).

When the data of the Father-Son relationship and the expanded intratrinitarian family language is admitted as evidence, then we see that love between the members of the Trinity is a dominant theme of the New Testament. This makes it much easier to understand the dual declaration in 1 John 4 that "God is love."

A Holy, Loving, Triune God (Order of Being)

Understanding Jesus as the center of the economic Trinity requires a theological move toward understanding the essence *(ousia)* of the ontological Trinity. This views love as expanding the concept of holiness. Love does not displace holiness as the *ousia* of God but amplifies it (Jn 17:11, 17, 23, 26). This parallels the expansion of Old Testament monotheism to New Testament trinitarianism. Later revelation does not destroy or obviate earlier revelation, but like a widening set of concentric circles expands it. Just as monotheism expands in the New Testament to incorporate the three persons of God in one being, so the holiness of God in the Old Testament is now expanded by love in the New Testament. Now love may be properly placed along with holiness as part of the *ousia* or essence of God.

There are two significant implications of this expanded *ousia*. First, the centrality of love further exposes the relational character of God's holiness. Shortly, we will discuss the various components of God's holiness, which is viewed by some as a static quality. But if love is the dominant expression of holiness, then holiness must be understood as a part of the essential relationality of God as a social being. Second, while holiness is expressed in the moral attributes of God in several key ways, the concept of love now conjoined with holiness shapes the character of these other moral attributes. This means that holiness and love should control our understanding of all other moral characteristics, including righteousness and purity, truth and faithfulness, and grace and goodness. These are not only expressions of God's holiness but also are controlled by his love.[24]

Relationships of the Components of Holiness

Summary of the expressions of holiness. There is good biblical evidence that holiness expresses itself in at least six different ways, and one of these has several derived meanings.[25] The six expressions of holiness include separation, power, brilliance, righteousness, goodness and love. Brilliance may be divided in such a way that the immanence of God is made known in truth but also in terms of grace and purity (see fig. 6.1).[26]

---

[24]On the relationship between holiness and love, see Thomas Oden, *The Living God* (San Francisco: Harper & Row, 1987), pp. 123-25.
[25]See Coppedge, *Portraits of God,* pp. 51-52.
[26]Ibid., pp. 134-39, 174-76.

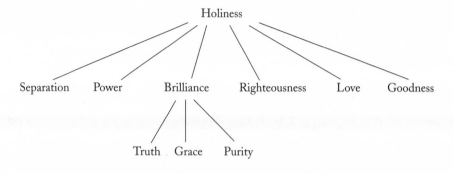

Figure 6.1. Six expressions of God's holiness

Some may wish to divide these expressions of holiness into moral and non-moral categories. Nonmoral expressions do not require the will of the persons for their expression, whereas the moral ones do. The supernatural Creator, separate from the universe, had power to create the world and all that is in it. So separation and power are nonmoral. Truth, grace, purity, righteousness, love and goodness, however, require relationships with other persons. Thus they are moral expressions of God's holiness (see fig. 6.2).

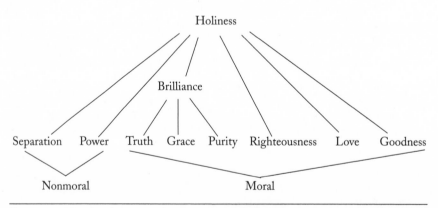

Figure 6.2. Moral and nonmoral expressions of God's holiness

Old Testament. In the Old Testament, holiness expressed in righteous relationships will also lead to purity. When holiness is expressed as love, it manifests itself in both the grace of God and his goodness toward others. And when holiness is understood as truth, it is closely connected with God's faithfulness. The relationship of these expressions of God's holiness can be seen in

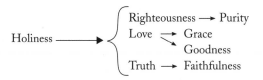

Figure 6.3. God's holiness in the Old Testament

figure 6.3. While these moral attributes of God are scattered throughout the Old Testament, they are best understood in light of the unifying and integrating holiness of God.

New Testament. In the New Testament the multiple expressions of holiness are centered on the person of Jesus. He is the model for what a holy God looks like. Above all he is the very expression of the holy, triune God in self-giving love. While Jesus is the Holy One of God (Jn 6:69), the earthly manifestation of the economic Trinity, he also reveals holiness and love as the essence of the ontological Trinity. Jesus' emphasis on love in relationship to holiness makes these the controlling concepts for understanding all the other moral attributes of God. This is illustrated in figure 6.4.

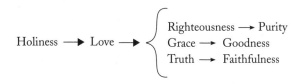

Figure 6.4. Holiness and love as controlling concepts

Having examined the two foundational elements of God's being—holiness and love—we are now ready to evaluate the other attributes of God.

7

THE ATTRIBUTES OF
THE TRIUNE GOD

Personal and Moral

I. THE ATTRIBUTES OF THE HOLY AND LOVING TRIUNE GOD

When we speak about the characteristics of God, we use the term *attributes*.[1] God's attributes have been organized in various ways, but the most satisfactory way of organizing them is according to his personal, moral, relative and absolute attributes.

One of the ways to understand the nature of God is to understand God's attributes in the light of his trinitarian nature. Focusing on the three-personed God entails a significant shift in understanding how the attributes relate to each other. The trinitarian approach, for example, affects the traditional order in which the attributes of God are described, with those coming first having some natural implications for those that are described later. We will look first at the traditional approach to the attributes and then at the trinitarian approach.

The Traditional Classification of Attributes

Traditionally, classifying God's attributes has taken this form:

1. Absolute attributes: aseity, spirituality, infinity, immutability

2. Relative attributes: omnipotence, omniscience, omnipresence, wisdom

3. Personal attributes: personhood

4. Moral attributes: holiness, love, righteousness, purity, truth/faithfulness, grace, goodness

---

[1] Other terms that have been used are *appellations*, *virtues*, *proprieties* and *perfections*.

This approach begins with the absolute attributes, that is, what God is in himself apart from his creation. Next come the relative attributes, which describe how God relates to the created world, then the personal attributes, and finally, the moral attributes, which express how God chooses to relate to other persons.[2]

The Trinitarian Approach to Attributes

While the traditional classification of attributes is the standard for writing systematic theology, a case can be made for beginning with a trinitarian approach, which would order the attributes like this:

1. Personal attributes

2. Moral attributes

3. Relative attributes

4. Absolute attributes

The rationale for this approach is that it more closely follows Scripture, which spends far more time revealing God's personal and moral attributes than his relative and absolute attributes. In fact, God's relative and absolute attributes are largely inferences drawn from what Scripture explicitly says about God's personal and moral attributes. The clear and explicit references should take precedence over the less direct inferences. But even more important, if God is a personal, trinitarian being, then his personal and moral attributes should be the primary way to understand God, not only in the order of knowing but also in the order of being.

The advantages of this trinitarian approach are significant. First, it gives the biblical data priority over the more philosophically oriented categories that emphasize the absolute and relative attributes of God. This is particularly significant because the absolute and relative categories tend to be more influenced by Greek philosophy than by biblical revelation. Second, a basic interpretive principle is followed in which the clear and biblically primary (personal and moral attributes) interprets the less clear (relative and moral attributes). Third, the trinitarian approach keeps the personal nature of the Trinity central, both from an economic as well as an ontological perspective. Fourth, this

---

[2]For the variety of classifications and language concerning the sequence of the attributes, see Thomas Oden, *The Living God* (San Francisco: Harper & Row, 1987), pp. 50-52.

approach, as we will see, allows us to address some of the problems of classical theism in articulating the relative and absolute attributes.[3]

II. THE PERSONAL ATTRIBUTES OF THE TRIUNE GOD

Trinitarian theism expands our understanding of the personal attributes of God. This begins by focusing on the three persons of God rather than on an abstract understanding of the unity of God. This classic approach of the Eastern church is being revived in the Western church by the recent interest in the Trinity.[4] Since the personal attributes of God relate not only to God but also to human persons, it is important to pay attention to them. Along with the moral attributes, these components of God's nature are reflected in men and women as God's image-bearers.

From a certain perspective the whole discussion of the Trinity is about how persons relate to persons. Therefore, this discussion of the personal attributes of God also helps us understand what personhood entails.

The Centrality of Jesus

In discussing the personal character of God we are immediately confronted with the meaning *person*. What are the defining characteristics of a person, or what constitutes personhood? Jesus is the key to understanding what it means to be a person.

Throughout this study we have worked with two basic principles: (1) the economic Trinity makes known the ontological Trinity, and (2) the Son is the key to understanding the economic Trinity. Thus we know the Father and the Spirit through Jesus (Jn 1:18). This is possible because they share the substance of God *(homoousios)*. As Jesus puts it, "If you had known me, you would have known my Father also" (Jn 14:7). As a result, to fully understand the personal nature of God, we look at the person of Jesus as he is revealed in the New Testament. One divine person, Jesus, makes known the other divine persons, the Father and Spirit, within the triune Godhead.

A corollary concept also illuminates personhood. Jesus is not only a divine

---

[3]This will become clearer in interpreting certain attributes such as the omnipotence and immutability of God. Approaching these from the personal and moral character of God rather than in terms of the absolute and relative attributes of a sovereign monarch casts an entirely different light on them.

[4]See Stanley J. Grenz, *Rediscovering the Triune God: The Trinity in Contemporary Theology* (Minneapolis: Fortress Press, 2004), pp. 218-19.

person but also a human person. Not only is Jesus consubstantial *(homoousios)* with the Father and the Spirit, he is also consubstantial with human beings. He is the God-man who tells us not only what God is like but what God intends us to be. Jesus is the key to understanding theology *and* anthropology.[5]

So while Jesus is the full revelation of personhood, divine and human, he is also the full revelation of the image of God, which men and women bear. This means that personhood is closely identified in humans with the image of God. God made women and men in his own image so they would be a reflection on the earth of what he—the personal God—is like. Sin has distorted this image, so we do not see clearly from sinful humanity what personhood ought to look like. But Jesus came in the full image of God *and* the full image of humanity. Therefore, he reveals in himself divine personhood and human personhood.

This full connection of the divine with the human in Jesus is called the *hypostatic union*. This makes it possible to understand what it means to be a person. In the hypostatic union, the divine and human Jesus reveals what a person is in the divine sense and in the human sense. According to God's original intention, one is a mirror image of the other. Human persons are designed to be like divine persons. That is, humanity is to be in the image of God. In this chapter, we will identify the component parts of personhood as they relate to the triune God.

Currently in both theology and the social sciences there is a growing interest in the concept of personhood. A critical point of departure is whether we describe the concept of person from below (as in anthropology) or from above (as in theology). We will take the latter course. One justification for this is that the concept of personhood underwent a seismic shift because of the trinitarian discussions of the fourth century. In the midst of defining how three persons could share one essence *(ousia)* in the Godhead, the specificity of personhood was developed. So the current interest in personhood, even if it does not recognize its historical roots, is deeply indebted to these trinitarian discussions.[6] With Jesus, fully God and fully human, there is the possibility of bridging the gap between studying personhood from above and from below. Jesus gives us both perspectives.

---

[5]On the development of the theological concept of person beginning with Jesus using the concept of *hypostasis*, see T. F. Torrance, *The Christian Doctrine of God* (Edinburgh: T & T Clark, 1996), pp. 156-61.

[6]See the previous discussion on *persona* in chaps. 3-4. For a discussion of the origin of the concept of personhood, see John D. Zizioulas, *Being as Communion* (Crestwood, N.Y.: St. Vladimir's Seminary Press, 1997), pp. 27-65.

The Components of Personhood

Persons are obviously complex beings. But this complexity comprises a whole that we recognize as persons. Understanding the component parts of personhood will help us understand the whole, which in turn will help us better understand the several parts and how they fit together. In addition, this discussion will also help us identify the personal attributes of God.

Social nature. The first thing Jesus makes clear is that there are no persons in isolation. Personhood always includes an intricate web of relationships. This means that social communion and fellowship are right at the heart of the concept of personhood.[7] In other words a person is someone who is in vital relationship with others. Therefore a person is not complete in himself, that is, completeness is found in social relationships with other persons. An isolated person is incomplete. Thus a person is always a "being in communion."[8] This of course helps explain the unity and diversity within the triune God. If persons are incomplete in themselves, the Father, Son and Spirit are only fully personal when they are joined together with other persons, which points to the unity of complete personhood within the triune God.[9]

We see the social nature of a person in both Jesus' human and divine relationships. From his birth Jesus related to his mother and father, and later to brothers and sisters. As he began his ministry, Jesus drew disciples around him. So he was always in relationships with other persons; he was not isolated. We cannot understand Jesus apart from this network of relationships.

From the divine side the birth narratives make it clear that the Father sent his Son into the world and that the Son was conceived by the Holy Spirit. The three divine persons were involved in the coming of Jesus. His unique relationship with the Father appears in his childhood when he asks his earthly parents, "Did you not know that I must be in my Father's house?" (Lk 2:49). At his baptism the heavenly Father blesses his Son with whom he is pleased, and the

---

[7]Referring to God as a social being does not mean endorsing all the current theories of the social Trinity. Some, following the lead of Moltmann, have so closely identified the relational nature of God with social human communities that the Trinity devolves into tritheism. By "social being" we are referring to God's relational nature within himself. The emphasis is on the perichoretic interrelatedness of the three divine persons.

[8]For a discussion of how Athanasius and the Cappadocians helped transform the concept of substance to give it a relational character see Zizioulas, *Being as Communion*, pp. 83-89.

[9]See Robert Jenson's discussion of the community of personhood (*Systematic Theology*, 2 vols. [New York: Oxford University Press, 1997-2001], 1:117-23).

Spirit of God anoints him for ministry. Jesus did the work of God within the parameters of these relationships. Clearly, he lived under the direction of the Spirit, and he constantly referred to his relationship with his Father.

At the end of his ministry, on his last night with the disciples, Jesus refers to God as his Father more than fifty times, and he prepares his disciples for the coming of the Spirit into their lives. In Acts 1—2 Jesus returns to the Father and then pours out the Spirit on his disciples. All of this is indicative of the close, intimate relationship between Jesus, the Father and the Spirit.

This biblical data drove the early church to say Jesus shares the *same being (homoousios)* with the Father and the Spirit. This means that when we know one member of the Trinity we know the others. Jesus is the key to the revelation of the Father and the Spirit, and his personhood makes them known as persons.

Further, when Jesus unfolds his own divine identity, he does it in terms of relatedness.[10] By describing himself as the Son of God who relates to God as Father, Jesus makes it clear that he is not self-originating. Thus the early church said he is eternally begotten of the Father. Nor is Jesus self-sustaining. His life is drawn continuously from the Father. Nor is he self-explanatory. By definition, a son finds his identity in relationship to his father. Nor is he self-fulfilling. He did not come to do his own will, but the will of his Father. His fulfillment is in doing his Father's will, not his own.

The social nature of being a person is expressed by Jesus in terms of reciprocal relationships of love. Jesus' relationship to the Father and the Spirit are by their very nature reciprocal. There is full interaction between them. God accomplishes revelation and redemption from the Father through the Son in the Spirit (Eph 2:18). Though they are uniquely distinct, they are not independent. They are always in relationship with one another, and they exist in a mutual giving and receiving.[11]

T. F. Torrance uses the term *onto-relational* to describe the relationship of God's social character to his essence:

> No divine person is who he is without essential relation to the other two, and yet each divine person is other than and distinct from the other two. They are in-

---

[10]For further discussion of personhood that connects individuals and relationships see David Coffey, *Deus Trinitas: The Doctrine of the Triune God* (New York: Oxford University Press, 1999), pp. 66-76.

[11]For persons in a relationship centered in love, see Jürgen Moltmann, *The Trinity and the Kingdom* (Minneapolis: Fortress, 1993), 171-74.

trinsically interrelated not only through the fact that they have one Being in common so that each of them is in himself the whole God, but also in virtue of their differentiating characteristics as Father, Son, or Holy Spirit which hypostatically intertwine with one another and belong constitutively to their indivisible unity within the Trinity. There is an indivisible and continuous relation of being between the Father, the Son, and the Holy Spirit so that the being of the Godhead is understood to be whole or complete not in the Father only but in the Son and in the Holy Spirit as well. These ontic and holistic interrelations between the three divine persons in virtue of which they are what and who they are as persons are substantive relations or "onto-relations."[12]

If God is a social being and his being *(ousia)* is identified with his holiness, then certain implications follow. First, holiness is transformed from a static quality to a relational category. The triune persons' shared holiness must be understood within a communion of relationships, and love is set in the forefront. This self-giving love becomes so central that God is described as love (1 Jn 4:8, 16). This is why Jesus talks about abiding in the love of the Father (Jn 15:10), and this is something Jesus desires to share with other persons (Jn 17:23, 26). The love that God shares with us is the mirror image of what God is in himself, or as Torrance puts it, "The love of God revealed to us in the economic Trinity is identical with the love of God in the ontological Trinity."[13]

So the love shared between the Father, Son and Spirit gives specificity to the triune God as social being. Richard of Saint Victor helps us understand the Trinity through the parallel of one human sharing love in mutual giving and receiving with another. But, Richard says, when the two are able to join their love and together share love for a third person, a new dimension of love takes place. This is an apt description of trinitarian intrapersonal love in which the Father and Son love each other and together love the Spirit. The Son and the Spirit love each other, and they also love the Father. The Father and the Spirit mutually love each other, and together they love the Son. Thus there is a dynamic of intrapersonal love within God himself that stands behind the declaration that God is love (1 Jn 4:8, 16).

What allows for the social nature of the Trinity where three persons are relating to one another? What makes it possible for the three members of the

---

[12]Torrance, *Christian Doctrine of God,* p. 157.

[13]See Torrance's excellent discussion on the giving and receiving of love within the triune God as a basis for God's expression of love toward us (ibid., pp. 162-67).

Trinity to share *being as communion?* Two further components of personhood seem to be particularly significant. One is life; the other is the functional capacities of personhood.[14]

Life. To be a person is to have life. Jesus makes clear that he possesses life in himself (Jn 1:4), and life is given to him from the Father and he shares this life with others (Jn 5:21). "For as the Father has life in himself, so he has granted the Son also to have life in himself" (Jn 5:26; 14:6). Within the triune Godhead this life is shared in a perichoretic way, and this perichoretic life is an essential component of personhood. Jesus brings the life of the triune God to men and women, and he models this life not only in its divine dimension but also in its human manifestation. Jesus comes not only to model divine and human personal life but to make it available to persons made in the likeness of God (Jn 10:10).

All persons have the capacity to perceive the reality in which they exist. All persons are self-conscious; that is, they have the ability to distinguish their own selves from the rest of reality. Through this self-consciousness, all persons understand their own identities. Each individual person is unique, and each recognizes that he is distinct from other persons and all other reality.

The same is true of Jesus. He not only is able to perceive reality—he is conscious of the world—but he also is aware of his own identity—he is self-conscious. His chief way of describing himself in relationship to God is as a Son to the Father (Lk 2:49). Thus he distinguishes himself from the Father (and from the Spirit). So when Jesus speaks about the Father, he always speaks about him as other than himself. When he talks about the Spirit and promises to send the Spirit as a gift to disciples, he clearly distinguishes the Spirit from himself (Jn 14:16-17). So he is not identical with either the Father or the Spirit; he has his own identity as the Son. At the same time, he does not see himself as separable from the Father or the Spirit. Because they interact perichoretically he identifies with the Father and the Spirit and yet is distinguished from them. The Father, Son and Spirit have a shared life, but the Son also has self-consciousness of who he is as a distinct person.

Human persons resemble the divine persons of the Godhead. We have life with both consciousness and self-consciousness. Our self-consciousness is re-

---

[14]Cf. this combination with a description of personhood by Arthur W. Wainwright, *The Trinity in the New Testament* (London: SPCK, 1962), p. 11.

lated to self-transcendence. This means that persons can distinguish themselves from themselves; they can stand outside of themselves and make eval-
uations. John Zizioulas speaks of *ecstasy* as the capacity to stand outside of
oneself, meaning that a personal subject can become its own object.[15] Self-
transcendence is particularly related to personal conscience, the ability to evaluate oneself by a moral standard.

So a person has (1) animate life, which includes (2) consciousness of reality,
(3) self-consciousness of one's own identity and (4) self-transcendence. Conscious life is related to the *ousia* of the triune God in terms of holiness as separation. One aspect of God's holiness is that he transcends creation; thus, by
extension, holiness, which is separation, can be viewed as self-transcendence.
This means that the holy God is self-conscious of his own identity, such that,
though he experiences *perichoresis* (shared life), he is also aware of a separateness or distinctness of life. So God's holiness is the overarching attribute that
makes possible the separateness of the persons within the triune Godhead.
Holiness is fundamental to the relational nature of the holy Trinity.

The heart: Functional capacities of personhood. There are four capacities in
which persons function. These are sometimes described in terms of the
psyche or personality, but we have avoided using these terms because of the
popular connotations attached to both. In the Old Testament all four are
covered by the Hebrew concept of *heart (lēb)*, and for ministry purposes, this
may be the best word for what is described. All four capacities of the heart
are clearly evident in the life of Jesus. They include reason, imagination,
emotions and will.

Reason. A thinking person is the embodiment of reason. Reason includes
logic (rules of correct thinking), memory (things impressed on the mind from
the past) and language (verbal communication between persons). Language is
the external evidence of the internal phenomena of logic and memory, all of
which are included under the rubric of reason. Jesus obviously used language
in his speaking and teaching, giving evidence of clear thinking and memory.
The Gospel of John describes Jesus as the Word *(logos)* of God, who existed
before the creation of the universe. This is a clear indication that within the
Godhead rational communication is part of who God is.

For centuries many in the church followed Boethius's definition of a person:

---

[15]Zizioulas, *Being as Communion*, p. 91; Richard of St. Victor was the first to use *ecstasy* in this way.

"an individual substance of a rational nature." While Boethius accurately discerned a key component of being a person, his definition is not broad enough. The intellect is a key to distinguishing between persons and animals, but there are other factors involved.[16]

Imagination. Imagination is so closely connected with reason that some see it as a subcategory of reason, similar to logic, memory and language. But there are good reasons to place it in a separate category. Imagination involves self-transcendence; it allows a person to envision something—a mental concept—that is distinct from what it is (or could be) in reality. It is a person's capacity to project in his or her mind something that is not yet in existence. For human persons it is envisioning something in the future; for divine persons, unlimited by time, it focuses on that which is possible but has not yet come to be.[17]

Jesus demonstrates his own imagination by envisioning the future when he says to Nathaniel, "You will see heaven opened, and the angels of God ascending and descending upon the Son of man" (Jn 1:51). Jesus is imagining (envisioning) what God intends to do, first Jesus' own life and then in the lives of disciples. When he looked ahead to the cross, to the pouring out of the Holy Spirit and to the work of disciples in fulfilling the Great Commission he was using his imagination. Within the Godhead itself, this capacity stands behind the creation of the world. First, the triune God imagines its possible existence, and then moves to create the world as we know it.

Emotions. The affective side of persons may be described as emotions or feelings. All person-to-person relationships involve some emotion, and this is true with regard to Jesus' personal interaction with others as well. Jesus clearly demonstrates the emotion of anger in his cleansing of the temple (Jn 2:13-16; Mk 11:15-19). Jesus looked on the rich young ruler and loved him (Mk 10:21). We see sorrow in Jesus' burden for the city of Jerusalem and the people of Israel (Lk 19:41) and in his agonizing struggle in the garden of Gethsemane (Mk 14:34). Both sorrow and love appear in the story of Lazarus's death (Jn

---

[16]Boethius's definition is also problematic in that a person is viewed as an *individual* instead of in relationship to other persons (see Colin Gunton, *The Promise of Trinitarian Theology* [Edinburgh: T & T Clark, 1991], p.94).

[17]For a helpful description of the variety of ways in which the term *imagination* may be used, see Garrett Greene, *Imagining God* (San Francisco: Harper & Row, 1989), pp. 62-66. In spite of his helpful treatment of imagination, Greene appears to want imagination to be the constituent of personhood, replacing the role reason played for Boethius.

11:35-36). Finally, along with his love, Jesus shared his joy with his disciples
(Jn 15:10-12; 16:24). So Jesus expressed the whole realm of personal emotions. This parallels God's emotional expressions toward the people of the Old
Testament. In light of Scripture, God's impassibility, meaning he is incapable
of emotion, is certainly problematic.

Will. The will, the capacity to choose, is obviously a significant part of personhood. All of Jesus' actions were determined by his choices. We see him, for
example, exercising his will in his first encounter with the disciples (Jn 1:35-
51), in turning water into wine (Jn 2:1-11) and in cleansing the temple (Jn
2:13-22). Clearly, a volitional element lies behind his choices, even though
Jesus repeatedly states that he has aligned his will with that of his Father (e.g.,
Jn 6:38). This indicates that his will does not belong to him alone but also to
his Father. This is a component of divine personhood that becomes central for
human persons.

A combination of capacities. These four capacities of the *heart* are central to
our understanding of personhood. Persons are not just rational creatures; reason is combined in a perichoretic way with imagination, emotions and volition. When one of these is isolated from the others, it results in a distorted
view of personhood. Full personhood is expressed in the unique blend of all
four, and with this we have a far better understanding of how persons relate
and work.

Moral capacity/conscience. *Moral capacity.* We have seen that a person is a
social being with conscious life and certain functional capacities. Not surprisingly, this combination produces a moral capacity within persons, which encompasses both a conscience and a will. The conscience arises out of one's separateness (self-transcendence), the ability to stand over our self and evaluate
our self morally and ethically. The conscience requires the use of reason, imagination and emotions. These three are essential for the sense of moral ought-
ness or awareness of right and wrong that is at the heart of the conscience.
Conscience presupposes the capacity to choose between alternatives that reason, imagination and emotions bring to the person. Conscience is the capacity
for knowing right and wrong and demands the moral exercise of the will.

We see this clearly in Jesus' conversation with his Father in Gethsemane.
His self-consciousness makes him aware that he is distinct from his Father. As
the Father speaks, Jesus becomes aware—through his reason, imagination and
emotions—of God's will for his life. This story is so powerful because Jesus

must choose to match his will with that of his Father's, and in this Jesus models the moral capacity that every person has, whether divine or human.

Moral holiness. Earlier we connected moral holiness with relationships to other persons. In order to express holiness in the moral dimensions, a person must be in relationships with other persons. All six dimensions of moral holiness are evidenced in Jesus' personal relationships with humans: love working through grace, goodness, truth, righteousness and purity. What is true of his relationships with humans is also true within the ontological Trinity as well. Indeed, this is what makes it possible to understand how moral holiness works.

Love is that component of holiness that permeates the relationships of the three persons of the Trinity. All dimensions of personhood are related to love. This thrusts love forward as the primary expression of holiness in moral choices. It is best to speak in terms of holiness as love, which expresses itself through grace, goodness, truth, righteousness and purity. Notice that in these love is other-oriented.

Therefore, the moral dimension of personhood cannot be reduced to one dimension or capacity (e.g., the will). There is a specific content to moral personhood: love expressing holiness and seen in grace, goodness, truth, righteousness and purity. And these demand other persons for their expression. Thus they are central to the relational Trinity.

Freedom. The components of a person already identified—sociality, life, functional and moral capacity—are intricately related to the concept of freedom. This is particularly true of the functional capacities of personhood. Freedom is closely identified with the will of a person, and volition also presupposes understanding and imagination and is often connected with feelings. Further, the ability to make choices presupposes the freedom of self-determination. This freedom is expressed in the social relationships and moral nature of the triune God in which the three members of the holy God freely relate to each other in love.

Our understanding of the ontological Trinity's freedom is derived from our awareness of Jesus' freedom. In the New Testament narratives, Jesus' freedom to choose is obvious. Staying behind in the temple to question and listen to teachers while still a boy is the first place we see Jesus exercising his will (Lk 2:41-52). Two other places where Jesus' will is particularly obvious are at the beginning and the end of his ministry. The first is in the temptation stories, where he chooses the will of God but clearly has the freedom not to do so. Indeed, this is the point of the temptation story. The other is in the garden of Gethsemane, where Jesus faces the cross and freely chooses to do the will of God, even though he has many reasons (and emotions) to avoid it.

These stories, which bracket Jesus' ministry, reveal his consistent choice to submit to his Father. He always chooses to align his will with the will of God. This is not predetermined by the Father but is freely chosen by the Son (Jn 6:38). Jesus models freedom for us. In him we see how to make moral choices: how to love, trust, be receptive to truth, care, obey and deal with temptation. We will also see that freedom is further expressed in our creativity and our responsibility for creation, which includes other persons.

Jesus' freedom is consistent with the other parts of being a person. So his freedom as a divine person does not include the impersonal or unholy. Jesus' freedom is consistent with the holy God. His freedom is "the effective energy inherent in God by which God is able to do all things consistent with the divine nature. The divine will is the infinite power of God to determine God's own intentions, execute actions, and use means adequate to the ends intended."[18] To be fully personal, one must have freedom of the will in self-determination.

Creativity. Personhood also has a creative component. Creativity is particularly intertwined with the functional capacities of personhood and freedom. To do anything creatively, one must have some understanding (reason), the ability to imagine something that does not yet exist, and the freedom of will to bring it into being. Creativity is often accompanied by emotions, although emotion does not seem to be as essential as the other elements.

The New Testament reveals that creativity was part of Jesus' existence in the ontological Trinity before the creation of the universe. He is identified as participating in creating the universe: "All things were made through him, and without him was not anything made that was made. In him was life, and the life was the light of men" (Jn 1:3-4). Paul says, "In him all things were created, in heaven and on earth, visible and invisible, whether thrones or dominions or principalities or authorities—all things were created through him and for him" (Col 1:16; cf. Heb 1:2).

But Jesus' creativity is not limited to the making of the heavens and the

---

[18]Oden, *Living God*, p. 90.

earth. Jesus also demonstrates creativity in his personal relationships. An obvious example is the way he put together and trained a band of disciples over a period of three years (Jn 1:35-51). The variety of methods Jesus used in teaching his disciples demonstrates remarkable creativity. His creativity in both the physical creation and in personal relationships is aptly illustrated in the story of the marriage at Cana (Jn 2:1-12).

Creative capacity involves imagining something (whether physical, relational, conceptual or experiential) not yet in existence and freely choosing to bring it into existence. Like Jesus, every person uses this capacity daily, even if only in the creative reordering of time and energy.

Responsibility. Closely connected to creativity is responsibility. Bringing something into existence entails responsibility for it. A person must understand what he is creating, imagine how to care for it, feel some emotion toward his creation, and freely choose to care for it. The freedom that makes moral choices and creativity possible also makes persons responsible for their choices and creations.

Humans are responsible for their physical creations, but more significantly they are responsible for how they relate to other persons. This is exemplified in the life of Jesus. He is not only responsible for sustaining creation (Col 1:17), but he is also responsible for the body of believers brought into existence through his creative life (Col 1:18). In the Gospels, after he calls his disciples, he assumes responsibility for them for the three years of his ministry, and after his ascension he continues to care for them through his Spirit (Jn 16:4-15).

Jesus' responsibility, woven together with creativity and freedom, is well illustrated in the stories recorded in John 1—2. Jesus first freely chooses disciples, creates a unique band of those following after him, and then assumes responsibility for those who are following (Jn 1:35-51). He then attends a wedding at Cana and creatively turns water into wine, which indicates that he takes some responsibility for the wedding feast at which he is a guest (Jn 2:1-12). Then while attending the Passover in Jerusalem, he drives out the money changers through creative disruption, thereby taking responsibility for his heavenly Father's house (Jn 2:13-22). This combination of capacities in Jesus is seen throughout the Gospel narratives.

Coinherent personhood: Perichoresis. The early church described the unity and diversity of the persons of the Trinity through *perichoresis*, a concept that is particularly appropriate in our discussion of personhood. *Perichoresis* means "coinherence" or "interpenetration." Thus the three members of the Trinity interpenetrate each other; that is, they share life together. No one of them is present without the others. This *perichoresis* is an expression of their social nature. Their lives coinhere in such a way that both the distinctness and oneness of their being is maintained. The relationships within the Trinity are always completely reciprocal. That is their nature.

The reciprocity of the three persons' natures clearly means they are completely open to each other as they share life together. The persons of the Trinity so interpenetrate one another in their openness that they are one being. Thus persons are only complete when they are open to sharing life with other persons. The perichoretic life of the triune God stands behind our understanding of God (and other persons) as being in communion.[19]

The persons of the Trinity share reason, imagination, emotion and will. They have eternally chosen to be in this state of shared life. This is why Jesus is described as the Word who was with God and who was God (Jn 1:1); in this case the sharing of reason allows for both uniqueness and oneness of these two persons of the Trinity.

The perichoretic sharing of life, and therefore personhood, is enveloped with holiness as love. In Scripture love is not just an emotional dimension of God's nature but relates to his will and presupposes both understanding and imagination. Part of being a God of love is sharing love, which is part of sharing personhood. Thus love, usually categorized as a moral attribute, is so intimately connected with the personal attributes of the triune God.

Scripture sometimes gives us glimpses of the triune persons perichoretically relating to each other through their reason, imagination, emotions and will. So Jesus converses (reason) with his Father, envisions (imagination) what the Father is going to bring to pass, expresses feeling (emotion) about what is coming and chooses to do God's bidding (will). We also see the triune God perichoretically relating to human persons with one mind, one imagination, one emotion and one will. This allows men and women to reciprocate, relating to God by relating to any one of the three members. When we relate to one, we relate to all three. Perichoresis is a conceptual tool that helps explain a great deal of data about the Trinity: how the three persons relate to each other, how

---

[19]Torrance believes that *perichoresis* is the key to the early church's development of the "onto-relational" concept of divine persons. This is at the heart of the concept of personhood in the working out of trinitarian theology (*Christian Doctrine of God*, p. 102).

they relate to us and how we relate to them.

***Defining* person.** We have observed the various components of personhood as the means of identifying the personal attributes of God. Persons are social beings who possesses life and consciousness and have the capacities of the heart: reason, imagination, emotion and will. Possessing a will means persons have the ability to freely choose among alternatives. This freedom is expressed not only in moral choices but also in creativity and responsibility. Persons also have a moral capacity, including a conscience, to relate to other persons in moral holiness through love, grace, goodness, truth, righteousness and purity.

Based on all this data, a working definition of *person* is a social being with conscious life who exercises reason, imagination, emotion and will in moral choices, freedom, creativity and responsibility.[20]

III. THE PERSONAL AND MORAL ATTRIBUTES OF THE HOLY, TRIUNE GOD

We have identified the personal attributes of God in a more extensive way than some in Christian theology because of the growing conviction that personhood lies at the heart of understanding these attributes. One implication is that the personal attributes highlight the moral dimensions of personal relationships. So the personal attributes naturally lead to a discussion of the moral attributes. Since one of the indicators of God's essence is his holiness, we need to examine the relationship of holiness to both the personal and moral attributes.

Personal Attributes and Holiness as Brilliance

Our beginning point in looking at holiness is the Hebrew word *qōdeš*. One of the possible etymological meanings of *qōdeš* is "brilliance" or "brightness." This is certainly connected in Scripture with the immediate personal presence of a holy God among his people.[21] We will trace the holy through the Old and New Testaments as an indicator of God's personal coming to those who be-

---

[20]Alternative definition of *person:* A living, self-conscious, social being with the functional capacities of reason, imagination, emotion and will to make moral choices in freedom, creativity and responsibility.

[21]Allan Coppedge, *Portraits of God* (Downers Grove: InterVarsity Press, 2001), pp. 134-35.

long to him. This will help us understand the personal or relational nature of God's holiness.

A holy God comes to his people. To Israel. The brilliance of God's holiness is often revealed in terms of God's glory. So when Isaiah sees the creatures declaring God's holiness, he exclaims, "the whole earth is full of his glory" (Is 6:3). Glory, representing God's holy presence, fills the holy of holies of the tabernacle at Mount Sinai (Ex 40:34-35). This is paralleled by the glory of God filling the temple at Jerusalem (1 Kings 8:11; 2 Chron 5:14; 7:1-2). The glory of God, which symbolizes the brilliance of his holy presence, is sometimes represented by a cloud, as at Mount Sinai (Ex 19:9, 16; 24:15) and in Ezekiel's vision of God's presence (Ezek 1:4; 10:3-4). This same brightness as glory may well be seen in Jesus on the Mount of Transfiguration (Lk 9:32).

At other times the brilliance of God's holy presence is symbolized by fire. God speaks to Moses through a burning bush on holy ground, that is, where the holy God is present (Ex 3:5). God comes down to make himself known on Mount Sinai in fire and lightning (Ex 19:6, 8; 24:15, 17). The children of Israel are led by the Holy One in the day by a pillar of cloud and at night by a pillar of fire (Ex 13:21-22; 40:36-38). Fire symbolizes the full presence of God through the Holy Spirit on the day of Pentecost (Acts 2:3-4), and in one of the final pictures of God in Scripture, seven torches of fire represent the Spirit of God where the creatures around the throne cry "holy, holy, holy" (Rev 4:5, 8).

These passages indicate that the brilliance of holiness is connected with the glory of God's personal presence. But it must be remembered that the symbols of cloud and fire represent the immanence of the personal God among his people. The focus is not so much on the physical phenomena as it is on the presence of God, who wants to be in relationship with his people. This is why God speaks when he comes in these powerful ways. Thus holiness as brilliance is not only related to God's personal presence but also to truth. So when God comes to Mount Sinai to offer a covenant to Israel (Ex 19—20), he brings instructions—the Ten Words—for his people. When his presence comes to the tabernacle (Ex 40:34-35) and the temple (1 Kings 8), it fills the holy of holies, where the Ten Words are kept. When the Holy One of Israel comes, he speaks to his people. The holy God is personal![22]

Through Jesus. The climax of God's brilliant presence in the world is found

---

[22]Ibid., pp. 135-38.

in the incarnation. The coming of Jesus as the representative of the Trinity is when the holiness of God is fully manifested to the world. "The Holy Spirit will come upon you, and the power of the Most High will overshadow you; therefore the child to be born will be called holy, the Son of God," the angel announces to Mary (Lk 1:35). This holy child comes as the perfect manifestation of God. "The Word became flesh and dwelt among us, full of grace and truth: We have beheld his glory, glory as of the only son from the Father. . . . No one has ever seen God; the only son, who is in the bosom of the Father, he has made him known" (Jn 1:14, 18). The disciples of Jesus came to recognize him as the "the Holy One of God" (Jn 6:69). This applies one of the most significant Old Testament titles of God (e.g., Is 12:6) to Jesus, who now represents the fullest expression of the holiness of God: the personal presence of God among his people. His coming is sometimes symbolized by light (Mt 2:2-9; Jn 1:4-5). Light, like glory, cloud and fire, represents the brilliance of holiness and sometimes is used as a symbol of the holy presence of God among his people.

Through the Holy Spirit. When Jesus was raised by the Spirit (Rom 1:4) and ascended into heaven, he poured out the promised Holy Spirit on his disciples (Acts 2:4, 33). Jesus had told them that the Holy Spirit would replace him as the immediate presence of God in their lives (Jn 14:16-17). Just as Jesus reflects the full personal and moral character of the triune God in the Gospels, so the Holy Spirit after Pentecost also reflects the full presence of the Trinity in creation. Just as God has made his holy presence known through the Son, now he makes it known through the Spirit. The Spirit filled the Twelve, just as he had filled Jesus (Mt 3:16), to accomplish God's purposes in the world through them just as God had worked through Jesus. Where the Holy Spirit is, the whole triune God is. Under the new covenant Jesus is the first revelation of God's personal holiness, and the Spirit is the second major expression of this holiness.

Holiness as brilliance: The personal and moral attributes of God. The brilliance associated with holiness is connected to the personal presence of God among his people. Since the full expression of this presence comes with the incarnation, Jesus is significant for understanding the implications of God's holy presence in the world. This is part of Jesus' full revelation of the economic Trinity, which is the reason we discussed the personal attributes of God in terms of Jesus' life. As a part of these personal attributes, Jesus reveals the moral capacity of personhood, which is exercised in freedom. Here the personal attributes of God open the door for understanding his moral attributes (i.e., those attributes that are related to choice). Will and freedom, components of personhood, are essential for making moral choices. They are therefore intimately related to any discussion of moral holiness. God continues to choose to be holy and loving, and out of his own personal and moral being he also continues to choose the other components of his moral holiness.

Holiness and the Moral Attributes of God

We have already seen that the components of moral holiness are love, righteousness, purity, truth, grace and goodness (see p. 165). The combination of holiness as love, which is expressed through the other five components, is of particular significance. Let's look carefully at each.

Holiness as love. The love of God expressed in the New Testament is built on God's holiness, which is expressed in the Old Testament by the words *ḥesed* and *'āhēb*.[23] The statement "God is love" presupposes God's declaration "I am holy." The New Testament writers did not repeat God's declaration because his holiness was a given. They built on this accepted premise by showing more fully what God's holiness implies, namely, that holiness is expressed in love. As Thomas Oden says, "The holiness which the Bible teaches is the holiness of the God who is love, therefore the truth of the holiness of God is completed in the knowledge of his love. This indissoluble connection between holiness and love is the characteristic and decisive element in the Christian idea of God."[24]

In the order of knowing it looks as though love is best understood as an expression of God's holiness. Both holiness and love are central to the moral attributes of God, even under the old covenant. But as the data unfolds, love becomes more and more prominent. The love of God is certainly present in the Old Testament, but from Mount Sinai on, the primary picture of God is built on his holiness. Some of the Old Testament writers, such as Isaiah, show clearly a picture of God's love as an expression of his holiness. As Walther Eichrodt says, "Hence for [Isaiah] love is a part of the perfection of Yahweh's

---

[23]Emil Brunner, *The Christian Doctrine of God,* Dogmatics, trans. Olive Wyon (London: Lutterworth Press, 1949), 1:183.

[24]Oden, *Living God,* pp. 123-25. Cf. Brunner, who correctly writes, "Thus the Holiness of God is the basis of the self-communication which is fulfilled in love," (*Christian Doctrine of God,* p. 164).

nature and a basic element in holiness."[25] But the full expression of God's love is not manifested until the advent of God's Son in the New Testament. Then the family categories that describe God and our relationship to him come to the fore (see pp. 197-200), and it is possible to arrive at a much more complete understanding of the love of God. Nevertheless, this expanded knowledge of God's love will be fundamentally unsound if it is not pictured against the backdrop of God's holy character. As we explore the biblical materials, God's love clearly comes as a natural expression of his moral holiness. As Skevington Wood says, "The supreme manifestation of holiness is in love."[26]

By the time we come to the order of being, Scripture, love and holiness are so interwoven that it is difficult to determine their sequence. Sometimes it looks as though love is an expression of God's holiness, and at other times as though holiness and love are interwoven within the *ousia* of God. In any case it is clear that these two dominate the other components of the moral attributes of God.

Holiness as brilliance: Truth, purity and grace. When Jesus comes as the Holy One of God in the New Testament (Jn 6:69), he also comes as the Word of God (Jn 1:1-3). He comes to speak the truth—the truth about God, ourselves and our world. Truth is always personal in Scripture. The same Hebrew word *(emet)* is used for truth and faithfulness. God's word can be counted as true because he faithfully keeps his word. Truth is wrapped in personal categories, not just abstract ideas. One dimension of holiness as brilliance is *truth*.

Holiness as brilliance is not only related to God's truth and faithfulness, it is also closely tied both to his grace and his purity. Holiness as *purity* is sometimes connected with fire, representing God's brilliant presence. This is the case when he comes to purify Isaiah (Is 6:6-7) for his mission. Fire also appears on the day of Pentecost when the disciples are filled with the Holy Spirit.

---

[25]Walther Eichrodt, *Theology of the Old Testament*, trans. J. A. Baker, 2 vols., 6th ed. (Philadelphia: Westminster Press, 1961-1967), 1:281.

[26]Skevington Wood, "Holiness," in *Zondervan Pictorial Encyclopedia of the Bible*, 5 vols., ed. Merrill Tenney (Grand Rapids: Zondervan, 1975), 3:183. On love as an expression of holiness see C. A. Beckwith, "Holiness of God," in *The New Schaff-Herzog Religious Encyclopedia*, ed. Samuel Macauley Jackson, 13 vols. (Grand Rapids: Baker, 1949-50), 5:318; J. Muilenburg, "Holiness," in *The Interpreter's Dictionary of the Bible*, 4 vols., ed. George Buttrick (Nashville: Abingdon, 1962), 2:622; Dale Moody, *The Word of Truth* (Grand Rapids: Eerdmans, 1981), p. 104; Otto Procksch, "ἅγιος" in *Theological Dictionary of the New Testament*, 10 vols., ed. Gerhard Kittel, Gerhard Friedrich and G. W. Bromiley (Grand Rapids: Eerdmans, 1964), 1:93; Thomas McComisky, "*qādôsh*," in *Theological Wordbook of the Old Testament*, 2 vols., ed. R. Laird Harris, Gleason L. Archer Jr. and Bruce K. Waltke (Chicago: Moody Press), 2:788.

Fire symbolizes purification from their self-centered orientation (Acts 2:1-4; see also Acts 15:8-9). The connection between holiness and purity is so strong that purity "becomes the principle content of holiness. This is shown sometimes in the realm of morals and sometimes that of ritual, and most often in both at once."[27] God's holiness as purity refers to his "separation from the impurity and sinfulness of the creature, or expressed positively, the clearness in purity of the divine nature."[28] Theologically, we may say that purity represents God's freedom from self-centeredness; this complements his other-oriented self-giving.

The last dimension of holiness as brilliance is *grace*, which must be understood in a twofold way. It is both the undeserved favor as well as the empowering work of God. God's grace is expressed toward his people all through Scripture, and nowhere more clearly than at Mount Sinai. There God makes his holiness known (Lev 11:44-45) and declares to Moses, "I will be gracious to whom I will be gracious, and will show mercy on whom I will show mercy" (Ex 33:19). Israel has already experienced God's grace in delivering them from the Egyptians. He did not deliver them because they deserved it but out of his undeserved favor. He redeemed them from bondage, empowering them to follow him and to be the people of God.

Grace and truth are two key characteristics of Jesus, the Holy One of God: "The Word became flesh and dwelt among us, full of grace and truth" (Jn 1:14). Thus holiness as brilliance is revealed in three significant moral attributes of God: truth, purity and grace.[29]

Holiness as righteousness. God's holiness as righteousness is expressed in the standard of right relationships that he gives to his people. Of course, this standard is patterned on the right relationships between members of the Trinity. So the righteous law of God becomes a description of the holy character of God. This was established at Mount Sinai when God tells Israel he is looking for a people who will reflect his own holy character (Ex 19:6; Lev 11:44-45). The expression of this holiness is worked out in a standard of righteous living: the Ten Words (Ex 20; Deut 5:1-21). These commandments express what a holy people ought to look like when they reflect the righteousness of a holy God.

Isaiah captures this connection between holiness and righteousness: "The

---

[27]Edmond Jacob, *Theology of the Old Testament* (New York: Harper & Brothers, 1958), p. 92.
[28]Gustoff Oehler, *Theology of the Old Testament* (New York: Funk & Wagnalls, 1883), p. 110.
[29]For further discussion of holiness as brilliance, see Coppedge, *Portraits of God*, pp. 134-41, 174-77.

LORD of hosts is exalted in justice, and the holy God shows himself holy in righteousness" (Is 5:16). In a similar way, the psalmist says of the Holy One of Israel, "Righteousness and justice are the foundation of thy throne," and so God's people are challenged to be those "who exalt in Thy name all the day, and extol thy righteousness" (Ps 89:14, 16).

The new covenant works on the same principle. God is still developing a holy nation (1 Pet 2:9) that will reflect his holiness (1 Peter 1:15-16). To be a holy people, Peter challenges Christians to follow the example of Jesus and so "die to sin and live to righteousness" (1 Pet 2:24).

God is not choosing some standard of right beyond himself; it is the very nature of the right relations within the triune God. Righteousness is established on relationships between the persons of the Trinity. This in turn is expressed in the right relationships with others. This righteous way of relating becomes the standard for all person-to-person relationships and thus is the standard for all human morality and law.

God's holiness as righteousness is seen in his relationships within creation. As one author states it, "God is, in his essence, by his very nature, holiness itself; and righteousness is the mode or way by which his essence is expressed toward his created world or toward anything apart from himself."[30] Emil Brunner says, "Righteousness, therefore, is simply the holiness of God, as it is expressed and confronted with the created world. The nature of God, which is holy, manifests itself over against his creature as the divine quality of righteousness."[31]

Understanding righteousness in relation to the Trinity shifts the focus from primarily being a legal term to being a relational category. We first perceive righteousness as about interpersonal relationships and only later find these codified in the law. In delineating the correct way for persons to relate to each other, righteousness is codified in Scripture. But God had been teaching people about right relationships (e.g., Genesis) before the law was given at Sinai (Exodus). So there is a prior relational base for righteousness in the order of knowing as well as the order of being.

From a trinitarian perspective our understanding of righteousness must begin with how the Father relates to the Son and Spirit, so family language is

---

[30]A. H. Leitch, "Righteousness," in *Zondervan Pictorial Encyclopedia of the Bible*, 5 vols., ed. Merrill Tenney (Grand Rapids: Zondervan, 1975), 5:105.
[31]Brunner, *Christian Doctrine of God*, p. 278.

fundamental to right relations with others. Therefore, righteousness can no longer be understood as only related to the roles of God as Judge or King. The righteous Father is the foundation for interpreting God's role as Judge, not vice versa.

Holiness as goodness. The connection between goodness and holiness begins with the synonymous use of these terms to describe God's holy presence in his temple: "We shall be satisfied with the goodness of thy house, thy holy temple!" (Ps 65:4). Then, in describing the benefits of God's "holy name," the psalmist includes that which is "good." We are to "bless the LORD," for the Holy One "satisfies you with good as long as you live" (Ps 103:1, 5). Furthermore, in calling all flesh to bless God's holy name forever, he declares that the people will "pour forth the fame of thy abundant goodness" (Ps 145:7). Clearly, goodness is an expression of God's holy name (i.e., his nature).

The giving of God's Holy Spirit is also connected to his goodness. When Isaiah extols God's "great goodness to the house of Israel," he describes God as the one who "put in the midst of them his Holy Spirit" (Is 63:7-14). In the New Testament Luke compares the good gifts of an earthly father with the heavenly Father's gift of the Holy Spirit: "If you then, who are evil, know how to give good gifts to your children, how much more will the heavenly Father give the Holy Spirit to those who ask him!" (Lk 11:13).[32] The writer of Hebrews also connects goodness with holiness in declaring that God "disciplines us for our good, that we may share his holiness" (Heb 12:10).

The goodness of God has its roots in the description of God's work at creation. After each day of the creation, God declares it to be good (i.e., in accord with his purpose and plan; see Gen 1:4, 10, 12, 18, 21, 31). Since his purpose and plan are based on his own nature, these good things are in accord with God's being. This is particularly apropos to the creation of man and woman in God's own image (v. 27). The goodness of God is further expressed in his provision of the Garden of Eden. God made it "pleasant to the sight and good for food" (Gen 2:9), indicating the abundant provision and care God provides for his people. His goodness is related to providing for basic needs like food, security, stability, companionship and making things beautiful (Gen 2:18).

The first direct reference to the goodness of God comes in connection with the revelation of God's glory and God's name, both of which are intimately

---

[32] Cf. Mt 7:11 which refers to the Father who gives "good things to those who ask him."

bound up with his holiness. When Moses asks God to reveal God's glory, the Lord responds, "I will make all my goodness pass before you, and will proclaim before you my name" (Ex 33:19). The psalmist makes the same connection between God's goodness and his name: "Praise the LORD, for the LORD is good; sing to his name, for he is gracious!" (Ps135:3). God's name—his holy nature—is consistently identified with goodness because, as W. B. Pope explains, holiness "is the standard of goodness." Thus it is the holy nature of God "that declares what is morally good." "The reason why good is good" is because the holy God is the eternal standard and foundation of all goodness.[33] In Greek philosophy the "good" may be an abstract idea, but in biblical revelation it is personal in nature and its meaning is governed by a holy and loving God.

Jesus declares, "No one is good but God alone" (Mk 10:18; Lk 18:19; cf. Mt 19:17). Good is not based on some standard higher than God, but goodness is an expression of his holy being. G. R. Lewis says:

> The good, the just, the pure, the holy is holy, not by reason of an arbitrary act of the divine will, nor of a principle independent of God, but because it is an outflow of his nature. God always wills in accord with his nature consistently. He wills the good because he is good. And because God is holy, he consistently hates sin and is repulsed by all evil.[34]

Donald Guthrie rightly warns us about defining what is good apart from the character of God. Jesus' statement that "only one is good, God," "makes clear that the character of God is such that it is itself the standard that should determine all human notions of goodness. And that goodness flows from the holy essence of God's being."[35]

IV. SUMMARY OF THE MORAL ATTRIBUTES

A review of the connection between holiness and the moral attributes is in order. A holy God expresses himself first in love, but also through the other moral attributes: truth, purity, grace, righteousness and goodness. These five moral

---

[33]W. B. Pope, *A Compendium of Christian Theology*, 3 vols. (London: Wesleyan-Methodist Book Room, 1880), 1:333.

[34]G. R. Lewis, "Attributes of God," in *Evangelical Dictionary of Theology*, ed. Walter Elwell (Grand Rapids: Baker Academic, 1984), p. 456.

[35]Donald Guthrie, *New Testament Theology* (Downers Grove: InterVarsity Press, 1981), p. 108; see also J. I. Packer, "Good," in *New Bible Dictionary* (Downers Grove: InterVarsity Press, 1981), p. 483.

attributes are expressions of a unique blend of holiness and love. Because moral attributes can be exercised only by persons, there is an intimate connection between them and the personal attributes of God. So the three divine persons are related in the ontological Trinity through love, truth in communication, purity from self-interest, gracious empowering of each other, righteous personal relationships and self-giving goodness. The moral attributes are expressed through the ontological Trinity's perichoretic relationships and then through the economic Trinity's relationships with human persons.

We began our exploration of God's attributes with the personal and moral attributes because these are the most explicit in Scripture. The Bible reveals God in personal terms; he makes moral choices and gives other persons the same capacity. Because the economic Trinity reveals the ontological Trinity, the moral attributes are true of both. Now, with our broadened understanding of the personal and moral attributes, we will look at the relative and absolute attributes.

8

THE ATTRIBUTES OF
THE TRIUNE GOD

Relative and Absolute

I. HOLINESS AND THE RELATIVE AND ABSOLUTE ATTRIBUTES OF GOD

Though the trinitarian perspective makes the personal and moral attributes of God primary, this does not mean that God's relative and absolute attributes are unimportant. However, because Scripture rarely addresses these latter attributes directly, their characteristics are primarily inferred from statements made about the personal and moral attributes of God.

Our trinitarian approach to the attributes of God not only expands our understanding of the personal attributes but also changes the order of the discussion of the attributes, and this is not just an academic exercise. Usually the attributes discussed first dominate the discussion of the others. In classical theism the absolute (infinity, immensity, eternity, simplicity, and immutability) and the relative (omnipotence, omniscience, and omnipresence) attributes are viewed as primary. Thus God's sovereignty is the controlling rubric. God's personal and moral attributes are subsumed under this approach, and their role in understanding the nature of God is minimized.

The trinitarian approach significantly changes our view of God by placing the personal and moral attributes first. Now God's sovereignty is seen in a different light. The absolute and relative attributes are governed by God's personal nature and moral character, which make person-to-person relationships much more important. This shift in perspective recognizes all of God's attributes as they function in a different and more biblical manner.

So, how do God's holiness and love relate to the relative and absolute attributes? The best approach is to connect holiness as power to God's relative attributes and holiness as separation to God's absolute attributes. Then the love of the holy, triune God informs and controls these other attributes.

Holiness as Power: The Relative Attributes of God

The relative attributes of God traditionally include God's omnipotence, omnipresence, omniscience, and wisdom. These attributes, sometimes called the communicable, operative or postrelational attributes, explain the way God relates to the created order.[1]

Omnipotence. Throughout Scripture God's holiness is expressed as power. When God delivers Israel from the Egyptians, the Song of Moses praises God, who is "majestic in holiness" and whose right hand is "glorious in power." The point is that the Lord has the strength to deliver his people (Ex 15:1-18). This is further evident in Israel's wandering in the wilderness, when they had to be constantly reminded of the Lord's power:

> They tested him again and again,
> and provoked the Holy One of Israel.
> They did not keep in mind his power,
> or the day when he redeemed them from the foe. (Ps 78:41-42)

Not only the psalmists but also the prophets declare that "the Holy One" not only creates people but delivers them "by the greatness of his might, and because he is strong in power" (Is 40:25-26). During the time of the exile God declares that he will one day vindicate his holiness before the nations by demonstrating his power to redeem his people from the exile (Ezek 36:23-24).

The New Testament reveals holiness as power even before the incarnation. In the birth announcement to Mary the angel says, "The Holy Spirit will come upon you, and the power of the Most High will overshadow you; therefore, the child to be born will be called holy, the Son of God" (Lk 1:35). Mary responds by praising God: "For he who is mighty has done great things for me, and holy is his name" (Lk 1:49). The same emphasis is seen in the resurrection of Jesus. Paul describes Jesus as the one who is "designated Son of God in

---

[1]The relative attributes are sometimes referred to as relational attributes, although this term may be confused with God's personal attributes. See Thomas Oden, *The Living God* (San Francisco: Harper & Row, 1987), pp. 50-51.

power according to the Spirit of holiness by his resurrection" (Rom 1:4).[2]

When the relationships of the triune God guides our understanding of holiness as power, then power takes on new meaning. Traditionally, power introduces the relative attributes of God, which normally begin with omnipotence and then proceed to omnipresence, omniscience and wisdom. Omnipotence is the controlling attribute, and when it is connected with the concept of God as sovereign King, as it is in classical theism, it implies autocratic, absolute power. This fits well with the Greek philosophical approach, but not with the Bible.

Our understanding of omnipotence is transformed when we begin with the triune God known through his holiness and love. Omnipotence is no longer seen as the absolute power exercised by a monarch. Instead, it is power exercised by the three members of the self-giving God who relates to creation in love. So God's power is guided by personal relationships motivated by unconditional self-giving. This does not diminish God's power but sets a completely new context for its exercise. Rather than viewing power in terms of God's control of all events, it is now understood as the triune God exercising his might by giving himself to others.

As a result, God is no longer pictured as an absolute monarch. For example, he does not elect some and condemn others through an arbitrary exercise of power. Rather, he is the Holy One who in self-giving love uses his power to enable all persons to enter into a relationship with himself. When omnipotence is the primary attribute, then God can arbitrarily elect some and reprobate others. In this classical model, power becomes more significant than holiness exercised in either righteousness or love (i.e., personal relationships). But the trinitarian approach redefines the way power is exercised, and salvation is necessarily reframed.

Traditionally, the other relative attributes—omnipresence, omniscience and wisdom—are subordinated to God's exercise of power. From the trinitarian perspective these attributes are in the service of God's personal and moral attributes, and how he relates to his creation. God's omnipotence is not re-

---

[2]For an exaggerated focus on holiness as power, see Rudolph Otto, *The Idea of the Holy* (London: Oxford University Press, 1928). Otto attempts to remove both the moral and the rational (and therefore the relational) elements of holiness, and concentrates on the overpowering presence that he describes as the *mysterium tremendum*. Otto attempts to find the common ground between ancient Israel's and its neighbors' concept of the holy. For an evaluation of Otto, see Allan Coppedge, *Portraits of God* (Downers Grove: InterVarsity Press, 2001), pp. 302-3.

duced or undercut but is set in a more biblical and relational framework.

By giving the personal attributes of God priority, the role of personal freedom, both divine and human, is elevated within our theology. Because God desires to freely interact with those who bear his image (i.e., personal attributes), then instead of using his power (omnipotence) to control human persons, he uses it to relate personally with them, respecting their freedom. The other three relative attributes also assume a different role. To relate to freely responding persons, God increasingly relies on his omnipresence, omniscience and wisdom. Because his power is subordinated to the personal and moral attributes, he accomplishes all of his purposes by being continually present and by using his full knowledge and wisdom. His omnipotence is not used to control personal relationships, but the reverse.

Omnipresence. Just as God's omnipotence is radically transformed in light of his personal and moral attributes, so is his omnipresence. Because God is a spiritual being and not limited by space (he is immense) and time (he is eternal), he may be simultaneously present everywhere (omnipresent). The trinitarian perspective helps explain how God, through his Spirit, can be immediately present throughout the whole universe.

The attribute of omnipresence connects God's transcendence (i.e., separation from the universe) with his immanence in our world of space and time. The supranatural God who created and oversees the universe is not contained in creation, but he nevertheless has the ability to be present in it for his purposes. So the psalmist exclaims:

> Whither shall I go from thy Spirit?
> Or whither shall I flee from thy presence?
> If I ascend into heaven, thou art there!
> If I make my bed in Sheol, thou art there.
> If I take the wings of the morning,
> and dwell in the uttermost parts of the sea,
> even there thy hand shall lead me,
> and thy right hand shall hold me. (Ps 139:7-10)

Obviously the psalmist feels an intimate connection between God's omnipresence and his power, and we must not fail to notice the trinitarian connection of both of these with the Spirit of God.

God's omnipresence makes it possible for him to continue his providential oversight of creation; he preserves it, supports its normal laws of operation, and in particular guides its affairs. Because God's personal and moral attributes govern his omnipresence, his omnipresence allows him to be available to all persons throughout the universe. He is not present merely to run the impersonal parts of creation, he is primarily present to interact with those made in his own image. So God's personal attributes are central to his omnipresence. Since the Trinity's relationships are always moral, his presence to others is always accompanied by his love and goodness in righteousness, purity, truth and grace. Further, he shares in the delights as well as the suffering and hurts of others. Omnipresence, from the trinitarian perspective, means God is present everywhere to relate to human persons in all aspects of their lives.

Omniscience. The triune God's desire to relate to all persons is also closely connected with his omniscience. God's omniscience begins with his perfect knowledge of himself and then extends to all other things. His understanding is infinite (Ps 147:5). God's infinite mind has intuitive, simultaneous and perfect knowledge of all that can be known. He is eternally cognizant of the actual, the possible and the contingent. All of God's works are known to him from the beginning of the world.[3] So divine omniscience spans the past, the present and the future.

The omniscience of God is inferred from the larger design of Scripture. The Bible opens with the story of creation (Genesis 1—2) and ends with the close of history (Revelation). The Bible spells out that God, who began and will end the world, has a design for and purposes to accomplish in creation. This broad view of Scripture provides the biblical foundation for all of history. Unlike the cyclical view of time in the ancient Near East, Israel's linear view of time provides the basis for progression in history, which presupposes that the God of Israel knows what is happening and therefore he can unfold his purposes.

Since God is omniscient he can reliably run the universe:

Behold, the former things have come to pass,
and new things I do declare;
before they spring forth
I tell you of them. (Is 42:9)

---

[3]W. B. Pope, *A Compendium of Christian Theology*, 3 vols. (London: Wesleyan-Methodist Book Room, 1880), 1:316 (see Acts 15:18).

Because God is present everywhere, his knowledge extends to all things. "All things are naked and open unto the eyes of him with whom we have to do" (Heb 4:13). This knowledge of all that is happening also extends to moral judgment: "The eyes of the Lord are in every place, keeping watch on the evil and the good" (Proverbs 15:3).

God's omniscience extends not only to the universe and the affairs of the nations but also to individuals:

> Thou searchest out my path and my lying down,
> and art acquainted with all my ways.
> Even before a word in my tongue,
> lo, O LORD, thou knowest it altogether. (Ps 139:3-4)

Jesus declared that the very hairs of our head are known to his Father (Mt 10:30).

God's omniscience even extends to interior motivations: "So you think, O house of Israel; for I know the things that come into your mind" (Ezek 11:5). Thus Paul states that God "searches the hearts" so he might know all that it contains (1 Cor 2:10). John confirms this, saying that God "knows everything" (1 Jn 3:20). God's omniscience is grounded in his personal attributes and is a direct expression of his reason and imagination, which are components of personhood. These include logic, memory, knowledge and language, and are interwoven in such an intricate way that the persons of the Trinity, who perichoretically share the same mind, also share the same knowledge. They think together, they remember together, they know together, they speak together. *How* the members of the Trinity do this is a mystery. But *that* they do is the clear witness of Scripture. Divine omniscience is grounded in the personal relationships of the triune God. This is one more witness to the personal nature of truth.

The omniscience of the triune God assures that his revelation and redemption will accomplish his purposes. The persons of the Trinity freely share and use their knowledge in a manner consistent with their moral attributes, beginning with self-giving love. So the omniscience of God is never separated from his personal and moral nature. Thomas Oden aptly summarizes God's omniscience: "God's knowing is said to be (a) eternally actual, not merely possible; (b) eternally perfect, as distinguished from a knowledge that begins, increases, decreases, or ends; (c) complete instead of partial; and (d) both direct and immediate, instead of indirectly reflected or mediated."[4]

God's omniscience carries a special implication for his foreknowledge. If God knows everything, he knows the past, present and future. This includes the so-called middle knowledge *(scientia media)* or knowledge of all contingent possibilities.[5] Isaiah is particularly strong in using the concept of foreknowledge to distinguish the God of Israel from all other gods. He argues that only the God of Israel can foretell what is to come:

> Remember the former things of old;
> for I am God, and there is no other;
> I am God, and there is none like me;
> declaring the end from the beginning,
> and from ancient times things not yet done;
> saying, "My counsel shall stand,
> and I will accomplish all my purpose." (Is 46:9-10)

God's ability to do all that he desires is not only based on his own decisions but also on his perfect knowledge of the choices and motivations of other persons. To limit God's foreknowledge to the choices that he is going to make, as in open theism,[6] is simply too partial in its description of God's understanding according to Scripture.

Unfortunately, the starting point of the Augustinian, Thomistic and Calvinistic traditions has been the absolute sovereignty of God. With such a beginning, foreknowledge becomes foreordination. So if God foreknows something, he must have previously ordained it to come to pass. With this view of God's sovereignty, it is difficult to conceive of something that God has not caused. So God foreknows because he forecauses. But this eliminates human freedom. If God knows what choices human persons will make, then that surely implies (from the classical traditions' perspective) that God has made all the choices. This makes human freedom an illusion.

Open theologians respond by declaring that the Bible clearly supports human freedom, so God's omniscience, and particularly his foreknowledge, must

---

[4]Oden, *The Living God*, p. 71, referring to Thomas Aquinas,*Summa Contra Gentiles* 1.63-71 (Notre Dame: University of Notre Dame Press, 1955-1957), pp. 209-38.
[5]See Luis de Molina, *The Concordia*, part 4, *On Divine Foreknowledge* (Ithaca, N.Y.: Cornell University Press, 1988), pp. 164-95.
[6]See, for example, Gregory A. Boyd, "The Open Theism View," in *Divine Foreknowledge: Four Views*, ed. James K. Beilby and Paul R. Eddy (Downers Grove: InterVarsity Press, 2006), pp. 13-37.

be limited. In doing this, though, they have bought into the classical view of the sovereignty of God—that is, if he foreknows something he must be its cause. So foreknowledge is equated with foreordination for the open as well as the classical theists.[7] The openness escape from the foreknowledge-freedom dilemma is to opt for freedom and reject foreknowledge. But is this our only option? Here our trinitarian theism serves us well.

Scripture passages that imply God expects persons to respond in freedom confirm the capacity for freedom that all persons, whether divine or human, possess. To be a person means to have freedom of choice. In Scripture, the tri-personed God repeatedly addresses men and women, expecting them to freely respond to his directions and invitations. The key to understanding fore-knowledge, then, is to begin with a trinitarian rather than a classical under-standing of God. Within the triune God, the three divine persons have knowledge and freedom, and persons made in God's image have the capacity for both. To be a person is to have freedom or choice. This triune understand-ing of God is incredibly helpful in cutting the thorny knot that connects fore-knowledge and foreordination. With this beginning point, God may fore-know something that he does not forecause. He may know the free choices of persons without foreordaining those choices.

The best analogy for God's foreknowledge is that earthly fathers can know with fairly reasonable certainty many of the decisions and choices their young children are going to make, which is possible because fathers know how their children think. And the fathers' foreknowledge is not based on forcing their children to make certain choices. If this is true in a limited way with earthly fathers, how much more is it true of the omniscient heavenly Father, who knows ahead of time what his created children are freely going to choose.

God's omniscience, like his omnipotence and omnipresence, is closely related to his ability to govern the universe, and particularly other persons. In terms of his providential governance, God must direct and order the cir-cumstances of creation to accomplish his purposes, particularly for persons made in his own image. Knowledge of all things is necessary for the accom-plishment of this objective. But since God's omniscience is governed by his personal and moral attributes, his omniscience serves all his personal rela-

---

[7]Clark Pinnock, *Most Moved Mover* (Grand Rapids: Baker Academic, 2001), pp. 84, 107.

tionships and is consistently confirmed in the biblical revelation of God's character and actions.

Here trinitarian theism challenges classical theism to reexamine its view of God's absolute sovereignty and how it affects foreknowledge and freedom. Trinitarian theism opens the door for a different evaluation of foreknowledge and freedom.

Wisdom. Wisdom is the practical application of God's omniscience. The coordination of God's knowledge with his infinite ability to bring about his ends is accomplished through his wisdom. "Oh the depth of the riches and wisdom and knowledge of God! How unsearchable are his judgments and how inscrutable his ways!" (Rom 11:33). Like the other three relative attributes, God's wisdom is closely bound up with his sovereign direction of the universe. God needs wisdom to know how to apply knowledge to accomplish his purposes within the universe: "With God are wisdom and might; he has counsel and understanding" (Job 12:13).

Wisdom, like omniscience, is controlled by God's personal and moral attributes. Therefore wisdom is applied knowledge that particularly relates to people in a way that is consistent with God's moral attributes. This confirms that truth in Scripture is never abstract but is always personal in nature. This is why Jesus is the key to understanding how God works in relationship to the world. In him the personal connects with truth, and he illustrates how God in his wisdom providentially desires to relate to all persons.

Finally, trinitarian theism protects us from the temptation to turn God's knowledge and wisdom into abstractions. Knowledge for knowledge's sake is not characteristic of God. Rather, knowledge is designed to be in the service of God's creation in general, and persons in particular. So our focus is on wisdom in personal relationships rather than truth as an abstraction. The fact that persons have an innate desire for knowledge and wisdom is a reflection of their being made in the image of God. But both need to be pursued in the context of a personal connection with God; then the human mind will be formed by the mind of the triune God.

Beginning with the Trinity makes God's personal and moral attributes primary, and significantly changes our understanding of God's relative attributes. In particular it keeps the exercise of power from being arbitrary, and it brackets the use of power, presence, knowledge and wisdom within God's relational and moral character. This approach is thoroughly consistent with the scriptural identification of these attributes as they are unfolded in the order of knowing and understood in the order of being.

Holiness as Separation: The Absolute Attributes of God

Holiness is conceived as separation when the Bible makes reference to God's transcendence over the world of space and time. God is not part of the natural world but is the supranatural One—the wholly other One (cf. Hosea 11:9). The Lord's Prayer illustrates this connection between God's holiness and his transcendence. It opens with "Our Father who art in heaven," which highlights his separateness from the universe. This is immediately followed by "Hollowed be thy name" (Mt 6:9). He whose name is holy is also the one who transcends the world.

The concept of holiness as separation is highlighted by one of the possible etymologies of the Hebrew word *qōdeš*. It may come from the root *qd* which means "to divide or separate." This suggests its original meaning may have been "cut off, withdrawn or set apart."[8]

Holiness as separateness points to God as Creator. Isaiah makes a strong connection between the holiness of God and his role as transcendent Creator:

> Thus says the LORD,
> the Holy One of Israel, and his Maker: . . .
> "I made the earth, and created man upon it;
> it was my hands that stretched out the heavens" (Is 45:11-12; cf. Is 17:7; 54:5)

The same picture appears at the close of Scripture where the enthroned God is worshiped as "holy, holy, holy" by the creatures who also declare, "for thou didst create all things, and by thy will they existed and were created" (Rev 4:8, 11).

Holiness as separation naturally emphasizes the role of God as Creator. In the order of knowing God is introduced as Creator at the very beginning of Scripture. This sets the tone for the rest of Scripture: the God who enters into relationships with people is the God who made all things. Shifting to the order of being we understand that before God became Creator, he was eternally triune. This means that God's personal nature—particularly his role as Father—takes priority over his role as Creator. The implication is that the per-

---

[8]Norman H. Snaith, *The Distinctive Ideas of the Old Testament* (New York: Schocken, 1964), pp. 24-25; cf. Coppedge, *Portraits of God*, pp. 54-57.

sonal and therefore the moral attributes of God are determinative in understanding how God creates and relates to the world he transcends. The personal nature of God, coupled with a focus on his moral attributes, has significant implications for our understanding of God's absolute attributes.[9] Particularly when God's holiness and love are given the emphasis that they have in Scripture, the absolute attributes of God cannot be divorced from certain significant characteristics of God that are constitutive of his being.

The absolute attributes of God normally refer to those components of who God is within himself apart from how he relates to the created universe. Sometimes these are called primary or essential attributes, while others refer to them as incommunicable, quiescent or prerelational.[10] These absolute attributes of a transcendent, triune, holy God include his spirituality, infinity, self-sufficiency and constancy.

Spirituality. The first of the absolute attributes is God's spirituality, which is highlighted by Jesus' description of God as spirit (Jn 4:24). What did he mean by this? Traditionally, God's spirituality has three components: unity, simplicity and incorporeality. In light of a trinitarian context for understanding the attributes, a fourth category needs to be added: spirituality as personhood. We will look at each of these dimensions of spirituality.

Unity. The unity of God is based on the monotheism of the Bible; it focuses on the oneness of God's triune essence. Thus the Lord declares:

> I am the LORD, and there is no other,
> besides me there is no God. . . . (Is 45:5)

Thus God's people are enjoined, "Know therefore this day, and lay it to your heart, that the LORD is God in heaven above and on the earth beneath; there is no other" (Deut 4:39). This fact undergirds the great Shema, the declaration of faith by God's people: "Hear, O Israel: the LORD our God is one LORD" (Deut 6:4; cf. Jesus' affirmation in Mk 12:29). This is echoed by the New Testament doxology "to the King of ages, immortal, invisible, the only God"

---

[9]Pope proposes that we cannot properly understand these absolute attributes without first understanding the personal attributes. Without this approach theology "must either renounce itself and abdicate, or accept a personal God, of whom these absolute attributes are to be predicated only as they are made consistent with his personality." He further makes the case that these personal attributes can only be properly understood in the light of the doctrine of the Trinity (*A Compendium of Christian Theology,* 1:306-7).

[10]Oden, *Living God,* pp. 50-51.

(1 Tim 1:17). Thus the New Testament as well as the Old teaches "there is one God" (1 Tim 2:5; cf. 1 Cor 8:6).

But the unity of God, so clearly unfolded in the order of knowing in the Old Testament, takes on a different cast in the light of the revelation of the triune nature of God in the New. While God does not cease to be one, three persons share one essence. This means there is a triunity within the nature of the Godhead. He cannot be divided into parts, but he cannot be seen as a monad either. So the relational nature of the triune God qualifies our concept of unity. Fresh light is also thrown on the unity component of God's spirituality with the full revelation that the triune God is a personal Spirit as well as Father and Son. The Holy Spirit elucidates more clearly what the spirituality of God involves.

Simplicity. The simplicity of God means he is not divisible into parts, which of course is reinforced by the concept of God's unity. Throughout church history simplicity has meant that God is not a composite being; he is one. Therefore all of God is present in all of God's activities.

This understanding of simplicity must be understood in terms of God's triune nature. God's simplicity must not be overdefined, that is, God is not a monad. God is not divisible into parts; he is three persons within one essence, which we understand through the concept of *perichoresis*—inner penetration of the persons in the shared nature of the one God. God is therefore simple in that sense. So, while a triune understanding of simplicity guards against focusing solely on the oneness of God, it also protects Christian theology against tritheism.

Incorporeality. God's spirituality also means he is immaterial and invisible. This distinguishes God from the created and material universe. When the Scriptures teach that God is pure spirit, it means that he does not have a literal body. As Jesus describes him, "God is spirit, and those who worship him must worship in spirit and truth" (Jn 4:24). Paul reinforces this with his declaration about the only God as immortal and invisible (1 Tim 1:17). This is further implied by the biblical picture of God as not being identified with any single part of the natural creation or its constituent parts. Rather, he is the transcendent Creator who is discontinuous with the physical universe of space and time.

This does not mean that God may not at times choose to enter the universe and take on a physical form, such as when he appeared to Abraham (Gen 18). We know that he particularly and uniquely came in Christ's incarnation. Further, God's incorporeality does not mean that he may not be described in anthropomorphic terms as a shepherd or a warrior or with body parts (e.g., God's arm). But these physical descriptions are not to be understood literally. They are metaphorical language to assist our understanding of how God works.

Our trinitarian perspective also qualifies our understanding of God's incorporeality. With the incarnation, we believe God assumed a human form, becoming visible and corporeal. While he remains a spiritual being, his incarnation broadens our understanding of his simplicity. God's assumption of human nature through the second person of the Trinity ensures that there is no dualism between God's transcendence and immanence, between his spiritual nature and his relating to human persons within creation. He has entered creation and experienced material existence in human form, and however mysterious this is, God has sovereignly chosen to let this experience have a permanent effect upon himself. It further allows humans, who only know personhood in a corporeal way, to know and relate to God through his incarnate Son. This certainly changes our concept of and relationship to God.

Personality. Another component of spirituality that arises from the meaning of *spirit*, demands our attention. Some believe that pure spirit is a mystery, that the content of a spiritual being is beyond our grasp.[11] But our trinitarian beginning point gives us fresh insight into this matter. If the tripersonal God has made persons in his own image, then the human spirit can help us understand what it means to made in the image of God. When we distinguish between human flesh and spirit, are we not distinguishing that which is corporeal from that which is incorporeal? And does that not imply that spiritual makeup of persons is really an alternative way of describing their personhood? If this is the case for human persons, it seems this is also true for understanding the divine personhood of God. God as spirit is incorporeal.[12] Defining God's spirituality in terms of personhood gives us some content of what spirituality means.

Earlier in our discussion of the personal attributes of God, personhood was defined in terms of a social being with conscious life who exercises reason, imagination, emotions and will in moral choices, freedom, creativity, and re-

---

[11] Pope, *A Compendium of Christian Theology,* 1:292-93.
[12] After the incarnation, though, God the Son is fully corporeal.

sponsibility (see p. 182). Since the triune God is first of all a relational, personal being and is the center of our discussion of spirituality, then this definition of personhood will help us understand what it means for God to be a spiritual being. It certainly gives spirituality far more positive content than the negative descriptions of God as incorporeal, invisible and without parts (simple). Further, it helps integrate God's personal attributes with the absolute attributes, which can be understood as the *perichoresis* of attributes.

God's personhood, part of his spiritual nature, helps explain the second commandment, which forbids the creation of any material image of God. God cannot be identified with creaturely matter, but he is represented within the created order by women and men made in his own image. "God is not matter" is part of the definition of God as spirit. Human persons, who embody spirituality in their own personhood, represent the spiritual nature of the invisible and incorporeal God.

Infinity. The infinity of God's divine nature means that he is without bounds or limits. Infinity is closely connected with the supranatural nature of God (i.e., he is beyond the natural world of creation). He is a supranatural being who is outside of both time and space. Infinity thus has a twofold reference point: first, God is eternal; second, God is immense.

Eternity. The eternity of God (i.e., infinity in relationship to time) means that God is without beginning or end; he stands outside of time.[13] He is the great and timeless "I AM." Thus, he is described as the first and the last (Is 41:4; 44:6). He is the everlasting God (Is 40:28). The psalmist exclaims:

> Before the mountains were brought forth,
> or ever thou hast formed the earth and the world,
> from everlasting to everlasting thou art God. (Ps 90:2)

In the New Testament, John speaks of grace and peace from "him who is and who was and who is to come" (Rev 1:4). The Lord God declares of himself, "I am the Alpha and the Omega, . . . who is and who was and who is to come, the Almighty" (Rev 1:8). Further, Jude describes Jesus as "before all time and now and for ever" (Jude 25).

Immensity. Whereas the eternity of God has to do with infinity in relationship to time, God's immensity is his infinity in relationship to space. God is

---

[13]For a discussion of several views of time, see Gregory E. Ganssle, ed., *God and Time: Four Views* (Downers Grove: InterVarsity Press, 2001).

not limited or circumscribed by space anymore than he is by time; he transcends both. As the Hebrews put it, "Behold, heaven and the highest heaven cannot contain thee" (1 Kings 8:27; 2 Chron 6:18). Though God transcends space, he is sometimes described as being in the universe without being localized or identical with any particular part of it (cf. Deut 4:39; Ps 139:7; Is 40:22; 66:1; Jer 23:24).

God's immensity implies his omnipresence. Beginning with the order of being, it is God's immensity that makes possible his omnipresence. God's lack of spatial limitation makes it possible for him to simultaneously accomplish his purposes throughout all of creation.[14]

God's infinity is particularly related to the holiness of God understood as separation. God is transcendent over (i.e., separate from) both space and time. So infinity is popularly understood as one of his supranatural attributes. Being infinite, God is separate (holy) from all that he has made, whether space, matter or time. Out of his own personhood the triune God freely chose to create a universe separate and distinct from himself and does not exist in created time and space. Nevertheless, God has chosen not only to share his personal life but also his love with persons in this creation. He relates especially to the personal part of the created world, even though he is clearly seen as distinct and separate from it. This connection expresses God's personal and loving nature, which gives rise to his creation of a world with whom he can share life and love.

Theologically, infinity elevates the supranatural character of God and protects us from pantheism (all is God) and panentheism (all is a part of God). In contrast to the rest of the ancient Near Eastern world, the God of the Bible is never identified with our world. He is separate and distinct from it. By being infinite, beyond both space and time, there is a clear distinction between the divine and the created. Today in much Eastern philosophy and theology, the line between the divine and created is blurred. In the contemporary West, pantheism and panentheism thrive in new forms, such as New Age thought and process theology.

God's infinity makes clear the distinction between God and creation, and particularly between divinity and humanity. But how then does the infinite God relate to finite humans? First, he does so by revelation. He makes himself

---

[14]Oden, *Living God*, p. 61.

known through the created order (general revelation) as well as through his rational communication (special revelation). So the triune God, who is a personal being, communicates to created persons through all the faculties of personhood that make such communication possible. This again places God's personal attributes in the midst of his absolute attributes.

The connection between the Creator and creation is completed and personalized with the coming of the second person of the Trinity in the incarnation. Here the triune God forever weds himself to the created world so there is a bridge from the infinite to the finite, from the Creator to the creation. This does not blur the distinction between the divine and the created or between God and humanity, but it unites the two in the person of Jesus, who is both God and man. This coming of the God-man prevents a dualistic separation between the Creator and the creation while maintaining a clear distinction between them. The infinite, supranatural God entered the natural world of space and time and provided a permanent connection between the two without blurring the discontinuity between them. Our trinitarian theism, then, balances God's infinity with his presence in creation, his transcendence and his immanence. The key to this theology is the relational, triune God, who created a world separate from himself so he could share triune life and love with other persons made in his image.

Self-sufficiency. The third absolute attribute of God is his self-sufficiency. This is sometimes described as his *aseity* or his *self-subsistence*, meaning that he possesses life in himself. God is not dependent on anyone or anything outside of himself for his own existence. There is no external cause of God; he simply and eternally is. God is without origin and can only be accounted for on the basis of himself. "There is no cause prior to God," explains Thomas Oden.[15] All existence and life find their cause in him. So Jesus says, "As the Father has life in himself, so he has granted the Son also to have life in himself" (Jn 5:26). This is surely part of what God had in mind when he revealed his name to Israel as "I AM WHO I AM" (Ex 3:14). Thus he declared, "Before me no god was formed, nor shall there be any after me" (Is 43:10), and "I am He, I am the first, and I am the last" (Is 48:12; see also Gen 1:1; Is 44:6). He alone is uncreated and the underived source of all (Ps 90:1-4).

This self-existence of God means that there is nothing above or beyond

---

[15]Oden, *Living God*, 1:55.

God that is responsible for his existence. The contrast is particularly clear in comparing the God of Israel to the gods of the ancient Near Eastern world. In a pagan worldview, above and beyond the gods was the metadivine, which may be variously described as a force, fate or primeval stuff. It was responsible for the gods' existence. But the God of Scripture is not part of the natural order nor is there any force, fate or metadivine above or beyond him. He exists only with himself, and he is solely responsible for all other things. There is no external dualism nor anything other than God that accounts for his existence.

The relationship of God's self-existence to his personal and moral attributes centers in the trinitarian nature of his being. While there is nothing that can be above or beyond God, there is an interrelatedness within himself. So in the Godhead self-existence is not that of a single individual but of a triune relationship. Each of the three persons of the Godhead was actively giving of himself in a moral way, especially in love, to the others before the universe was created. Understanding the priority of God's personal attributes, expressed in the three divine persons' self-giving love, removes any temptation to think of God before creation as either a monad or some impersonal force out of which everything else emerged. Rather, in his triune being there is "infinite variety of life, in the mutual knowledge, love, and communion of the Father, the Son, and the Holy Ghost."[16] The self-sufficiency of God along with his spirituality and infinity make up the heart of his transcendence. These comprise the basis of the supranatural being of God.

Constancy. The fourth of the absolute attributes is God's reliability. This refers to the fact that there is no change in any attribute of God's nature. As the psalmist declares, "Thou art the same, and thy years have no end" (Ps 102:27; Heb 1:12). The Lord declares of himself, "For I the LORD do not change" (Mal 3:6; also Heb 6:17-18; Jas 1:17). Jesus, who is the full reflection of the Father, is described as "the same yesterday and today and forever" (Heb 13:8). The unchangeableness of God is our guarantee that the One we trust today will not be different tomorrow. Our faith is built on the trustworthiness and sameness of God's character.[17]

Classical theists usually describe this attribute as "immutability," defining it

---

[16]Pope, *A Compendium of Christian Theology*, 1:301.
[17]While some descriptions of God's work may seem to imply that he changes (e.g., God repented of an action), this is not to be understood in terms of a change in his essence, attributes, purposes or character.

in terms of absolute changelessness. If God changes, they argue, he could not be a perfect being. Change implies he could become more or less perfect, which is an impossibility. Since God is the most perfect being, change must be excluded. A third option remains, however. Change for God is just different; it does not imply either more or less perfection as it might in reference to creation. But some theologies make God's immutability such that he never changes at all, either in his relationships or in himself.

From the trinitarian perspective God's unchangeableness must be understood in personal terms, where freedom and choice are an integral part of what is being described. When we do this, the terms divine *constancy* or divine *reliability* more adequately describe this attribute.[18] The three-personed God has a will and therefore freedom, and in all person-to-person relationships there is variation of interaction and so in some degree a kind of "change." No personal relationships are static; they are all dynamic. Person-to-person relationships cannot be frozen; they adjust or change in some respects. Because our relationship with God changes, it has some kind of effect on him and us.

In light of this, the biblical passages that imply God's constancy must be understood in regard to his personal and moral attributes. He is not personal now but some impersonal force at another time. He is not loving and faithful today but unloving and unfaithful tomorrow. Further, the personal nature of his being is not going to change, nor will the relative or absolute attributes of God. In particular, because of the personal and moral dimensions of his nature, his character and his purposes both for himself and for the world do not change. But the relationship between God and other persons change in some respects, depending on their responses to him. Because God's nature is constant, it is possible for him to relate to human persons who are changing in their historical circumstances. Because he is reliably the same, he can adjust to the change that occurs within persons, relations and history. Beginning with the personal and moral attributes of God requires a much more dynamic understanding of immutability, one that fits well with the biblical picture of the faithful God who is the same in his character, basic nature and purposes in all his relationships.

This trinitarian approach to divine constancy carries with it several implications. First, God's essential being is not "developing," as is suggested by

---

[18]Oden does not place this attribute under the absolute attributes but under the moral attributes because it must not be divorced from God's moral and relational character (*Living God*, 1:110-11).

process theology. God's purposes and character as well as his essence is not changing in some new way. Second, from a trinitarian perspective this approach to God's unchangeableness allows dynamic and interactive relationships between God and human persons. This sets the context for understanding the few passages about God "repenting" of his actions. We will return to this issue soon.

Finally, this approach also allows for the significant change that comes with the incarnation. While God's purposes, character and essential nature do not change in the incarnation, some change certainly takes place. At the incarnation God forever weds himself to his creation and permanently eliminates any absolute dualism between the divine and the created order. So though the Son of God experiences change—coming into the world, living, dying, rising, ascending and waiting for a second return—it is a very qualified and nuanced change that reveals rather than alters his character, purposes and essential nature.

This trinitarian perspective facilitates understanding the Scriptures that describe God as "repenting" (Gen 6:6-7; Ex 32:14; 1 Sam 15:35; Jer 26:3, 13, 19; Amos 7:3; Jon 3:10). Do these imply a change in God's basic attributes, character or purposes? No. These Scriptures speak in an anthropomorphic way to describe God's response to human persons; that is, they speak of God as if he were another human being changing in a relationship. A supranatural God of course knows what he is going to do and how others are going to respond all along. But he condescends to relate to us in an easily understood (human) way; thus we describe him using human categories such as "changing his mind." Understanding these few passages (and there are only a few) in this light is far more satisfactory than ignoring the massive biblical data that supports God's foreknowledge, which controls his own actions and his governance of the world. Rejecting God's foreknowledge in order to explain God's "changing his mind" is a bit like straining out a gnat and swallowing a camel! By placing the accent on God's personal attributes we strengthen our understanding of his constancy in responding to people, and this makes it possible to understand these passages without falling into the foreknowledge-denying trap of open theism.[19]

---

[19]For further discussion see Jay Wesley Richards, *The Untamed God: A Philosophical Exploration of Divine Perfection, Simplicity and Immutability* (Downers Grove: InterVarsity Press, 2003); and Steve Roy, *How Much Does God Foreknow? A Comprehensive Biblical Study* (Downers Grove: InterVarsity Press, 2006).

II. THE NATURE OF THE TRIUNE GOD

One of the benefits of a triune approach to understanding the nature of God is that it holds together the biblical data on both the transcendence and the immanence of God. The triune God, who created the universe and stands outside of space and time, enters creation in the person of the Son. This protects us, on the one hand, from making God so transcendent that he seems unconcerned with the world, and, on the other hand, it guards us from the kind of immanence that identifies God with the world (see the theological spectrum in fig. 8.1).

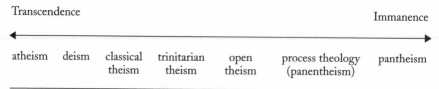

Figure 8.1. Theological spectrum from transcendence to immanence

The trinitarian approach addresses the concern of classical theism to preserve the sovereignty of God. God the Creator has made a world of which he is not a part but over which he rules. This has been a crucial tenet of Christian theology from the beginning. However, the trinitarian approach redefines changes God's sovereignty by shifting the focus from God as King to God as Father. So God's sovereignty is not first connected with majesty and power but with personal and family relationships—God seeking fellowship with those he has created to be like himself. Because God is Father (metaphysically) within the ontological Trinity, he is able to assume the role of Father (metaphorically) within the economic Trinity to those persons who enter into an appropriate relationship with him.

This also addresses the concern of open theism that classical theism has made God (the sovereign King) too remote and distant from his people, especially in their pain and suffering. But a father is intimately involved in the life of his family, and the coming of the Son on behalf of the Father through the power of the Spirit is the way the triune God identifies himself with his children. In fact, Jesus' interaction with persons in his own day is the living illustration of how the triune God desires to interact with persons of every generation. Certainly Jesus' loving response to the pain and suffering of those around him demonstrates the triune God's involvement with us. This trinitarian view of God is a more adequate response to the openness critique than the suggestion that we need a more compassionate King.[20]

The trinitarian paradigm gives us a picture of the relationality of God and also protects us from two problems. First, it keeps us from a view of God's sovereignty that makes him distant and aloof. While classical theism is certainly not deism, it sometimes so elevates God's transcendence that the open theists' complaint is given legitimacy. Second, it protects us from pantheism or panentheism and over-emphasizing God's immanence (process theology). Neither is an adequate description of the biblical God. Open theists attempt to protect themselves from the dangers of process theology, but by limiting God's foreknowledge as they do, another biblical line is crossed, making God too immanent without enough attention given to his transcendence.

Trinitarian theism balances God's transcendence and immanence. The triune God certainly transcends the world he has created. But the advent of Jesus binds God to his people in a graphic and permanent way. God clearly desires to not only relate to his people but to identify with them. In Jesus he identifies with every component of human life: relationships with families, friends, congregations, culture, government, education, commerce, travel and so forth. God is concerned about pain and suffering in our sinful, fallen world, which became obvious in Jesus' life, death and resurrection. In light of this, the abstract concept of impassability has to be drastically revised. The triune God does identify with suffering and even participates in it. The older view that Jesus suffered only in his human nature simply is not adequate; it disregards the biblical data and the theological implications of the triune God who comes into the world.

Since all of life is a gift from God, he not only identifies with pain, hurt and suffering but also with joy and delight in the fullness of the experiences of life, family, growth, knowledge and so on. He wants to participate in all of life's dimensions with those in relationship to himself. So trinitarian theism speaks to the cry of those who want God personally involved throughout life's journey.

This trinitarian reconfiguration of God's attributes reframes the relative and absolute attributes. They no longer control the personal and moral at-

---

[20]John Feinberg, *No One Like Him* (Wheaton, Ill.: Crossway, 2001), p. 701.

tributes but are themselves guided by these two. This means that our idea of God is not primarily conceived in terms of power and transcendence but in terms of appropriate person-to-person relationships. Nowhere is this more apparent than in the interaction between human freedom and God's sovereignty.

When we understand freedom as an essential part of personhood and therefore part of the nature of the tripersonal God, we view freedom in a new way. When sovereignty is primarily defined in terms of the absolute and relative attributes, the focus of God's absolute control becomes the chief factor. As a result, the personal attributes, which include freedom, take second place. Classical theism struggles with the biblical picture of persons freely responding to God while maintaining its view of God's absolute sovereignty. Some within that tradition minimize human freedom so that God's sovereignty might not be compromised. So while they admit that God is truly free, humans do not have genuine freedom.

However, if we begin with Jesus, who freely operates as a human being made in the image of God and as the Son of God who shares in God's divine freedom, then the freedom that God possesses has to be mirrored in some realistic way in human persons. Placing God's personal attributes *before* the absolute and relative attributes gives the freedom of the tripersonal God priority over his sovereignty. From the triune perspective God's sovereignty is redefined by the personal nature of God, including his freedom.

Thus God is no longer understood primarily as a sovereign King demanding that his subjects do his will. Rather, sovereignty is discussed in terms of the interrelationships within the tripersonal God who freely bestows on human persons certain capacities that reflect his own nature. God gives people free will so that he might enter into person-to-person relationships with them. Because they are made in his image, meaning they reflect his personal and moral nature, he interacts differently with them than he does with the rest of creation. Within creation the unique freedom that persons possess is an essential component of God's relationship with them.

This perspective does not mean that God is not sovereign. But it is a redefined sovereignty, self-chosen by God, that allows persons to choose to submit to God's sovereign direction for their lives. In his providential oversight of humanity, God still can accomplish his ultimate purposes, but in their divinely given freedom some people may choose less than God's best for their lives.

Person-to-person relationships cannot be forced. They must be freely chosen. God opens the door for human persons to freely receive his life and grace and to establish and maintain an ongoing relationship with him. Freedom of choice is central to exercising all the components of personhood, including creativity and responsibility, as those made in the image of the tripersonal God. This removes any determinism in understanding human nature.

In our understanding of how all of the attributes fit together, trinitarian theism expands the role of two of the moral attributes: holiness and love. This move is justified by the emphatic roles they play in Scripture.

Holiness is no longer identified only as a megacategory for righteousness, but in fact becomes a controlling rubric for all four categories of attributes. Because holiness relates to all four, this is a better way to understand God's statements about himself as holy (Lev 11:44-45; 1 Pet 1:15-16). Love is also elevated and understood as essential to the interrelationships of the ontological Trinity. Thus we see the implications of love for all the other attributes of God.

From this perspective, then, the holy and loving triune God, who as personal being relates to others in a moral way, is the foundation for understanding the relative and absolute attributes of God. By beginning with God's holiness and love, a much more biblical picture of God is articulated, and we have a much different understanding of how the economic Trinity relates to us.

The last implication of this reordering relates to the variety of roles God plays in relationship to us. So we now turn our attention to the roles of God in the economic Trinity.

THE ROLES OF THE TRIUNE GOD

The Way the Economic Trinity Works

Historic Christian orthodoxy has always believed that to properly understand the nature of God, we need God's revelation. Without divine assistance, human reason and perception, which are limited to this world, cannot comprehend the supranatural, transcendent and personal triune God who stands outside of the universe of space and time. By its very nature Christianity is not based on what we think about God but on what God has made known about himself. Biblical faith is rooted in God's self-disclosure.[1] Since the church believes this special revelation has come to us in Scripture, the Bible is the source of all legitimate attempts to comprehend the nature and character of God. But the question remains: How does God speak through this special revelation in language that we can understand?[2] The answer lies in the work of the economic Trinity, that is, the triune God making himself known.

I. HOW DO WE KNOW THE SUPRANATURAL GOD?

Because the triune God is a supranatural being and ordinary human perception is limited to the natural world, how is it possible for people to know God? Can humans comprehend a God who is outside the world of space and time? Human language is necessarily confined to the world of creation. Recognizing

---

[1]"A human knowledge of God can be a true knowledge that corresponds to the divine reality only if it originates in the Deity itself. God can be known only if he gives himself to be known. The loftiness of the divine reality makes it inaccessible to us unless it makes itself known. Hence the knowledge of God is possible only by revelation" (Wolfhart Pannenberg, *Systematic Theology*, 3 vols., trans. Geoffrey W. Bromiley [Grand Rapids: Eerdmans, 1991-1997], 1:1; cf. Emil Brunner, *The Christian Doctrine of God*, Dogmatics, trans. Olive Wyon [London: Lutterworth, 1949], p. 118).

[2]In this chapter I am following substantially the materials in chap. 1 of my *Portraits of God* (Downers Grove: InterVarsity Press, 2001), pp. 21-38.

our dilemma (particularly the finiteness of our perception), God has condescended to use human language to describe his own transcendent being. Working with terms from creation, and particularly from personal relations, God tells us what he is like. So God's self-revelation in Scripture (special revelation) uses words we are familiar with, words and images that come from our own world (general revelation). Both general and special revelation are from God and are used in complementary ways.

The best way to describe the transcendent God is by use of *analogical language* (i.e., using terms that are alike in some but not all ways).[3] So, for example, from the natural world we understand what *power* is, and that assists us (by comparison) to understand God's work as all-powerful (almighty) or omnipotent. So by analogy the use of *power* in relation to God is similar to our use of *power* in this world. But it is also dissimilar; *power* is often impersonal, as in the power of electricity. So God is connected with power in his omnipotence, but he is not a mere force—an impersonal power. Analogy is particularly helpful in comparing the way God works in relationships.[4]

There are many kinds of analogies.[5] For our purposes the analogy that has particular relevance for us is *metaphor*. Aristotle aptly captured the significance of metaphor: "If one wants to master speech, one must master metaphor."[6] A metaphor is a specialized form of analogical language in which one thing (a subject) is compared to another (a symbol).[7] When God is described using metaphors, there is an analogy between God (the subject) and something in the created world (the symbol) that is based on the similarity of being, action or relationship.[8] God, for example, is called a rock (Ps 31:2-3). While the comparison is limited, this metaphor helps us understand that God is un-

---

[3]On analogy see Thomas Aquinas *Summa Theologica* 1.Q.13, ed. Thomas Gilby (Garden City, N.Y.: Image, 1969); *Summa Contra Gentiles* 1.32-34 (Notre Dame: University of Notre Dame Press, 1955-1957); E. L. Mascall, *Existence and Analogy* (Hamden, Conn.: Archdon, 1967), pp. 92-121; P. Sherry, "Analogy Reviewed," and "Analogy Today," *Philosophy* 51 (1976): 337-45, 431-46.

[4]Cf. Alan J. Torrance, "Analogy," in *Dictionary for Theological Interpretation of the Bible,* ed. Kevin J. Vanhoozer (Grand Rapids: Baker Academic, 2005), pp. 38-40.

[5]For discussions of the analogies of proportionality and attribution see Battista Mondin, *The Principle of Analogy in Protestant and Catholic Theology* (The Hague: Martinus Hyjhoff, 1963), pp. 51-61, 100-102.

[6]Aristotle, cited in Ian Paul, "Metaphor," in *Dictionary for Theological Interpretation of the Bible,* ed. Kevin J. Vanhoozer (Grand Rapids: Baker Academic, 2005), p. 507.

[7]Metaphors are analogies of extrinsic proportionality.

[8]See P. W. Macky, *The Centrality of Metaphors to Biblical Thought* (Lewiston, N.Y.: E. Mellen Press, 1990), pp. 26, 49. Macky lists ten different types of metaphor used in Scripture.

changing and provides a firm foundation for whatever we do. It may well be that metaphorical analogy is used more frequently than any other mode of description of God.[9]

The metaphors that imply the greatest degree of correspondence between God (subject) and a symbol from this world are those that are taken from personal relations.[10] These personal metaphors describe God's being, actions and relationships as similar in many respects to a human's being, actions and relationships. This kind of "human" metaphor for God may be called a *role*. These roles (a metaphor itself borrowed from the theater) indicate truths about God by comparing him to the way human persons act and relate to others. Each of these indicates that this is the way God *is*, this is the way God *acts* and this is the way God *relates to others*. The use of these role metaphors allows the Bible to graphically depict God as King, Father, Judge and the like. These metaphorical roles of God are one dimension of analogical language.[11] They are the primary description of the way the economic Trinity relates to creation.[12]

God's active doing, speaking and relating seems best captured with the word *role*. Accordingly, we are going to use *role* as the primary term to describe these personal images of God, while *metaphor, analogy, portrait* and *identity* will be used as secondary terms.[13]

In *The Language and Imagery of the Bible* G. B. Caird calls attention to the fact that God uses human categories to help people understand himself. Caird points out that the metaphors/roles derived from human relationships have special significance because they work as a two-way traffic in ideas:

> When the Bible calls God Judge, King, Father or Husband it is, in the first instance using the human known to throw light on the divine unknown, and particularly on God's attitude to his worshippers. But no sooner has the metaphor

[9]B. Mondin, *Principle of Analogy*, p. 94. For significant discussion of metaphors and God see Walter Kasper, *The God of Jesus Christ*, trans. Matthew J. O'Connell (New York: Crossroad, 1999), pp. 93-99.

[10]On limits on using analogy and metaphor see H. Palmer, *Analogy, A Study of Qualification and Argument in Theology* (London: Macmillan, 1973), pp. 85-96.

[11]Cf. Richard Baukham's use of "The Identity of God" as an alternative label in *God Crucified* (Grand Rapids: Eerdmans, 1998), pp. 7-8. John Frame refers to them under the rubric of images of God (*The Doctrine of God* [Phillipsburg, N.J.: P & R Publishing, 2002], pp. 368-78).

[12]Cf. Barth's use of the analogy of relation that corresponds to the analogy of extrinsic proportionality. Kasper, *The God of Jesus Christ*, pp. 97-98.

[13]Three kinds of metaphors are used for God: inanimate objects (God is a rock), animals (Lion of the tribe of Judah) and persons (King, Father, Shepherd). On a continuum, inanimate objects clearly are least like God and personal metaphors are most like him.

traveled from earth to heaven than it begins the return journey to earth, bearing with it an ideal standard by which the conduct of human judges, kings, fathers and husbands is to be assessed.[14]

Caird's valuable insight is that while God draws from this world to describe himself, when we understand his full revelation to us, the metaphors are reshaped by God's own being and become the standard for a new understanding of human roles. So from our knowledge of human kings we know that the King of the universe is somewhat similar—he gives direction, exercises authority, provides order for those under his responsibility, directs personal relationships, provides protection for those under his care and so forth. But once we understand the nature and character of the triune God better, we better understand what a good king should be like. God is the model for human kings; they should base their behavior on the way the holy, loving, triune God relates to his creation.

God uses multiple metaphors/roles because none is fully adequate in itself. In addition, because no human judge, king or father is ideal, our perception of these roles is often distorted. Yet enough is known about each of these human roles to give us a better understanding of some aspect of the nature of God.[15] God is like them in some ways but (in accord with the way analogy works) not in every way.

Once we begin to reflect on the nature and character of the economic Trinity as revealed through roles, a much more perfect model is given to us of what an earthly judge, king or father ought to be. So while we begin to understand God with the use of these extended metaphors, our more comprehensive understanding of him is not conditioned by our knowledge of any of these human portraits, which might be faulty. In fact, the human roles of necessity

---

[14]G. B. Caird, *The Language and Imagery of the Bible* (Grand Rapids: Eerdmans, 1997), p. 19.

[15]There is a growing list of literature on metaphor in general. Some of the more significant works include I. A. Richards, *The Philosophy of Rhetoric* (New York: Oxford University Press, 1936); E. Bevan, *Symbolism and Belief* (London: Collins, 1938); Max Black, *Models and Metaphors* (Ithaca, N. Y.: Cornell University Press, 1962); I. Barbour, *Myths, Models and Paradigms* (New York: Harper & Row, 1974); P. Ricoeur, *The Rule of Metaphor* (Toronto: University of Toronto Press, 1977); G. Lakoff and M. Johnson, *Metaphors We Live By* (Chicago: University of Chicago Press, 1980); and E. R. MacCormac, *A Cognitive Theory of Metaphor* (Cambridge: MIT Press, 1985). Several works specifically relate metaphor to religious language. In addition to the sources cited in the text see C. S. Lewis, *Miracles: A Preliminary Study* (New York: Macmillan, 1947), and "Bluspels and Flalanfferes," *Rehabilitations and Other Essays* (New York: Oxford University Press), pp. 135-58; E. R. MacCormac, *Metaphor and Myth in Science and Religion* (Durham, N.C.: Duke University Press, 1976); and J. M. Soskice, *Metaphor and Religious Language* (Oxford: Clarendon, 1985).

must be corrected in the light of a larger understanding of what God is like.[16]

II. THE ROLES OF THE TRIUNE GOD

The Major Roles of the Economic Trinity

Eight major roles of God dominate the biblical data. This does not mean that no other roles are used to describe God and our relationship with him, but in terms of quantity of material and theological significance, eight of them stand out. The eight roles are *Personal Revealer, Father, Creator, King, Priest, Judge, Redeemer* and *Shepherd.*

Each role has a language category that describes not only God but people and the divine-human relationship. The language category connected with each term forms an extended metaphor system that helps illuminate the relationship depicted in each role. For example, when speaking of God as *Creator* we use the language of creation with a focus on giving life. In describing God as *King* we use language of the royal court to describe his majesty. Here the focus is on authority—the King rules.

Table 9.1. Roles of the Triune God

Role	Personal Revealer	Father	Creator	King	Priest	Judge	Redeemer	Shepherd
Language	personal relations	family	creation	majesty	sanctuary	legal	slavery/ freedom	pastoral scene
Focus	fellowship/ communi- cation/ truth	love	life	authority	grace/ purity	law	deliverance/ service	care

From table 9.1 we can see that the chief emphases of God as Personal Revealer are fellowship and personal communication of truth in interpersonal relationships. The term *Personal Revealer* indicates several things. The economic Trinity is making himself known to the world, so this role features the three *persons* within the Godhead. But it also highlights one of the major responsibilities of the triune God: to *reveal* himself.

While this role is essential for our understanding of the economic Trinity—

---

[16]For discussion of biblical figures of speech, including metaphor, see B. Keach, *Preaching from the Types and Metaphors of the Bible* (Grand Rapids: Kregel, 1972); E. W. Bullinger, *Figures of Speech Used in the Bible—Explained and Illustrated* (Grand Rapids: Baker, 1968); and C. F. Pfeiffer, "Figures of Speech in Human Language," *Bulletin of the Evangelical Theological Society* 2, no. 4 (1959): 17-21.

it is the most pervasive in Scripture and draws from the analogy of persons in general, it is not quite as concrete as the other roles in describing who God is. Though God reveals himself in a personal way through each of the other seven roles, he often does not communicate as King or Father or Judge but simply speaks to people in a personal way. The subcategories of Personal Reveals give it a bit more definition. They are the roles of God as *Teacher*, *Prophet* and *Friend*. Each focuses on some dimension of a tripersonal God communicating and entering into relationships with other persons.

When we relate to God in his role as Father, we use the language of family. This is the portrait of intimacy and of the home, and naturally focuses on love. When God functions as Priest, the language is borrowed from the temple or the sanctuary, and the focus is on grace and purity. When he is described as Judge, the language is from the courtroom and is legal in nature. The language of slavery and freedom describes God as Redeemer and focuses first on deliverance and then on service. Last, pastoral language assists us in understanding God as Shepherd and focuses on care.

The Subroles of the Economic Trinity

These eight major roles of God do not exhaust the biblical metaphors that describe the economic Trinity. But while these are among the most extensively used in Scripture, certain other metaphors may be understood as subcategories of these eight. For example, as *Physician* or *Healer* God is one who restores health and life. Thus this role may be reasonably understood as a subcategory of the role of Creator and giver of life.

There are several other categories that refer to God's role in relationship to creation. One is the role of God as *Farmer* or *Agriculturist*. Farmers work the land to grow crops, flocks or herds. The focus is on growing. As *Builder* God is making something, in this case out of existing materials. The language is that of construction and the focus is on building. The last category connected with God's role as Creator is that of *Potter*, whose focus is on shaping something. So the language of potter is a subcategory of the language of creation.

Likewise, the *Lord of Hosts*, or God's warrior role, is a subcategory of God's role as King. Kings often led their armies to battle, so the language category is taken from the military and its focus is on warfare.

We have already mentioned that God as Personal Revealer has several subroles. God as *Teacher* focuses on the teacher-student relationship, with language centered on learning and a focus on truth. The subrole of *Prophet* uses the language of proclamation and its focus is on revelation. The role of *Friend* uses terms of close personal relationships, and the focus is on faithfulness. God as *Lawmaker* is a subcategory of God as Judge. Here the language is legal in nature; its emphasis is on the giving of the law. Obviously, there is significant overlap between the roles of Lawmaker, Judge and King.

Under the family category there is the subrole of God as *Husband*. Here the language of the home is used with a focus on love. A second family subrole is God as *Bridegroom*, where nuptial language is used and the focus is on intimacy.

Among the subroles, the most prominent are those that depict God as Husband, Warrior and Physician. Table 9.2 includes the key subroles, their language categories and the major focus of each.

Table 9.2. Subroles of the Triune God

Role	Personal Revealer	Father	Creator	King	Priest	Judge	Redeemer	Shepherd
Language	personal relations	family	creation	majesty	sanctuary	legal	slavery/ freedom	pastoral scene
Focus	fellowship/ communica- tion/truth	love	life	authority	grace/ purity	law	deliverance/ service	care
Subrole	Teacher	Husband	Physician	Lord of Hosts/ Army		Lawmaker		
Language	learning	home	medicine	military		legislation		
Focus	truth	love	healing	warfare		giving law		
Subrole	Prophet	Bridegroom	Farmer					
Language	proclama- tion	marriage	agriculture					
Focus	revelation	intimacy	growing					
Subrole	Friend		Builder					
Language	friendship		construc- tion					
Focus	faithfulness		building					
Subrole			Potter					
Language			pottery					
Focus			shaping					

The Reasons for Multiple Roles

Each of the roles conveys significant information about God, but no single one gives us a complete picture. This is the reason Scripture uses many different metaphors to describe God and our relationship to him.[17] Multiple images are necessary for a holistic picture of God. One of the major problems in the history of the church may be the tendency of different segments of the church to emphasize certain roles. When one or two roles are accentuated, an unbalanced picture of God results. In an extreme form this approach leads to heresy. In milder forms it leads to various groups focusing on only part of the truth.

When we embrace all of the metaphors for God, we get a fuller picture of what he is like, which in turn leads to a more balanced theology. Further, since incomplete as well as distorted views of God ultimately lead to a stunted or imbalanced Christian experience, a more complete understanding of the triune God will hopefully lead us to a deeper personal knowledge of God. Caird rightly expresses the conviction that the theological knowledge of God should lead to our being conformed to God's image. He is convinced that beginning with the familiar situations of home and community we derive metaphors to illuminate the activity of God. But God subsequently reframes these terms, and they become absolute standards that are used to remake persons in God's likeness. The ultimate justification for anthropomorphic imagery (analogies, metaphors and roles) lies in the contribution it makes to the attainment of that goal.[18]

This happens when the full range of God's roles is explored along with corresponding attributes that give us a holistic view of God—his being, character and works. This fuller vision of God gives us the richer and more accurate view of the image God wants to produce in us. An image that allows us to work in parallel ways to his economic roles.

One of our purposes is to provide a fuller understanding of who God is from his roles so that we will be drawn into a deeper relationship with him, an experience that results in being more perfectly conformed to God's likeness and more adequately prepared to serve him in ways that are similar to his roles toward the world.

---

[17]See Vern S. Poythress, *Symphonic Theology* (Grand Rapids: Zondervan, 1987), pp. 16-17.
[18]See Caird, *Language and Imagery of the Bible*, pp. 177-78.

III. THE ROLES AND THE TRIUNE GOD

All Three Persons of the Trinity Work in All the Roles

In our survey of the biblical evidence underlying the doctrine of the Trinity we noted that all three persons work in all eight major roles. Although, in terms of their titles, a particular divine person may be identified with a specific role (e.g., Father = Creator and Son = Redeemer), we have seen that, in the way the members work, all three members of the Trinity do some of the same activity in each of the eight roles. Seeing all three persons in all eight roles broadens our understanding of the trinitarian nature of God. When our Christology and pneumatology are related to the various roles of God, not only are these individual doctrines enhanced but we develop a more holistic theology, a fuller view of the triune God. Let's explore this further.

Person of Christ. Christology is connected to the Old Testament by the fact that all of the roles of God revealed under the old covenant are more vividly and completely expressed in the person of Christ. The roles Jesus plays under the new covenant parallel each of those Yahweh demonstrated about himself under the old covenant. By this parallel use of roles for God and for Jesus, the identity of God is given fresh meaning and clearer illustration.[19] In other words, the categories we have for understanding Jesus come from the roles of God already revealed in the Old Testament. So those who know their Old Testament have the basis for understanding how Jesus works as Creator, King, Redeemer, Shepherd and so on.

Because Jesus works in every major role of God, there is a natural connection between the Old and New Testaments. Further, because of the union of the divine with the human (the theandric union) in Jesus, he demonstrates more clearly both who God is and God's design for human beings. Accordingly, very often both Jesus' divinity and his humanity play a part in each role. In the creation metaphor, for example, Jesus is not only the Creator of the cosmos and the image of God but also the image of the perfect human being. Similarly, Jesus is the King of the universe and also the Servant of God. He reveals God as the divine Word, frequently as a Prophet and Teacher. But in his humanity he models friendship with God, cultivating a relationship by listening to him in prayer and being receptive to all God has to say.

---

[19]Cf. Bauckham, *God Crucified,* pp. 6-13.

Jesus serves as the High Priest while also modeling a perfect sacrifice. As God he is Judge, but he also models perfect obedience to the law. In familial terms Jesus is the Son of God as well as the Son of Man. As divine Redeemer, Jesus is the Savior of the world, but after setting people free he models a human servant of God (note the overlap with the role of King). Finally, in his divinity he is the good Shepherd, while in his humanity he shows us how to follow God. Table 9.3 illustrates the relationship between the roles of God and Christology.[20]

Table 9.3. Christ and the Roles of God

Role	Personal Revealer	Father	Creator	King	Priest	Judge	Redeemer	Shepherd
Christ's Divinity	Word, Teacher, Prophet	Son of God	Creator, Image of God	King of kings	High Priest, Mediator	Judge	Savior	Good Shepherd
Christ's Humanity	Friend	Son of Man	Image of Man	Subject of God	Perfect Sacrifice, Intercessor	Advocate, Obedience to law	Servant	Following God

Person of the Holy Spirit. A parallel case can be made for understanding the Holy Spirit. One of the Spirit's major responsibilities is to call attention to the Father and to the Son rather than to himself (Jn 16:13-15). Some have observed that the images used of the Spirit are far less noticeable than those of the other two persons of the Trinity. He is sometimes called "the imageless" member, reflecting the fact that the descriptions of the Spirit are certainly less vivid than the way the roles describe both the Father and the Son.

However, an examination of the data reveals that in terms of *function*, the Spirit's work parallels all eight roles of the Father and the Son. In the Old Testament, the "Spirit of God" works in all the roles that God does. This prepares us for the fuller revelation in the New Testament. Under the new covenant the work of Jesus illuminates the roles of the Spirit. Just as the incarnation makes more vivid the several roles of God the Father (Jn 1:18), so too Jesus brings alive the roles of the Spirit. Through the second person of the Trinity we know the first, and we similarly come to know the third. In other words Jesus highlights the person and work of God the Father and God the Holy Spirit.

---

[20]For tables 9.3 and 9.4 see Coppedge, *Portraits of God,* pp. 367, 370.

In terms of God's economic activity the Spirit plays the role of Creator in Genesis, and then he is the ruling presence of the Godhead in the lives of the believers (King). He is also the Spirit of truth who makes God's revelation possible in this world (Personal Revealer). The Spirit intercedes for people (Priest), and he serves as the Counselor and Advocate for them before God (Judge). At the same time he is the agent of the new birth that brings us into God's family (Father). The Spirit empowers people to serve God (Redeemer), and he gives direction to the lives of individuals (Shepherd).

The Spirit's work can only be understood in the light of all these categories. A fully orbed pneumatology is impossible until all these roles are considered. All of the data of the Old and New Testaments must be incorporated in a truly Christian theology of the Spirit. The roles of the Holy Spirit are illustrated in table 9.4.

Table 9.4. The Spirit and the Roles of God

Role	Personal Revealer	Father	Creator	King	Priest	Judge	Redeemer	Shepherd
Holy Spirit	Spirit of Truth	Agent of New Birth	Agent of Creation	Executive of Godhead	Intercessor	Advocate	Spirit of Power	Good Spirit
	Spirit of Glory	Spirit of Sonship Assurance	Eternal Spirit		Spirit of Grace	Counselor	Spirit of Freedom	Guide
	Spirit of Wisdom Knowledge/ Counsel		Spirit of Life		Indwell-ing Spirit	Witness	Spirit of Might	

The roles of God and Christian theology. The development of systematic theology includes other steps, but to be biblically grounded it must begin with the correlation of all of scriptural materials. Once there has been a correlation of all of the data (e.g., about the person of Christ or the person of the Spirit), the next task of systematics is to find the unity and coherence of these materials. How does the data fit together and what are the implications? Through this approach the early church developed the doctrine of the Trinity.

But the roles of God also serve other purposes in our understanding of the triune God. They provide a theological unity of the two Testaments. They demonstrate that the God who revealed himself in the Old Testament is the same God who reveals even more about himself in the New Testament. In the incarnation and then at Pentecost God's way of working gets much clearer. The roles of God are categories for understanding how progressive revelation has expanded our view of God and his works. As we move from the old covenant to the new, the roles help us understand that we are not leaving behind one view of God and shifting to a radically different one, but we are expanding our view of God. So while the material in the New Testament adds to what we have already seen in the Old Testament, it also unifies the way God works throughout revelation history. The result is that we have a stronger theological unity of both Testaments.

The roles also assist us in understanding the unity within the economic Trinity. All three persons work in the world in similar ways. While each divine person has a distinct focus or terminus, all three are perichoretically involved in the eight roles.

Finally, in the incarnation Jesus vividly demonstrates each of the eight roles; he is therefore the key to our understanding of both the Father and the Spirit. Jesus' function opens up our understanding of how the Father and the Spirit work more fully in each of these roles.

Roles of God in the Economic Trinity Correspond to the Ontological Trinity

We see the roles of God primarily in relationship to the economic Trinity because this is where God works in relationship to us. But with our rule of thumb that the economic Trinity is the same as the ontological Trinity, we expect a correspondence between the way God works in the world *(opera ad extra)* and the way God exists within himself *(opera ad intra)*.

In two of the roles—Personal Revealer and Father—this is particularly obvious. God is Personal Revealer to us in the economic Trinity, and this certainly describes the interpersonal relations of the ontological Trinity. It emphasizes the personal nature of truth and the importance of verbal communication, which are part of person-to-person relationships within the triune being.

Jesus makes God known as his Father in the economic Trinity, and this naturally leads to understanding the eternal relationships of the ontological Trinity. The Son is eternally begotten, and the Father eternally begets. The Spirit is the Spirit of the Father and of the Son. This familial love relationship describes a key dimension of God's personhood within the ontological Trinity. It involves love that is self-giving and other-oriented.

While the other roles of God made known through the economic Trinity do not have the same ontological grounding as Personal Revealer and Father, there are hints of how they reflect the three persons of the ontological Trinity. God's role as King relates to structure and order; God wants to be the authority in our lives through the economic Trinity. This also points to structure or order within the ontological Trinity. The Son is sent by the Father and the Spirit processes from the Father through the Son. So there is an implicit structure within the ontological Trinity, albeit this is set in the context of equality in essence and attributes.

God's role as Priest in the economic Trinity is particularly highlighted in Jesus' role as Mediator. This role directs our attention to holiness in terms of grace and purity, and it points to the activity within the ontological Trinity of the Son and the Spirit interceding for us to the Father. So priestly intercession takes place within God himself (Rom 8:26-27, 34). This role also accents the sacrificial self-giving that is characteristic of the inner nature of God.

The role of God as Judge/Lawmaker is linked to God's holiness as righteousness. This role in the economic Trinity points to a standard of rightness (righteousness) in all personal relationships, beginning within the ontological Trinity. It also suggests a shared moral nature in which the three divine persons perichoretically share a will that is the basis of right relational choices.

The role of God as Redeemer/Servant is connected in some measure to the concept of holiness as power within the economic Trinity. This is the power found in the freedom to serve, and is closely connected to self-giving service within the ontological Trinity. Finally, the role of God as Shepherd, made known by the economic Trinity, is closely tied to the concept of holiness as goodness. Within the ontological Trinity it functions through the shared self-giving care of the three members for one another, as well as the moral nature of God as good within himself.

The conclusion is that the God who makes himself known in the economic Trinity *(opera ad extra)* is the same God within himself, which we call the ontological Trinity *(opera ad intra)*. Because he is the same triune God, there is a correspondence between who he is in his work toward us *(pro nobis)* and who he is in his trinitarian being *(in se)*. One of the ways to see these corresponding dimensions of God's being is through the roles that he plays in revealing himself through the economic Trinity. The most obvious indicators of this are his roles as Personal Revealer and Father. God clearly acts in these ways within himself before he relates to the created world in these capacities. But the other six roles, while metaphorical in nature rather than metaphysical, at least point to some key dimensions of the way God relates within his own being. Who God is ontologically is consonant with who he is economically.

IV. HOW THE ROLES RELATE TO THE THEMES OF CHRISTIAN THEOLOGY

An examination of each role and its accompanying language category reveals that, in addition to the trinitarian nature of God, a significant amount of other Christian theology is described under each. This is because the metaphors at the heart of each role have an extended language system. Caird spells out how this works:

> Some metaphors readily lend themselves to a high development because they belong to a metaphor system, i.e., a group of metaphors linked together by their common origin in a single area of human observation, experience or activity which has generated its own particular sub-language or jargon. Farming, commerce, law, welfare, family, weather, love, health, nature, sport—each of these has a recognizable language of its own and any metaphor drawn from anyone of these areas invites embellishment by the addition of others.[21]

Because of these metaphor systems, each of the roles provides biblical terms or theological language that explicates a number of themes in Christian theology.[22] We have already seen how the biblical materials reveal that in each role there is language that describes the triune God (Father, Son and Spirit). The next stage is to note that there is also language that describes *human persons, sin, the atonement, salvation, growth in Christian experience, the church, full sanctification* and *glorification*.

It works like this. We have already seen how the Father, Son and Holy Spirit are described as the *Creator. Human persons* are described as creatures

---

[21]Caird, *Language and Imagery of the Bible*, p. 155.

[22]For a different use of metaphor to build Christian theology from a contemporary feminist perspective see Sally McFague, *Metaphorical Theology* (Philadelphia: Fortress, 1982). For a critique of McFague's restricted use of metaphorical theology see C. Gunton, "Proteus and Procrustes: A Study in the Dialectic of Language in Disagreement with S. McFague," in *Speaking the Christian God*, ed. A. K. Kimel Jr. (Grand Rapids: Eerdmans, 1992), pp. 65-80.

who are given life and made in the image of God. *Sin* is described in terms of marring the image of God in people, worshiping creation instead of the Creator and destroying life. The *atonement* has to do with Christ as the new head (recapitulation) of the human race who brings the life of God again to men and women. *Salvation* is that which begins to remake the image of God in persons or the giving of the life of God in the soul. *Growth* in Christian experience is a progressive rebuilding of the image of God while learning to live the godly life. The *church* is the body of Christ, while *full sanctification* is a more complete remaking of the moral image of God in individuals. *Glorification* is the final restoration of persons as well as the creation of a new heaven and new earth. The complete set of terms relating to creation language is outlined in table 9.5.

When all the roles are put together with all the themes of Christian theology under each role, a very full conception emerges of the triune God and how we relate to him. Who God is obviously dominates Christian theology and is the connecting link between its various themes.[23] An abbreviated outline of the total picture is provided in table 9.6.

This data reveals that many theological truths are described biblically and theologically in multiple ways. Scripture sets this pattern. This gives us the full picture of God and of other crucial truths we need to understand. The roles of God gives us language categories that allow us to develop and understand Christian theology holistically. For example, these multiple roles show that we cannot be content with describing sin or salvation in only one or two ways. In order to have a fully biblical theology, each subject needs to be described using all of these language categories as well as any additional terms that are used in Scripture for that particular theological truth.

V. THE MIXTURE OF ROLES IN SCRIPTURE

In the Bible these extended metaphors or roles are often mixed together in the same passages. Rarely do we find only one role used in any single passage (although certain authors tend to use one or two of the roles more frequently than the others). We separate these roles for the sake of analysis, which we hope will lead to a clearer picture of the triune God and our relationship to

---

[23]"God is all in all throughout the whole compass of theology: everywhere both its subject and its object and the unity of these" (W. B. Pope, *A Compendium of Christian Theology*, 3 vols. [London: Wesleyan-Methodist Book Room, 1880], 1:233).

Table 9.5. God as Creator

Father	Son	Spirit	Persons	Sin	Atonement	Salvation	Growth	Church	Full Sanctification	Glorification
Creator	Creator	Agent of creation	Made in image of God	Marred image/ idolatry	Recapitulation	Remaking image Life	Growth in image of God	Body of Christ	Full remaking of image	New Heaven/ Earth

Table 9.6. Roles of the Economic Trinity

Role	Personal Revealer	Father	Creator	King	Priest	Judge	Redeemer	Shepherd
Language	Personal	Family	Creation	Majesty	Sanctuary,	Legal	Slavery/Freedom,	Pastoral Scene
Focus	Fellowship, Communication, Truth	Love	Life	Authority	Grace/ Purity	Law	Deliverance/ Service	Care
Son	Emmanuel, Word, Teacher	Son, Bridegroom	Creator	King	High Priest, Mediator	Judge, Advocate, Witness	Savior	Good Shepherd
Spirit	Spirit of Truth	Agent of new birth	Agent of Creation	Executive of Godhead	Intercessor	Advocate	Spirit of Power	Good Spirit
Humans	Person	Child	Creature in God's image	Subject/ citizen	Worshiper	Made for law, order	Freedman/servant	Sheep

Table 9.6. Roles of the Economic Trinity (continued)

Role	Personal Revealer	Father	Creator	King	Priest	Judge	Redeemer	Shepherd
Sin	Alienation, rejection	Self-love, disobedience	Marred image, idolatry	Rebelliousness, rebellion	Defilement, uncleanness	Lawlessness, transgression	Bondage, yielding	Lostness, straying
Salvation	Reconciliation, accepting Christ	New birth/life	Regeneration, life	Pardon, enter kingdom	Forgiveness, cleansing,	Justification	Redemption, ransom/delivery	Being found
Atonement	Reconciliation	Moral influence	Recapitulation	Governmental, Anselmic satisfaction	Propitiation	Penal satisfaction	Ransom	Example
Growth	Developing relationship	Maturity	Growth in image	Kingly rule	Continuous cleansing	Obeying law	Serving God	Following
Church	Communion of saints	Family household	Body, building	Assembly, kingdom	Kingdom of priests	Community under law	Community of redeemed	Flock
Sanctification	Fullness of God, infilling of Spirit	Perfect love, perfection	Full remake of image	Full submission, lordship	Cleansing from sin, purification	Full obedience	Full redemption	Total following, rest of faith
Glorification	Eternal fellowship	Final inheritance	New heaven/earth	King of kings	Eternal worship	Final judgment	Final redemption	Eternal rest

him. God's nature, of course, is not divisible, and so the biblical passages that mix these roles come as a healthy corrective to our analytic treatment of them. God is one, and so he is, in some measure, like all of these portraits. Each role modifies the others. A holistic view of the economic Trinity must include all of the roles of God and also must consider their mutual effect on each other.

No analogy or role from this world will be perfectly adequate to explain the transcendent God. There is always a component of mystery in knowing God. This is one of the reasons why so many different analogies are used. The various roles condition one another and help us see God more perfectly.[24] Usually, we press these roles only as far as Scripture does, but there are certain circumstances when the theological implications of certain roles may be pressed even further. But in doing so, we need to proceed very cautiously, lest we err by pressing an analogy too far. After all, an analogy is by definition like something in some respects but not in all.

In our discussion of the various roles, we noticed that there is some overlap from one role to another. So as Father and as Creator, God brings life into being. Both the roles of King and Judge have some responsibility for making law and establishing order in society. Thus some activities of God and some relationships of people to God may fit in more than one category. The lines between these categories must be flexible and porous because many times the categories bleed into one another. This should not surprise us. After all we are studying and relating to one God, and there is a unity to his being even if he works in multiple ways in creation.

VI. THE TRINITY AND FOUNDATIONAL ROLES

We have seen that the roles of God are analogies. This analogical language may be divided into two types: metaphysical and metaphorical.[25] A metaphysical analogy has to do with the essence of God's *being*, whereas a metaphorical analogy describes the way God *works* in relationship to others. The former relates initially to the ontological Trinity, and the latter primarily to the economic Trinity.[26] So far, we have mainly discussed the metaphorical roles used

---

[24]On how metaphor and analogy qualify one another see J. F. Bethune-Baker, *Introduction to the Early History of Christian Doctrine* (London: Metheun, 1942), p. 160.

[25]These correspond to analogy of intrinsic attribution and analogy of extrinsic attribution.

[26]This does not mean that there are no hints within the ontological Trinity of how God works in all the roles, even in the metaphorical roles. See pp. 226-28.

of the economic Trinity—Creator, King, Priest, Judge, Redeemer and Shepherd—and their subroles—Physician, Farmer, Builder, Potter, Warrior, Teacher, Prophet, Friend, Husband, and Bridegroom. Now we will look a bit closer at metaphysical analogy and the two major roles associated with it.

Metaphysics has to do with the essence or being of something. When we talk about the metaphysical nature of God, we are talking about that which belongs to his essence, the ontological Trinity. We have begun analyzing the essence of God's nature in relationship to his holiness and love, including the expression of such attributes as grace, purity, righteousness, truth and goodness. When we use these expressions in relationship to God (e.g., God is good), we are using a metaphysical analogy that is literally true of God's being.

Two of God's roles are metaphysical analogies: Personal Revealer and Father. While both of these analogies include metaphorical elements (that God is like a person who verbally communicates [Personal Revealer] and like a Father), he not exactly like either. He does not have a physical body like all other persons in the created world, nor does he have a consort with which to beget children. So like the other metaphorical analogies, God is like a Personal Revealer and a Father in some ways but unlike them in other ways. The added dimension in these two roles is that there is something within the inner being of the triune God that they describe, something of his essence is revealed that is not true in the same way as with the metaphorical roles. This is not to say the metaphorical roles do not give us hints about how God works within his triune nature, but they are not basic, not part of his essence, in the same way as the metaphysical roles are.

As Personal Revealer the three members of the Trinity relate to each other within one ontological Trinity; particularly, they are in constant communication with each other. The personal relationships and communication within the Trinity are central to the very essence or being of God. The same is true of the relationship between the Father and the Son. Classic Christian theology understands this distinction between the Father and Son: one begets and the other is eternally begotten. Thus there was fatherhood in the ontological Trinity before it was expressed toward us in the economic Trinity. Since Personal Revealer and Father reveal the very essence of God's being, these two roles are properly designated as metaphysical analogies.

Because *Personal Revealer* and *Father* have to do with the basic essence of God's nature, there is a sense in which God is more like these two roles than any of the others. These roles more accurately and more fully describe who God is as well as the way he works. We could refer to them as foundational roles for the Christian faith. When their priority is taken seriously, it has profound implications for the rest of our theology. For example, when we begin with God's personal nature and his fatherhood, rather than God's role as Creator or King, these become the heart of our perception of God. This has very practical implications for how God relates to our world.[27]

This understanding of God also affects the order of his attributes. The centrality of God as *Father* means that God expresses himself as a God of love. Love, previously understood as one component of God's holiness, now is pushed to the forefront. The holy, triune God expresses himself through six moral attributes, but God's self-giving love, which is most characteristic of the inner nature of the Trinity, is dominant. So the metaphysical significance of the role of God as Father is that God's love is connected with his holiness, and these two attributes control his other attributes.

VII. A WHOLE VIEW OF GOD ESSENTIAL

What God Is Doing with Multiple Roles: The Economic Trinity and Revelation

Making himself known. There are many ways to understand the holy, loving, triune God who reveals himself in Scripture. God has chosen to make himself known through a number of roles in order that we might fully understand his being and character. To do this God uses our world of experience to tell us about himself.

For example, everyone has made or created things, and most people know about kings or political rulers. Everyone has had personal relationships, such as friends and teachers, and priests or intermediaries are familiar to most. Virtually all understand the role of a lawmaker and a judge.

Father is probably the most universal role in human experience. Most know

---

[27]These implications will come to the fore in our discussion of the doctrine of providence in chaps. 12-13.

about slavery and what it means to be set free, and the pastoral setting of a shepherd looking after his sheep is easily recognized. So, from the everyday experiences of the vast majority of people, God has chosen figures of speech by which to reveal his own person and character.

God's use of general and special revelation. Because these roles are taken from our general experience, we should understand their use in Scripture to be special revelation's complement to general revelation of nature and experience. We see here a good example of the coordination of special and general revelation. Without special revelation, the roles that we see in general experience are not fully adequate to tell us what God is like, but with special revelation our experience of these roles contributes to our understanding of God. This is not to say that general revelation is on an equal basis with special revelation, but that when special revelation in Scripture illuminates general revelation, there is a more significant and holistic understanding of God's truth. There is a match between the two. This parallels the dual witness required in the Old Testament to confirm a truth.

The fact that God chooses a number of roles to make himself known is important. While he is like all to some degree, he is not to be perfectly identified with any single one of them. He resembles each role in certain respects, but we cannot press the analogy too far. For example, God is like a shepherd in many respects, but he is unlike a shepherd in the sense that a shepherd cannot relate to his sheep as persons. So while each role is valuable, each has limits. None of them can be made to stand alone or be pressed too far without distorting the full picture of what God is really like.

Why God Uses Multiple Roles

Roles are necessary for knowing God. God reveals himself in multiple roles so we can properly relate to him. To do so we must have the whole picture of what he is like. Sometimes people tend to see God in only one or two of the roles and therefore relate to him in a limited way. A much more holistic understanding of God's character and way of working is necessary if we are to properly relate to him as he desires. For example, some relate to God only as a righteous Judge or a sovereign King. The problem with such an approach is that it does not allow for the intimacy and affection that God desires to express toward those who belong to him. The roles of Judge and

King must be balanced with God's immanence, which we find in his roles as Father and Friend.

The reverse is also true. Some try to relate to God only as a loving Father and do not understand his commitment to righteousness as the Lawmaker and Judge. In this case they remake the loving Father into a permissive parent who makes little or no demands on his children. Again, a false picture of God often leads to a very faulty relationship with him. So we can know and relate properly to him fully only when all of the major roles are taken into consideration.

This holistic view of God does not rule out the possibility that one or more roles might be dominant or the key for interpreting the others. We have already suggested that the roles of Personal Revealer and Father are central for understanding the Trinity, and that the trinitarian view of God ought to be our starting point for understanding God, including his other roles. Even beginning with a trinitarian view of God as three persons, Father, Son and Spirit, we must understand how God works in all his other (metaphorical) roles. The full picture is essential to formulating a sound theology of God and relating to him as he desires.

People are familiar with different roles. God also uses multiple roles to reveal himself because people usually are more familiar with certain roles than they are with others. Some may be more familiar with kings than shepherds, while others may understand fathers better than creators. But because these figures are drawn from everyday experience, everyone knows, at least to some significant degree, something about several of the roles. By the very nature of their experience people first relate to God through certain roles. They may know him initially as a Father who gives them new life, or as a Judge who declares them not guilty. However, if they are to know him properly and fully, their understanding needs to be expanded to include all of the roles. This means that the teaching ministry of the church is very significant, for it makes it possible for people to respond more adequately to God. While some of this teaching may be done before people come into a believing relationship with God, a great deal more needs to be done after they establish a right relationship with him.

Roles are necessary for a whole theology. Once we understand the eight major roles, we need to synthesize the data under each theme of Christian theology. Theology without the biblical materials from all eight roles and their language categories is inadequate.[28] The church must present a holistic portrait from each of these categories for preaching, teaching and other ministry purposes.[29] For teaching, preaching and discipling purposes today, the entire biblical picture must be taken into account for people to understand God properly and respond to him adequately. Since the application of biblical truth to life is a matter of special concern for the church, we hope the use of the roles of God will make a significant contribution to this end.

---

[28]This approach to the biblical data fits between the final stages of biblical theology and the beginning stages of systematic theology. It is the task of biblical theology to collect the fruits of exegesis, first within books and then within authors. But most biblical theology stops with the collection of certain significant data under authors or time periods. An exception to this has been Donald Guthrie's *Theology of the New Testament* (Downers Grove: InterVarsity Press, 1981) in which he attempts to summarize the biblical data under the categories of systematic theology. As valuable as Guthrie's work is, it is limited only to the New Testament. The next step must be taken to include the Old Testament materials in order to gain a holistic view of subjects like God, human persons, sin, salvation, the atonement, growth, the church, sanctification and glorification.

[29]This, of course, does not rule out taking progressive revelation into account or giving significant consideration to how much revelation was available at any particular period in biblical history.

10

THE TRIUNE GOD
CREATES A COSMOS

The overarching approach of this book is to look to Jesus as the theological beginning to understanding the nature of the triune God, a trinitarian focus that sets the stage for knowing his attributes and his economic roles in relationship to the world. Two components of the work of the economic Trinity round out our view of God: the doctrine of creation and the doctrine of providence.[1] In this and the following chapter we give our attention to understanding the triune God in creation, and chapters twelve and thirteen are devoted to God's providential care for the creation he has brought into existence.[2]

I. THE BASIS OF THE DOCTRINE

The Christian church's basic view of creation is expressed in the Nicene Creed,

---

[1]In some branches of classical theism the works of God include not only creation and providence but also his decrees (e.g., John Feinberg, *No One Like Him* [Wheaton, Ill.: Crossway, 2001], pp. 501-36; and John Frame, *The Doctrine of God* [Phillipsburg, N.J.: P & R, 2002], pp. 313-39). This had been especially true in Reformed theology (see Louis Berkhof, *Systematic Theology* [Edinburgh: Banner of Truth, 1958], who discusses the degrees and predestination before creation and providence [p. 8]). A triune approach to God does not speculate on a set of decrees in the mind of God before creation. Rather, it places the doctrine of predestination under soteriology. The focus of the triune approach is how grace is applied in salvation. In this context salvation comes from the triune God through the Son, and the fruits of the atonement are applied by the Spirit in the lives of responding men and women. This approach keeps the soteriological questions centered around the person and work of Christ and gives appropriate attention to the large biblical data that his salvation comes to freely responding human persons who have faith, rather than being based on arbitrary decrees of a sovereign monarch.

[2]A first draft of some of the materials in this chapter were developed by Dr. John Oswalt. He has graciously allowed me to use his work as the basis for this chapter. I have expanded his work, rearranged materials, altered its style in numerous places to fit my own, and worked to make it consistent with the rest of this book. The result is that I am fully responsible for the final form of all the content, but I am deeply grateful to him for allowing me to use the spadework that he has done in developing a chapter on cosmology for a separate project.

which gives a triadic structure to the role of God as Creator. It confesses one God, the Father almighty, maker of heaven and earth, one Lord Jesus Christ, through whom all things were made, and the Holy Spirit as the Lord and giver of life. So a trinitarian structure is built into the Christian understanding of the created order. How did the church come to this consensus?

Introduction: Creation from the Order of Being

The Gospel of Matthew opens by connecting the New Testament with the history of Israel found in the Old Testament: "The book of the genealogy of Jesus Christ, the son of David, the son of Abraham" (Mt 1:1). Matthew then provides the genealogy of Jesus from Abraham to Joseph, the husband of Mary. Under the providential leading of the Spirit, the church placed Matthew first in the New Testament canon because it presents Jesus as the fulfillment of God's plans and purposes for Israel. This approach is highlighted by the opening genealogy, which serves as a brief "history" of Israel. Matthew is clearly making the case that Jesus is the long-promised Messiah who completes God's will for Israel and the world.

In God's progressive revelation, the ongoing unveiling of God through Israel, Matthew is a bridge to the Old Testament. The advent of the Messiah, Jesus, is the next step in what God wants his people to know, so they can properly relate to him, to each other and to the world.

This same progressive revelation is used by Mark and Luke, though with some variations. Mark's opening statements are shorter than the other two Synoptic Gospels, but his quotes from Malachi and Isaiah, and the use of John the Baptist to introduce Jesus make clear connections with the Old Testament (Mk 1:1-8). Luke too connects Jesus with the history of Israel by means of the birth and ministry of John the Baptist. Luke complements this with the songs of Mary and Zechariah (Lk 1), which connect John and Jesus to the way God has been working in Israel.

Though the three Synoptic Gospels primarily use the order of knowing, they give us hints about another way of viewing Jesus. Matthew and Luke in particular do this by identifying the conception of Jesus as a unique and unrepeatable miracle. The story of Jesus being conceived by the Holy Spirit and born of the virgin Mary gives us clues as to his preexistence. This story also prepares the way for identifying Jesus with Yahweh, the Lord of the Old Testament, the God who created the world and is now sending his Son into it.

The references to Jesus as the Son of God in Mark (Mk 1:1) and Luke (Lk 1:35) also lay this groundwork. At the end of his genealogy Luke's reference to the first Adam, who was also "the son of God" (Lk 3:38), strengthens the parallel between Jesus and the first created man. But this has to be understood in light of the conception of Jesus by the Holy Spirit, in distinction from the physical creation of Adam from the dust of the earth in Genesis. Matthew points to the role of Jesus before creation through the title "Emmanuel," which means "God with us" (Mt 1:23).

These hints from the first three Gospels are expanded in the prologue of the Gospel of John. Here John shifts the story from the order of knowing to the order of being. John does not begin with Yahweh progressively adding a bit more information about himself, as he has done all along throughout the history of Israel. In order to explain Jesus, John shifts to what God was like before creation: "In the beginning was the Word, and the Word was with God, and the Word was God" (Jn 1:1). This identification of Jesus with the Word who was with God and was God begins to unfold the Johannine data that will lead to a doctrine of the Trinity. Here John describes who God is apart from his creation and apart from the order of knowing. John then explains that the second person of the Trinity was one of the agents of God in the work of creation: "All things were made through him, and without him was not anything made that was made. In him was life" (Jn 1:3-4).

John does not dismiss the connection of Jesus with the history of Israel, as is clear from John the Baptist's introduction of Jesus. John the Baptist serves as the bridge to what God has been doing throughout the old covenant. Yet the Gospel of John reveals that there is an understanding of Jesus that is distinct from the order of knowing, and this approach tells us something about what God is like apart from his self-revelation in Israel's history.

This understanding of Jesus through the order of being leads to the fuller unveiling of the triune God, which in turn sets the stage for a more significant understanding of God's work in creation.[3] We move beyond the monotheistic

---

[3]Since systematic theology must work with all of biblical revelation, the order of being is its preferred way of treating themes in Scripture (i.e., determining what all of the biblical data says and how it fits together). This is why Emil Brunner begins the discussion of creation with John 1 rather than Genesis 1 (see his *The Christian Doctrine of Creation and Redemption*, Dogmatics, trans. Olive Wyon [London: Lutterworth Press, 1952], 2:6). Cf. the same approach that begins with Jesus in Karl Barth's *Church Dogmatics* 3/1, ed. G. W. Bromiley and T. F. Torrance, trans. G. T. Thompson and Harold Knight (Edinburgh: T & T Clark), pp. 28-29.

picture of Yahweh creating the world (Gen 1—2) to the triune God using the person of the Son to create. With further revelation of Jesus (particularly in the end of the Gospel of John and in Acts), we see the more personal nature of the Holy Spirit, and this gives us a fresh appreciation for the work of the Spirit in the Old Testament. Particularly, it clarifies that the Spirit in Genesis 1:2 is the third person of the Trinity and not just some force or energy of God. With this fuller information about the Spirit and the Son as agents of God's creation, we have a biblical and theological basis for understanding creation in an entirely new light. The work of making the universe was not that of the Father alone but, as Irenaeus graphically puts it, it was the work of the Father through the "two hands" of God, the Son and the Spirit.[4] All three persons of the Trinity were involved in creating the world.

The significance of the prologue to John's Gospel is that it not only identifies Jesus before creation and in the act of creation, but it also identifies him as coming from God into creation and thereby wedding God forever to the universe he has made: "The word became flesh and dwelt among us" (Jn 1:14). The Son of God came into the world, according to John, for two major purposes. First, he came to fully reveal the triune God to those whom he has created. Thus Jesus was "full of grace and truth; we have beheld his glory, glory as the only son from the Father" (v. 14). Jesus brought the truth to help us see what God is really like: "No one has ever seen God; the only Son, who is in the bosom of the Father, he has made him known" (Jn 1:18). The first thing that Jesus revealed is the Father-Son relation that existed in the triune God before the creation of the world.

Second, the Son came to bring life (Jn 1:4, 12-13). The triune God, who perichoretically shares life within himself and gives life to the world, now sends one of its members to regive life to those whom he has made. This re-creation of the spiritual life of human persons is part of the reason for the coming of Jesus into the world. Thus one of God's primary reasons for creation is to share the triune life with those made in his own image. John reveals that the living, triune God sent the Son into the world to share the life God originally intended for men and women. According to the Gospel of John, God through Jesus came to provide revelation and life, one leading to the other, so that we

---

[4]Irenaeus *Against Heresies* 4, Preface, Ante-Nicene Fathers, ed. Philip Schaff and Alexander Roberts (Peabody, Mass.: Hendrickson, 1994), 1:463.

might participate in God's purpose at creation—the giving of his triune life.

Before we work out the implications of a trinitarian understanding of creation, we must ponder the unique worldview that birthed trinitarian theism. The stage was set, of course, with the absolutely unique worldview of the Old Testament. If we are going to understand how Jesus affects our cosmology, we must pause to understand the intellectual viewpoints of Israel and its neighbors. This will help us understand the basic worldview of Scripture, which in turn sets the stage for a clearer understanding of this supranatural worldview from a trinitarian perspective.[5]

Understanding Worldviews

In all parts of the world, every generation faces some basic human questions. These include: Where did the world come from? What is the nature of reality? Is this world all there is to reality? What is the relation between the seen and the unseen worlds? How did this world come to be? Why is there something rather than nothing? Who or what made this world? How can we explain the existence of evil? Surprisingly, there seem to be only two basic sets of answers to these questions. While there may be a large number of variations, they all seem to be based on just two approaches, and British theologian Colin Gunton argues that this is because there *are* only two possible ways of thinking about reality. "The choice is inescapable," he says, "either God or the world itself provides the reason why things are as they are."[6] Either the cosmos is all there is, or there is something beyond it. There are only two options: natural or supranatural.

By far, the naturalist view is the most common. It is found in the most primitive cultures and is the one that prevails today in some of the most advanced cultures. In fact, although there have been various attempts to imagine a reality beyond the cosmos, there are only three systems of thought in which the supranatural view is thoroughly and completely carried out: Judaism, Christianity and Islam. All three derive their understanding of reality from a single source: the Scriptures of Israel. Thus *there is only one place in all human history where an alternate view to the prevailing naturalistic one has emerged and has been consistently applied, and that is in ancient Israel.*

---

[5]For a survey of the various theories of origins, see Feinberg, *No One Like Him*, pp. 540-51.
[6]Colin Gunton, *The Triune Creator* (Grand Rapids: Eerdmans, 1998), p. 36.

The naturalistic worldview: Continuity. The uniqueness of the biblical perspective is all the more surprising because of the absolute dominance of the other viewpoint in the ancient Near East. From Sumer in southern Mesopotamia in 2500 B.C. to Rome in A.D. 300, the most brilliant thinkers were agreed. They expressed themselves in varying ways, but their understanding of reality was essentially naturalistic (i.e., the cosmos came from within the natural order of space and time). The Israeli biblical scholar Yehezkel Kaufmann has called this the worldview of "correspondence" (or continuity).[7] He uses this term to describe an understanding of reality in which all parts of reality are continuous with all other parts. Thus there is no fundamental distinction between the divine, the human and the realm of nature. All components flow from the same primeval "stuff," some natural element in the cosmos. Therefore, whatever happens in one of these areas is a reflection of, and is reflected in, the other two. Whatever the gods are doing is reflected in what humans are doing, and whatever humans do is somehow reflected among the gods. And if certain natural events occur, it is understood that they are paralleled in "heaven."

William Albright suggests that this particular expression of the naturalistic worldview is the result of reasoning by analogy.[8] The train of thought goes something like this: if we are to explain why things happen as they do in this visible reality, we must assume that there is an invisible reality. But how are we to understand invisible reality? If that reality were radically different from this one, we could not understand it or use it to our own advantage. Therefore, it *must* be continuous with this visible reality, and it must be capable of being understood in terms of this one.[9] Once that decision is made, several consequences inevitably follow.[10]

Consequences of naturalistic continuity. What are the consequences of the view that the invisible world is continuous with the visible world and can be

---

[7]Yehezkel Kaufmann, *The Religion of Israel,* trans. M. Greenberg (Chicago: University of Chicago, 1960), pp. 35-36.

[8]William F. Albright, *History, Archaeology and Christian Humanism* (New York: McGraw Hill, 1964).

[9]The point must be made that this analogical reasoning about the invisible world is not a result of a "primitive mentality" that could not master elementary logic. Throughout the ancient world and in "primitive" cultures today, basic logic is used in daily life. Only in the invisible realm, the metaphysical realm, are the normal laws of logic suspended and analogy brought into play. This is not just primitive thinking.

[10]The fact that these same consequences are found around the world, in cultures far removed from the ancient Near East, implies that borrowing or diffusion is unlikely. This argues for their inevitability.

understood by analogy? The following are inferences from this worldview:

- There are multiple gods. Outside of Israel everyone believed in many gods. Polytheism, with many gods behind all of reality, was the standard fare of the day. With multiple gods there is no unity to ultimate reality. This was reinforced by thinking that where humans could see no unity in the visible world, there was no unity in the invisible one either.[11]

- Invisible cosmic forces are identical with natural elements. Thus the stars, sun, moon and oceans are gods. Every god was some natural element, and all significant natural elements were gods.

- Conflict is intrinsic to all reality. Such conflict is between chaotic matter, which has always existed, and the gods, who have emerged from chaos and attempt to impose order on it. The visible cosmos is the result of this constant conflict.

- It is possible to manipulate the invisible realm by mechanically manipulating nature. Ritual manipulation, by magic or cult, is the fundamental way to exercise power over the gods.

- There is an absolute beyond the gods—power. The gods themselves seek to use this power (the metadivine) on one another.

- Sexuality is at the heart of all life. Since sex is so fundamental to human reality, it must be fundamental to all reality.

- Ethics are insignificant because they are utterly relative. Again, the logic is plain: humans often act in unethical ways, therefore the gods must be even more ethically inconsistent.

- Individual persons and events are of little or no significance. This is drawn from the endless cycles of the cosmos. Things or persons that occur only once are of no value. Even humanity in general is of little significance. In the great scheme of nature, humans are very fragile and insignificant.

- The study of history is unimportant. Seeking the causes of events within the visible cosmos is hopeless. These events are determined by events in

---

[11]Greek thinkers, who strove mightily to apply basic logic to metaphysics, were convinced that there had to be a fundamental unity behind all things. But in spite of Herculean efforts on the part of some very brilliant minds over a span of some three hundred years (from Thales in 625 B.C. to Aristotle in 325 B.C.), they were never able to reach agreement on what that unity was, and Greek culture reverted to the views that had prevailed prior to this great attempt.

the invisible world. Records of past events may be interesting, but they are not history. History is the analysis of past human behavior (understanding human beliefs, attitudes and actions) with the goal of having a better future. Such study is fundamentally impossible from a naturalistic worldview in which all events are endless cycles of meaninglessness.

Of course there are differences in the way these conclusions are developed and applied in various cultures, but it is very impressive to find the basic ideas appearing repeatedly around the world in settings that otherwise are very different.[12] The apparent reason for this is that the same naturalistic process of thought has been followed in all these settings.

The biblical worldview. Israel emerged from this naturalistic worldview at the end of the Early Bronze Age, and two thousand years later, when the church was formed, the same naturalistic worldview dominated the Roman Empire. Yet Israel and the church embraced a worldview diametrically opposed to this naturalistic one. This different understanding is found in the Israelite and Christian Scriptures. The Bible insists that God is radically other than the cosmos and is not to be identified with any natural element in it. Furthermore, the Bible declares that God is one and has no consort or rival. In particular he is not rivaled by some independent entity of evil. This God is utterly consistent and has no internal conflict. He has no body, is not sexed and cannot be manipulated through magic. Furthermore, the Bible insists that there is an absolute standard for human ethical behavior, a standard based on the character of God. The Bible depicts individual humans and the events of history as having great significance. God has a purpose in human existence and is directing history toward this goal. People make real choices that are not fated by something outside the visible realm. Still more dramatically, human understanding of the nature and character of God comes through the context of history.[13]

It is highly unlikely that this unique worldview was developed by analogy. Everywhere else, starting with the visible cosmos and drawing inferences about ultimate reality led to a naturalistic worldview. How then did Israel develop a unique worldview that contradicts that of its neighbors? Their own explanation was that they had not discovered it but that it was revealed to them.

---

[12]Kaufmann, *Religion of Israel,* pp. 21-59.
[13]Ibid., pp. 60-121.

Transcendence and its consequences. Israel's worldview is based on one underlying concept: the principle of transcendence. This means that the basic reality shaping and conditioning the cosmos is not ontologically continuous with the cosmos. In other words the explanation for the natural world is not within but outside the cosmos; the answer lies in the supranatural. The character of ultimate reality is not dictated by the cosmos. Out of the supranatural realm the following was revealed to Israel:

- There is one God who transcends the universe of space and time and who is responsible for all that exists. While the naturalistic worldview has many gods, only in Israel do we find transcendent monotheism, where one God is the Creator of but remains separate and distinct from the entire cosmos.

- Ultimate reality begins and ends with the transcendent God; there is no metadivine power, force or being beyond God. Therefore God cannot be manipulated by magic or sacrifice or the cult.

- Evil comes from within the created order. There is no parallel evil entity or being that is greater than or equal to the transcendent God.

- The character of the transcendent God, understood in essence to be holy, is the basis for the moral standards and character of humans. There is no appeal to any other rule of right and wrong.

God's transcendence is foundational for all biblical thought. All of the other unique characteristics of Israelite and Christian thought can only be understood in the light of the one God who is outside the universe of space and time.

But if God is transcendent, there must be an absolute gulf between God and the cosmos. If God is utterly other than the cosmos, a truly supranatural being, then it seems impossible for anything in the cosmos to cross the barrier between us and him. The only way to overcome this difficulty is for God to enter space and time while still maintaining his own transcendence. In other words the transcendent God intercepts his cosmos at any and every point. The Bible insists that although it impossible for humans to find and explain him, it is not a problem for him to find humans and explain himself to them. Thus, when Israelite believers were queried as to the source of their unique convictions about reality, they responded that God revealed himself to them in history. If we do not accept this answer, we must look for a better one. The only alternative is to suggest that the Israelites constructed their religion in the same manner as did their neighbors, and the differences are merely accidental.[14] But in light of the differences discussed, such a position seems highly unlikely.

The Hellenistic form of naturalistic continuity. The Christians who formulated the church's doctrine of creation encountered the same naturalistic worldview in their Greco-Roman context as did their Israelite forbears among the Canaanites. The most pervasive expression of this worldview was provided by Plato.[15] On the surface, his beliefs seem different from those of the ancient Near East. Plato's thought is much more abstract and sophisticated than the others' myths. Indeed, Plato and the other Greek philosophers of the fifth and fourth centuries B.C. were very contemptuous of these "stories of the gods," which they dismissed as being childish and crude. In part this reaction was the result of the Greeks' elevation of reason to the status of a first principle. Whereas their predecessors could find no basis for universal ethics, the Greek philosophers, beginning with Socrates and Plato, believed they could find some rational basis for the moral life. Likewise, the Greeks claimed that if reason was at the heart of all things, then the squabbling and fornicating of the so-called gods was an offense.

However, beneath the surface there is an underlying continuity between Hellenistic thought and that of its predecessors. In the *Timaeus* Plato asserts that the Demiurge fashioned the visible world by imposing copies of the Forms—eternal, rational principles—on matter, which exists eternally. Furthermore, this was not a matter of choice or thought, but simply the necessary expression of the rational principles themselves. So the invisible Forms constitute reality, while the visible and necessarily defective reproductions of those Forms in nature are less than real. The ancient Sumerians would have found this view fully intelligible, though somewhat boring. Likewise, Plato's idea— the farther one gets from pure idea (by moving into the material and sensuous world), the more one sinks into disorder and corruption—was entirely consonant with what the other peoples of the ancient Near East believed, even if they expressed it in much more concrete ways. To be sure, his explanations were a considerable advance on anything that anyone before him had pro-

---

[14]A recent example of this attempt is found in Mark Smith, *The Origins of Biblical Monotheism* (Oxford: Oxford University Press, 2001).

[15]Plato did not form these ideas out of thin air. He was heir to the thought of Greek philosophers of the previous two hundred years. Furthermore, it is impossible to say how much his teacher Socrates was responsible for the distinctives of Plato's works.

posed. Nevertheless, the basic ideas were not different than what others had believed. Plato took the worldview of his day, divested it of its cruder anthropomorphisms and some of its logical contradictions and presented it as a seemly logical and coherent system.

Nevertheless, in essence Plato's is still a naturalistic worldview that begins from within the universe (with reason) to explain ultimate reality. Plato's successor, Aristotle, recognized two problems with eternal Forms: (1) the visible world, by definition not eternal, becomes unreal by comparison, and (2) it is difficult to know how the perfect gave rise to the imperfect. So he argued that the present cosmic system has always existed, and within that system an "Unmoved Mover" set all things into motion but is not itself moved by any other thing. The problem here is that his system seemed to leave no room for the eternal values that Plato was arguing for. With this impasse at about 300 B.C. Greek philosophy seemed to reach as far as it could. Here was the highest pinnacle of human thought. But despite their brilliance, neither of these men conceived of a God who genuinely transcends the cosmos and created the universe as an expression of his own free will. They remained within a naturalistic worldview.

II. THE BIBLICAL UNDERSTANDING OF CREATION

It is important for us to look in more detail at the biblical data. What precisely does the Bible say that is relevant to the formulation of the doctrine of creation? The most important truth of the Bible is that the one God eternally exists in three persons. This truth shapes every other Christian doctrine, including that of creation.[16] Not only does the concept of the Trinity make it possible to avoid the pitfalls of the naturalistic worldview, it also provides the solution to a number of problems that monotheistic transcendence raises.

The Triune Creator

Creation as the work of the Trinity. The Bible makes it plain that all three persons of the Trinity are involved in creating the cosmos. At the outset the Spirit is said to be an agent of creation (Gen 1:2). This idea is further developed in Job 33:4, where Job says, "The spirit of God has made me," and in Psalm 104:30 the psalmist declares, "When thou sendest forth thy Spirit, they are cre-

---

[16]For an illustration of a classical work of theology that frames the doctrine of creation in trinitarian terms, see W. B. Pope, *A Compendium of Christian Theology*, 3 vols. (London: Wesleyan-Methodist Book Room, 1880), 1:362-63.

ated." Since the Hebrew word *rûaḥ* means "spirit," "wind" or "breath," God's Spirit, like the breath of a person, is intimately bound to God's life and being. The etymological links of "spirit" with "wind" and "breath" are important. Job 33:4 makes this explicit: "the breath of the Almighty gives me life." The well-known image of the Spirit giving life to the bodies in the valley of dry bones in Ezekiel 37 lends further support to this idea. The third person of the Trinity brings created beings to life and preserves them. In the New Testament the Spirit of God gives life (2 Cor 3:3, 6). This same life-giving Spirit is also involved in recreating the spiritual lives of persons (Rom 8:11; Gal 5:25).

In addition to the Spirit, the Son is involved in creation, as Colossians 1:16 so forcefully puts it: "For in him all things were created, in heaven and on earth, visible and invisible, whether thrones or dominions or principalities or authorities—all things were created through him and for him."[17] It seems clear that Paul is excluding any other possible mediators between God and creation. Further, when he describes Jesus as the agent of creation, the apostle is also denying that Jesus is thereby something less than fully God, for in the previous verse Paul asserts that Jesus is "the image of the invisible God." In these two verses, the gauntlet has been thrown before the finest of Greek philosophy. God is Creator, yet the creation is neither an effusion of God nor is it an evil (or less-than-good) place.[18]

The relationship of Christ to creation is expanded in the Gospels in a variety of ways. He uses natural images, like soil or wheat, to describe the kingdom of God; the creation miracles (e.g., stilling the storm, multiplying the loaves and the walking on the water) reveal he is Lord of creation; he casts out the demons and restores ill people to full health and life, suggesting that he has come to reestablish God's rule over creation. These symbolic actions reveal that Christ is restoring creation to God's original design.[19]

---

[17]See also Hebrews 1:2-3, where Jesus is described as the agent and sustainer of creation.

[18]On how the role of the Son clarifies the role of the Father in creation, see T. F. Torrance, *The Trinitarian Faith* (Edinburgh: T & T Clark, 1995), pp. 76-84.

[19]See Gunton, *Christ and Creation* (Grand Rapids: Eerdmans, 1992), p. 18. Cf. Barth's discussion of *opera trinitatis ad extra sunt indivisa:* "Hence the proposition that God the Father is the Creator and God the Creator the Father can be defended only when we mean by 'Father' the 'Father with the Son and the Holy Spirit.' He is not without his Son but as the Father of Jesus Christ that God bears the name of Father in Scripture and the creed. And again, the Holy Spirit of God is the self-communication of his fatherhood as well as his lordship as Creator, so that without him God could not partake of the name of Father and Creator. How else can the proposition that God the Father is the Creator be understood except in the sense that by appropriation, but also by implication, its true reference is to the triune God?" (*Church Dogmatics* 3/1, pp. 49-50).

T. F. Torrance describes the relationships of the triune God as Creator succinctly.

> Owing to this oneness of nature between the Father, the Son and the Holy Spirit there is a oneness of activity between them, although each in accordance with his own *hypostatic* reality engages in the creative work of God in his own distinctive way. It is then of this one God in his intrinsically *homoousial* and perichoretic relations as Father, Son and Holy Spirit, that we are to think of him as sovereign Creator.[20]

Relationships within the Trinity. The high god of the various pagan religions was often referred to as "the father of the gods," and for that reason it is significant that no such description of Yahweh appears in the Old Testament. In fact, the term *Father* is rarely used of him in connection with creation. Given the context of paganism around Israel, this may be intentional. There is no hint that the cosmos had somehow emerged from the divine being or was somehow coterminous with him. God is not the world, and the world is not God. *Apostate* Israelites says "to a tree, 'You are my father,' and to a stone, 'You gave birth to me'" (Jer 2:27). When *Father* is associated with creating something, it is usually in reference to the emergence of the nation rather than some ontological procreation (Ps 89:26; Is 63:16; Mal 2:10). Otherwise *Father* is normally used in reference to fatherly care and compassion (Ps 68:5; 103:13; Jer 3:4). In other words, the personal and family roles of God as Father stand out rather than his work as Creator.

God's fatherhood gains prominence in the New Testament because of the Son. But the Father is not the procreator of the Son; the absence of a divine mother underlines this fact. Despite the elevation of the virgin Mary to this status in some parts of the church, the Bible will have none of it. Mary is a human being who is "overshadowed" by the Holy Spirit. She is the guarantee of Jesus' humanity, not his divinity. *Father* and *Son* describe relationships—mutual coinherence and self-giving—within the Trinity. The Father entrusts the revelation of himself to the Son. Without reservation he shares the divine glory with his Son. And the Son does nothing but what the Father tells him. He is ready to lay aside his own glory in order that the Father might be fully known. The Spirit says nothing of himself but points to the Son and the Father (Jn 16:13-15). The Spirit has been sent in order for the world to share the

---

[20]T. F. Torrance, *The Christian Doctrine of God* (Edinburgh: T & T Clark, 1996), p. 212.

kind of relationship that the Father and the Son share. This has profound implications for a doctrine of creation.[21]

Creation as an act of self-giving love. The Bible reveals that all three persons of the Trinity were involved in the act of creation. This is precisely as it should be. Because the holiness of the Trinity is especially manifested in self-giving love, creation cannot be the work of a single divine person but is an expression of the relations found within the Trinity. Love as we know it in the Bible is always reaching outward in multiplying concentric circles. The Trinity always seeks others on which to pour love.[22] It is no accident that procreation occurs in the context of human love. Whereas in the animal world, copulation is an act of the moment triggered by hormonal changes and instinctual behavior, in humans it is designed to be the apex of a process of "knowing," of progressive self-revelation and surrender built on a foundation of trust and deep mutual affection. Children born into this kind of a relationship grow up whole and healthy. Why are animal and human procreation different? Because men and women are made in the image of God and our procreation images his creation.

God, who shares life within the Trinity in self-giving love, created the heavens and earth to express this self-giving love to others. He has chosen to create human persons with whom to share life and love as an outward expression of what happens within his own being.[23] So, contrary to some approaches to creation, the making of the universe by the triune God was not first of all about his power and omniscience, but about his self-giving expression of life and love.[24] This foundation sets the parameters for describing God's creative work. Then his relative attributes (omnipotence, omniscience, omnipresence and wisdom) are appropriately set in their place. This is consistent with our Nicene confession of "God the Father, the Almighty, maker of heaven and earth." Before God is Creator, he is Father, and his almighty power is exercised under

---

[21]Cf. Basil of Caesarea's trinitarian description of creation: "The original cause of all things that are made, the Father; . . . the creative cause, the Son; . . . the perfecting cause, the Spirit" (*On the Holy Spirit* [Crestwood, N.Y.: St. Vladimir's Seminary Press, 1980], p. 15, cited in Gunton, *Christ and Creation*, p. 46).

[22]"It is to the ultimate love of God the Father that the 'reason' for the creation is to be traced, why it exists at all. There is no reason why the creation came to be, why there is something and not nothing, apart from the eternal movement of Love in the inner Life of God, which in love freely overflows from God who does not will to exist for himself alone but for others also" (Torrance, *Christian Doctrine of God*, p. 212).

[23]See T. F. Torrance, *The Trinitarian Faith* (Edinburgh: T & T Clark, 1995), pp. 89-95.

[24]Emil Brunner identifies the love of God as the *causa finalis* of the creation (*Christian Doctrine of Creation and Redemption*, p. 13).

the control of his trinitarian fatherhood. So the creation of the universe certainly involves God's omnipotent power, but this is not a raw, unlimited power exercised in sovereignty. Rather, it is "the living power of the eternal Father flowing from his intrinsic nature as love, as the movement of the love that God is ever in himself as Father, Son, and Holy Spirit."[25]

Creation from the trinitarian perspective. A christological beginning point leads to a trinitarian theism that controls all Christian thought, including the doctrines of creation and providence. Thus our trinitarian theology is different from classical theism, which finds its center in God as sovereign King. It moves from emphasizing the relative attributes of God to his personal attributes. This does not denigrate the relative attributes and their significant role in creation, but it does change our perspective of the role they play.

From this christological and trinitarian perspective, priority is given to personal relationships. Persons are created for two kinds of relationships: with God and with each other. Creation is derived from the shared life of the Trinity. The divine life is relational in its essence; therefore created life reflecting God's image is designed to be relational. The climax of Genesis 1 is the creation of man and woman, who, designed in the image of the triune God, experience this personal life of love. In the Gospel of John it is clear that Jesus came to bring the triune life of loving relationships to fallen persons. The rest of creation is set in the context of the creation of persons in God's image. Nature is not an end in itself but a means for people to relate to others, both divine and human. Thus persons and their relationships are central to a proper understanding of the created order. This shift in perspective means the nature of personhood is our first concern. Accordingly, we will examine each of the components of personhood as they relate to a doctrine of creation.

We have seen that the triune God is a *social being*; the three divine persons share life perichoretically within the Godhead. Human persons, made in God's image, are also social beings, designed for person-to-person relationships.

Personhood within the triune God also encompasses *life*, including the components consciousness and self-consciousness. God himself is living and aware of each distinct person of the Trinity. Thus human persons too have life

---

[25]Torrance, *Christian Doctrine of God*, pp. 209, 211.

(shared from the triune life), consciousness and self-consciousness, all of which make them aware of their distinctness as well as their need for others. When the first man, Adam, was given life as a social being, he was aware of his own distinctness and his need for human relationships. God then created Eve, another person with conscious life, to complete Adam's personhood.

The personal attributes of God include reason, imagination, emotions and will. The triune God obviously uses his reason through his omniscience and wisdom in the creation of and providential care for the world. Imagination was essential for creation, for the image always comes first and then the reality. This is true not only for human persons but also for God. God not only experiences the emotions of joy and delight in the Trinity but also in his creation, and particularly in women and men who love and obey him. Finally, God willed to create the world he imagined. Theses functional capacities of personhood, subsumed under the Old Testament term *heart*, are clearly shared by human persons. The heart of God makes it possible for him to exercise three other dimensions of his personhood.

The first of these is his *freedom*. His will makes it possible for him to create or not to create. God is not limited by anyone or anything equal to or greater than himself. God is ultimate reality. Thus he can create freely out of the self-giving love of his own triune nature. He did not have to create. He creates in complete freedom.[26] This is crucial for understanding human persons. They are made to freely respond to the love offered them by the triune God.

A second expression of God's heart is his *creativity*. This was fully exercised in making all the components the universe, and especially its highly complex living creatures, humans. The relative attributes of God come into service in his creativity. He uses his omnipotence, omniscience, omnipresence and wisdom to create the heavens and the earth. But these, of course, are governed by God's personal attributes. Human beings exercise the same creativity, but it is used within the confines of created existence.

God's heart also expresses itself in *responsibility*. He is responsible for what he has made. He has delegated some responsibility for creation to men and women (Gen 1:26, 28), but he remains ultimately responsible for it. Here again he uses his omnipresence, omnipotence, omniscience and wisdom to

---

[26]For an excellent discussion of the freedom of God in creation see Torrance, *Christian Doctrine of God*, pp. 216-18.

care for the universe. But the accent is on his *care for creation* rather than his *rule over creation*.

So beginning with the triune God carries enormous implications for the doctrine of creation. Primarily, creation is about persons who are lovingly created to share life with the triune God. We must not miss the fact that creation is not first of all about stars or atoms or even about planet earth. If we begin with God's sovereignty, we are tempted to see creation in terms of God's power. When we start from that perspective, it is easy to see God treating people as puppets or automatons, things to be manipulated. The trinitarian perspective provides a healthy corrective to this approach. The focus on relationships within the Trinity means that personal relationships are central to the purpose of creation. Creation is about the triune Creator who enters into relationships with the men and women he has made.

Creation

***The meaning of* creation.** Creation is literally the very first subject we encounter in Scripture; it is the second word in the Hebrew text of Genesis 1:1. The first word is *bĕrēʾšit*, "in the beginning," but immediately following is the third-person masculine singular verb *bārāʾ*, "he created."[27] A study of the term shows that it carries the meaning of "bringing into existence something that did not exist before."[28] So in Numbers 16:30 God says, "if the LORD creates something new," the earth will open its mouth to swallow Korah, Dathan and their followers. Likewise, Isaiah says that just as the Lord brought the world into existence as a new thing, so he can do a new thing in the life of his people (Is 43:1, 7, 15; 45:7-8, 12, 18). In the same way, the prophet speaks of God's ability to "create new heavens and a new earth" (Is 65:17; 66:22). Creation involves bringing something into existence that has not been.

In light of the meaning of *bārāʾ* it is obvious that the writer of Genesis is at pains to insist that humanity is a new "creation." No less than four times he asserts that God "created" persons (Gen 1:27; 5:1-2; 6:7). This is in direct contrast to the statements that the "waters bring forth swarms" of fish (Gen 1:21)

---

[27]The verb occurs fifty-four times in the Hebrew Bible, most frequently in Isaiah (17 times) and Genesis (8). The other books where the term appears frequently are Psalms (6) and Ezekiel (5).

[28]Helmer Ringgren, "בָּרָא" in *Theological Dictionary of the Old Testament*, 15 vols., ed. G. Botterweck and H. Ringgren (Grand Rapids: Eerdmans, 1974), 2:247; cf. Thomas McComiskey, "בָּרָא" in *Theological Wordbook of the Old Testament*, 2 vols., ed. R. Laird Harris, Gleason L. Archer Jr. and Bruce K. Waltke (Chicago: Moody Press, 1980), 1:127.

and the earth "bring forth" the beasts (Gen 1:24). The author is asserting that
people are a new order of being direct from the heart of the Creator.[29]

Clearly, the author of Genesis is emphasizing the new thing that God has
done in creation.[30] If there were any doubt that this was uppermost in the author's mind, it is dispelled by the *final clause* (Gen 2:3) of the opening account,
which says that God "rested from all his work which he had done in creation."
The structural pattern used is called *inclusio*, meaning that the passage is
bracketed by references to God's creation of the world (Gen 1:1; 2:3). The
purpose of *inclusio* is to indicate that everything inside these brackets is influenced by a certain concept, in this case the creation *(bārā')* of something, the
world, that did not exist before. The author's chief purpose is to assert that
God purposely did a new thing when he brought the cosmos into existence, a
concept foreign to Israel's neighbors.

Creation out of nothing. But there is an issue that the Hebrew word bārā'
does not solve: what existed before the moment of creation? Was the "new
thing" created from preexistent stuff?

The Hubble telescope, with its convincing evidence that there was a distinct moment when this cosmos began (the so-called big bang), has caused
many physicists to reconsider creation. But what preceded the big bang?
Though it is impossible to prove, many scientists assume that some physical
entity existed. It was, they surmise, infinitely dense and compact, no larger
than a period on this page. This option clearly lies within a naturalistic framework because the cosmos begins with some physical (natural) stuff.

This naturalistic view prevailed in the ancient world, although their explanation was much more colorful and interesting than the current one. Just like
many moderns, the ancients held that matter was eternal, with the default
condition being chaos. Furthermore, they believed that spirit proceeded out of
matter and subsequently subdued and ordered matter. Creation, or more correctly, "beginnings" in ancient Near Eastern paganism, was a matter of the
gods defeating the various chaos monsters and reorganizing the stuff of those
monsters' bodies into the present world order.[31] This process did not happen

---

[29]This same thought is repeated in Deut 4:32 and Is 45:12.

[30]The same thing is true in Gen 2:4-25, which introduces the Fall narrative (Gen 3:1-24). There too
the opening sentence emphasizes that the heavens and earth were created by God.

[31]For example, see the Babylonian creation story *Enuma Elish* in *Ancient Near Eastern Texts*, ed. James
Pritchard (Princeton: Princeton University Press, 1955), pp. 60-72.

once in ancient times, so that we now enjoy the present effects of some past event. Rather, it happens continuously as we rehearse and act out the myths our origins.

The church fathers were at great pains to disassociate the biblical doctrine of creation from pagan myth. Thus they promulgated the doctrine *creatio ex nihilo*, "creation out of nothing." They began with the triune God, who is spirit and who precedes all things as a supranatural being. Matter was brought into existence from nothing else, and it continues to exist by the will of this transcendent God. There is no eternal struggle between opposing forces inherent in matter. The only struggle is whether created beings are going to obey the will of the Creator.[32]

In formulating this doctrine of creation the early church was careful to distinguish between God's roles of Father and Creator. They clearly acknowledged that God is always Father, but not always Creator.[33] But when he does create, he creates as the Father through the Son and by the Spirit. But the work of God generating the Son is distinct from that of creating the world. So when the Father, Son and Spirit create the universe, God is making something new, even for God. Before the creation, we must conceive of God as the ontological Trinity, the self-giving, tripersonal God of Father, Son and Spirit. Once God creates, he relates to his creation as the economic Trinity. *Creatio ex nihilo* clearly implies the unlimited freedom of God to go beyond his ontological being by choosing to create something outside of himself.[34]

Creatio ex nihilo was in part based on the conviction of the biblical writers that the world was created by the Word of God (Ps 33:6; Heb 11:3).[35] Creation by a word from God implied to the early church that God created everything out of nothing. He was not shaping preexistent stuff, but he spoke and the cosmos, including time and space, came into existence out of nothing.[36] This did not preclude working with and shaping matter after it was created

---

[32]For the connection between creation out of nothing and a trinitarian understanding of creation, see Colin Gunton, *Cambridge Companion to Christian Doctrine* (Cambridge: Cambridge University Press, 1997), pp. 141-42.

[33]Torrance, *Trinitarian Faith*, pp. 84-89.

[34]Torrance, *Christian Doctrine of God*, p. 208.

[35]On the scriptural foundation of a doctrine of *creatio ex nihilo*, see Feinberg, *No One Like Him*, pp. 552-57; see also Pope, *A Compendium of Christian Theology*, 1:367-95.

[36]See Colin Gunton, *The Triune Creator* (Grand Rapids: Eerdmans, 1998), pp. 73, 92.

(see Gen 1—2). Thus the early church rejected the eternity of matter and its corollary, eternal dualism.[37]

Recent challenges. The church's position faced no real challenge until recently. The Septuagint, the Greek translation of the Old Testament, was clear and unambiguous: "In the beginning, God made the heavens and earth." And although this might not be the only way to translate the Hebrew *bērē'šît bārā'*, it was certainly a good translation. But a question arose because the form *bērē'šît* takes appears to be a "construct," and if that is correct, we would expect it to have a genitive relation with the following word, thus "in the beginning of . . ." This is the way the word is used frequently in Jeremiah ("In the beginning of the reign of . . ." [Jer 26:1; 27:1; 28:1]) and elsewhere. If this were the correct understanding of the construct, a literal translation would be "In the beginning of God created. . . ." A smoother translation would be, "When God began to create the heavens and the earth, the earth was without form and void" (cf. NRSV and REB). This rendering, of course, suggests that the earth was "without form and void" *before* God began to make something completely new of it, suggesting an eternal dualism of God and some natural elements, like darkness and water. An alternative understanding of the meaning of the structure would be that God's *first* creative act was to create formless matter.[38]

Response to the challenges. Those who advocate this translation generally believe that Hebrew religion evolved from earlier pagan religions. Therefore, they say, we should not be surprised if the Israelite view of the beginning showed traces of the idea that matter had always existed and that "creation" was simply the imposition of form on what had previously been chaotic. There are two major problems with this point of view. First, while it may be possible to show a number of commonalities between the pagan religions of the ancient Near East and the religion of the Bible, it is all but impossible to account for their differences on the basis of the evolution of cosmological ideas. Second, it is very difficult to imagine how later editors let this supposed recrudescence of paganism stand in the text. This is especially hard to understand if one accepts the thesis that the doctrine of creation arises very late in Israelite history, only emerging after the encounter with Babylonian "creation" theology during

---

[37]See Robert Jensen, *Systematic Theology* (Oxford: Oxford University Press, 1998), 2:11-12.
[38]See the discussion on "without form and void" below.

and after the exile. It is simply unthinkable to believe that the supposed creators of the "priestly" theology, with its insistence on the absolute transcendence of God, would either not see the implication—that matter precedes or at least is coeternal with God—or, seeing it, would allow it to stand.

This means that, just as the Septuagint translation shows, the writer of Genesis 1:1 did not think of *bĕrē'šît* as a construct form. He intends it to be taken in a freestanding, absolute sense. That the form can be used as an absolute is shown by Isaiah 46:10, which says, "I make known the end *['ahărît]* from the beginning *[bĕrē'šît]*."[39] Thus it seems highly likely that in Genesis 1:1 the author intended something like "At the first (of all things)," or "At the first (moment of time)." Again, the translation of the Septuagint must be taken with great seriousness. "At the first *[en archē]*, God created the heavens and the earth."[40] Thus there is good reason to believe that the writer of Genesis was indeed advocating *creatio ex nihilo*. Nothing preceded God and nothing coexisted with him. He created out of nothing.[41]

Without form and void. But we must consider one final point before leaving this topic, the phrase "without form and void" (Heb *tōhû wābōhû*). Did God first create chaotic matter? Isaiah 45:18 very explicitly says that God did not create the earth as a *tōhû*. The problem may well lie in our assumption that the phrase does indeed connote chaotic matter.[42] In view of Isaiah's statement, it seems much more probable the intent is simply to say that the earth did not exist. God did not first create chaos, and then, secondarily, decide to make something of it. The Isaiah passage tells us that it was God's intent from the beginning to create a cosmos that was inhabitable by his creatures, specifically human persons. Thus it seems the intent of Genesis 1:1 is something like this, "At the beginning of all things, God created the heavens and the earth, neither of them having existed before."

---

[39]The occurrence in Proverbs 4:7 is probably to be taken in the same way, "Wisdom is first *[bĕrē'šît]*; acquire wisdom." While it is not conclusive, it is also important to note that *bārā'* is a finite verb and it is very unusual to place a noun in a construct relation with a finite verb. The construct form of *bĕrē'šît* is not used with a verb elsewhere. Deuteronomy 33:21 suggests the possibility that some ordinal sense is intended. That verse reads, "He chose the first for himself." It is understood that "first portion" is intended, but "first" stands alone.

[40]This translation makes it possible to read Genesis 1:1 "as the caption of the following narrative, both summarizing and introducing it" (Jenson, *Systematic Theology*, 2:3).

[41]This is the position of Claus Westermann in *Genesis 1-11: A Commentary*, OTL (Minneapolis: Augsburg Publishing House, 1984).

[42]Since the phrase only occurs three times in the Old Testament, it is difficult to determine its precise connotations on the basis of usage.

The point is further corroborated by the method of creation: speech. While this point most clearly denies the emanation of creation from the being of the Creator, it also suggests the coming into existence of something that had not existed previously. There was no light until God spoke it into existence. So it is for the other elements of the cosmos. Just as a word has no independent existence outside the mind until it is spoken, so creation had no prior existence until it was spoken into being.

The implication of *creatio ex nihilo* is that there is no eternally existing matter that coexists with God.[43] God alone is ultimate reality, so there is no eternal dualism to explain the problem of evil. Evil has to be explained in terms of some distortion or perversion of the good that God has created.[44] The triune God is the ultimate source of all things, and all must answer to him.[45]

The origins of the invisible world. While the Bible has little to say about the origins of the invisible world, the world of spirits, there is every reason to infer that these are created entities as well. There is no evidence that the Israelites or the early Christians considered any part of the spirit world to be self-existent or somehow independent of God's creative will. This applies to those spirits which do his will, such as the cherubim (Ezek 1:5-21) and the seraphim (Is 6:2-4), and to those who seek to thwart his will, the demons.

The divine council. There has been an attempt in recent years to argue that the Old Testament gives evidence of a "divine council" of the gods, such as is found in Canaanite religion. In the Canaanite religion, the gods, many of whom are considered to be children of the high god, El, frequently join together to alter El's purposes. But this is not the case in the Bible. Take, for example, 1 Kings 22:19-23 and Job 1:1-12; 2:1-6. In 1 Kings, it is said that "the host of heaven" are standing on the right and left of the Lord, who sits on his throne (v. 19; the same verb is used of the seraphs in Is 6:2). God gives a di-

---

[43]Some have suggested that darkness and water were preexistent natural elements when God began to create the universe (e.g., Edmond Jacob, *Theology of the Old Testament* [New York: Harper & Row, 1958], p. 140). For an examination of the entire biblical data as to whether darkness is an uncreated element, suggesting an eternal dualism, see Allan Coppedge, "An Inductive Study of the Concept of Darkness in the Old Testament" (master's thesis, Asbury Theological Seminary, 1969), pp. 18-26, 70, 76, 80.

[44]For further discussion of the implications of the doctrine of *creation ex nihilo*, see Gunton, *Triune Creator*, pp. 87-92.

[45]For a scientific account of *creatio ex nihilo*, see William Lane Craig, "The Caused Beginning of the Universe: A Response to Quentin Smith," *The British Journal for the Philosophy of Science*, 44, no. 4 (1993): 623-639, cited in Torrance, *Christian Doctrine of God*, p. 207.

rective and selected representatives carry it out. Though the "host of heaven" represented the pagan gods for Israel's neighbor, that was not the case for Israel. The hosts of heaven in the Bible are creatures of God who exist to respond to his calling. They are specifically not in the same category as God (cf. Is 40:25-26). The apostle Paul forcefully says that everything that is, visible and invisible, and every power was created by Christ (Col 1:16).

Job 1—2 makes the same point regarding the heavenly beings. There they are referred to as "the sons of God," which the Septuagint translates as *angelloi*, or "angels."[46] They "present themselves" before God in the manner of courtiers and are expected to give a report of their activities. There is no sense that these beings are on par with God, counseling him on actions to take or vetoing his plans. They exist to do his bidding and can take no action apart from his directive.

Much of the same could be said about angels in general.[47] They are messengers of God and are described as spiritual creatures without bodily existence. Apparently they are endowed with free will, which makes them susceptible to temptation. The good angels are often used by God as messengers to the world (Dan 8:16-26; Lk 1:11-20, 26-38). There is no suggestion in Scripture that angels are eternal beings, but they, like other things visible and invisible, are created by the triune God (Col 1:16).[48]

The origin of Satan. It is certainly intentional that the serpent of Genesis 3, which Christian theology has regularly associated with Satan (Rev 12:9; 20:2), is said to be a creature (Gen 3:1). The tempter is probably described as a serpent because the enemy of the "creator" god in the myths of the ancient Near East, the god or goddess of chaos, is typically depicted as a dragon, a kind of serpent. But if the comparison is intentional, then it is also apparent that a very decisive contrast is also made by means of that description. The serpent of Genesis 3 is not a cosmic monster from whom God himself originated. The serpent is a creature of God, one among many. Thus, while he may pose a threat to God's creatures, he poses none whatsoever to God himself.

Historically, Isaiah 14:4-21, especially verses 12-14, and Ezekiel 29:1-19

---

[46]That "sons" need not refer to biological descendants is shown by the fact that bands of prophets were called "the sons of the prophets," with no suggestion that they were the biological children of prophets (cf. 2 Kings 6:1).

[47]For an expanded discussion of angels and spirits, see Pope, *A Compendium of Christian Theology,* 1:408-16.

[48]Oden, *Living God,* pp. 240-41; Torrance, *Christian Doctrine of God,* pp. 229-34.

have been said to describe the fall of Satan. Unquestionably they describe the disastrous consequences of creaturely pride, and they do so in highly figurative language that presents such pride as a challenge to the very throne of heaven. However, in both cases human kings are being addressed, the kings of the two commercial powers of the ancient world: Babylon and Tyre, respectively. Thus it is not clear that these passages describe the circumstances in which some created spirits became the enemies of God. Jesus, though, said that he saw Satan fall "like lightning" (Lk 10:18), and this gives some support to a literal interpretation of Revelation 12:7-9, which says that as a result of war in heaven Satan and his angels were expelled from heaven.

The passages from Job present a somewhat different but complementary picture than that derived from Isaiah and Ezekiel. Here "the accuser" (Heb *haśśāṭān*), is said to be one of the "sons of God" (*bēn ʾĕlōhîm*) who "came to present himself before the LORD" (Job 2:1). Here Satan is simply one of the heavenly creatures who takes a cynical view of all the motivations behind human service to God. He cannot believe that God would be served out of love. This attitude is entirely consistent with that manifested by the serpent in Genesis 3. We are given no hint as to where such an attitude originated. But again, Satan is not a cosmic god from whom all evil originates. Apparently, Satan's fall from heaven does not prevent him from having access to God or preclude interaction between them.

In any case, the Bible does not support pagan ideas of the source or power of evil. That there are evil spiritual powers in the cosmos that wish us ill, the Bible presents as fact. Though these powers are in rebellion against God, they are neither greater than nor equal to God. They have been decisively defeated in Jesus Christ, as every one of his encounters with the demonic world demonstrates (cf. Mt 12:25-29) and as Paul resolutely states (Rom 8:38; Col 2:15).

Attempting to Integrate Hellenistic and Biblical Thought

Serious problems result when Platonic and Neo-Platonic cosmologies are merged with the biblical doctrine of creation. The first and the most serious is the failure to distinguish adequately between Creator and creation. The greatest distinction between the biblical and other understandings of reality is that in biblical thought God is *not* the world. Any system that compromises this truth is unbiblical. The God of Scripture is not part of the natural world, he is supranatural.

A second problem is identifying evil as an eternal cosmic entity. The Bible insists that evil does not exist on its own, and it is defined in negative terms: that which does not conform to the will and nature of God. The tendency to equate reason and the spirit with good, and the sensuous and the material with evil is another problem. The Bible insists that all creation is good and that salvation does not mean moving from the material to the spiritual. Fourth, Neo-Platonism posited successive degrees of beings who served as mediators between God (pure spirit) and absolute evil (pure matter). Once again, the Bible asserts that there is only one mediator between God and humanity, the God-man Jesus Christ, in whom there is no sin at all. A fifth problem is the tendency to view perfection as a static state. But the Bible pictures life within God as a dynamic, perichoretic interaction of divine persons. For human persons, Genesis 17:1 expresses it well, "Walk before me, and be perfect" (my translation). This is a relational, and therefore dynamic, perfection, like God himself.

The biblical position differs dramatically from Platonism and Neo-Platonism.[49] The Bible insists that God and his creation are two very different orders of being. The world did not emanate from God but exists because God spoke it into existence. Though the cosmos exists because of God, it is not identical with him. Nevertheless, it is real and not ephemeral. The importance of the distinction between the natural and supranatural cannot be overestimated. Creation had a beginning and will have an end; it is limited. Furthermore, it is good, and the Fall did not destroy that goodness, even though it marred it. Good is not restricted to reason and the spirit. Rather, goodness inheres in the entire creation because it conforms to the will and the purposes of the Creator. Salvation is not a change in essence (from matter to spirit) but redemption from the consequences of sinful choices and the divine enablement to share the holy character of God. Final salvation is not an absorption into God or the static contemplation of the good. Rather, it is the continuation of a dynamic dialogue of love, worship and praise.[50]

---

[49]For further comparison of the Greek and biblical conceptions of creation, see Gunton, *Triune Creator*, pp. 14-40.

[50]For a history of the development of the doctrine of creation, see Colin Gunton, *The Cambridge Companion to Christian Doctrine* (Cambridge: Cambridge University Press, 1997), pp. 148-55.

11

THE NATURE OF CREATION

I. THE NATURE OF A TRIUNE CREATION

The Goodness of Creation

The recurring theme of the first chapter of Genesis is that God created a good world. But what does this mean? Does it mean that it is a moral creation or an obedient creation? Neither of these seems to be the case. Rather, it is an artist's pronouncement that what was imagined and now exists is "good"; that is, the creation conforms exactly to the artist's preexisting vision. Thus "good" (Heb *tôb*) in the Old Testament is first of all that which conforms to God's purposes, while "bad"[1] (Heb *ra*ʿ) is anything that does not conform to those purposes. "Good" and "bad" are not expressions of some arbitrary decision by a distant sovereign. Rather, they reflect the fact that creation has an inherent design. That which follows the design is "good" and that which does not is "bad." This demonstrates that "good" and "bad" are not eternal entities. They are simply categories that exist to describe being in relation to the Creator. As ultimate reality, God determines what is good and bad.

What does the Bible mean, then, when it says God is good? Does it also imply that he could be "bad" if he chose? It certainly implies that the Hebrews could conceive of him acting in such a way. The pagan gods of their neighbors certainly could be bad. But whatever the possibilities may be, it became apparent through the Israelites' ongoing encounters with this Creator that he is entirely self-consistent: he never acts in ways contrary to his

---

[1]The translation "bad" is to be preferred because in its usages this English word conforms better to the range of meanings of the Hebrew term than does the traditional but much more restricted "evil." "Bad" extends all the way from the unfortunate ("I'm having a bad day") to the morally evil ("Nero was a bad man."), just as *ra*ʿ does, whereas "evil" does not extend as far as "unfortunate" or "calamitous."

original purposes. Thus they said, "The Lord is good."

The Bible also refers to God as good in a second, moral sense. This is closely related to the nature of the triune God, who is good in his caring for others. What is true of the ontological Trinity is true of the economic Trinity. God who is good and caring in himself is also good in relationship to created persons. Goodness takes on a moral quality when it involves personal relationships. God's goodness toward inanimate, plant and animal creation is a secondary expression of this moral goodness. But his goodness toward persons is a deeper expression of his inner goodness, and as we have seen earlier, this goodness is closely associated with God's holiness and love.[2]

For the early Christians the goodness of creation (i.e., its design) contradicts the Neo-Platonic view of nature, where the world of time and space is not good. From that perspective creation, having evil and imperfection in it, does not conform to the intentions of one who is absolutely good. At best, it is a mistake; at worst, it is absolutely evil. Its existence can only be explained as the result of an infinite number of mediators, each one slightly more evil than the previous. The Bible denies this. The heavens and earth were created good, and though sin—human rebellion—has marred it, that marring is not absolute.[3] The Bible declares that even after the Fall persons dwell in a good world (e.g., Ps 19; 104), for it continues to be an expression of God's creative intention and a place where he manifests himself. This has significant implications for our soteriology.

Because God is good, Christians appreciate the goods of this world. There are multiple components of God's created world, such as the ecological environment, sexuality, food and drink, culture, and the like, that may be used by humans in a perverted way and in that sense become bad. But *bad* in this case means a wrong use of the good that God has originally designed. The gifts of creation are not right or wrong in themselves but are designed to be used according to God's purposes. When Christians use these goods appropriately, they are the most life-affirming of all people, thankfully praising God for good gifts which bring great enjoyment (Ps 16:11).

Therefore, asceticism, which denies the normal use of God's gifts, is inap-

---

[2]For holiness expressed in goodness, see Allan Coppedge, *Portraits of God* (Downers Grove: InterVarsity Press, 2001), pp. 332-35.

[3]On the goodness of creation and the entrance of sin, see Thomas Oden, *The Living God* (San Francisco: Harper & Row, 1987), pp. 252-57.

propriate for Christians. Nor should they adopt a world-denying attitude, withdrawing from the cultures that emerge from human interaction within creation. There are certain components of life and culture that have been perverted, and Christians should not participate in those components. But at the same time they should never reject the good gifts of creation or culture in general.

The Distinctness of Creation

The biblical view of the cosmos is very different from naturalism; it insists that the cosmos is ontologically distinct from its Creator. God transcends it, he is not part of it, and he cannot be manipulated through it. This radically different worldview is articulated a number of ways in the Bible, but none of them are philosophical arguments. Rather, the distinction between Creator and creation is inferred from the biblical data, which we will examine presently.

The mode of creation: Speech. The mode of creation is God's speech. Though words have their origin in the mind of their speaker, once they are spoken they have a life of their own. They can be manipulated and recombined by the speaker, but they are no longer identical with the speaker. An oration has an identity independent of the orator. The words are not an effusion from the speaker; they are an expression of thought, will and choice. But once made, they are distinct from the one who speaks. To be sure, the words are not totally separate from the speaker; after all, they continue to be the words *of* the speaker. But they are now distinct and have an existence of their own. So when God spoke reality into existence, he gave creation an existence of its own.[4]

No idols. The distinction between Creator and creation is also found in the second commandment: "You shall not make for yourself a graven image, or any likeness of anything that is in heaven above, or that is in the earth beneath, or that is in the water under the earth" (Ex 20:4). When Israel took this commandment seriously, they were driven to the conclusion that there is a fundamental distinction between God and the world. The line of reasoning is fairly obvious. We cannot represent God in any form of this visible world because he is radically other or different from the world. He is discontinuous with it. The Bible is diametrically opposite to the naturalistic under-

---

[4]See Robert Jenson, *Systematic Theology,* 2 vols. (New York: Oxford University Press, 1997-2001), 2:6-7.

standing of reality. The Bible insists that God is ontologically distinct from the cosmos; nonetheless, the cosmos shares in his goodness because is his creation![5]

While God forbade persons from making anything within creation (e.g., wood, stone, metal, animals, geographical features, etc.) to represent him, this does not mean that God left himself with no witness to what he is like in the world. Women and men are made in his own image and likeness (Gen 1:26-27). So the only thing within the created order that is "like" God is humanity, which reflects his image. Though God and creation are distinct, Scripture hints that he is related to creation through the persons he created. This hint was fully exposed when God took on human flesh in the person of the Son (Jn 1:14). Therefore, while the distinctness between God and creation is ontologically clear, through the incarnation the triune God entered the created world to represent himself as a person. Thus there is no radical dualism between God and creation.

No characteristics of creation in God. The Bible refuses to attribute to God any of the characteristics of creation. He does not correspond to any natural element; he cannot be manipulated by magic; there is no conflict within him; he transcends sexuality. He alone can say, "I am, and there is no other." Thus he is never identified with anything in creation. He is not the sun or the moon, or the sea, or the earth or the heavenly hosts. He is not passion or war; he is neither pleasure nor power. He is not to be understood by reference to heaven and earth. Rather, heaven and earth are to be understood by reference to him. He causes the sun to move and calls the host of heaven by name. He "sits above the circle of the earth" and sets the boundaries for the sea. In Scripture, this barrier between Creator and creation is never breached. Whereas in other religions of the ancient Near East, the gods are identified with some natural element in creation, not once is God confused with the cosmos in the Bible.

Some might respond, God *is* said to be love. But what happens with this apparent continuity? Rather than conforming God to the fallen expressions of love in this world, God, who is distinct from this world, demonstrates an entirely different kind of love that transforms our earthly conception of it. The

---

[5]Because Judaism, Christianity and Islam have all been shaped by the Scriptures of Israel, they are the only three iconoclastic religions in the world.

love manifested by the Trinity is not grasping but giving, not self-serving but self-denying, not passionately devouring the beloved but seeking the best for the other no matter the cost to oneself. Further, love existed within the ontological Trinity before creation. Love is not a created thing, so it is not a natural element projected onto God. Love is something within the triune God that, like personhood, is shared with the created order.

Miracles of the exodus and Jesus. One of the clearest expressions of the distinction between the Creator and creation is found in the plagues on Egypt (Ex 7—12). The text clearly shows that these events were an attack on the gods of Egypt, all of whom were personifications of various aspects of the cosmos (Ex 12:12; 18:11). These gods were not just symbolized by natural elements, they corresponded to them. Yet through the plagues, Yahweh demonstrates that he is "the one who causes things to be" (one meaning of the name "Yahweh") rather than any of those contingent, though deified, cosmic elements of the Egyptian pantheon.

The miracles of Jesus establish the same point, although from a positive rather than a negative side. The plagues demonstrate that the cosmos does not have the power of life. Thus all those forces that the Egyptians sought for life and blessing are shown to be death-dealing apart from the grace of Yahweh. On the other hand, Jesus demonstrates that he has the power to take all that is death-dealing in the world, whether the demonic or deformity or illness or nature run amok or even death itself, and turn it into life (e.g., Lk 4:31-41; 7:11-16). Thus all that is in the cosmos, from life to death, is in the absolute control of the One who is not the cosmos but is its Creator.

Without exhausting the data on the distinctness of God, we have shown that the biblical data clearly indicate this: God created the universe by an act of speech; no images of God from the natural, nonpersonal creation were permitted in Israel; there are no characteristics of creation that are attributed to God; and the miracles of the exodus and in the life of Jesus clearly indicate God's power over all of the natural forces within the universe. Whereas all the gods of the ancient Near Eastern world corresponded to some natural element, the unique biblical worldview is that the God of Israel made the created order but is not to be confused with it. From the perspective of the New Testament we know that the triune God made and shares his life with this world, but he remains ontologically distinct from it.

The Being of Creation

One of the great ironies of the pagan naturalistic view is that it ends up achieving the very opposite of its original intent. This worldview assumes that all reality is similar to that which is observed in time and space—there is a continuity between the spiritual realm and nature. Thus ultimate reality is a reflection of this visible reality. So, like the seasons of nature, ultimate reality is cyclical. Ultimate reality is also purposeless. Ultimate reality has only one absolute: power, as this reality does. But embedded in the naturalistic worldview there is an unintended consequence. If ultimate reality and the natural world are image and reflection, which is the image and which is the reflection? The answer is obvious. The visible cosmos is clearly the reflection, since it is conditioned by the invisible one. Plato's famous illustration of the cave is the most dramatic expression of this conviction.[6] This changing, decaying world cannot be the real one. The real one is where all things are constant. Therefore, what is done here in the natural world only has significance to the degree that it escapes what is taking place here and succeeds in connecting with "the real world."

The biblical perspective is in direct opposition to this view. Genesis 1 leaves no doubt that God created the natural world. The use of the day-and-night time frame shows that, in contrast to Origen, who maintained that the original creation was outside of time and space, creation did not occur apart from time.[7] The naming of the rivers in Genesis 2 demonstrates that the Garden of Eden was not in some primordial, continuous space but in our space. The Fall narrative is even more dramatic. Sin, which corrupted cre-

---

[6]Plato uses the cave to illustrate the unreality of the present world. A group of people are in a cave, although they do not know it. Behind them is a great fire, and silhouettes of objects are being carried back and forth before the fire, projecting shadows on the wall before the people. But the people do not realize they are shadows. They analyze what they see with great care because they understand it to be reality. One of those objects they describe as a tree. But one of the people turns around and discovers the fire and the silhouettes. He tries to tell the others, but they have no interest. He now imagines that he has discovered true reality. But eventually he wanders back behind the fire and sees another light a long distance away. He struggles toward this light and finally comes to what he realizes is the mouth of the cave in which they have all been living. The true light is so dazzling that he falls to the ground blinded. When he opens his eyes, he sees before him not a shadow or a silhouette, but what he takes to be a real tree. Actually, he is looking at a reflection of a tree in a puddle of water. Finally he raises his head and sees the real tree. What we take to be reality is only a shadow of a silhouette of a reflection of reality *(The Republic 7)*.

[7]For the classical connection of time with creation see Oden, *Living God*, pp. 259-62. See also Gregory E. Ganssle, ed., *God and Time: Four Views* (Downers Grove: InterVarsity Press, 2001).

ation, did not take place in some timeless, spaceless eternity. As Genesis 2—3 makes clear, the first sin took place in our world. Not only that, it was a result of human choice, a choice made out of fear that God could not be trusted to supply our basic needs. It is hard to imagine a more stinging rebuttal to the idea that the only events of real consequence occur outside time and space.[8]

The incarnation confirms the reality of history and nature. God's Son became human and lived in our world. The apostle Paul seems to take delight in declaring that Jesus Christ became flesh (Rom 8:3; Eph 2:15; Col 1:22; 1 Tim 3:16). The apostle John says belief in the incarnation is necessary for salvation (1 Jn 4:2). Paul and John apparently are intentionally targeting all those views, Greek and otherwise, that understand reality to be somewhere else than in the visible world. After all, God subjected himself to the limitations of time and space: "The Word became flesh and dwelt among us" (Jn 1:14). Could there be a stronger witness to the reality of this world?

II. THE PURPOSES OF CREATION

The repeated statement that the creation is "good," even "very good," hints at the fact that the cosmos is not the necessary expression of impersonal creative energy. Rather, creation is designed. This implies thought, reason and planning. What is the plan? In the alternate, naturalistic worldview, humans are an afterthought of the gods, made to serve them. The Bible, though, paints a dramatically different picture. Far from being slaves, human persons are the very apex of creation, only a little lower than God himself (Ps 8:5), and made to receive the blessing of God (Gen 1:28). Moreover, the trinitarian fellowship of the three divine persons is enlarged to include fellowship with human persons. T. F. Torrance describes it this way:

> We do not know any God who is completely locked up in himself, but only the God who interacts with us. We learn from his incarnate self-revelation that God does not will to exist for himself alone and does not wish to be without us, but has in his eternal purpose of love freely created a universe, within which he has placed human beings made after his own image and likeness in order that he may share his love with them and enable them to enjoy his divine fellowship.[9]

---

[8] See Francis Schaeffer, *Genesis in Time and Space* (Downers Grove: InterVarsity Press, 1972).
[9] T. F. Torrance, *The Christian Doctrine of God* (Edinburgh: T & T Clark, 1996), p. 207.

The Chief Purpose: God's Desire to Fellowship with Other Persons

God's desire to include others in his fellowship is evident throughout Scripture. After creating human life as the climax of creation, God seeks them in the garden (Gen 3:8-9). He invites Abraham to walk with him (Gen 17:1) and to consider with him the appropriate treatment of a sinful city (Gen 18:16-19). Furthermore, the real goal of the exodus events was to bring people to himself (Ex 19:4-6). Once the Hebrews had escaped Egypt, we would expect immediate entry into the Promised Land. However, something intervened, something that reveals God's ultimate goal. First, through a covenant (Ex 19—24) God invites the Hebrews into a committed relationship with himself, which would be marked by living in ways that reflect God's character. Then God delivers instructions for building the tabernacle (Ex 25—31; 35—40). Why does God do this? In order to take up residence in their midst: the tabernacle is a symbol of God's immediate presence. This was the goal of the exodus.

But this Old Testament data pales alongside its expansion and development in the New Testament. "God with us" is no longer symbolically expressed through a house of worship. Now God has come in the flesh and invites men and women to walk with him. The importance of discipleship in the ministry of Jesus underlines this fact. God is not so much interested in imparting facts about reality as he is in fellowshipping with and blessing persons. To do this, Jesus first chose a very small group with whom to relate closely. The mission he gave them was to teach, preach and baptize, but these are means to a more important end—making disciples. Disciples are baptized "in the name of the Father and of the Son and of the Holy Spirit" (Mt 28:19), so the life and close fellowship within the Trinity is shared in the lives of the disciples.

If Jesus' work of making disciples is understood to be re-creating what God intended for persons in the original creation, then we may rightly affirm that God created the world in order to share himself with other persons. Thus his self-giving love, which characterizes his triune nature, is experienced by persons both in relation to God and to other human beings.[10] This explains the importance of humanity in the Bible. People are what the entire cosmos is all

---

[10]See Robert Jenson's discussion of the purpose of creation as "thus at once God and his creatures united in Christ." Jenson identifies himself both with Jonathan Edwards and Karl Barth in this trinitarian work of God that connects God's work at creation with his work at redemption (*Systematic Theology*, 2:19-20).

about.[11] To paraphrase Jesus, people are not made for creation but creation is made for people. This is in shocking contrast to the pagan worldview, which concluded, as do many modern people, that against the backdrop of the vast universe, human beings are insignificant.

From the biblical perspective, creation provides the context where human beings can seek God's face, experience a growing relationship with him, share his character and ultimately live with him in unbroken fellowship. Creation is the stage on which God relates to other persons. God's chief purpose in creation is *to share his life and love in fellowship with other persons.*[12]

Complementary Purposes

This central purpose in creation is complemented by five secondary purposes for creation, and especially human persons.

The first purpose is that persons are made for fellowship with God to share his moral character. In our earlier discussion of the attributes of God, his moral attributes immediately followed his personal attributes. As persons relate to persons, moral questions arise, first within the triune nature of God and then in all other person-to-person relationships. This means that when persons share the life and love of the triune God, they reflect God's moral attributes, which are primarily defined by his holiness and love.

God made men and women in his image so his moral attributes would be reflected in the created order. God's holiness and love are subsequently expressed in his other moral dimensions: righteousness, truth, grace, purity and goodness. The most significant model of what these look like comes in the life of Jesus. He embodies the character of holiness and love in all its expressions. His human nature models perfectly what they look like in his divine nature.

The second purpose for those in fellowship with God is developing the mind of God. God shares reason and imagination, which are central to personhood, with those who are made in his image. Through the mind, persons

---

[11]This is the logic of Genesis 2, with its placing of the world under the control of Adam and Eve. It is also the logic of the book of Revelation, which links the destiny of the cosmos with the destiny of humanity. The two pictures bracket (inclusio) all Scripture.

[12]For an alternative in the Reformed tradition that sees the purpose of creation as God sharing his glory, see Karl Barth, *Church Dogmatics* 3/1, ed. G. W. Bromiley and T. F. Torrance, trans. G. T. Thompson and Harold Knight (Edinburgh: T & T Clark, 1958), p. 95. It should be noted that Barth follows the discussion of God's glory with a discussion of God creating and sharing out of his love (pp. 95-97).

are able to enter into relationships, and through relationships human understanding is developed even further, so there is a reciprocal relationship between the mind and personal relationships. This capacity to understand is especially important for living in the created order and having the ability to face reality. To do this properly, a person must see reality as God sees it, understand it as God understands it; he must have the mind of God. Jesus, who was a rabbi or teacher, demonstrates what it means to have the mind of God (Phil 2:5). He communicates how God understands all of created reality.

The third purpose is that God wants people to have close person-to-person relationships. We have touched on this in our discussion of God's sharing his triune life and love in fellowship with created persons. This is not only between God and human persons but also between human persons and other people. This is necessary because we are social beings who reflect the character and mind of the holy, triune God. The need for close relationships is built into the nature of personhood as part of God's design for creation.

The need for close relationships has two great models in Scripture. The first is the family. Because persons are incomplete in isolation, Adam was not complete until Eve was made (Gen 2:18). The second model is the spiritual family. Jesus gathered twelve disciples around him for close personal relationships, sharing a common life of love, learning and service. These personal relationships were extended in the larger community of faith, which served as the foundation of the church.

The fourth purpose is that God desires people to serve him in their work. God gave the first man and woman the task of caring for the earth (Gen 1:28), particularly to "till and keep" the garden and raise a family (Gen 2:15). Creatively serving one another in work as a means of serving God was a part of God's plan even before sin entered the world.

Jesus models this in his multiple ministries to other persons through preaching, witness, teaching, discipleship, healing and deliverance. He demonstrates to disciples how they may work for God by serving other persons. Being made in the image of God, who creates and providentially oversees his creation, persons are designed to care for creation as they serve others.

The fifth purpose is that God wants people to delight in the created order. God made the world so he might delight in human persons (Ps 35:27) and also in the rest of creation. He made the earth beautiful, indicating his own creative and aesthetic nature. God made sights, sounds, tastes, textures and smells that we too might delight in his good creation.

David Bentley Hart observes, "God's greatest action in creation belongs from the first to that delight, pleasure, and regard that the Trinity enjoys from eternity, as an outward and unnecessary expression of that love; and thus creation must be received before all else as gift and as beauty." Hart continues, "This beauty of the Trinity, this orderliness of God's *perichoresis* is the very movement of delight, as the divine persons within one another, and so the analogy that lies between worldly and divine beauty is a kind of *analogia delectationis*."[13]

Eden in Hebrew is the word for pleasure. God created a pleasant garden for Adam and Eve to enjoy with him. For humans this means taking special delight in other persons, which is central to God's design, and also in the rest of creation. This delight in God's good and beautiful creation is the basis of all art, music, architecture, manufacture and exploration. God's creation is good and meant to be enjoyed by those who bear his image (Ps 16:11).

Many Christians feel that the chief purpose of human beings is to glorify God.[14] All of creation glorifies God by calling attention to his ability to create and sustain a universe such as ours. When they are fulfilled, creation itself and God's other creative purposes glorify God before other persons; that is, persons are drawn to acknowledge God for who he is and what he does.

But is glorifying God a creation purpose or a result of creation? If glorifying God is God's own purpose, it would seem to be a self-centered purpose rather than a self-giving purpose. Does God have some innate need to be glorified and constantly have others' attention? Alternatively, if glorifying God is a natural result of God's purposes in creation, its role changes. If glory is a result of what God has done, it leads others to God's purposes for them, and it is therefore an other-oriented factor rather than a self-centered one. From the nature of the triune, self-giving God, it seems that God's glory as a result of creation is preferable. If this is the case, then God does need to be glorified, but as a result of what he has done, not as a chief end in itself.[15] Our shift in perspective

---

[13]David Bentley Hart, *The Beauty of the Infinite* (Grand Rapids: Eerdmans, 2003), pp. 249, 252.

[14]See the Westminster Shorter Catechism: "The chief end of man is to glorify God and enjoy him forever." The chief end in this context is God's choice for human persons and is to be understood as identical to his chief purpose for humans.

[15]This position is echoed by nineteenth-century Lutheran Gottfried Thomasius, who said that the teaching "usual since Anselm, that the glory of God is the final end of creation, seems to me to confuse the outcome with the founding purpose. For the creation is indeed a glorification of God, . . . but what moves him to create is not this glorification of himself, that he does not need, but love alone" (*Christi Person und Werk* [Erlangen: Dreichert, 1886], pp. 144, cited in Jenson, *Systematic Theology*, 2:18).

comes with a move from seeing God primarily as sovereign King to understanding him as the tripersonal God.

III. WHAT IS WRONG WITH CREATION?

Corruption of Creation

The Bible sees creation as now existing in a corrupted state that is not everything God created it to be. This is first expressed in Genesis 3 when God tells Adam and Eve the consequences of their rebellion. The ground is "cursed" because of their sin. It will no longer submit to their stewardship. Now it will produce "thorns and thistles" (Gen 3:18). Furthermore, having come from the dust (Gen 2:7) they will return to the dust in death (Gen 3:19). Pain, frustration, domination and death entered the world. These were not inherent in the nature of creation, nor are they an expression of an eternal conflict between creative and discreative forces. In contrast to all other ancient thought, these evil things exist as a corruption of the original plan because of human action in history. Some have suggested that the serpent introduced evil into the world (Gen 3:1-5). But the Bible clearly says the sinful choice of Adam and Eve brought about a creation in which life is cut short by death.[16]

Genesis 3 and Romans 8 are the chief passages describing the ways creation has been corrupted. Clearly, creation still testifies to the existence and character of its Creator. In the Old Testament this is expressed in Psalm 19, where it is said that without a sound "the heavens are telling the glory of God" in words that reach "to the end of the world." Paul says in Romans 1:18-21 that the clarity of creation's witness to God leaves human beings without any excuse for their refusal to acknowledge and worship him. But the apostle also says that creation has been "subjected to futility" and awaits freedom from its "bondage to decay" (Rom 8:20-22). But he does not define exactly what he means by "futility" and "decay." How does he see these manifested, and what

---

[16]Some offer the argument that since death only entered the world through the sin of Adam and Eve, the events of creation could not have occurred over a long period of time. However, this is to take too limited a view of "death." In a pre-fallen world, would all life forms have been immortal? This raises very serious questions about the nature of time and of development within time. As Paul says, "sin is the sting of death" (1 Cor 15:56). This may imply that it is not the cessation of life in one form and its transformation into another form that is the problem, but rather that corruption of life and its vital relationships that now occurs because of the destructive power of sin. Ultimately, it is not so much physical cessation that is the result of sin as it is "the second death": eternal separation from God (Rev 2:11; 20:4, 14; 21:8).

will it mean for creation to be purposeful and pure? Given his association of "decay" with death elsewhere, he probably is implying that these phrases refer to a creation where death, disease and decay rule. It may also imply destructive changes within nature as well, such as earthquakes, volcanoes, tornadoes, storms and the like.

Creation and Evil

The doctrine of the Trinity also shows how the cosmos can be both a direct creation of a good God and yet be the temporary domain of evil, that which is contrary to God's creation purposes. Both for Plato and the Neo-Platonists, the only way to explain the presence of evil in the world while maintaining the essential goodness of the First Principle was to hypothesize a series of mediators. As they descended in succession ever farther from the First Principle (or God), each mediator was less perfect. While for Plato the number of mediators was more limited, the number for the Neo-Platonists was very high. Thus the material world is evil because its immediate creator was all but completely evil.

The Bible counters this way of thinking. The world is good because it is the creation of a good God, who freely created in keeping with his own design. The agents of creation—the Son and the Spirit—are fully God, and there is no distance between their work and the plan of the Father. Therefore, creation is the work of the triune God. But then, what is the source of evil in creation?

Free, self-giving love characterizes the relations among the persons of the Trinity. Furthermore, the Trinity's chief purpose in creation is that persons may experience that same fellowship, both among themselves and with God. But such fellowship is only possible in the context of freedom. This is graphically illustrated by Jesus. Only because he freely chose to obey the Father can the world be redeemed from evil. If that obedience had been coerced or in some other way necessitated, it would not have been an expression of self-denying love. But if self-giving can never be coerced, then self-love must remain a real possibility, and self-centered love is the essence of sin.

This is what has happened to the world: We have taken the freedom given us by a loving Creator and turned it against him and others. Evil is not a cosmic reality necessitated by a flawed creator. Rather, it is a diseased way of relating, which resulted from our freely turning from the purposes of God.

Although evil is a tragic deviation from God's wishes by the misuse of personal freedom, it did not come as a surprise to God, nor did it entail some drastic revision of an original plan that made no provision for evil. Love, by its very nature, has a plan for countering evil. As Jesus says, those who love only those who love in return do not have the love of the Father (Mt 5:44-48). Thus, through the Spirit, who sustains a grasping, scheming world; and through the Son, who gives his life for a demanding, thankless world; and through the Father who waits to welcome home children who have squandered the wealth he has showered on them, the Trinity overcomes sin within himself and more fully shows what self-giving love is really like.

Restoration of Creation

Paul says that although creation has been corrupted because of human sin, it will participate in the final redemption of humanity (Rom 8:19-22). However, he does not specify how the re-creation will take place. In light of his previous description of the corruption of creation, we can imagine that in the renewed creation there will be no dissolution (decay), and life will be triumphant, intense and fulfilling.

Such an inference would be entirely consistent with the pictures drawn from the Old Testament about the restoration of creation. Isaiah in particular sees a new heaven and a new earth in which there is no harm or destruction (Is 11:9; 65:17, 25; 66:22). He sees this as the kingdom of the Messiah where wickedness will have no place and where justice will be the norm (Is 11:1-5). Isaiah also sees it as a place where aggression and violence will have no place in the animal kingdom. In other words, the restoration of creation may have more far-reaching implications than we might think. All we have known is decay in the ongoing life on the planet. If that was not the case before the entry of sin, what a very different creation it was and will be again.

In any case, Isaiah and Revelation see a creation in which there will be no more human death. Isaiah speaks of the last great feast at which God will remove the shroud that covers all faces (Is 25:7-8), and Revelation sees a world in which there will be no more death (Rev 21:4). Isaiah speaks of a time when a hundred-year-old person will be considered a child (Is 65:20), and Revelation envisions a world where there will be no more curse (Rev 22:3).

Is it possible that two related but different scenarios are being discussed in these passages? Revelation 20 speaks of a thousand-year reign of Christ on earth. But then Revelation 21—22 looks forward to a "new heaven and a new earth" in which there will be neither sun nor moon nor sea. Could it be that

we will first see a redeemed creation in which many of the same features we
know will be present, but without human death, and then we will see a completely new creation in which the very nature of physical being will be
changed? It is impossible to answer this question definitively. Suffice it to say
that the Bible does not see this present creation in which death reigns supreme
as being God's final work. He who made the world for life and love is not going to be content until sin, distortions and death are removed from it, and his
life and love flow through it unchecked once again.

IV. IMPLICATIONS OF THE TRINITARIAN VIEW OF CREATION

In our survey of a biblical understanding of creation we have looked at the
Creator, the act of creation, the created world and the future restoration of creation. It remains to draw out some of the implications of looking at creation
from a triune starting point.

A Dynamic View of Reality

The idea that creation was originally perfect and static and that final redemption involves a return to that state owes more to Plato than it does to the Bible.
Personal relationships are never frozen; fellowship presumes both freedom and
dynamism. Growth and development are at the core of the creation account.
The plants are to bear fruit after their own kind, and humans are to reproduce
and multiply, filling the earth that has yet to experience fullness. Furthermore,
having dominion over the earth (Gen 1:26-30) is not so much about bringing
the earth under authority as about "husbanding" it, enabling it to reach a potential that was not fully realized in creation itself. This is one explanation of
the statement that Jesus Christ was slain from the foundation of the earth.
God was prepared to do whatever was necessary for the purposes of creation
to be achieved, not all of which were fully complete in the first act of creation
in Genesis 1.

The nature of the Trinity, who desires redemption and sustenance, is further testimony that creation was not merely the arbitrary expression of a sovereign King concerned to manifest his glory. It is apparent that redemption
and sustenance would be meaningless in a perfectly static cosmos. Only in a
dynamic setting in which potential must be realized, nurtured and maintained,
or possibly lost, are God's redemption and sustenance necessary. This means
that evil is not an unfortunate failure in God's creative plans, an unexpected

thwarting of his original design or a necessity in the plan of an implacable and impassible sovereign. Instead, creation is the unfolding of a relationship between God and created persons in which persons could increasingly share God's character, in particular by participating in love, the most central expression of holiness. For this purpose to be realized, its opposite was not necessary, but it must have remained a real possibility. Thus the Fall of the human race did not come as a surprise to God, but neither was it required for creation's purposes to be achieved.

Creation of Men and Women

Because the Creator is triune—three persons in one Godhead—and makes persons in his own image, he makes people personal just as he is personal. People have the personal attributes of God. Further, the moral attributes of God ought to be reflected in persons as well. Because God is a social being, people also are social beings. By definition, individual people are incomplete in themselves and therefore need other persons. This is probably why God designed created persons male and female, so that an awareness of their individual incompleteness was built into their very being. While God himself transcends sexuality, he is completed by the triune relationships within his own being. So that persons would not miss this lesson, individually they are either male or female, each one complements and completes the other (Gen 1:22-25). So the trinitarian perspective on creation carries significant implications for human relationality.

It also carries implications for human freedom. If the purpose of creation is to realize the glory of an absolute sovereign King, then creaturely freedom may be an impossibility. The will of the sovereign would be determinative and must be realized in all its details. Thus if something happens in the cosmos, whether good or bad, it must be an expression of the King's will. Select passages of Scripture might appear to support such a position, but from a trinitarian perspective such an interpretation is problematic.[17] We have seen that in the personhood of each member of the Trinity there is freedom. The Son's choice to

---

[17]See particularly Isaiah 45:7 and Amos 3:6. It is important to remember the Old Testament context of passages like these. Paganism asserted that there were good and bad gods, and that bad things were brought about by the bad gods, the good gods being unable to prevent them from doing so. The Old Testament makes it very clear that there are no effective beings in the world other than the Lord. All that happens in the world must ultimately lead back to him. But this is an oversimplification in service of an important point. It does not preclude secondary causation and choice.

lay aside the prerogatives of heaven and come to earth was an act of freedom. Likewise, the Spirit's choice to say nothing about himself but to point solely to the Son is an act of freedom. There can be no compulsion in love. If one of the purposes of creation is to have persons share in the fellowship of love, then freedom is an absolute necessity.[18] God desires that we know his fullness. That fullness is love. To suggest that some persons are compelled to love God and that others are compelled to hate him makes a mockery of love, of the fullness of God and of personal freedom.

Creation and Sin

In trinitarian theism, sin is first of all relational in nature. Sin negatively affects the relationship between people and God. Though it also has implications for other human relationships, sin primarily breaks fellowship with God. Second, sin curves a heart in on itself *(cor incurvitas ad se)*, moving it from self-giving love toward others to self-centered love. This is clearly out of sync with God's created design. A proper understanding of the Creator and creation helps us understand sin's distortion.

Understanding God's desire for creation—the experience of and growth into self-giving love—explains why the sin of the first couple had such cosmic dimensions. People were created to experience the blessing of God by fully trusting him for all their needs. As they and their offspring lived and grew in such a relationship, the purpose of the entire cosmos would be realized. What they did instead struck at the heart of the entire plan. They decided, with the serpent's prodding, that the Creator could not be trusted to supply their needs. The entire cosmos felt the effects of this act. According to God's original design, nature was in submission to humanity because persons were in submission to God. When persons refused to depend on God, the natural order was undone. When the ones for whom the cosmos was created were living in rebellion, the design for which the cosmos was created was thrown askew. It could no longer bless those who were no longer living in keeping with that design.

Creation and the Atonement

Since sin breaks relationships, distorts the image of God by making people self-centered instead of other-oriented and ends in death, the atonement has

---

[18]See the role of freedom as an essential part of personhood in chap. 7 on personal attributes.

to address these same issues. Thus our view of the atonement focuses heavily on life. God's original purpose is to share life in fellowship with other persons, therefore restoring life and relationships is central to Jesus' purposes for the world. So the atonement has life as an overarching theme. In an expanded version of the recapitulation theory, Jesus walks through every phase of human life and existence in order to restore it to God's original intent. Of course, we need to understand God's original purposes for creation in order to comprehend what Christ is doing to bring about a "new creation."

Creation and Salvation

Our understanding of salvation focuses on having a life-giving relationship with Jesus. The Gospel of John is important to this perspective because it describes salvation in terms of finding life in Jesus (Jn 3:36; 20:30-31). Salvation is also described in terms of regeneration, or the remaking of persons as God intended them to be (Tit 3:5). Paul also describes salvation as becoming a new creation (2 Cor 5:17). The triune God, who originally gave life at creation, sent his Son into the world to make it possible for persons to be re-created in his image. Through the Spirit, people are made alive in Christ and remade in the image of the Creator (Eph 2:5; Col 3:10). Salvation is about transformation and relationships, not just position or status.

Creation and Growth in Christian Life

After becoming new creations, Scripture encourages Christians to grow more like Christ. Personal growth implies that the creation was originally designed for maturing. It was not a completely static and finalized entity. Persons who have found new life in Christ have the opportunity to grow and mature toward a more fully developed form of God's purpose within the created order.

This is where Christian responsibility for the stewardship of the created order arises. God gave men and women responsibility to care for the earth. They are not to exploit creation but to use it for God's purposes, and they will be held accountable for that stewardship. Proper environmental and ecological concerns therefore have a significant place in the lives of committed Christians.

Creation and Sanctification

The creation story gives us God's original design for men and women, which of course was distorted by sin. The New Testament's teaching regarding full sanctification implies that God is continuing to transform people in a more complete way to remake his image in their lives (Eph 4:22-24). When fallen women and men are re-created, the personal attributes of God reflected in them are reshaped as God originally intended; then persons may be freed from the self-centeredness of sin so that the moral characteristics of God, especially holiness and love, might be fully reflected in them. Full sanctification is another transforming work of God to reverse the impact of sin on human lives.

Creation and Glorification

The doctrine of creation comes to fruition in eschatology. Sometime in the future, God will bring history to a close and will re-create the world, forming a new heaven and a new earth (Is 65:17; 66:22; Rev 21:1). This new creation will be the context for the faithful ones who have been raised from the dead. Here they will enjoy life in the transformed creation. The restoration of creation is the fulfillment of God's purpose in creation—people enjoying life and love with other persons.

Thus a significant number of Christian doctrines are affected by our trinitarian perspective on the doctrine of creation.[19] Getting it straight "in the beginning" is obviously significant for the whole Christian faith.

V. NATURALISM VERSUS SUPRANATURALISM: IMPLICATIONS FOR THEOLOGY

The biblical doctrine of creation is radically different from the "creation" accounts of the ancient Near Eastern world. The biblical perspective highlights the fact that one God created the universe and is responsible for it, yet he remains separate from it. There is discontinuity between God and the cosmos. God is not part of the natural world of space and time. He is best described as supranatural.

In contrast, the ancient Near Eastern perspective and much of contemporary thought stresses the immanence of God. In the ancient world the gods were identified with different aspects of nature. There was even continuity between the primeval "stuff," from which the gods emerged, and nature, including humankind. Immanence leads to continuity. In contemporary terms, this

---

[19]For more detail on how the trinitarian perspective on creation affects other doctrines see, Coppedge, *Portraits of God*, pp. 71-88.

is a naturalistic worldview, which explains everything within terms of space and time and matter.

There are, C. S. Lewis reminds us, two basic worldviews: supranaturalism and naturalism.[20] These worldviews have widespread influence on all thought. In this section we will briefly review some of the implications of naturalism and supranaturalism on the Christian faith, ministry and practical life.

Anthropology

In naturalism, men and women must be accounted for within the system of the cosmos. In the ancient Near Eastern perspective, they emanated from the same primordial stuff that produced the gods and nature. Humans were the last in the chain of evolving reality, and this is why men and women have no particular significance or value.

Evolution explains humanity from the contemporary naturalistic worldview. Humans are a slightly higher form of the ever-evolving animal kingdom. Thus humans are animals. But this does not provide satisfactory answers to the basic human questions, Who am I? Why do I exist? and What is my purpose? It leads to a fairly bleak philosophy of life. In Francis Schaeffer's words, "Man is reduced to a zero."[21] This view has led in contemporary times to the Holocaust and slave-labor camps. This philosophy stands behind both abortion and euthanasia. The significance of human life is gone. This is manifested in the Playboy philosophy: Women are used for temporary pleasure and then discarded. It is a philosophy of life without absolute moral values. In the end, might makes right.

From the biblical, supranatural worldview persons were created within the parameters of space and time, but life is not an accidental occurrence. People have a unique relationship with the Creator. They alone are made in the image of the triune Creator. Persons exist to share life and love in fellowship with God and with one another. Thus people are of greater value than natural creation, plant life and animal life. In other words, from a supranatural perspective unborn babies are more significant than spotted owls. We care for the old, the infirm and the handicapped, even if they are no longer "productive" members of society. God has made men and women to be like himself, which includes shar-

---

[20]C. S. Lewis, *Miracles* (London: Fontana, 1947), pp. 9-15.
[21]Francis Schaeffer, *He Is There and He Is Not Silent* (Wheaton, Ill.: Tyndale House, 1972), p. 11.

ing in his moral character. This provides a standard of absolutes and moral values in human relationships that does not exist anywhere else.

One's worldview guides how persons relate to the rest of creation. For the naturalist, a human is merely an advanced animal. This makes it possible to treat men and women like animals and vice versa. In some parts of the East where this naturalistic worldview prevails, rats are allowed to eat food that should be reserved for starving children. The rats are not killed because they might be reincarnations of ancestors. In the West some people are more concerned about animal rights than human rights. This is the logical fruit of naturalistic thinking.

The supranatural perspective directs the appropriate use of creation by human persons. From this biblical perspective nature is neither a god nor alive like persons; it is, rather, neutral. The Creator has given humankind the responsibility to care for and rule over creation (Gen 1:26-28). This is the basis for modern science. From the biblical perspective all creation is legitimate for investigation, use and enjoyment under God's direction. It is no accident that modern science was developed in the West, which was founded on the biblical perspective. Unfortunately, because of the decline of biblical influence in the culture, people are moving in one of two directions: toward mysticism or scientism. The implications for anthropology are very significant.

Revelation

The doctrine of revelation centers on how we know reality (i.e., epistemology). From a naturalistic point of view, careful observation of and rational reflection on the natural order leads to knowledge and understanding. That's all we have to go by.

From a naturalistic point of view, then, "sacred" scriptures are merely products of natural human thought within the world of space and time. So scriptures, which may contain wisdom and human insight, are basically human books with authority delegated to them by a community of believers.

The biblical explanation of its Scripture is that the supranatural God has revealed himself to his people. Thus knowledge does not come merely through observation and reflection but through revelation from that which is beyond space and time. We know what God is like because he has revealed himself to us, not because we "discovered" it within our world. The biblical view is that God's self-revelation, centered in Jesus Christ and made explicit in the Old and New Testaments, is the basis for understanding not only God and creation but all reality. The Scriptures carry an authority that is grounded in God. Although God used human authors to convey his words, parallel to the incarnation of the Word, the ultimate author is the triune God himself.[22] This truth gives Scripture its unity in thought and theology, making possible systematic theology and a coherent Christian perspective on all of its themes. Though each sentence, paragraph, chapter and book of the Bible are carefully examined in order to understand nuances and differences of approach, Christians believe that behind them there is an overarching unity, because through them God has unveiled himself to give us a whole picture of who he is, who we are and how we should relate to him.

The implications are enormous. From a naturalistic point of view, the truthfulness of Scripture is evaluated through the most up-to-date methods of literarily criticism, anthropology, sociology, philosophy and so forth. But from a supranatural perspective God has made himself known in the Bible, and therefore it is to be gladly received and submitted to. Christians are not free to select on the basis of some other standard what they will accept as true in Scripture but are to receive it as a whole as truth from God.

Sin

Hamartiology, the study of sin, presupposes a standard of right and wrong. Sin is clearly a deviation from that standard. In the naturalist worldview, right and wrong are determined within space and time. Typically a group—a family, clan or nation—establishes the norm by which attitudes, conduct and relationships are evaluated. Depending on the situation, the standards may be determined by economics, politics, psychology, education or social custom.

The biblical worldview judges sin by the character of God's holiness and love. This, and not something within the cosmos, provides a supranatural standard for right and wrong. The moral attributes of the triune God are central. Righteousness, purity, grace, truth and goodness are expressions of God's holy and loving nature. Sin is that which is contrary to the will and character of this God. So when David sinned he cried to God, "Against thee, thee only, have I sinned" (Ps 51:4). David's sin certainly had consequences for others.

---

[22]Telford Work, *Living and Active: Scripture in the Economy of Salvation* (Grand Rapids: Eerdmans, 2001), pp. 8-10.

But, according to the Bible, sin is primarily an offense to God. Once this is understood, the devastating effect of sin on other persons can be seen in its appropriate light. Sin is not primarily political correctness, conforming to social norms, psychological harmony or economic justice. All of these things are affected by sin, but they are not the essence of sin.

John Wesley said that the doctrine of original sin is the first distinguishing point between heathenism and Christianity.[23] If you do not understand the problem (sin), you will never get the solution right. Naturalism and supranaturalism approach the basic human problem from entirely different perspectives, and not surprisingly their respective solutions diverge radically.

Christology

Christ is the solution to the human problem. Christology centers on the question, Who is Jesus? Jesus' influence is so great that every thinking person at some time asks this question. Was he a mere man (the naturalistic view)? or Is he human and divine at the same time (the supranatural perspective)? C. S. Lewis declares that naturalism has only three options for interpreting who he is: a psychotic, a deceiver or a fabrication of the early church.[24] The first option says Jesus was a mentally unbalanced person so disturbed that he spoke and acted as if he were God. But from reading the Gospels, which is our only source, we see that Jesus is anything but a psychological "case."

Was Jesus a deceiver? This means he deliberately led people from the truth—about himself and about his relationship to God. However, most people, even naturalists, who read the Gospels realize that he was a great moral teacher. But he cannot be both a great moral teacher and falsely make claims that he was divine, the Son of God in the supranatural sense. Lewis points out that great moral teachers do not lie or knowingly mislead others. Either he is a great moral teacher or a deceiver. If he is a great moral teacher, then all of his claims must be true, including his divine nature.

Is Jesus a creation of the early church? This is the position of some scholars who believe Jesus' miracles, predictions and much of his life were invented by the early church to shore up its own authority. But what then accounts for the origin of the church itself? Since its founder was Jewish and lived and taught

---

[23]John Wesley, *Standard Sermons*, 2 vols., ed. E. H. Sugden (London: Epworth, 1921), 1:222.
[24]C. S. Lewis, *Mere Christianity* (New York: Macmillian, 1958), pp. 40-41.

in a Jewish context, which was uniquely and profoundly monotheistic, and the church's earliest members were Jewish, it is difficult to see how they could make a plausible case for Jesus to be divine.

The biblical perspective, which is open to the supranatural, presents Jesus as divine as well as human. Those Jews who knew him best—his disciples—were driven to the verdict that Jesus was a human person who shared in the very being of God, his Father. On this basis the church developed the doctrine that Jesus was fully God *and* fully human at the same time. This makes plausible accounts of Jesus in relation to creation, miracles, the power to forgive sins and to give and transform spiritual life.

Salvation

Our soteriology (study of salvation) is dependent on our view of the basic human problem. From a naturalistic perspective the problems people face are derived from the natural world, so the solutions are also found within nature. If the problem is psychological, then "salvation" is found in counseling, therapy or psychotropic drugs. If the problem is economic inequity, redistribution of the world's resources would be an appropriate solution. If the problem is ignorance, then education is the answer. Human problems are solved by human effort.

From the biblical perspective, the basic human problem is sin, which crosses over from the natural world to the supranatural. Sin is first of all against God. It breaks our fellowship with God and we are incapable of fixing it. Salvation then must originate from the triune God. Through the person of Jesus Christ, God entered the world to redeem humankind from sin. Jesus' entire life—advent, teaching and ministry, death and resurrection—provides atonement for sin and offers salvation to men and women.

The solution to sin, which lies at the root of all human problems, begins with Jesus' supranatural work and is actualized by the Holy Spirit in human life. Those who respond in faith not only receive a new standing before God but are also transformed from within by the holy and triune God. Salvation is not achieved through human effort but is accomplished by the Father, the Son and the Holy Spirit.

The Christian Life

From a naturalistic perspective, human transformation is the result of human effort to solve problems according to whatever standards society might set.

Human relationships are governed by ethical norms that vary—and change—from society to society. Nothing is based on absolute values that are crosscultural and crossgenerational.

From the supranatural perspective the Christian life consists in working out the purposes of God for all of creation. Life is not random, nor is life's purpose determined by an individual or a social group. Rather, it is determined by the nature and character of God as known in Jesus Christ. Further, the transforming work of God in salvation is worked out as God accomplishes his will for each individual life in the context of community. Jesus Christ incarnate is the standard for life, work and relationships. The absolute standard for ethical conduct is based on God's holiness and love, which are revealed in Jesus Christ. The Spirit applies this standard transgenerationally and transculturally.

The Church

From the naturalist perspective, the church is just another sociological phenomena to be accounted for in human terms. It is a human organization on par with schools, hospitals, businesses, political organizations and so on. The church is a human attempt to organize religious ideas and expressions.

Biblically, the church is no mere human organization; it has a divine origin. Because persons are social beings, reflecting the triune nature of God, they join with other persons to be whole. When God transforms persons in his own image, they become aware of the social nature of all persons. This begins with natural families but extends to the family of believers. This larger group forms the basis of the Christian church. The church is designed to reflect the triune nature of God as a place for Christians to fellowship with and serve others to accomplish God's purposes in the world.

Ministry

Within the church Christians are challenged to be involved in multiple ministries. The naturalist views such activities from a completely different perspective than those who are Christian supranaturalists. The ministries of counseling and preaching will provide examples of this difference.

Counseling. From the naturalistic point of view counselors draw upon insights from leading psychologists and psychiatrists who study the human psyche and behavior. Through a variety of therapies, these counselors attempt to help persons find their problems and come up with a solution within the natural world. So, for example, Rogerian psychology helps the patient clarify his needs and make choices, but it does not suggest or propose solutions from outside the client's own self.

The biblical perspective is that the ultimate answers to life's problems come from God. The problems people face often have a sin component or are the result of a sinful environment. The Christian counselor believes that there is a supranatural dimension to healing and wholeness in the counseling room. While valuable techniques and insights may be learned from secular psychology, there is an additional element that the Christian counselor brings to the table: God. He has not left us on our own to find our own solutions. Scripture is a source for addressing human problems and finding God's principles for living full and productive lives.

Preaching. From a naturalistic perspective, there is not much difference between preaching and giving a political address or an after-dinner speech. All three involve communication, persuasion and perhaps some entertainment. Preachers, like all other public speakers, craft their speeches using the best rhetorical and communication techniques available.

From the biblical perspective, preaching involves rhetoric and careful preparation, but there is a supranatural dimension both in preparation and delivery. The Spirit of God anoints the preacher as he works with God's Word, and quickens the spirits of those who are listening. So there is more than crowd psychology at stake: God's Spirit witnesses to the truth as it is preached so that people can appropriately respond to what God is saying.

There are many people involved in ministry who are theoretical supranaturalists, but their approach to ministry makes them practical naturalists. Because they do not expect God to have answers or to speak and witness to his truth, they prepare, work and minister with their own resources and by their own power. A consistent supranatural perspective involves dependence on the Spirit and trusting God to address human need through whatever medium of ministry is currently being employed.

Conclusion

Obviously, there is a vast difference between naturalism and supranaturalism. This is played out in theology and ministry. Sadly, many in the church are theoretical supranaturalists but practical naturalists. We—all Christians—need to critically examine our thinking to be sure that our theology and practice are consistent with a supranaturalist perspective, which teaches that the holy, triune God created, redeemed and is transforming the world through Jesus and the Holy Spirit.

12

THE TRIUNE GOD'S
WORK OF PROVIDENCE

INTRODUCTION

The Function of Providence

The term *providence* comes from the Greek *pronoia* and the Latin *providere*, meaning "to see ahead" or "to be able to anticipate." Thus providence has to do with God's ability to foresee and think ahead about what will be needed in his creation. It is also coupled with his ability to provide and care for the needs of the world he has made. To fully develop this doctrine, we must make an extensive examination of the Old and New Testaments. A relational view of the triune God as revealed through Jesus Christ is the key to understanding providence. God's identity is the controlling factor in understanding how he relates to the world and specifically to human persons.

Four Errors Countered by Providence

The doctrine of providence examines and explains the interaction between the triune Creator and his creation.[1] A trinitarian view of providence protects Christians against several erroneous views of God's work within creation: deism, pantheism, fatalism and chance.

Deism, which primarily views God as Creator, severely limits his interaction with the world once it is complete. God's transcendence so dominates deism that he is virtually separated from creation's ongoing operation. Deism's Creator is like a watchmaker who winds a new watch and then leaves it to run on its own.

---

[1]Colin Gunton, "Creation and Providence," in *The Triune Creator* (Grand Rapids: Eerdmans, 1998), pp. 175-92.

Though deism begins with supranaturalism, it ends with practical naturalism. The biblical concept of providence counters this view by showing that God has not left his creation to run its own course. He interacts with his creation by sustaining it, preserving it, caring for it and governing its operations. The biblical doctrine of providence is a healthy antidote to a deistic worldview.

The biblical doctrine of providence also counters *pantheism*. Pantheism is the identification of God with the created order itself. God is in all things. Whereas the God of deism is totally transcendent, pantheism's God is completely immanent. Both hold elements of truth, but both are in error. The biblical view of providence addresses this by revealing the transcendent Creator who interacts with his creation without being identified with any of its parts. Biblically, God is transcendent and immanent.

Fatalism teaches that things are absolutely predetermined, either by impersonal fate or by a supranatural God who has predetermined all the choices and events of creation. Either way, the practical effect of fatalism is the same: it undercuts human freedom and responsibility. The biblical doctrine of providence demonstrates that God relates to persons who make free and spiritually significant choices. A scriptural view of providence undercuts the ground of fatalism.

That life is based on pure *chance* is a variation of fatalism. According to this view, everything is the result of the impersonal plus time plus chance. There is no governing principle whatsoever. Things happen without plan or purpose; life is truly random. The concept of providence makes it clear that the world does not operate by chance. Providence declares that life is not purposeless but has God-designed purpose and meaning, and that significance is found in fellowship with the triune God.

Providence Addresses Two Major Theological Issues

The doctrine of providence not only addresses errors regarding the doctrine of God, it also speaks to two major issues that arise in every generation: theodicy and miracles.

Theodicy tries to justify God's ways in the face of continuing evil. How can an all-powerful and good God allow evil in his creation? Why does he allow it to ravage the world? Providence, which addresses how God relates to the world "as it is," speaks directly to this issue and provides an adequate balance of perspective between God's nature and the nature of the world we live in.

The miraculous is the other issue on the minds of many. Does God work miracles in our world? Does he intervene in the natural order, which normally runs on the basis of cause and effect? If he does intervene in this way, when, where and how does he do this? Providence specifically addresses God's interaction with our world, and the miraculous is a significant part of it.

Pastoral/Practical Significance

The doctrine of providence has enormous pastoral implications. Thinking Christians cannot help but ask how God is working in their personal lives, their families, their churches, their nations and the world. They want to know how God works and how this affects them and others. This becomes particularly acute when painful circumstances occur. Spiritual leaders must assist those who wonder what is God doing, why is he doing it and how he is accomplishing some meaningful purpose amidst pain, loss and even death.

The doctrine of providence, then, protects Christians against theological error, helps us understand the problem of evil and miracles and has practical significance for people who wonder whether God is working in our world. Before we move to a discussion of the trinitarian approach to the concept of providence, we will examine its component parts.[2]

I. THREE COMPONENTS OF PROVIDENCE

The doctrine of providence is traditionally divided into three interrelated parts: (1) the work of God in preserving his creation, (2) the way God cooperates with natural and secondary causes to run the universe in an orderly fashion, (3) how God governs all things, including free agents, to accomplish his purposes. So providence may be understood as the activity of God in sustaining this creation *(preservation)*, in cooperating with creation *(concurrence)* and in guiding the events of creation *(governance)* toward his chosen ends.[3]

---

[2]Wayne Grudem, *Systematic Theology* (Grand Rapids: Zondervan, 1994), p. 315; Emil Brunner, *Christian Doctrine of Creation and Redemption,* Dogmatics, trans. Olive Wyon (London: Lutterworth Press, 1952), 2:148; N. M. de S. Cameron, "Providence," in *New Dictionary of Theology* (Downers Grove: InterVarsity Press, 1988), p. 541; Thomas Oden, *The Living God* (San Francisco: Harper & Row, 1987), pp. 277-78.

[3]For variations on the ordering of the components of providence see W. B. Pope, *A Compendium of Christian Theology,* 3 vols. (London: Wesleyan-Methodist Book Room, 1880), 1:437, on "conservation, care and governance"; and Gunton, *The Triune Creator,* p. 176, on "conservation, governance, perfecting, rest." Using the traditional order are Oden, *Living God,* pp. 270-3; Grudem, *Systematic Theology,* p. 315; Wolfhart Pannenberg, *Systematic Theology,* 3 vols., trans. Geoffrey W. Bromiley (Grand Rapids: Eerdmans, 1991-97), 2:35-59; Karl Barth, *Church Dogmatics* 3/3, ed. G. W. Bromiley and T. F. Torrance, trans. G. T. Thompson and Harold Knight (Edinburgh: T & T Clark, 1958), pp. 58-238.

Preservation

Preservation is God's work of maintaining, upholding and sustaining what he has brought into existence, which logically follows from his role as Creator: what he makes, he also preserves (Ps 138:7).

The objects of God's preservation of his universe include (1) inanimate creation, (2) living plants, (3) animals and (4) human beings. In the work of preservation, God is upholding all four of these in existence and preserving each in its basic way of being that was ordered according to God's purposes for it.

Two Bible texts reveal the intimate connection between the triune God and this work of preservation. Both come in key christological sections. The first is Colossians 1:15-19, where Jesus is described as "the image of the invisible God" through whom all things were created. He is the Son in whom "all the fullness of God was pleased to dwell" (v. 19), and "in him all things hold together" (v. 17). Through Jesus we understand that the Trinity was not only involved in the act of creation but in sustaining all things, holding them together after they are made.

The second christological passage is Hebrews 1:1-5. Here Jesus is presented as the Son of God (v. 2), through whom God "also created the world" (v. 2). Within creation Jesus reflects the glory of God as the image of his nature and upholds "the universe by his word of power" (v. 3). By his identification as the Son of the Father, Jesus is directly involved in both the creation and preservation of the universe.

As Creator, God is the prime cause of all things. But his work of preservation is carried out through multiple secondary causes. When God created the cosmos, he set the laws of cause and effect in place, and he works through these to maintain his creation.

Among the secondary causes is the gift of human free will. God's providence does not exclude the will but works through it and sustains it. Even after the Fall, God by his prevenient grace sustains the human capacity to make free choices.[4] Part of God's design for human beings, made in his image, is the ability to choose how they relate to him and others, and this freedom is sustained in his act of preservation.

God's preservation of the cosmos undergirds modern science. By establishing secondary causes, God has created a universe that is not only orderly but

---

[4]See pp. 274-79 and 312-15 for a discussion of sin and human freedom.

largely predictable. The scientific method of observing nature and testing hypotheses presupposes that the so-called "laws of nature" will function in the same way given the same set of conditional elements.[5]

The preservation of God's creation, like the other parts of the work of providence, is based on his omnipresence, which allows him to know the state of everything in the world, his wisdom (including omniscience) and his power (omnipotence), which allows him to bring about what his goodness determines is best for his creatures.[6]

Concurrence

In the order of causality, God is the primary cause of all things, but he has created a world in which there are also secondary causes that operate in the natural, rational and moral dimensions of life. These do not work on their own but are dependent on God's ongoing care. The doctrine of concurrence focuses on God's continuous work through secondary causes, sustaining them and using them to accomplish his purposes for each kind of created being.[7]

The doctrine of concurrence has particular significance for humans. By sharing the triune God's personal attributes, they possess reason, imagination, emotions and will along with corresponding freedom, responsibility and creativity. God maintains the same human capacities with which they were originally created in spite of their sin. Thus the secondary cause of human free will is preserved and honored by God as a part of normal human activity. God does not override human freedom, but rather works concurrently through that freedom to accomplish his purposes.

Sometimes humans make bad choices and fall into sin. But because human freedom is essential to all personal relationships, God concurs with their freedom even though he does not approve of their sin.[8] Though God permits people to choose sin or evil, he does not directly cause either. He chose to create

---

[5]See Oden, *Living God*, pp. 279, 281, 288; Grudem, *Systematic Theology*, pp. 316-17; John Wesley, *Letters* (London: Epworth Press, 1931), 2:256-62. For discussion of the concept of preservation in the early church see Pannenberg, *Systematic Theology*, vol. 2, 35-36.

[6]John Wesley, "On Providence," *Works* (BI) (Nashville: Abingdon, 1985), 2:538-40.

[7]The concept of concurrence is an extension of preservation, and indeed some theologians treat concurrence under the heading of preservation. See John Calvin, *Institutes of the Christian Religion* (Philadelphia: Presbyterian Board of Christian Education, 1813), 1:223-25.

[8]Augustine, *On Continence*, NPNF 1 (Peabody, Mass.: Hendrickson, 1994), 3:377-90; Calvin *Institutes* 3.22-24; Thomas Aquinas *Summa Contra Gentiles* 3.77.1 (Notre Dame: University of Notre Dame Press, 1955-1957).

persons who might choose that which is contrary to his will.

The doctrine of divine concurrence protects the holy God from the charge that he is the source of evil. If God caused humans to sin or choose evil, then he would be directly responsible. But because persons freely choose to sin, the responsibility is theirs. Nevertheless, God's creatures are not left to themselves. God is present with his creatures even though he is not the cause of their actions.[9] Through his Word and the ministry of the Holy Spirit, God cooperates with his creatures in their actions and uses secondary causes to work within nonpersonal creation.[10]

Governance

In his providence God guides and directs every part of creation to his purposeful ends. Scripture clearly reveals God's work in the affairs of individuals and nations. Creation, the Fall, the flood, Babel, the covenant with Abraham, the exodus, Mount Sinai, the conquest, the Davidic monarchy, the exile and return, the incarnation, the cross and resurrection, Pentecost and the establishment of the church: all of these events testify to God's providential governance of the world.

God's providence is crucial to the doctrines of sin and redemption. God foresaw the entry of sin and evil in creation and made provision for redeeming persons from it. Christ is God's response and solution to sin, and his work opens the door to understanding God's governance of all creation. The doctrine of God's providence is the central link between creation, sin, redemption and the consummation.

Nothing in creation is beyond God's providential care, but the various parts of creation are treated according to their own properties and God's purposes for each. There is a major distinction between God's governing the impersonal (matter, plants and animals) and the personal (humans) parts of creation. For the most part God works through the ordinary channels of secondary causes, but with humans he also works through their choices. He accomplishes his purposes by working appropriately with each part of creation.[11]

God works through "natural" law to accomplish his purposes in impersonal creation. Physical laws normally govern inanimate creation. This enables the

---

[9]Pannenberg, *Systematic Theology,* 2:48.
[10]Oden, *Living God,* pp. 281-85; Grudem, *Systematic Theology,* pp. 317-22.
[11]Oden, *Living God,* pp. 286-89.

study of physics, chemistry, geology and astronomy, which depend on physical forces that are reliable and do not vary. Lifeless matter also makes possible living plants, and the natural laws of biology (e.g., cell division, reproduction and photosynthesis) govern this area. Animals are sentient and mobile beings, yet they are not persons. They too are governed by laws appropriate to their being, which we study through the discipline of zoology. Thus God gives integrity to the nonpersonal aspects of creation through secondary causes.

Every person and every human group is in some way under the governing hand of God. But Scripture indicates that God respects the freedom he has given to individuals, so he manages their affairs without being directly responsible for the choices that they make. How is this possible?

In order to understand this, we need to take a fresh approach—a trinitarian approach—to the way God governs human persons.[12]

II. JESUS AS THE MODEL: THE WAY OF UNDERSTANDING PROVIDENCE

As with the rest of this book, Jesus is our model for understanding the way providence works. As God, he provides the divine perspective, and as a man, he provides a human perspective on how providence works. Both perspectives are important for understanding God's governance of creation. This is the fresh approach we will take to understand the nature and workings of providence.[13]

Jesus' Model of Providence from the Divine Perspective

The context of providence: Jesus and the Trinity versus God as sovereign King. The Trinity, personhood and roles of God. We have seen that the Bible presents God as a social being. The three persons of the Trinity are intimately related to each other (ontological Trinity) and work to build relationships with others (economic Trinity). The social nature of God is concretely revealed in the life of Jesus. God seeks persons with whom to establish relationships. Thus God designed human persons with two kinds of relationships in mind: (1) relationships with the triune God, and (2) relationships with other human

---

[12]Oden, *Living God*, pp. 286-93; Grudem, *Systematic Theology*, pp. 327-32; Pope, *A Compendium of Christian Theology*, 1:440-43; Pannenberg, *Systematic Theology*, 2:54-59.

[13]For a discussion of Jesus as the way of understanding of a trinitarian view of providence, see T. F. Torrance, *The Christian Doctrine of God* (Edinburgh: T & T Clark, 1996), pp. 221-22.

persons. Thus our discussion of governance must be wrapped in relational categories.

A proper discussion of providence does not begin with God's power but with his relationality. The Trinity is a perichoretic interaction of love; there is no power struggle among the three divine persons. Because of this and because God's personal attributes govern his relative attributes, the triune God does not begin with the exercise of omnipotence over his creatures (see chap. 7). Rather, he begins by developing relationships with human persons.

In chapter seven we saw that the personal attributes of the Trinity include God's social nature; life; the capacities of reason, imagination, emotion and will; freedom; responsibility; and creativity. Jesus, the God-man, models these attributes and is therefore the key to understanding personhood, both divine and human. Because God and humans are personal, God governs people in a different manner than he does the rest of the created order. This is particularly true of the human will (freedom of choice), which God always respects in his person-to-person relationships.

In chapter nine we discovered that two of God's roles—Personal Revealer and Father—are primary because they are metaphysical, not just metaphorical. This is significant for understanding providence: it means that the focus of providence is personal; God is the divine parent who cares for his children. Thus governance is not so much a matter of control, fiat, power and authority as it is one of communication, self-giving, love, respect and trust.[14] When God's roles of Personal Revealer and Father are taken seriously, the whole discussion of God's governance is radically altered. In fact, it calls into question whether *governance* is the proper term. It may be that *guidance* and *direction* are more suitable terms for the Father's relationships with human persons.

Providence: Moving from God as sovereign King to God as triune being. Most treatments of providence begin with the role of God as sovereign King.[15] The King accomplishes his purposes by governing his citizens through

---

[14]Of course authority is exercised within this context of communication, self-giving, love, respect and trust.

[15]E.g., John Frame, *The Doctrine of God: A Theology of Lordship* (Phillipsburg, N.J.: P & R, 2002), p. 276. See also John S. Feinberg, *No One Like Him* (Wheaton, Ill.: Crossway, 2001). Feinberg's extensive study on the doctrine of God does not treat the doctrine of the Trinity until chap. 10, and the trinitarian understanding of God seems to make almost no difference to the rest of the discussion. His primary focus is on God's role as sovereign King. The same is true of Frame, who treats the Trinity last (*Doctrine of God*, chaps. 27-29).

power. But before God was King (economic Trinity), he was the eternal Father (ontological Trinity). So the priority of God's role as Father, anchored within a trinitarian Godhead, is obvious. When the larger biblical perspective of God as triune being is brought into focus, it modifies God's role as King (see pp. 232-34).

This shift from the sovereign King to God as Father sets God's omnipotence, sovereignty and authority in an entirely different context, that of a loving Father who cares for and guides the growth of his children. So God's personal attributes take precedence over his relative attributes. God still has power and authority, but these now service the Father's loving heart.

The trinitarian perspective makes it easier to understand the biblical narratives about personal as well as historical providence. God as Father is not only concerned with nations, peoples and his overarching purposes for the world, but he is also intimately concerned with individual men and women. So the Bible includes multiple stories about God's relationships with individuals and how he coordinated the circumstances of their lives to accomplish his purposes (e.g., Joseph and Esther).

The triune Father reveals his purposes for creation. Understanding God's purposes for the world is essential to his providential work in and through creation. His purposes are the ends for which he is working through his providential oversight of the world.

We must distinguish between God's purposes for impersonal and personal creation. God sustains the impersonal creation—matter, plants and animals—and cooperates with it through secondary causes to bring it to good ends. Because these parts of creation do not have freedom of the will, they may be managed or governed through secondary causes without any threat to their basic existence. But even here our shift from God as sovereign King to that of Father means that God cares for and is concerned about impersonal creation, which is legitimate in itself. God models stewardship of the created order in that he takes responsibility for it. And being made in God's image, Adam and Eve were given dominion over and responsibility for God's good creation (Gen 1:26-28).

God made impersonal creation the context for personal creation. The universe was designed by God for those made in his own image. So in Genesis 1—2, once all other components are properly established, the creation of man and woman serves as the climax. The created order is made for human sustenance, delight, enjoyment and use. They are to care for creation, not exploit, destroy, mismanage or waste it. All the while, the triune God providentially cares for creation that it might serve as the context and atmosphere for the most important aspect of the whole created order—human persons, who are designed to relate to him personally.

In Scripture, God has six purposes for human persons.[16] Primarily, he desires that they share life and love out of a close personal relationship with himself. The other five flow from this desire: (2) that men and women might be a living reflection of his own character, (3) that they develop godly thinking, (4) that they have other close personal relationships, (5) that they serve others, and (6) that they delight in and enjoy his good creation. In spite of the entrance of sin into the world (Gen 3), it is clear that God's purposes for women and men have not changed. The realization of these purposes for them is accomplished through God's providence.

The distinction between God's means and God's purposes. When providence centers on God's role as sovereign King, there is a temptation to equate God's means with his purposes. It is assumed that a sovereign monarch has the power (means) to accomplish whatever he purposes. The trinitarian understanding of God as Father reveals the distinction between purpose and means. While the Father purposes (desires) good for his children, he limits the use of his power (means) to actualize it because he is unwilling to override their freedom of choice.

From the trinitarian perspective, God's chief purpose is that all persons live out of a close relationship with himself. The Trinity, whose divine persons share the closest and most intimate relations, made human persons in his own image so they too might share life in person-to-person relationships. God, who is love, shares love and desires love in return. T. F. Torrance says that the triune God does "all in fulfillment of the purpose of his measureless Love not to exist for himself alone but to bring other beings into coexistence with himself that he may share with them his triune fellowship of love."[17]

God's chief means, then, in light of his chief purpose, is to enable all persons to choose a shared life of love with himself. Love, to be genuine, must be freely chosen. So the Father, who respects the freedom of his children, does

---

[16]See a more extensive discussion of God's purposes for creation, see pp. 270-74.
[17]Torrance, *Christian Doctrine of God*, p. 221.

not force his purposes on them, but invites them into a relationship of love, and this is possible because they are providentially designed to make such a choice and thereby experience his chief purpose for life.

This trinitarian and familial language helps us understand why God's *plan*—to enable all persons to choose what he desires for them—is accomplished while his *chief purpose*—that they lovingly relate to him—is not accomplished with all.

God's secondary purposes for people (nos. 2-6) are evident in the creation narrative and are illustrated again in the life of Jesus. So God has made known his desire that these purposes be realized in the life of every human being. But they are dependent on God's chief purpose being carried out. Until a person shares a relationship of love with God (beginning with saving grace), it is not possible for God to accomplish his other purposes in that particular person's life. When persons freely respond to the Father's love, the door is opened for God's other purposes to be accomplished in them.

God's primary means undergirds each of his secondary purposes: he enables all humans to choose each of his purposes and to let him bring them to fruition in their lives. So out of the actualization of God's chief purpose, his secondary purposes can also be actualized.

God has five *secondary purposes* for us once his *first purpose* is accomplished. In each case he enables us to choose each of his desires. All six purposes are best understood in terms of God as Father rather than God as sovereign King. Though the Father desires his best for his children, he does not force his purposes on them. He respects their right to accept or reject his plans. So some of the Father's purposes may not be perfectly accomplished for all people. But his means—the enabling power through grace for every individual to freely choose his purposes—are accomplished.

Jesus, the Trinity and the role of the King. While God's primary roles are that of Personal Revealer and Father, he still works in creation as the sovereign King. God certainly governs Old Testament Israel as a ruler. Further, at the consummation of history, God again will serve in the role as King, exercising the final word in sovereign authority over his creation. Scripture provides many examples where God's governing rule over the nations in general and Israel in particular is illustrated (e.g., Is 6; Rev 4).

Jesus appeared at a time when many Israelites expected the arrival of the Messiah, a Davidic ruler anointed by God. While Jesus used much of this terminology to initially identify himself, he radically transformed it by modeling a different view of sovereignty and kingship. He did so by identifying his own relationship with God as primarily that of a Son to a Father. God is sovereign, but Jesus set before his disciples a trinitarian sovereignty. The role of Father is so central to Jesus' that the disciples and the early church used *Father* as the primary way to refer to God. Sovereign kingship, therefore, was seen against the backdrop of God as Father.

This reframing counters the temptation to think of sovereignty in terms of transcendence. God as Father is separate and distinct from his people, but like a Father he interacts with them as well and is personally involved in their daily lives. So God's immanence and his transcendence are kept in balance.

This means that any connection between the sovereign King and providence has to take into account the relationship of divine persons of the Trinity. The model of sovereignty is no longer the emperor of Rome, the governor of Judea or the king of Galilee, but the interactive communication, self-giving, care, love and right relationships between Jesus, the Father and the Spirit. Trinitarian sovereignty is not about omnipotence but self-giving, holy, loving relationships.

Providence and the triune God's purposes. The triune God works in the world to accomplish his primary purpose by enabling, by grace, all persons to choose a shared life of close relationship with himself (redemption). If they choose what God has made available, he enables them to choose his other purposes for them. Clearly, the whole discussion of providence is connected with redemption. God cannot bring about his purposes for persons apart from redeeming them.

God provides for this chief purpose in two ways. First, *historical providence* establishes the setting for redemption. God worked through Abraham, the exodus, the Davidic kingdom, the exile and return, Jesus, and the pouring out of the Spirit at Pentecost. These are the providential acts of God in history that provide a context for human redemption. God chose one nation, Israel, in order to reach all. The culmination of this plan is seen in Jesus, on whom God focused all of history so that he might serve as a basis for the redemption of the world.

Second, *special* or *personal providence* makes it possible for individuals to choose fellowship with God and all of its benefits. This relationship begins with the initial experience of salvation by faith in Christ, continues in growth as his disciple, moves on to deeper levels in full sanctification and a life full of the Spirit, and goes on to greater stages of development in spiritual maturity. Through God's agents, personal providence arranges the circumstances of life in order for redeemed persons to continue to choose growth in their relationship of love with God.

The triune God's personal agents in providence. Each member of the economic Trinity has special functions in relationship to the created order. The Father, for example, indicates the purposes of the Godhead and is most closely identified with the means God uses to make those possible. But the Son and the Spirit are God's chief agents for interacting with creation and in providentially accomplishing his purposes.

The Son of God, through the incarnation and life of Jesus, models the triune life of God and the six purposes of God for people. He demonstrates fellowship with God, he illustrates godly character, he reveals how to think as God thinks, he models close human relationships, he serves God in ministry to others, and he delights in life.

The Son is also the means through which persons can accomplish these purposes: the grace of God. This grace was made available through Jesus' incarnation, life, death and resurrection. The atoning work of God in Christ releases God's grace to persons so that they are enabled to receive what God desires to do in and through them. The Son's provision of grace enables persons to freely respond to what God wants to give them.

The Spirit also plays two roles in the economic Trinity's providential work in the world. First, he *orders the circumstances* of life so that God's purposes can be accomplished. He coordinates the affairs of the nations and more specifically the personal lives of individuals so they are in the place to make appropriate choices and receive God's best for them. Second, the Spirit *applies God's means*—God's grace—to individuals so they can freely choose to respond to God, and God can accomplish his work in them and fulfill his purposes. The Spirit consummates or actualizes the work of Christ. What is made possible by the Son, is made actual by the Spirit.

A biblical understanding of providence includes all three persons of the economic Trinity. The Father is connected with God's purposes in creation. The Son models God's purposes and makes provision for their accomplishment through grace. The Spirit orders the circumstances for God to work in people's lives and applies the grace to individual persons so they might appropriate God's gifts.

The triune God's providential means. God's grace and providence go hand in hand. Grace has two components. First, it is the unmerited favor of God toward persons; thus it is a relational term. Through grace we receive something that is not due to any merit or work on our part. Rather, it comes as a gift of God. Grace is the self-giving of God in which all of the favor of his personal presence works in relationship to us.

Second, grace is the holiness of God as enabling power. In his omnipotence God creates and preserves the universe. But when power is wrapped in the personal categories of the triune God (i.e., holiness), it is described as grace. From this perspective grace is God's enabling of persons to make choices that allow him to accomplish his purposes in their lives.

Grace is provided through the Son and is actualized by the Spirit when he enables individuals to choose God's purposes. Notice that grace is not a *thing;* it is not something people possess. Rather, it is a relational reality with the holy, triune God. When we are in fellowship with God through the Spirit, God's enabling power works through this relationship to empower us to do what he longs for. This enabling power, which comes from our relationship with God, is grace.

God's grace enables even the fallen human will to function with relative freedom. *Prevenient* grace is the grace with which God works with persons prior to salvation. The Spirit providentially orders life's circumstances so nonbelievers have the opportunity to respond to the invitation to fellowship with the triune God. In the book of Acts, for example, people at Antioch of Pisidia, who had not yet believed, heard the gospel proclaimed in the synagogue (Acts 13:16-43). After the initial proclamation of the gospel, but before anyone has responded in faith (Acts 13:48), God in his prevenient grace had already been at work in their midst, so that Paul and Barnabas "spoke to them and urged them to continue in the grace of God" (Acts 13:43). The same grace had been at work when Apollos crossed to Achaia and on his arrival was able to greatly help "those who through grace had believed" (Acts 18:27). Grace—*prevenient grace*—had already been operative to bring them to belief. These illustrations make it clear that in spite of the drastic impact of sin, a person's will has enough freedom restored to it by grace to respond to God's revelation in faith. After the initial response of faith, grace does not cease. Rather, it is enlarged with saving grace and growing grace as the person's relationship with the triune God more fully enables him to respond even further to God's desires.

Jesus' Model of Providence from the Human Perspective

Jesus, the God-man, helps us understand providence not only from the divine perspective but also from the human perspective. We have already hinted at how his earthly life opens our understanding of providence, but now we will look at this more closely.

General versus specific providence. Jesus: The model of historical providence. Jesus is the key to understanding God's providential work in history. After Adam and Eve's fall into sin (Gen 3), God initially does not work with a specific group of people (Gen 4—11), but beginning with Abraham (Gen 12—35) God primarily works through one nation—Israel—to accomplish his plans. The plan of God for people comes to fruition in the person of Jesus, who models what God desires for the whole nation.[18]

The New Testament opens with the genealogy of Jesus, tracing his lineage from Abraham through David to the birth of Christ.[19] This shorthand history is a declaration that God has been working throughout history to accomplish his purposes through Jesus. In Acts, Paul's overview of historical providence includes God's choice of the patriarchs, their sojourn in Egypt, the exodus, the wilderness wandering, the conquest of Canaan, the leadership of the judges and Samuel, the establishment of the monarchy under Saul and David, and the ministry of John the Baptist as the last forerunner of Jesus. Jesus is the fulfillment of God's purposes throughout this significant history (Acts 13:16-31).[20]

Paul not only sees God's providential plan for Jesus extending back through history but also through the future to the end of the age. The work of Jesus, culminating in his death and resurrection, plus the Spirit's work at Pentecost extend God's work in Israel to all peoples, both Jews and Gentiles. Paul illustrated how this works on his missionary journeys to the Gentiles (Acts 13—28). The gospel of Jesus Christ changed lives and in a matter of a few hundred years changed the whole world. So the Old Testament illustrates how historical providence worked to prepare for Jesus' coming. The Gospels present his incarnation, life, death and resurrection, and the rest of the New Testament illustrates how Jesus changes lives, touching all of the

---

[18]N. T. Wright, *Jesus and the Victory of God* (Minneapolis: Fortress, 1996), pp. 147-97, and *The Challenge of Jesus* (Downers Grove: InterVarsity Press, 1999), pp. 34-53.

[19]Luke's genealogy does not begin with Abraham but with Adam (Lk 3:23-28).

[20]Other sermons in the book of Acts also trace God's purposes through Israel to Jesus (cf. Acts 7:2-53).

nations of the world. So the whole sweep of history centers on the person of
Jesus. The triune God is working through both historical and eschatological
providence to accomplish his purposes in the world by enabling everyone to
enter into a close relationship with himself. If they choose to do this, God
arranges circumstances to accomplish his secondary purposes in their lives.
This is God's historical providence.

Jesus: The model of personal providence. While the metanarrative of Scripture is a testimony to general providence (i.e., God works in history to accomplish his overall purposes from creation to consummation), it is also a
testimony to God's personal or specific providence for individuals. A proper
understanding of this is related to the multiple ways God intends Scripture
to be read. At every major turning point in biblical history (especially the
history of Israel) God has at least one person who models proper human and
divine relationships.

Thus we should not only read Scripture to see how it serves God's general
historical purposes but also to observe his relationships with individuals,
which are the basis for our understanding of personal providence. As Paul
surveys Israel's history in Acts 13, his audience would have been aware of
God's personal interaction with Abraham, Isaac, Jacob, Joseph, Moses,
Joshua, Samuel, Saul, David and John the Baptist. And of course Jesus is the
center of the narrative and thus the primary illustration of God's personal
providence.

Jesus' birth, life, death, resurrection and ascension demonstrate God's personal interaction with persons. Jesus, fully human, illustrates in principle
God's desire to relate to every person. His experiences, including his historical
and cultural setting, are uniquely ordered by God's personal providence. Jesus'
life and ministry were part of God's personal ordering.

Some have suggested that God's providence is general but not personal.
John Wesley's response was that a general providence that excludes personal
providence is "self-contradicting nonsense."[21] For Wesley Scripture was so
clear about God's specific work with individuals that to give this up meant giving up providence all together.

> Either, therefore, allow a particular providence, or do not pretend to believe in
> any providence at all. If you do not believe that the governor of the world gov-

---

[21]Wesley, "On Providence," sermon 67, *Works* (BI) 2:548.

erns all things in it, great and small; and all the individuals whereof they are composed (and yet without forcing the wills of men, or necessitating in their actions) do not affect to believe that he governs anything.[22]

God's providential ordering of circumstances for individuals. Jesus, the God-man, reorders all of our thinking about providence. When he taught his disciples about God's providence Jesus started with familiar terms and concepts, but then he shifted to new and less familiar concepts.

The Old Testament makes large use of royal language when speaking of God's providential work. God governs the created order as sovereign King. Jesus used much of this language to discuss the kingdom of God and his messianic role within it. But once he identified himself as the long-expected Messiah in the line of David, he filled these terms with new meaning. When speaking of God, Jesus introduced family language, speaking of God primarily as his Father. When his disciples ask Jesus to teach them how to pray, he instructs them to address God as their Father (Mt 6:9; Lk 11:2). Just prior to the crucifixion, when Jesus addresses the disciples for the last time, he refers to God as Father more than fifty times (John 13—17).

Following Jesus' example, the early church also addressed God as Father. All but three New Testament epistles begin with a reference to the Father. And of the three that do not, two refer to the Father within the first few paragraphs. Significantly, no epistle begins with a reference to God as King, Creator or Judge. Clearly, Jesus' relationship to his Father changed the way his followers relate to God and changed their perspective of how God relates to the world.

This shift to family language requires a corresponding shift in the ordering of the roles of God and the attributes of God. When royal language is dominant, the relative attributes (omnipotence, omniscience, omnipresence, wisdom) are seen as primary. The temptation is to view God as an absolute dictator who can arbitrarily choose whatever he wants without consideration of others. The focus is on power and authority; the King always gets what he wants.

The fact that God has multiple roles (e.g., Redeemer, Shepherd, Teacher and Friend) modifies this portrait of God as a despot or dictator. Scripture presents the multiple roles of God for this very reason. No one role is absolute,

---

[22]John Wesley, "An Estimate of the Manners of the Present Times," in *Works*, 3rd ed. (London: Wesleyan-Methodist Book-Room, 1831), 11:160.

each being modified by the others.[23] When Jesus introduced God as Father, this changed his disciples' perspective on God's sovereignty. The emphasis shifted from God's relative attributes (omnipotence, omniscience, omnipresence, wisdom) to his personal (sociality, life, reason, imagination, emotions, will, freedom, responsibility, creativity) and moral attributes (holiness and love expressed in righteousness, truth, purity, grace and goodness). Thus the disciples' relationship with God did not begin with his omnipotence but with his personal attributes and the corresponding moral attributes.

Christian theology, based on Jesus' teaching and salvific work, must take into account all of the attributes of God, and all of God's attributes are pertinent to the doctrine of providence. However, from the trinitarian perspective, which begins with God as Father, the relative attributes (e.g., omnipotence) are subordinate to the personal attributes (e.g., freedom) and moral attributes (e.g., love, righteousness, goodness). The coming of the Son of the Father has irrevocably altered our view of God and his providence.

God's providential ways: A summary. Because we have examined a lot of material in this section, a brief summary is in order.

First, we looked at God's *purposes* for his people. God wants the best for all of his creatures, especially men and women. He desires that all people have a close personal relationship with himself, even after the Fall. If people respond to his offer of salvation and a life related to himself, then the door is open for his secondary purposes to be accomplished in them. His secondary purposes are (1) godly character, (2) godly thinking, (3) close personal relationships with other persons, (4) service to others, and (5) delight in life and God's purposes in living.

Second, God places *self-limitations* on his providential work. The triune God is a social being, with interpersonal relationships at the heart of who he is. The freedom to relate in love is a crucial component of his personhood. God made people in his own image, that is, for freely chosen personal relationships. God the Father has sovereignly chosen, therefore, to limit his own freedom, particularly in terms of interpersonal relationships, by giving free will to his children. Thus the self-limitation of God is an important factor in the doctrine of providence

---

[23]On the variety of roles, spanning from distance to intimacy, see Coppedge, *Portraits of God*, pp. 394-95.

Third, God uses *means* in his work of providence. The Son provides the grace of God and the Spirit actualizes this grace in individual lives. In his trinitarian role as Father, God's use of means helps us understand that not all of his purposes are accomplished, because persons can choose whether or not to have a relationship with him. Nevertheless, God's desire to be united in a fellowship of holiness and love with persons will be fulfilled, though not fulfilled for all. If an individual chooses to respond to God's invitation of fellowship, then God enables that person to continue to choose God's other purposes for Christian growth and maturity.

Finally, through his providence God has a *plan* for individual lives. Here we find a tension between God's desire for the absolute best and the reality of human choices, which may limit the appropriation of God's desire. Since our trinitarian perspective does not permit an arbitrary decision on God's part to make choices for us, he may have to modify his plans for individual lives, but he does so in light of his foreknowledge of our choices. The Father knows the choices of his children without causing them. But through the agency of his Son and his Spirit he uses means (grace) to order life's circumstances for individuals in light of their free choices.[24]

Great wisdom is required to accomplish God's plan for individuals in light of the choices they make. If they freely choose his will, their lives more closely match his ideal plan. If they choose not to follow his perfect will, there are fewer blessings and goods that God can effectively accomplish in their lives.

How the triune God providentially works. *Jesus illustrates the work of providence.* God's relationship to Jesus as a man is an indicator of how he desires to relate to other men and women. One key example of this comes in the garden of Gethsemane. On this last evening of Jesus' life, God in his providence had coordinated all the circumstances of his life, including the free choices of those around him. So God's providence includes wrong choices: the sinful choices of the Jewish leadership, the Roman governor and a disciple. But God was able to use even the sinful choices of Caiaphas, Pilate and Judas to accomplish his specific plan for Jesus. Without overriding their freedom, God used their choices to bring his plan for Jesus to fruition.

In his garden prayer, Jesus models the appropriate human response, using

---

[24]For more on foreknowledge and freedom, see Feinberg, *No One Like Him,* pp. 735-75, and James K. Beilby and Paul R. Eddy, ed., *Divine Foreknowledge: Four Views* (Downers Grove: InterVarsity Press, 2001).

the most intimate form of address to God—"Abba, Father"—in his request that this cup be removed from him (Mk 14:36). So this petition is not primarily to the sovereign God but to his Father, with the full acknowledgment that the Father may have a plan Jesus does not fully understand. He approaches God's providential role in trust and thereby demonstrates total obedience to the will of God. "Not what I will, but what thou wilt." This response of trust and obedience makes it possible for God to accomplish his full and best purposes for him.

The value of using Jesus as an example is that it removes the temptation to always consider God's providence in terms of blessing, prosperity, health and lack of pain. For Jesus, the cost is high; pain and death were part of God's plan for him. Apparently, the providential working of God as Father does not exempt his children from all difficult circumstances. If Jesus had sought God primarily as sovereign King, he could have called for twelve legions of angels to deliver him from his circumstances (Mt 26:53). But he relates to God as Father and therefore completely trusts his fatherly providence.

Ordering circumstances. How does God order the circumstances of life around the personal freedom of individuals? We know his plans include his purposes, he limits himself by human freedom, and he uses his means. But more specifically, he orders circumstances through permission, restraint, overruling, prevention and guidance.

1. As Father, God limits his own choices by *permitting* persons to make free choices. He desires this freedom to be properly used to seek him and therefore get his best. But he permits poor and even sinful choices that lead to suffering. Genuine freedom can be misused. As a Father, God permits people to choose sin and evil, even though he does not approve of those choices. We must live with our choices, and the drastic consequences of wrong choices are part of his providential education.

2. The Father also works in the lives of individuals by *hindrance.* Though he does not coerce humans, he may put obstacles in their way when they are about to hurt themselves or others. Human parents often protect their children from harm by limiting the toys they can play with or by fencing them in.[25] This hindering does not involve overriding the freedom of individuals, but it may involve the coordination of the free choices of many people as

---

[25]Of course, in spite of a parent's best efforts, a child may still find a way to do harm.

well as some parts of the impersonal creation to hinder a person from certain harmful consequences to himself or others (Gen 20:6).

3. Sometimes God may *overrule* the consequences of choices, especially when they are drastically negative. This is not an overruling of free and rational choices, but involves such things as lapse of memory, confusion, distractions and alternative thoughts coming to mind. God sometimes overrules to keep sinners from harming themselves and others and indirectly nudges them toward decisions beyond their own understanding. Sometimes God overrules consequences of wrong choices. An example is the story of Jacob's sons selling Joseph into slavery. God did not approve of the wrong choices and the threat of murder. So he overrode the consequences of their decision in order to get Joseph to a place where he could fulfill God's plan to save the Hebrews and bless Egypt (Gen 50:20). So God is regularly working through circumstances, relationships, events and impersonal creation to override or prevent some of the drastic implications of evil in some circumstances.

4. God also *prevents* temptation from becoming overpowering and prevents evil from having its full way. Because, as 1 John states, "Greater is he that is in you than he that is in the world" (1 Jn 4:4), God can externally open ways of escape or internally provide grace to resist temptation (1 Cor 10:13).[26] He often coordinates the free choices of others and external circumstances of impersonal creation to prevent individuals from being unduly harmed or missing God's way.

5. God also *guides* people. The Spirit of God, working through prevenient grace, arranges the circumstances of Christians, and to some degree even non-Christians, so that they are guided to make appropriate decisions. The Spirit coordinates activities, events, natural laws, secondary causes and so forth to optimize the opportunities people have to choose what God wants for their lives.

To arrange certain circumstances in an individual's life, God's guidance does not necessarily require that the individual chooses correctly. But many times (if not most) this is the case. The more godly decisions a person makes, the greater the probability of getting God's best in his life.

---

[26]Oden, *Living God*, pp. 300-202.

The means of guidance God has at his disposal are legion. The most significant for Christians, and sometimes even nonbelievers, is his Word. Guidance also comes through other persons, impressions on the mind, imagination, emotions, events, circumstances, interruptions, changes and even distractions. It may come through finances, reading books or the media. Sometimes God's guidance comes through sickness, accidents, tragedy or death. These and other circumstances of our lives may be part of God's providential guidance. While God does not override human choices, he made delay, hinder, prevent or override the consequences of certain poor choices.

These tools of providence are used by God through his relative attributes. He is able to work in our lives because of his omnipresence and omniscience. By using his self-limited omnipotence and wisdom, he is able to coordinate all the circumstances of life. As Wesley said, "The whole frame of divine providence is so constituted as to afford man every possible help, in order to his doing good and eschewing evil, which can be done without turning man in to a machine; without making him incapable of virtue or vice, reward or punishment."[27]

In summary, the trinitarian perspective on providence is primarily shaped by Jesus' relationship to God as his loving Father. Thus in his providential work in persons, God does not force decisions but respects their freedom to choose. Nonetheless, he works through the circumstances of their lives to give them the opportunity to fellowship with him. God the Spirit, working through the prevenient grace that has been provided by God the Son, orders circumstances through various means so that God can enable persons to freely choose his design for their lives. If this freedom is used appropriately, the Father's purposes and best plans will be actualized.[28]

---

[27]Wesley, "On Providence," *Works* (BI) (Nashville: Abingdon, 1985), 2:541.
[28]Pope, *A Compendium of Christian Theology*, 1:440-44.

13

THE TRIUNE GOD,
FREEDOM AND PROVIDENCE

I. PERSONS AND FREEDOM

God's Trinitarian Sovereignty and Human Freedom

Persons and freedom of the will. One of the classic discussions in Christian theology centers on how a personal God can exercise sovereignty and accomplish his purposes on the one hand and how persons can exercise freedom of the will on the other. Can both be simultaneously possible? Philosophers ask a similar question: Are persons free to make their own choices or are they determined by other forces? Biologists and social scientists face a similar problem: Are persons simply products of their heredity or environment, or do they have both the capacity and responsibility to make choices concerning their own lives?

The basic options are (1) people do not make real choices because their lives are determined, or (2) persons have free will and therefore make real choices. The two positions may be described as *determinism* and *indeterminism*, and different theological traditions fall within one of these positions.

Indeterminism posits that real human freedom is not compatible with causal determinism. In other words, because a person has free will, he is not determined by other causes or forced to make choices or do particular things against his will. It is always possible to choose something different. Because this position is incompatible with causal determinism, it is sometimes referred to as *incompatibilism*. It is also called *contra-causal free will, libertarian free will* and the *free-will defense of human personhood.*[1]

---

[1]Alvin Plantinga, *The Nature of Necessity* (New York: Oxford University Press, 1978), pp. 170-71; John Feinberg, *No One Like Him* (Wheaton, Ill: Crossway, 2001), pp. 626-31.

The key point of indeterminism is that persons control their own acts. This does not mean that there are no natural or supranatural influences on them, but that no causal factor or combination of antecedents, laws of nature or other factors is sufficient to force a person to choose one option over another. A human could always choose to do otherwise, even if he does not.

The basic idea of *determinism* is that for everything that happens there is such a context of conditions that nothing else could happen. Three forms of determinism can be identified.

Fatalism is the most extreme form of determinism. Fatalism usually applies to both nonpersonal and personal creation. Often connected with inevitability, fatalism maintains that no matter what a person does, the outcome will not be affected by his efforts. The implication is that everything that ever happens has been determined in advance and nothing can stop it, including human choice. In some forms of fatalism, even God seems unable to control events and circumstances.

A second form of determinism is *hard determinism*. This position too holds that all is causally determined. But hard determinism it is more removed from the idea of inevitability than fatalism. Usually it makes God the omnicause of all that happens. The result, however, is that there is no personal freedom of the will.

Soft determinism is another variation of determinism. This position concurs that everything is causally determined but attempts to provide some room for human freedom. This position teaches that causal determination is compatible with some human freedom and so is sometimes called *compatibilism*. Soft determinism attempts to provide room for genuine human choices by suggesting that the will is at liberty to make free choices because a person's will is not determined. People do not make choices contrary to their own wishes or desires. But from a soft determinist's perspective, human wishes or desires are caused by God, so in that sense they are causally determined. By redefining freedom, soft determinists are able to say that persons can do whatever they wish or desire and thus have freedom of choice. But in reality, these determinists have shifted the focus of causal determinism from the will to the wishes and desires of a person, and the effect is exactly the same. A person is determined and could not do otherwise. Thus genuine personal freedom does not exist with this position.[2]

---

[2]Feinberg, *No One Like Him*, pp. 631-39.

Whether one is a determinist or indeterminist seems to rest on how one approaches the doctrine of God.[3] Normally, the determinist's position begins with a view of God as sovereign King and defines sovereignty primarily in terms of God's omnipotent will. The will of the absolute sovereign cannot be thwarted, and by his acts of power he forces his subjects to do exactly as he desires. This view attempts to give glory to God by focusing on his transcendent sovereignty and power, and the price to be paid for defining sovereign kingship in this way is genuine human freedom.

Beginning with the Trinity produces an entirely different result. The triune Creator, whose three persons eternally relate to each other in mutual love, makes persons in his own image and likeness. Therefore people are made for personal relationships. Personhood, whether divine or human, involves the will, which is intimately connected to freedom. Freedom is an essential component of personal relationships. So our trinitarian starting point has shaped our understanding of personhood, and that in turn demands genuine freedom for persons to relate to other human persons, or to the triune God.

Logically, those who begin from a trinitarian starting point are indeterminists.[4] They believe that there is no incompatibility between the triune Creator and the genuine freedom that he has given humans. As a result, beginning with a triune God redefines the concept of God's sovereignty. Before God is sovereign King, he is God the Father, God the Son and God the Holy Spirit. So the interpersonal dimension of God is determinative in understanding how God's sovereignty works. Many in the Western church follow the Augustinian view of the Trinity, which focuses on God's oneness. So they begin with God as sovereign King rather than as Father, Son and Spirit. Thus God has the characteristics of an absolute ruler, similar to the emperor of Rome.

From the trinitarian perspective, the world is governed by the three-personed God, who desires relationships with those he has created. God has sovereignly chosen to limit his own freedom by giving freedom to human persons. Because of human freedom, God's perfect will may not be realized in all

---

[3]For the current state of the debate on this issue, see Jerry L. Walls and Joseph R. Dongell, "Calvinism and the Nature of Human Freedom," in *Why I Am Not a Calvinist*, ed. Jerry L. Walls and Joseph R. Dongell (Downers Grove: InterVarsity Press, 2004), pp. 96-118; and Robert A. Peterson and Michael D. Williams, "Freedom: Incompatibilist or Compatibilist?" in *Why I Am Not an Arminian*, ed. Robert A. Peterson and Michael D. Williams (Downers Grove: InterVarsity Press, 2004), pp. 136-61.

[4]This does not mean that everyone who is a trinitarian follows this logical progression to its conclusion. This may be because their trinitarian view of God is secondary to their view of God as sovereign King.

human lives. Though God desires that all persons be saved (1 Tim 2:4), all are not. God enables people to freely choose a right relationship with him so that his other purposes can be fulfilled. But many do not choose to do so. While this position is anathema to those who start with God as sovereign King, from the trinitarian perspective it is part of the beautifully dynamic world created by the loving and holy Trinity, who desires fellowship with those who reflect his own image.

The trinitarian perspective also supports and enhances the other roles of God such that a complete picture of how God works in relationship to creation is developed. Take, for example, God as the righteous Judge. From the determinist perspective persons do not have free will, but why then does God offer rewards and punishments for those who obey and disobey him? Scripture, which shows God offering rewards and punishments, is thus undermined. However, Scripture is given its proper due when we believe that people are free to make those choices. Otherwise righteousness and justice are completely subverted. God is just when a person chooses to obey and is rewarded, but God is also just when he punishes those who disobey.

The role of God as Father is also properly understood from the trinitarian perspective. A father loves his children and invites them into an intimate relationship with himself. But biblical love is only possible when it is freely chosen. Forced love is not love at all. So if persons are going to love God as Father, they must be free to choose to love him. Of course, this means they are free not to love him as well. Therefore genuine human freedom is an essential part of relating to God as Father.

So a trinitarian starting point carries very significant implications for God's sovereignty and human freedom. It redefines sovereignty, making it more biblically sound. It integrates and balances God's sovereignty with his other roles, such as righteous Judge and loving Father. This supports Scriptures that presuppose humans have genuine human freedom.[5]

Foreknowledge, Freedom and Providence

Foreknowledge as foreordination. Determinists usually equate God's foreknowledge with his foreordination. To protect the concept of an absolute sov-

---

[5]Allan Coppedge, *Shaping the Wesleyan Message* (Nappanee, Ind.: Evangel Publishing House, 2003), pp. 103-6.

ereignty, this position holds that God knows something ahead of time because he foreordained it to come to pass. What God wills he knows will happen. From this perspective it is inconceivable that God could foreknow something that happens differently from his will, because that would mean God did not cause it. Again, this comes from a concept of sovereignty that does not allow people to freely choose something God does not want. As John Feinberg puts it, "God foresees because he decrees. He decrees actions and events and means to both; hence, he foresees causes in each case that will bring about the act or event. Moreover, having decreed all things, he also knows what he himself will do at various points in history."[6]

Foreknowledge distinguished from foreordination. God's sovereignty is transformed by the trinitarian perspective because of its emphasis on person-hood. The three-personed God chose to limit himself in order to enter into genuine personal relationships. His choice to freely create persons is a part of this freely chosen limitation. Therefore, God's sovereignty does not have to be absolute or fully deterministic.

Since God does not have to cause all events, foreknowledge and foreordination can be separated. From the trinitarian position, foreknowledge can work with human freedom so that God can still accomplish his general purposes by enabling individual persons to freely choose his specific purposes. The crucial distinction here is that God can foreknow something he did not cause. He may observe free human choices that not only does he not cause but even desires they would have chosen differently.[7] But with foreknowledge of those choices and the events surrounding them, the sovereign and all-wise God can work through his Word, use the influence of others and order circumstances to accomplish his "adjusted plan" for individuals in light of their free choices. His plan is to continue to enable them to make good choices and thereby give them his best.[8]

---

[6]Feinberg, *No One Like Him*, p. 741.

[7]On the possibility of middle knowledge, or the Molinist approach, to God's foreknowledge of all possible choices, see William Lane Craig, "Middle Knowledge: A Calvinist-Arminian Rapprochement?" in *The Grace of God, the Will of Man*, ed. Clark H. Pinnock (Grand Rapids: Zondervan, 1989), pp. 141-64. See also William Lane Craig, *The Only Wise God: The Compatibility of Divine Foreknowledge and Human Freedom* (Grand Rapids: Baker, 1987).

[8]For a discussion on the way indeterminists understand the relationship between foreknowledge and freedom, see Feinberg, *No One Like Him*, pp. 742-75. Trinitarian theists would be comfortable with either the Boethian solution, the concept of middle knowledge (the Molinist solution) or the Ockhamist resolution.

For indeterminists, foreknowledge is significant for understanding providence. God's foreknowledge of free human choices makes it possible for him to coordinate the circumstances of life so he can accomplish his plan for the good of persons without undermining their freedom.[9]

II. LIVING WITH TRIUNE PROVIDENCE

Pastoral Implications of Triune Providence

God's providence has enormous practical implications for individuals. First, nothing arises in the life of an individual without God's knowledge and permission. God's guidance of individual lives is coordinated with his overarching historical purposes, and through various means he is able to providentially structure the circumstances of each person's life to enable him to make the best choice. God's foreknowledge of all contingent things makes it possible for him to coordinate circumstances so that "in everything God works for the good" for each person (Rom 8:28).

Second, at no time and in no circumstances is God's Spirit absent from a Christian who is in fellowship with him. In other words God is in the midst of every event of the lives of those who are rightly related to him; they are never left alone. God is also present with nonbelievers, but their awareness of his presence and working is severely limited.

Third, all the circumstances of an individual's life are used by God to accomplish his six purposes for him. Once God brings an individual into a relationship with himself, he will provide every opportunity for the person to develop godly character, thinking, relationships, service and delight in life. So a believer who has responded to God's chief purpose—fellowship with God—can be assured that God is doing everything possible to accomplish his other purposes.

A Christian also may move forward with the knowledge that God's purposes can be accomplished. This means that through his Spirit God has enabled every individual to continue to respond to him in an appropriate way. This ability of God to fully accomplish his purposes in an individual's life depends on the person's responses to God's enabling grace. Thus we need to receive this empowering grace in trust and obedience so that God may continue

---

[9]Coppedge, *Shaping the Wesleyan Message*, pp. 109-10.

to work through our circumstances to accomplish his desired ends.

Obviously, to accomplish God's full purposes, an individual would have to make a proper response on all occasions, to all of the opportunities available. Realistically, this does not always happen. We either choose wrongly or we are ignorant (i.e., we intend to do right but make wrong choices because of a lack of knowledge). In either case, God's adjusted plan accomplishes as many of his purposes for us as possible given our individual responses. So when we make mistakes or sin, we must ask, What is God's best from this point on in my life? How can I respond appropriately so that he can accomplish all he desires as fully as possible from this time forward?

God's providence reassures us that we are not alone when facing difficulties, and that God desires to use all circumstances, both positive and negative, for our good. While his love and goodness assure us that he has our best interest at heart, his power and providential work assure us that he is doing all that he can to accomplish his best for us. This assurance is designed to draw us into an even closer relationship with him.

Positive and Painful Providences

There are two kinds of providential circumstances: positive and negative. With positive providential circumstances the blessings of God are obvious in relationships, opportunities, health, fulfilling work, financial rewards, recreation and so forth. Very often positive providential circumstances are taken for granted, and we sometimes do not stop to respond appropriately to God because all is going well.

Negative providential circumstances are usually painful. Because we live in a fallen world, we are affected by natural evil, moral evil (including the sinful choices of others) and poor choices due to ignorance or infirmity. When this happens, we often raise questions related to God's providence. How can a good God, who loves us and has such significant power, allow these things to happen? This is the classic problem of evil. But sometimes these painful experiences call our attention to God's providential working in the world.

What is the proper response to God's providence, whether positive or negative? The overall response should be the same, although there may be slight variations in the application of each. Three responses seem particularly appropriate to both positive and painful providential circumstances.

The first response should be *thanksgiving*. When we experience positive occasions of providence, we have no real problem with giving thanks. But often we need to be encouraged to give thanks to God, which reminds us our circumstances are not primarily due to ourselves. All good comes from God, and he needs to be praised and thanked for his multiple blessings and favor (Col 3:17; Jas 1:17).

Giving thanks in response to negative occasions of providence, however, is quite a bit more difficult. Sometimes it seems emotionally impossible to thank God directly for the immediate circumstances causing the pain, especially when this involves sin or evil. Nevertheless, thanksgiving is the appropriate response. We can thank God for who he is, for the positive experiences that surround the negative ones and for all the ways we know God is working positively on our behalf. The value of thanksgiving in this context is that it focuses our attention on God rather than on ourselves. We acknowledge that God is in charge of life and has provided far more blessings than we deserve, in spite of what is currently happening to us (1 Thess 5:18). When we do not respond with thanksgiving, we focus on ourselves, reinforcing our self-centeredness. This in turn makes it more difficult to see how God is providentially working in our lives.

The second appropriate response is *trust*. This is always the bottom line in our relationships with God and is certainly an issue of providence. Again, positive experiences increase our confidence in God and strengthen our faith that he is working for us. When faced with negative providence, trust is essential. This is especially true when we do not fully understand what he is doing or why he is allowing certain things to happen. These are the times he invites us to trust him in a deeper way. Negative circumstances force us either to trust, which draws us nearer to God, or distrust, which pushes us away from him. God's desire is obviously the first, but of course we may choose either.

Finally, we must *listen* to what God is communicating to us in the midst of positive and negative circumstances. In either case we must ask, What are you saying to me in the midst of this? Are there some things that I need to learn from these circumstances? How should I appropriately take advantage of these circumstances that I might learn, grow and develop your other purposes more fully for my life? When we experience negative providence, the message from God may be painful, but sometimes he uses the pain to help us understand our status more perfectly so we might receive his message in trust and allow him to accomplish his purposes more fully in our lives.[10]

Properly responding to God's providence allows God to accomplish more of his desires for us. When we respond to positive and painful experiences appropriately (i.e., through thanksgiving, trust and listening), we develop a closer relationship with God. Out of this deeper relationship he is able to do more to shape our character, sharpen our minds, deepen our relationships with others and use our lives in his service.

The Role of Mystery

No attempt to holistically comprehend the scriptural data is completely satisfactory. While we know many things because God has revealed them in his Word and through his general revelation (creation, reason, conscience and experience), we do not know everything. So we have true knowledge but not full knowledge of all of the ways that he works. Thus we have *true* truth about God's providence, but not *exhaustive* truth.

For example, the sovereign God clearly respects the freedom of other persons, but we do not know every detail about *how* he does this. From the scriptural data we infer that he works this way, but it nevertheless remains a mystery. From Scripture we know that we worship a loving and good heavenly Father who desires the best for his children. We also know that he has the wisdom, presence and ability to order life's circumstances, including those encompassed by sin and evil, to accomplish his major purposes for us if we respond appropriately to him.

While these truths are richly illustrated in Scripture, the details of God's providence are often hidden from us. This is undoubtedly for the best. We have just enough information to assure us that he loves us and we can trust him in all circumstances. Thus we are encouraged to draw nearer in our relationship with him, which is the very thing he desires most. More knowledge on our part might cause us to rely more on ourselves and thereby trust God less. Trust is a crucial ingredient in developing an intimate relationship with our Father. Therefore the appropriate response to the mystery of providence is, Thanks be unto God!

---

[10]John Wesley believed the appropriate responses to God in providential circumstances are to (1) put one's whole trust in God, (2) be thankful, and (3) walk humbly/closely with him ("On Providence," *Works* (BI), 2:548).

III. TRINITARIAN THEISM AND OTHER VIEWS OF PROVIDENCE

The doctrine of providence examines how God relates to his creation. The best way to approach this providence is through a trinitarian perspective, which we have termed *trinitarian theism*. In this section we will compare this perspective with three other major ways of viewing providence: classical theism, process theology and open theism.

Classical Theism

Much of our previous discussion of providence shows how trinitarian theism contrasts with classical theism's view of God. Here we will highlight some of the key points of classical theism as the basis for our discussion of process theology and open theism.

Classical theism—the position of Augustine, Aquinas and Calvin—is one of the major influences in Western Christianity. Augustine (and most classical theists) starts with the unity of God rather than the three divine persons, and he particularly focuses on the role of God as sovereign King rather than God as Father. So while Augustine, Aquinas and Calvin give assent to the Trinity as a central doctrine of the Christian faith, their own theologies are more controlled by the view of God as sovereign monarch than by the Trinity, which features God as Father.[11]

From this perspective, God providentially controls everything. In his omnipotence God has the power to do whatever he wants.[12] His will is irresistible and his purposes are always accomplished. Before the creation of the world God decreed that what he purposes to do will come to pass. Thus his plan for history in general and for the individuals within it is immutable.[13]

In classical theism, God's omniscience is subordinate to his omnipotence.

---

[11]For a contemporary illustration of the same phenomena, see Feinberg, *No One Like Him*, a theology of the doctrine of God. Feinberg delays his discussion of the Trinity until chapter 10. And his discussion of the triune God has almost no effect on the rest of his doctrine of God. His controlling motif is that of a "caring King" (p. 32), which emphasizes God's transcendence and omnipotence. God transcends the created world and rules over it in power.

Sometimes this theology is coupled with the Greek view of God as the "perfect Being." From this starting point God's transcendence and omnipotence become controlling attributes. Thus God is viewed as absolutely immutable, impassible, omniscient and atemporal. See the same approach in John Frame's *Doctrine of God*.

[12]Though God cannot do the logically impossible.

[13]For variations on God's decree from the Calvinist and Arminian perspectives see Feinberg, *No One Like Him*, pp. 501-7.

God's foreknowledge is based on his decrees. As John Feinberg says, "God foresees because he decrees."[14]

Process Theism

Reaction to classical theism. Process theology has its roots in the thinking of philosophers Alfred North Whitehead and Charles Hartshorne, who used the theory of relativity, quantum physics and evolution to shape their worldviews. Contemporary science, they said, makes modern humans uncomfortable with the transcendent God. As a result, the God of classical theism is inadequate for the contemporary world. Whitehead asserts that classical theism conceives of God as an "imperial ruler (associated with the Roman Caesars), a hypostatization of moral energy (the Hebrew Prophets) and an ultimate metaphysical principle (Aristotle)."[15] Process theologians not only feel that viewing God as sovereign King ("Imperial Ruler") is improper, they also believe that classical theism is too closely aligned with the metaphysics of Plato and Aristotle, making God timeless, immutable and impassible. God's immutability, they contend, makes it impossible for God to enter into real relationships with his creatures. Divine impassibility implies that God cannot have emotions or be moved by what his creatures do.[16]

From the process perspective, the transcendent and unchangeable God of classical theism neither fits the biblical picture of God nor the commonsense experience of modern persons.[17]

The process concept of God. In an attempt to hold the transcendence and immanence of God together, process theology views God as dipolar (or bipolar). God's immaterial, primordial nature (his conceptual pole) is permanent. But God also has a physical nature (his consequent pole), which is changing and impermanent. This is the concrete side of God's nature that is manifested in the world. Sometimes process theologians refer to the world as God's body. So

---

[14]Ibid., p. 741. Cf. Richard Rice, "Biblical Support for a New Perspective," in *The Openness of God,* ed. Clark Pinnock (Downers Grove: InterVarsity Press, 1994), pp. 14-15.

[15]Alfred N. Whitehead, *Process and Reality* (New York: Macmillan, 1929), pp. 519-21, quoted by Feinberg, *No One Like Him,* p. 153.

[16]On Whitehead's influence on process theology, see Veli-Matti Kärkkäinen, *The Doctrine of God: A Global Introduction* (Grand Rapids: Baker Academic, 2004), pp. 179-82. Cf. John B. Cobb Jr., *Christian Natural Theology Based on the Thought of Alfred North Whitehead* (Philadelphia: Westminster, 1965).

[17]For a review of the contrast between process theology and classical theism, see Ronald H. Nash, *The Concept of God: An Exploration of Contemporary Difficulties with the Attributes of God* (Grand Rapids: Zondervan, 1983), pp. 24-30.

God and the world interpenetrate each other, which is sometimes referred to as *panentheism*. Since the world is always changing, God's consequent pole is always in the process of becoming. Thus God is in process.

God, therefore, is not distant and aloof from, but engaged with, his created order. God continues to grow and develop because he is so intimately involved with this world. God changes and improves as he learns and grows along with his creatures. Process theologians reject *creatio ex nihilo* since matter, God's consequent pole, is eternal. Nevertheless, God is creative because he continually shapes matter through his involvement with it. God is very much a corporeal being, not fully distinct from the universe he has made.

Since God has a physical pole, he is clearly not immutable in the classical sense. He not only changes in his relationships but also in his being, attributes and knowledge. God is passible; he identifies with the suffering and emotions of his creatures and clearly is involved in time. The process God is neither omniscient nor omnipotent. Because he is involved in time, his knowledge is limited, and because humans exercise real freedom, God does not have foreknowledge of what they will do in the future. According to its proponents, this process view of God is far more attractive to contemporary persons than classical theology.

Providence, then, is God's ongoing creative involvement in the growth of the world, including the changes due to human free choices. God is limited by his lack of foreknowledge but actively identifies with the emotions of his creatures. He is always present to assist his creatures in facing whatever comes their way. God does not exert too much power in his relationships; he uses persuasion rather than coercion.

By means of the dipolar concept of God, process theologians desire to distinguish themselves from both classical theists and pantheists. They declare that God is neither totally independent of the world (as in traditional theism) nor identical with it (as in pantheism). Thus they are *panentheists*. Panentheism is the view that "deity is in some real aspect distinguishable from and independent of any and all relative items, and yet, taken as an actual whole, includes all relative items."[18] While God is not literally identified with the world (as in pantheism), he penetrates it and is present in everything such that he

---

[18]Charles Hartshorne, *Divine Relativity: A Social Conception of God* (New Haven: Yale University Press, 2003), p. 89.

and the world are mutually interdependent.[19]

Open Theism

Reaction to classical theism. Open theism, sometimes known as *relational theism*, *presentism* or *neotheism*, is another reaction to classical theism.[20] Open theologians believe the classical view of God overemphasizes God's transcendence to the detriment of his immanence. They hope to redress the balance between transcendence and immanence without overemphasizing immanence.[21] From the open theist's perspective, classical theism

- does not give an accurate picture of what the biblical God is like
- makes God remote, distant from his from people and unresponsive to their needs
- deemphasizes the relationality and social dimension of who God is within himself and in his interaction with human persons[22]

---

[19]For more on process theology, see Feinberg, *No One Like Him*, pp. 67-69, 149-79; cf. John B. Cobb Jr. and David R. Griffin, *Process Theology: An Introductory Exposition* (Philadelphia: Westminster Press, 1976).

[20]Open theism dates to the publication of Richard Rice's *The Openness of God* (Minneapolis: Bethany, 1980), which was reprinted as *God's Foreknowledge and Man's Free Will* (Minneapolis: Bethany, 1985). But its real impact did not begin until the publication of *The Openness of God* (Downers Grove: InterVarsity Press, 1994) by five authors. Richard Rice introduces the volume with biblical support for the openness view. John Sanders gives an historical overview of issues that have led to this position. The heart of the book is by Clark Pinnock on the systematic theology of the openness perspective. The philosophical perspective is covered by William Hasker and the practical implications by David Basinger. Since that time other publications that have promoted this point of view are John Sanders, *The God Who Risks: A Theology of Providence* (Downers Grove: InterVarsity Press, 1999); Gregory Boyd, *God of the Possible: A Biblical Introduction to the Open View of God* (Grand Rapids: Baker, 2000), and *God at War* (Downers Grove: InterVarsity Press, 1997); Clark Pinnock, *Most Moved Mover: A Theology of God's Openness* (Grand Rapids: Baker Academic, 2001); and William Hasker, *God, Time and Knowledge* (Ithaca, N.Y.: Cornell University Press, 1989).

Some responses to openness theology are Bruce Ware, *God's Lesser Glory: The Diminished God of Open Theism* (Wheaton, Ill.: Crossway, 2000); Jon Tal Murphree, *Divine Paradoxes: A Finite View of an Infinite God: A Response to Process and Open Theologies* (Camp Hill, Penn.: Christian Publications, 1998); Feinberg, *No One Like Him;* and Norman Geisler and Wayne House, *The Battle for God: Responding to the Challenge of Neotheism* (Grand Rapids: Kregel, 2001).

Some open theists question the legitimacy of the title *classical theism* and prefer to call it *conventional theism*. The argument is that classical theism is a recent designation developed by contemporary Calvinists. The larger Christian tradition includes more positions than that of Augustine, Aquinas and Calvin (see, e.g., Pinnock, *Most Moved Mover*, p. 6). Kärkkäinen agrees (*Doctrine of God*, pp. 10-12).

[21]Clark H. Pinnock, "Systematic Theology," in *The Openness of God* (Downers Grove: InterVarsity Press, 1994), pp. 105-7, 111-13.

[22]This particular criticism is by Pinnock, *Most Moved Mover*, pp. 1-3.

- does not place enough emphasis on God's love or his interaction with people
- does not provide room for human free will (a criticism of both strong determinism and compatibilism)
- makes God the cause of all things, including human choices and therefore sin
- defines immutability in a way that makes God a static, immovable and distant ruler rather than a responsive and personal being
- defines impassability (i.e., God cannot suffer) in such a way that God does not identify with the suffering and pain of his people
- inadequately explains how God changes his mind, repents of his actions and corrects his plans[23]

Basic Proposals of Open Theism

Open theists reject the classical view of God, which makes him "an aloof monarch." Instead, they present God as a "caring parent" with an emphasis on his "love and responsiveness, generosity and sensitivity, openness and vulnerability, a person . . . who experiences the world, responds to what happens, relates to us and interacts dynamically with humans."[24] Feeling that the classical view is captive to Greek philosophy, these theologians claim that the open view of God is much more closely aligned with Scripture. Their view leads them

> to depict God, the sovereign Creator, as voluntarily bringing into existence a world with significantly free personal agents in it, agents who can respond positively to God or reject his plans for them. . . . God rules in such a way as to uphold the created structures and, because he gives liberty to his creatures, is happy to accept the future as open, not closed, and a relationship with the world that is dynamic, not static.[25]

Open theists note that, historically, Christian doctrine has tilted toward divine transcendence, and while they believe in God's transcendence, they also believe it needs to be balanced with God's immanence. God's immanent role as a caring parent means he lovingly identifies with the persons he has created.[26]

---

[23]Cf. Richard Rice's summary of open theism's rejection of classical theism ("Biblical Support for a New Perspective," in *The Openness of God* [Downers Grove: InterVarsity Press, 1994], pp. 11-12).
[24]Pinnock, "Systematic Theology," p. 103.
[25]Ibid., p. 104.

The focus on God's love makes it possible to think

of God's relation to the world as dynamic rather than static. . . . It means that God interacts with his creatures. Not only does he influence them, but they also exert an influence on him. As a result, the course of history is not the product of divine action alone. God's will is not the ultimate explanation of everything that happens; human decisions and actions make an important contribution too. Thus history is a combined result of what God and his creatures decide to do.[27]

While some attempt is made within openness theology to show that this love is related to the Trinity, the connection between trinitarian thinking and the role of God as Father is not accentuated. Starting with the Trinity certainly serves as an appropriate basis for challenging classical theism's view of God as sovereign monarch, but it does not necessitate an open view of God.[28]

Open theists believe God has given humans freedom of the will and has thereby limited his omnipotence. Here openness theology shares with the trinitarian perspective the belief that God allows persons to make real and significant choices. Because of the gift of freedom of choice, God has chosen not to cause everything to happen.[29]

One important feature that separates open theism from classical theism is open theism's rejection of God's foreknowledge. (In fact, this separates open theism from traditional orthodoxy of all kinds.) Open theists believe that God has not only limited his omnipotence but is also limited by time. They reject the concept of a timeless God.[30] Because God is time bound, he does not know the future and therefore is not omniscient. This conviction explains why open theism is sometimes called *presentism*, because God knows all things that are past and present. But since future human choices do not really exist until they are chosen and acted on, God cannot know them. His knowledge of the future

---

[26]Rice, "Biblical Support for a New Perspective," pp. 15, 18, 22; Pinnock, "Systematic Theology," p. 108; Pinnock, *Most Moved Mover*, pp. 3, 81-82.

[27]Rice, "Biblical Support for a New Perspective," pp. 15-16; cf. Pinnock, *Most Moved Mover*, pp. 26-31, 79-81.

[28]It is interesting to observe that Pinnock does not refer to God as *Father* in this discussion of Trinity, but he nevertheless describes God's love as "like the tender love of a nursing mother." God is elsewhere referred to as *mother* and *Godself* (Boyd) but not as *Father* or *himself*. It appears as though open theism is politically correct! See Pinnock, "Systematic Theology," pp. 108-9; Gregory Boyd, *Trinity and Process* (New York: Peter Lang, 1992), pp. 332-333.

[29]Pinnock, *Openness*, pp. 109-111; 113-117.

[30]Pinnock, "Systematic Theology," pp. 118-21; Pinnock, *Most Moved Mover*, pp. 96-99.

is limited to his own plans and his best predictions of what people will do in the future. Thus the future is truly open. This limited foreknowledge is a key component of the openness perspective.[31]

Because God limits his omnipotence, has limited knowledge of the future and has given persons genuine freedom of choice, he is taking significant risks with creation. To providentially work for the good of creation, God has to respond "on the spot," as it were, to the choices humans freely make. God nevertheless thinks the risk of facing an open future is worthwhile if people will respond to him in love. God's "openness" to the future, in which God does not know what is going to happen, is where the designation "openness of God" arises.

Open theists also reject the traditional concept of God's immutability. They believe God's existence, his nature and his character are unchangeable. But in his interactions with the world, he does change. "God is dynamic in respect to his experience of the creaturely world, his response to what happens in the world, his decisions about what to do in the world and his actions within the world. He is deeply affected by what happens to his creatures."[32] Openness theologians take literally the Bible's portrayal of God as changing his mind, and therefore his actions and experience.[33] Further, as a result of his identification with the world through suffering, they also reject God's impassability.[34]

Open theists hope "to correct this imbalance in the handling of the transcendence and immanence of God." In making this shift, they recognized the danger of overcorrection. As Clark Pinnock says, "Let us seek a way to revise classical theism in a dynamic direction without falling into process theology."[35]

Trinitarian Theism

In contrast to classical, process and openness theologies, trinitarian theism begins with a different view of God, which facilitates our understanding not only God himself but also how he relates to the world he has created. The trinitarian perspective begins with the person of Jesus, and thereby addresses two major issues in the theological debate among the other theologies. First, Jesus

---

[31]Pinnock, "Systematic Theology," pp. 121-24; Pinnock, *Most Moved Mover*, pp. 99-102.
[32]Rice, "Biblical Support for a New Perspective," p. 48.
[33]Pinnock, "Systematic Theology," pp. 117-18. Pinnock calls this "changeable faithfulness" (*Most Moved Mover*, pp. 85-88).
[34]Pinnock, "Systematic Theology," pp. 118-19; Pinnock *Most Moved Mover*, pp. 88-92.
[35]Pinnock, "Systematic Theology," p. 107.

demonstrates that we should primarily approach God not as sovereign King but as our loving Father. This drastically transforms our understanding of God's sovereign reign. The Father, Son and Spirit govern the universe through personal relationships of love.

Second, trinitarian theism balances transcendence and immanence. Again, Jesus is the key to holding these two biblical truths together. In the incarnation the transcendent, supranatural God entered into the world of space and time. Jesus demonstrates that God is intimately involved in the lives of those he has created. Personal relationships are never static; change is inevitable. Thus while God's essence, character and purposes are immutable, he changes in terms of the relationships he has with human persons. Further, relational change may well affect God's emotions. Impassibility must not preclude the triune persons' identification with the suffering and pain of persons. The classical identification of the sufferings of Jesus with his humanity alone simply does not do justice to the divine-human nature of Jesus. When he suffered in his humanity, he also suffered in his divinity. A modification of classical impassibility clearly is called for from the trinitarian perspective.

Third, the trinitarian view of God highlights God's relationality. Because God is ontologically a social being, when he created persons in his own image, they were designed to interact with him and other persons. This relational view of God certainly fits with the biblical picture of God's intentional and consistent interaction with persons in our world. It also takes seriously the fact that God, a free being, made persons who also have freedom to make choices. People are free to respond to God, to love God and to take moral responsibility for their actions. There is a certain "risk" in this, but it is a limited risk because God does have complete foreknowledge of the future. Thus he is able to providentially order the circumstances of life, the world and history to accomplish his purposes in light of human freedom.

Trinitarian theism is vastly different from open theism and process theology. Many of the objections of open theism (and some of process theology) to classical theism are answered by trinitarian theology. Trinitarian theism believes that God created the cosmos, including time and space, out of nothing. Thus he stands outside of both (i.e., he is transcendent) but can enter into both (i.e., he is immanent). The incarnation of Jesus illustrates how God enters the world of space and time without being controlled by either. The trinitarian perspective also preserves God's unlimited foreknowledge of the future.

One of the ways God distinguishes himself from false gods is in his ability to foreknow the future (e.g., Is 41:21-29).

Trinitarian theism is critical of openness theology's inability to separate foreknowledge from foreordination. Open theists rightly reject foreordination (forecausation) as inconsistent with God's giving his creatures freedom of the will. But because open theists believe God cannot foreknow something without causing it, they reject God's foreknowledge of the future. Trinitarian theists, on the other hand, believe that though there is some mystery in *how* God can know the future of free human choices, Scripture teaches that he does. The most helpful analogy in understanding this is that human fathers who know their children well know with a great deal of certainty the choices their children will freely make. Thus God, the infinitely wise Father, has no difficulty in foreknowing human choices that he has not caused.[36]

Through its dipolar view of God, which blurs the distinction between creation and Creator, process theology easily slips into pantheism. Alternatively, trinitarian theism holds transcendence and immanence together via the God-man Jesus Christ. In him the transcendent Creator has come into our world while not being identified with it. Trinitarian theism thereby avoids panentheism and pantheism.

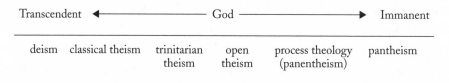

Figure 13.1. Spectrum of views on providence

Figure 13.1 illustrates the spectrum of views of God's role in providence. In terms of God's providence, the trinitarian view, which holds God's transcendence and immanence in balance, avoids many of the problems of the other positions. It provides the best and most coherent view of the total biblical data regarding God and his interaction with the world. Because it is grounded in Scripture, trinitarian theism's view of God's providential involvement in the world is the most attractive alternative on offer.

---

[36]See Coppedge, *Shaping the Wesleyan Message*, pp. 109-10.

EPILOGUE

The cumulative effect of the evidence is overwhelming. When the broad base of Scriptural data is set in its proper light, God's triune nature is obvious. Support for trinitarian theism is not confined to a handful of isolated texts but is drawn from the whole corpus of the biblical materials. The references to the Father, Son and Spirit not only run through the entire New Testament, they form an overarching theological umbrella that best captures the complete biblical perspective on God.

The early church wrestled with the relationship of Jesus with God the Father. Their theology was driven by the biblical witness that Jesus is the divine Son, who shares the very essence of God. The biblical text (which is primary) and the witness of the early church are two anchor points that fix our doctrine of God. Our view of God is the single most influential concept for all Christian theology; therefore the triune nature of God carries enormous weight and has broad implications.

We have presented a sustained argument that when we begin with Jesus as the center of the Christian faith, we inevitably move to a triune view of God, and this affects how we conceive of God's nature, attributes and roles. These in turn shape our understanding of creation and providence, the ways in which God relates to us. In particular this means we no longer give God's role as sovereign King pride of place in our theology. Following Jesus' lead, we begin with God as Father, Son and Holy Spirit. God's trinitarian nature preceded his roles as Creator, King, Judge, Redeemer and so forth. Recognizing this fact radically alters all of Christian theology.

All major branches of the Christian church are trinitarian, so we are not proposing anything new. Rather, we are calling the church to take seriously what it already knows, and let the Trinity control how it thinks about and experiences God. The triune starting point for the doctrine of God is just the beginning! It will change the way we think about anthropology, sin, revelation, atonement, salvation, growth in Christian life, sanctification, predestination, the church and last things. So there is ample room for more theological work and practice. This is the task that lies ahead of us.[1]

Fortunately, we do not have to wait to personally experience God in this triune nature as Father, Son and Spirit. Remember that theology has two components: knowledge and appropriation. A book like this one provides knowledge. But once we have knowledge, we have to decide what to do about it. Are we ready to apply it to our lives? So we close this study with a challenge and an invitation. The challenge: Do not let your knowledge of the triune God become an end in itself. The invitation: Begin to draw near to God as Father, Son and Holy Spirit in listening, prayer, worship and personal relationships. If the challenge is taken and the invitation is received, get ready to know the triune God in such remarkable ways that it will produce the richest spiritual experience in your life.

---

[1]For an introduction to what this might look like, see Dennis Kinlaw, *Let's Start with Jesus* (Grand Rapids: Zondervan, 2005).

Name Index

Albright, William, 242

Alexander of Alexandria, Bishop, 83, 89, 93, 240

Apologists, 89, 90

Aristotle, 215, 243, 247, 321

Arius, 84, 85, 93, 96, 97

Athanasius, 89, 93, 94, 95, 96, 97, 100, 101, 102, 103, 108, 109, 111, 132, 140, 170

Augustine, 16, 17, 101, 102, 103, 104, 105, 108, 145, 146, 320, 323

Aulén, Gustaf, 156

Barth, Karl, 14, 15, 19, 109, 110, 216, 239, 248, 269, 270, 291

Basil of Ancyra, 94

Basil the Great, 97, 98, 99, 101, 103, 250

Berkhof, Louis, 109, 237

Boethius, 104, 108, 174, 175

Brunner, Emil, 28, 109, 154, 155, 184, 187, 214, 239, 250, 291

Caird, G. B., 216, 217, 221, 227

Calvin, John, 16, 17, 116, 293, 320, 323

Cappadocian Fathers, 97, 100, 109

Clement, 92

Descartes, René, 109

Didymus the Blind, 132

Eichrodt, Walther, 155, 184, 185

Feinberg, John, 16, 109, 211, 237, 241, 255, 296, 307, 311, 315, 320, 321, 323

Fletcher, John, 110

Forsyth, P. T., 156

Frame, John, 16, 55, 57, 59, 61, 63, 65, 67, 69, 71, 73, 75, 77, 109, 216, 237, 296, 320

Gregory of Nazianzus, 98, 99, 106, 132

Gregory of Nyssa, 98, 99, 100

Grudem, Wayne, 26, 106, 109, 291, 293, 294, 295

Gunton, Colin, 14, 27, 73, 108, 110, 175, 227, 241, 248, 250, 255, 258, 261, 289, 291

Guthrie, Donald, 189, 236

Harrison, Everett, 153, 156

Hart, David Bentley, 18, 105, 110, 114, 272

Hartshorne, Charles, 321, 322

Irenaeus, 89, 90, 91, 240

Jacob, Edmond, 66, 67, 68, 69, 151, 186, 258,

304, 309

Jenson, Robert, 15, 36, 65, 108, 110, 149, 170, 257, 264, 269, 272

Kant, Immanuel, 109

Kasper, Walter, 14, 30, 64, 87, 90, 106, 108, 110, 114, 135, 140, 216

Kaufmann, Yehezkel, 123, 242

LaCugna, Catherine, 15, 100, 105, 110, 140, 149

Lewis, C. S., 217, 281, 284

Lewis, G. R., 189

Lonergan, Bernard, 83, 84, 85, 93, 97, 109

Moltmann, Jürgen, 15, 91, 108, 109, 110, 114, 139, 170, 171

Nicene Fathers, 83, 86, 89, 240

Oden, Thomas, 26, 36, 74, 83, 84, 109, 163, 167, 184, 192, 196, 206, 263, 267, 291, 293

Origen, 88, 92, 93, 267

Palamas, Gregory, 109, 140

Pannenberg, Wolfhart, 15, 24, 28, 38, 109, 110, 118, 149, 214, 291, 293, 295

Paul of Samosata, 83

Pinnock, Clark, 16, 17,

Subject Index

Scripture Index